Modern Erasures

Modern Erasures is an ambitious and innovative study of the acts of epistemic violence behind China's transformation from a semicolonized republic to a Communist state over the twentieth century. Pierre Fuller charts the pedigree of Maoist thought and practice between the May Fourth movement of 1919 and the peak of the Cultural Revolution in 1969 to shed light on the relationship between epistemic and physical violence, book burning and bloodletting, during China's revolutions. Focusing on communities in remote Gansu province and the wider region over half a century, Fuller argues that in order to justify the human cost of revolution and the building of the national party-state, a form of revolutionary memory developed in China on the nature of social relations and civic affairs in the recent past. Through careful analysis of intellectual and cultural responses to, and memories of, earthquakes, famine and other disaster events in China, this book shows how the Maoist evocation of the "old society" earmarked for destruction was only the most extreme phase of a transnational, colonial-era conversation on the "backwardness" of rural communities.

Pierre Fuller teaches history at Sciences Po Paris. He is the author of *Famine Relief in Warlord China* (2019).

Modern Erasures

Revolution, the Civilizing Mission,
and the Shaping of China's Past

Pierre Fuller

Sciences Po, Paris

CAMBRIDGE
UNIVERSITY PRESS

Shaftesbury Road, Cambridge CB2 8EA, United Kingdom

One Liberty Plaza, 20th Floor, New York, NY 10006, USA

477 Williamstown Road, Port Melbourne, VIC 3207, Australia

314–321, 3rd Floor, Plot 3, Splendor Forum, Jasola District Centre, New Delhi – 110025, India

103 Penang Road, #05–06/07, Visioncrest Commercial, Singapore 238467

Cambridge University Press is part of Cambridge University Press & Assessment, a department of the University of Cambridge.

We share the University's mission to contribute to society through the pursuit of education, learning and research at the highest international levels of excellence.

www.cambridge.org
Information on this title: www.cambridge.org/9781009012935

DOI: 10.1017/9781009026512

First published 2022
First paperback edition 2023

A catalogue record for this publication is available from the British Library

Library of Congress Cataloging-in-Publication data
Names: Fuller, Pierre, author.
Title: Modern erasures : revolution, the civilizing mission, and the shaping of China's past / Pierre Fuller, Monash University, Victoria.
Other titles: Revolution, the civilizing mission, and the shaping of China's past
Description: Cambridge ; New York, NY : Cambridge University Press, 2022. Includes bibliographical references and index.
Identifiers: LCCN 2021056167 (print) | LCCN 2021056168 (ebook) | ISBN 9781316515723 (hardback) | ISBN 9781009012935 (paperback) | ISBN 9781009026512 (ebook)
Subjects: LCSH: China – History – 20th century – Historiography. | Collective memory – China. | Communism – China – History – 20th century. | Revolutions – China – History – 20th century. | China – Rural conditions. | Mao, Zedong, 1893–1976 – Influence.
Classification: LCC DS773.94 F85 2022 (print) | LCC DS773.94 (ebook) | DDC 951.04072–dc23/eng/20220112
LC record available at https://lccn.loc.gov/2021056167
LC ebook record available at https://lccn.loc.gov/2021056168

ISBN   978-1-316-51572-3   Hardback
ISBN   978-1-009-01293-5   Paperback

To Eleanor

Contents

Figures and Maps

Figures

Maps

Acknowledgments

This endeavor has been enriched by many friendships and conversations along the way. I'm indebted to advice at various stages starting with world history colleagues at the University of Manchester, among them Ana Carden-Coyne, Peter Gatrell, Christian Goeschel and Georg Christ. I also wish to thank in various ways over the years Pierre-Étienne Will, Daniel Hausmann, Anthony Garnaut, Barry Parsons, Martin Heijdra, Chris Courtney, Sabine Dabringhaus and Janet Hunter. In China, I'm most grateful to the archivists and librarians at the provincial archives and libraries in Lanzhou and Yinchuan for their graciousness and for pointing me in research directions; to the staff at the Peking University Library over numerous trips and to the archivists at the Divinity Library Special Collections at Yale University; to Fan Lingjuan and Xue Zhengchang in Yinchuan; to my taxi driver in and around Haiyuan for opening doors there; and, as always, to Guan Yongqiang at Nankai.

Hosts and participants at various conferences and seminars offered invaluable support and advice, including the Social History Society Conference held at Newcastle; the Interdisciplinary Centre for East Asian Studies at Goethe University, Frankfurt; the European Association for Chinese Studies 20th Conference in Braga and Coimbra; the Shelby Cullom Davis Center and Department for East Asian Studies at Princeton University; the 6e Congrès Asie at Sciences Po; the Department of History at the University of Freiburg; the Asia Research Institute at the National University of Singapore; the Manchester China Institute at the University of Manchester; and the Mondes Communistes / Mondes Soviétiques seminar series at Sciences Po.

Writing and research support came from Manchester's School of Arts, Languages and Cultures and Princeton's Davis Center; travel funds from the Manchester China Institute; production costs from the School of Philosophy, History and International Studies at Monash University; and most importantly from Joan Trengove, whom I thank for the vacant but truly welcoming home on Melbourne's Mornington Peninsula where much of the manuscript was written.

I also warmly thank the two anonymous reviewers for Cambridge University Press whose suggestions were remarkably helpful, Lucy Rhymer for her patience over the years as this project evolved, Nick Scarle in Manchester for again creating maps for me, Alexander Macleod for his careful and thoughtful copyediting, and Ruth Boyes, Priyanka Durai, Michael Watson and Rachel Blaifeder for shepherding the book along in its final stages.

And finally my deepest appreciation goes to Eleanor Davey, my wife, for being there for me all this time, for the golden advice, and for bearing with long silences when I poked away at all the things this work involved. I lovingly dedicate this book to you.

———

Parts of Chapter 2 were originally published in Pierre Fuller, "Writing Disaster: a Chinese Earthquake and the Pitfalls of Historical Investigation," *History Workshop Journal* 80 (Autumn 2015), 201–17; and parts of Chapter 3 were originally published in Pierre Fuller, "'Barren Soil, Fertile Minds': North China Famine and Visions of the 'Callous Chinese' Circa 1920," *International History Review* 33/3 (September 2011), 453–72. The author gratefully acknowledges Oxford University Press and Taylor & Francis, respectively, for the republication of this material.

Note on the Text

To assist the reader, titles or names of Chinese books, articles, organizations and artworks are given in translation. The only exception are Chinese names for periodicals, which are retained throughout the text.

Introduction

This book brings two sets of ideas into conversation. The first was central to the civilizing mission of colonial projects around the globe. It could be found circulating in European and American editorial rooms early in the twentieth century during the height of the imperial era. The second was part of revolutionary programs shared by previously colonized or semi-colonized peoples, which, in the case of China, culminated in the human and epistemic destruction of the Cultural Revolution half a century later. The two modes of thought were unlikely allies in the ideological struggles that mark the modern period. Together they would constitute the practice of social erasure underpinning important facets of the modern identity itself.

———

In 1923, the Parisian publishing house Librairie Félix Alcan published a book entitled *Les Chinois: essai de psychologie ethnographique*. "They do not have our respect for human life," Jean Rodes explained of his Chinese subject – barely five years after a generation of Frenchmen had been lost to the gas, shells and rot of so many Great War trenches – adding, "among them pity is entirely unknown." "All who have written on the Chinese have spoken about their lack of character, their cowardice," he continued elsewhere (under the heading "The Chinese Sensibility") in a chapter titled "The Chinese as He Is."[1]

Echoing a generation of Yellow Peril literature from the turn of the century, Rodes' characterizations were hardly novel. But two aspects of his work are especially revealing: its use of scientific authority to couch gross generalization, and the intrepid timing of its claims, coming as France took stock of one of the bloodiest episodes in its own history.

---

[1] Jean Rodes, *Les Chinois: Essai de Psychologie ethnographique* (Paris: Librarie Felix Alcan, 1923), 151–52, 177, 186–89. All translations into English are my own, unless otherwise noted.

1

The likes of Rodes' assertions nonetheless had staying power as well as transnational appeal. They crossed over into Anglo-American circles, where they were adopted in civilizational and racial terms. "Instinctive sympathy is another trait which we in the West are prone to regard as normal in creatures above the brute," Ralph Townsend wrote in *Ways That Are Dark: The Truth about China*, published by New York's G. P. Putnam's Sons in 1933. "But this view certainly cannot include all the human family," he asserted, adding that "the Chinese appear to be one of the notable exceptions to the higher zoology"; "They failed to develop any credo of fellow sympathy. It is that they appear to have in the very crib and core of their molecules almost complete insulation against its infection."[2]

The idea of Chinese inhumanity soon appeared in the Germanic world, as well: "The East Asians' ability to endure very great physical pain may go some way towards explaining the cruelty of the Chinese and their indifference to the sufferings of their fellowmen," the psychologist Lily Abegg's *The Mind of East Asia* explained in 1952 (published in translation by London's Thames and Hudson from the original *Ostasien Denkt Anders* of 1949). "Many times one imagines one had attained a fair measure of understanding of the Chinese only once more to be reminded of the cruelties that interpose an unbridgeable gap between ourselves and this anciently civilized people," she added, not yet five years since German society had engineered a system for leading millions of innocents to their deaths. "All peoples racially akin to the Chinese possess the same inhuman tendency."[3]

Tracing the basis for these European claims leads to a third observation: they all cross-referenced a small circle of earlier works from both sides of the Atlantic, revealing thin foundations, at best, to their authority. Both Rodes and Townsend cite *Chinese Characteristics*, a book from 1894 by the Shandong-based missionary and New Englander Arthur H. Smith.[4] Abegg's appraisal of the East Asian character in turn cites Townsend's study, along with two other works: *Thunder out of China* by

---

[2] Ralph Townsend, *Ways That Are Dark: The Truth about China* (New York: G. P. Putnam's Sons, 1933), 51–54.
[3] Lily Abegg, *The Mind of East Asia*, trans. J. Crick and E. E. Thomas (London: Thames and Hudson, 1952), 281–83.
[4] Arthur H. Smith, *Chinese Characteristics* (New York: F. H. Revell, 1894). Smith's work was in 1920 still one of the top five books on China for resident foreigners. It appeared in a French version later in the decade. Arthur H. Smith, *Moeurs Curieuses des Chinois*, trans. B. Mayra and Le Lt-Cl de Fonlongue (Paris: Payot, 1927). Lydia Liu, *Translingual Practice: Literature, National Culture and Translated Modernity* (Stanford, CA: Stanford University Press, 1995), 51.

the TIME magazine reporters Theodore White and Annalee Jacoby, and philosopher Bertrand Russell's *The Problem of China*.[5]

This brings us to a fourth observation on this transatlantic reductive exercise on the Asiatic character: that it formed generalizations of everyday life and behavior from moments of acute social distress. This involved violence in its varied forms: the voluminous books and photographs of the Boxers come to mind, or the place of torture and beheadings in the Western imagination – what Jérôme Bourgon has called the "making of a myth" regarding "the Chinese 'thirst for blood.'"[6] But it also involved famine. White and Jacoby's work famously brought the Henan famine of 1942–43 to the world's attention, while Russell produced his book immediately following his lecture tour of China conducted over the course of the northern famine of 1920–21. These were merely some of the more prominent Western writers who touched on Chinese famine in the early twentieth century. And they almost invariably presented Chinese as inert, at best, in the face of others' suffering.

But most importantly, Anglo-European diagnoses of the Chinese character would be internalized by Chinese writers and social reformers. This cross-fertilization of ideas would happen, no less, at a watershed moment in China's troubled republican experiment, one underway since the fall of the Qing dynasty (1644–1912). This sensitivity became especially acute with Beijing's failure to maintain the integrity of Chinese territory despite contributing to the winning side of World War I. After some of the first shots of the war were fired in Germany's concessions in the coastal province of Shandong, Tokyo, eyeing those possessions for Japan, had prevented Beijing from committing troops to the Allied effort and thereby having a diplomatic hand to play at war's end. So, instead, Beijing had offered muscle in the form of 140,000 Chinese, hired and sent to the western front to dig trenches, bury French and British dead, and, eventually, mend tanks and other materiel.[7]

It was the injustice of losing Shandong to the Japanese, despite China's contribution to victory, that famously triggered the Chinese student movement on May 4, 1919. This began as a series of nationwide

---

[5] Theodore Harold White and Annalee Jacoby, *Thunder out of China* (New York: William Sloane, 1946).

[6] Jérôme Bourgon, "Obscene Vignettes of Truth: Constructing Photographs of Chinese Executions as Historical Documents," in Christian Henriot and Wen-hsin Yeh, eds., *Visualising China, 1845–1965: Moving and Still Images in Historical Narratives* (Leiden: Brill, 2013), 87. On "oriental" torture generally, see Timothy Brook, Jérôme Bourgon and Gregory Blue, *Death by a Thousand Cuts* (Cambridge, MA: Harvard University Press, 2008).

[7] Xu Guoqi, *Strangers on the Western Front: Chinese Workers in the Great War* (Cambridge, MA: Harvard University Press, 2011).

demonstrations over Beijing's impotence at the negotiating table at Versailles. But, immediately at its launch, the movement went far beyond politics, questioning all aspects of Chinese thought and practice. May Fourth would become, in short, a diagnostic exercise on the fundamental reasons for China's weakness on the modern international stage. Collectively, it prescribed the transformation of China and the Chinese – culturally, socially, morally and otherwise – through programs that subsequent revolutionary regimes would seek to carry out for the remainder of the century.

—

Over ten days in late April 1969, Ma Zhongtai was ritually beaten on a village stage and then left for dead at the base of a nearby hill.[8] His accusers hardly knew him. They were some forty years his junior, probably not even born until after Ma's family had lost its immense wealth at the time of the revolution. The summer of 1947 had seen local "landlord power" "destroyed," in the words of Joseph Esherick, and Ma soon after left for town, and then for a distant city.[9] His landlord status nonetheless remained grounds – twenty years after land reform – for a public show trial and execution.

Ma's death occurred in an area of northern Shaanxi bordering Inner Mongolia and Ningxia, but it could have been pretty much anywhere in the People's Republic at the time. Anywhere "between 492,000 and 1,970,000" people were killed in fields, village outskirts or other rural settings across China in the 1960s, according to Yang Su, and "possibly as many as three million."[10] Andrew Walder's estimate for total killings between 1966 and 1971 is 1.1 million to 1.6 million. Nearly three-fourths of these deaths were "due to the actions of authorities," Walder has determined, in the Cleansing of the Class Ranks Campaign of 1968 and 1969 and other measures.[11] The remainder were victims of battles between political factions or targeted by local activists acting "in the name

---

[8] Jiangsui He, "The Death of a Landlord: Moral Predicament in Rural China, 1968–1969," in Joseph W. Esherick, Paul Pickowicz and Andrew G. Walder, eds., *The Chinese Cultural Revolution as History* (Stanford, CA: Stanford University Press, 2006), 147–48.

[9] Joseph Esherick, "Revolution in a 'Feudal Fortress': Yangjiagou, Mizhi County, Shaanxi, 1937–1948," in Feng Chongyi and David S. G. Goodman, eds., *North China at War: The Social Ecology of Revolution, 1937–1945* (Lanham, MD: Rowman and Littlefield, 2000), 77.

[10] Su bases this range, in part, on the contents of 1,530 volumes of county gazetteers. The continued secrecy around this most sensitive series of events accounts for this broad and tentative range. Yang Su, *Collective Killings in Rural China during the Cultural Revolution* (Cambridge: Cambridge University Press, 2011), 2, 37.

[11] Andrew G. Walder, "Rebellion and Repression in China, 1966–1971," *Social Science History* 38 (Winter 2014), 517, 521, 533.

of their community," Su writes – a phenomenon he consequently calls collective (as opposed to mass) killing.[12]

How it comes to be that neighbors are killed over a bygone social status is one of the questions pursued in this book. Part of the explanation comes down to a shift in the dominant moral compass of the community. Maoism replaced a "pattern of customary social ethics in action, which placed a sacred value on loyalty generated by kinship, friendship, and charity" with "communist morality [...] derived not from daily life but from abstract theoretical doctrine,"[13] He Jiangsui explains in a study of Ma's 1969 killing. "Moral transformation was central to the reconstruction of Chinese society."[14]

Behind these contending moral discourses were competing visions of the past. As Red Guards swept in and set about dynamiting a memorial arch, a Buddhist temple and an ancestral hall, Ma's fellow villagers put mud over two stone stele before they could be spotted, covering them with bricks, and painting an image of Mao Zedong on top. As recently as the 1940s, nearly the entire village had worked for or rented from Ma's extended family, which had dominated the village for generations from their fortified hilltop compound. The stele recorded how Ma's family used this wealth to set up soup kitchens for neighboring villages during times of famine.[15] Yet in land reform struggle sessions, Ma family members were denounced, in songs taught to the villagers, for being "as rapacious as a wolf and savage as a cur," and, by the middle of 1966, *Renmin ribao* (People's Daily) editorials were broadcasted over village loudspeakers exhorting people to "Sweep Away All Monsters."[16]

A weaponized, morally charged discourse was at play in the everyday violence of late sixties China. This way of speaking was in turn based on a way of viewing communal relations in the past – another focus of this book.

———

So far we have touched on aspects of Anglo-European ethnographic writing during the peak of colonialism, and then political movements at the peak of Maoism. The two sets of ideas they present on prerevolutionary Chinese social relations come together in the words of a prominent journalist of the late twentieth century. Writing in the pages of the *New York Times* in the aftermath of the Tiananmen massacre

---

[12] Yang Su, *Collective Killings in Rural China*, 5.
[13] The use of square brackets with the ellipsis, throughout the work, to indicate my omission of text is intended to draw attention to the vulnerability of texts to manipulation.
[14] Jiangsui He, "The Death of a Landlord," 125, 126, 129.   [15] Ibid., 129, 137.
[16] Ibid., 132, 136.

of June 1989, Harrison E. Salisbury characterized Chinese history through the eyes of the son of Deng Xiaoping, who was crippled by Red Guards during the Cultural Revolution when his father fell out of favor:

Deng Pufang has had plenty of time to think about China and its cruelty. He believes that much of Chinese violence stems from a lack of humanity and humaneness. He believes China has no tradition of helping the misfortunates. Too often, lepers or cripples were simply clubbed to death as a burden on society. China developed no great philosophy of charity, aid to the downtrodden or an obligation to help the less fortunate [. . .]. More than anything, Deng Pufang has said, China needs to be educated in the philosophy of humanitarianism. Without it, China will remain bogged down in medieval darkness.[17]

What is most telling about Salisbury's piece from after Tiananmen is the neatly circular nature of its logic: it uses Cultural Revolution violence driven by a rejection of the Chinese heritage to embody the values of that same Chinese heritage. (Salisbury echoed this point in a book on Mao and Deng published a few years afterwards: "Charitable inclinations had very spindly roots in China," his *New Emperors* reads. "The only people who had really taken an interest in the unfortunates were Christian missionaries" while "the Chinese response to the disadvantaged was cruel and brutal.")[18]

Modern Erasures endeavors to take this circular idea and travel its full circumference. It does this by charting the pedigree of a perception that took hold of Chinese nationalism in its formative stages: one of Chinese deficiencies in public or civic morality relative to their Western peers. To do this, it covers the fifty years between the May Fourth movement sparked in 1919 and the peak of the Cultural Revolution in 1969. It has long been recognized that May Fourth, together with the New Culture movement (circa 1915–25) that preceded and overlapped with it, left a legacy that, in the words of Rana Mitter, "underpins the whole history of twentieth-century China."[19] What this book aims to do is shed light on the epistemic violence behind the process of enlightenment (*qimeng*) and awakening or being awakened (*juewu* or *juexing*), epistemic loss that cultivated certain perceptions of Chinese social history in ways that justified the enormous bloodletting of the Nationalist and Communist revolutions.[20] It does this by exploring the extent to which political

---

[17] Harrison E. Salisbury, "In China, 'A Little Blood,'" *New York Times*, June 13, 1989.
[18] Harrison E. Salisbury, *The New Emperors: China in the Era of Mao and Deng* (Boston: Little Brown, 1992), 419–20.
[19] Rana Mitter, *A Bitter Revolution: China's Struggle with the Modern World* (Oxford: Oxford University Press, 2004), 4.
[20] On these respective concepts, see Vera Schwarcz, *The Chinese Enlightenment, Intellectuals and the Legacy of the May Fourth Movement* (Berkeley: University of California Press, 1986); Xiaoming Chen, *From the May Fourth Movement to Communist Revolution: Guo Moruo and the Chinese Path to Communism* (Albany: State University of New York Press,

campaigning in the People's Republic was indebted to more than half a century of commercial, academic, evangelical and other seemingly less politicized forms of writing and erasure of aspects of Chinese life.

This timeline is not meant to enshrine the New Culture and May Fourth movements any further than they have been in scholarship, or likewise fixate on the Cultural Revolution, or draw a simple teleological path between the two. Our investigation could easily reach back to the social and political critiques offered by post-Boxer fiction or deeper still into the Qing period. There we would find precedents for the types of political diagnoses and cultural memory formation and documentary erasure discussed here.[21] But (hi)stories have to start somewhere. This one starts in the immediate wake of May 4, 1919, the movement long recognized for catapulting China into its twentieth-century formulations. It does this for what it reveals about social revolution in its embryonic stages and the sense of modernity these twentieth-century movements sought to bring into being. It ends with the Cultural Revolution, but not to suggest it presented the totality of the Chinese revolution and its achievements. Rather, reconsidering the terms on which violence was practiced in the 1960s brings out what Maoism most closely shares with the colonial project. It was through this denial of prerevolutionary capacities for civic values and pursuit of the common good that aspects of the Maoist revolution emerged as an offshoot of the civilizing mission. The erasures that emboldened this aspect of the Maoist program are "modern" only in the particular movements and identities they served to inspire.

Disaster and Community

Modern Erasures pursues several lines of inquiry into the social context and theory of the Chinese revolution for what they reveal about key premises on which Maoism, and by extension modernization in China more broadly, have been based. Behind the reasoning of the revolution and its civil violence, behind its theorizing and the day-to-day "keywords" of

2007); and John Fitzgerald, *Awakening China: Politics, Culture, and Class in the Nationalist Revolution* (Stanford, CA: Stanford University Press, 1996).

[21] See, for example, Li Boyuan, *Modern Times: A Brief History of Enlightenment*, trans. Douglas Lancashire (Hong Kong: The Chinese University of Hong Kong, 1996); Andrea Janku, "Preparing the Ground for Revolutionary Discourse from the Statecraft Anthologies to the Periodical Press in Nineteenth-Century China," *T'oung Pao*, Second Series, 90 (2004), 65–121; Beatrice S. Bartlett, "Qing Statesmen, Archivists, and Historians and the Question of Memory," in Francis X. Blouin, Jr., and William G. Rosenberg, eds., *Archives, Documentation, and Institutions of Social Memory: Essays from the Sawyer Seminar* (Ann Arbor: University of Michigan Press, 2006), 417–26.

political mobilization was a range of premises on the nature of things in Chinese life.[22] These premises could be traced back to at least the early twentieth century. Then, using the tools of the emerging discipline of sociology, the social survey movement took stock of China's human diversity and categorized it into a coherent whole, one readily employable in theory and emerging national narratives. This meant that the birth of the Chinese Communist Party in 1921 and the subsequent rise to power of the Guomindang (Nationalist Party) over the 1920s took place within a broader set of conversations on the health of the Chinese nation as it was conceived vis-à-vis the imperial powers and in relation to its own imagined past. In short, in order to gainfully revisit the context and the theoretical underpinning of the Chinese revolution, one must retread the intellectual footsteps that crisscrossed the country after May 4, 1919, in search of the social ailments of republican China.

The reason this is worth doing is that May Fourth-era reformist writing on Chinese life was not limited to the well-trod ills of China's petty capitalist system, to the structural causes for Chinese impoverishment or to imperialism. Nor did reformist writing end with the patriarchal family unit, with the Confucian regulation of family life (*qijia*) and interpersonal ethics (*lijiao*) and their stultifying effects on the individual – women and girls in particular, as epitomized by foot-binding, arranged marriage and female seclusion and illiteracy. Reformist writing went further, extending into the nature of Chinese communities. (And with this third area of inquiry, the movement entered an area that has posed considerable difficulties for scholars to critically assess.) From these perceptions of communal relations would spring a whole constellation of operative terms through which prerevolutionary old society (*jiu shehui*) would be cast over the following decades: this included the evil gentry (*lieshen*), landlord (*dizhu*) and peasant (*nongmin*) as political subjects acting within a broader feudal (*fengjian*) framework through which recent Chinese history was increasingly interpreted.

From the start, the diagnoses behind China's revolutionary programs were as moralist as they were materialist in nature. Collectively, the May Fourth movement imagined a "new social order," writes Shakhar Rahav, a nation-building mission that was to "communicate moral lessons to others" on a range of things, from egalitarian values and romantic love to the treatment of women.[23] But these lessons also involved claims about social conduct and community, on ethics and civic action. Here the

---

[22] On keywords in modern Chinese political culture, see Wang Ban, ed., *Words and Their Stories: Essays on the Language of the Chinese Revolution* (Leiden: Brill, 2011).

[23] Shakhar Rahav, *The Rise of Political Intellectuals in Modern China: May Fourth Societies and the Roots of Mass Party Politics* (Oxford: Oxford University Press, 2015), 47.

movement's writers almost invariably saw Chinese communities falling short compared to their Western counterparts. In her groundbreaking social history of the foundations of Chinese communism, Wen-hsin Yeh casts student activists from hinterland communities as "engaged enough by traditional values" in their home districts "to be shocked by the disjuncture between the community's professed norms and its actual practices." In this way, May Fourth was, in Yeh's words, "a consequence of the dialectical interaction between the quickening pace of modernization and the petrifying weight of traditionalism."[24] Similarly, in his recounting of the rise of socialist realism in 1930s China, the literary scholar Wang Ban writes:

In the transition from the Qing to republican China, Chinese realist writers of the May Fourth culture evinced a [...] break with the Confucian ethico-political order. With this break as part of their new understanding of reality, writers began to approach the world not from inherited moral presumptions, but through *direct personal experience and by rigorously investigating what they encountered as real.*[25]

Several questions come to mind here: How was moral disjuncture substantiated? Or petrified traditions? What, in practice, was direct personal experience? How rigorously were conclusions drawn?

As Charles Hayford has warned of a term popularized in the 1930s for use in writing on rural China: "too often we mistake 'peasant' for a primary category of nature rather than a contingent intellectual tool; the term is what Raymond Williams calls a 'keyword,' one that encapsulates and collapses history and argument."[26] What has been lost in the collapse of a complex prerevolutionary rural landscape into "peasant culture"? Have scholars taken at face value the social premises behind China's reformist and revolutionary programs?

At the heart of all these questions are perceptions of rural communities a century ago. It was there, in villages and small towns of China's interior, that the vast majority of Chinese lived out their lives well into the twentieth century. And yet life in China's countryside remains considerably less understood by historians than life in the country's urban sphere. To illustrate how this might be, we might turn to one of the most empirically driven scholars of the Chinese revolution and its social origins, Lucien

---

[24] Wen-hsin Yeh, *Provincial Passages: Culture, Space and the Origins of Chinese Communism* (Berkeley: University of California Press, 1996), 5.

[25] Wang Ban, "Socialist Realism," in Wang Ban, ed., *Words and Their Stories*, 109; emphasis added.

[26] Charles W. Hayford, "The Storm over the Peasant: Orientalism and Rhetoric in Construing China," in Jeffrey Cox and Shelton Stromquist, *Contesting the Master Narrative: Essays in Social History* (Iowa City: University of Iowa Press, 1998), 152.

Bianco. In the 1960s, Bianco sought to trace the Communist revolution to the "living conditions that prevailed from one end of rural China to the other," in the material and moral conditions stemming from "the exploitation of man by man."[27] Yet Bianco has also written at length about the scarcity of numbers for anyone looking into prerevolutionary rural life, and the extent to which available data are skewed toward urban events, especially along the country's more cosmopolitan coast:

> By and large, a Jiangnan [greater Shanghai] riot involving 100 farmers stood a better chance of ever coming to my knowledge than a 200 to 300-man uprising in Subei (northern Jiangsu) or Zhexi (Western Zhejiang) and a 1,000-man rebellion anywhere in Gansu. Or should I say 1,000 men around Lanzhou, 2,000 men anywhere else in Gansu?[28]

Coming from someone with a long career mining rural gazetteers (*difangzhi*) and other local records for the richness of rural life, Bianco's observation reflects the grip that urban perspectives held over the course of the modern period – even in countries with rural majorities – largely due to the growth of city-based media. But, of course, this – the process of "coming to one's knowledge" – is also due to the positioning of most modern scholars in urban contexts, physically and socially.

This brings us to the approach that *Modern Erasures* takes to the study of this period. Geographically, it begins in the region around Guyuan, Gansu, in today's southern Ningxia Hui Autonomous Region. In time, it begins the moment this mountainous area hosted one of the most dramatic geological events of the twentieth century, the great Haiyuan earthquake of December 1920. Through the earthquake, the second deadliest of the twentieth century, little-known communities in China's Northwest caught, if only briefly and partially, the attention of writers and readers around the country, and the world. They did so at a crucial juncture in modern Chinese history. Late 1920 was midway into China's New Culture movement of the 1910s and 1920s, and just over a year after the start of the May Fourth movement. It was also six months ahead of the founding of the Chinese Communist Party. The earthquake also struck midway into the North China famine of 1920–21, which menaced more than twenty million Chinese over the same winter.

The intersection of these events brings numerous threads in modern Chinese and world history together. It also presents a historiographic

---

[27] Lucien Bianco, *Origins of the Chinese Revolution, 1915–1949*, trans. Muriel Bell (Stanford, CA: Stanford University Press, 1971), 87, 90.

[28] Lucien Bianco, "Numbers in Social History: How Credible? Counting Disturbances in Rural China (1900–1949)," in Eberhard Sandschneider, ed., *The Study of Modern China: A Volume in Honour of Jürgen Domes* (London: C. Hurst, 1999), 264.

problem. The historical field is relatively rich in social histories of the late Qing or of the Guomindang era after 1928, periods marked by robust state bureaucracies. But in 1920, early in China's so-called warlord period, state record-keeping was at a low point. Consequently, the historian's grasp on everyday life in rural China – Bianco's quandary – is at its weakest in the years around the New Culture and May Fourth movements, the very moment of modern China's greatest intellectual and cultural ferment.

Disaster events, and communal responses to them, are a way around this problem as they offer entry points into otherwise elusive social landscapes. Generally speaking, riots or other types of conflict attract the attention of journalists or record-keepers in ways welfare measures do not. If violence becomes less and less visible the further the researcher goes from the city – and so more difficult to document – as Bianco points out, acts of assistance pose challenges of a much higher order. Capturing intervention in people's material needs in the countryside often requires an almost forensic disentangling of discourse (representation of the "nature of things") from empirical evidence (of human actions and events themselves). This is especially challenging when the former is voluminous, say in city-based media and public debate, and the latter often impossibly thin on the ground.

What allows interaction and exchange in the countryside to reveal itself – what enables the historian to peer into otherwise inaccessible or obscure social terrain – are moments of ecological distress such as earthquakes, and similar crises like floods or drought. Disasters are times when the very fabric of communities is tested. Yet responses to distress at the immediate and local level do not involve an invention of social ties or cultural norms or practices; they simply amplify them, and raise their visibility in the records that communities generate and safeguard. In times of disaster in republican China, existing structures like soup kitchens and shelter systems were ramped up, and so became more notable and therefore visible in records. Ideally, relief was performed by capable members of the afflicted community itself; when this failed to happen sufficiently, when the community and its networks failed to maintain the moral and social order that disaster relief was designed to maintain, then agents of the state (in the form of the district magistrate or higher authorities) were charged with intervening and maintaining local moral and social order – ideally only as a last resort. Either way, the cultural practices, values, methods and social networks behind relief structures existed, and continued to evolve, before and after each crisis. For this reason, extraordinary events like disasters achieved the visibility that allows us to peer into the ordinary, in other words into communal values and decision-making.

This is particularly important in the case of peripheral communities whose traces in the historical record are especially few and far between.

But of course, residents of afflicted regions and their social networks were not the only sources of news and commentary on disaster events. Journalists, geologists, Christian mission workers, student investigators and others fanned out into the hinterland to sound the alarm on disaster conditions and report on ravaged communities. And we know – researchers know – much more about what these outside observers said about life in the afflicted interior than we do about what people in the interior recorded themselves. So my focus is on instances in which extant local accounts of earthquake and famine in the form of letters, stone stele transcriptions and gazetteer biographies can be held up against reports by university students, geologists, missionaries and others reporting on, roughly, the same time and place. My aim is to juxtapose accounts from different social networks in early republican China for what it reveals about journalistic practices at a pivotal moment in twentieth-century revolutionary politics.

As remote as the disaster-struck communities explored here were in 1920, they were in fact close to the centers of cultural production in the formative stages of the Maoist program: Guyuan lay a few days' trek west across the loess plateau from Yan'an, the early Communist Party stronghold that served as the incubator for the Maoist project. Zhili, the most severely affected province in the 1920–21 famine (named Hebei from 1928), would form part of the Jin Cha Ji border region in the 1940s; the region's Communist propaganda unit would evolve into the party mouthpiece *Renmin ribao*. These events allow us to trace the lineage of certain ideas on rural life over various stages of the revolution and over, roughly, the same social geography.

By doing this, one can better understand the basis on which assessments were made on the health of rural Chinese communities vis-à-vis Anglo-American, French or German civic cultures of the time. It was one thing to decry the material conditions of the petty capitalist system of prerevolutionary China. Behind its bewildering range of tenancy, debt and labor arrangements lay acute ills of malnutrition, disease and near servitude suffered by multitudes of Chinese. But it is quite another to make unique moral claims about that same system: that it had lost, or never had, any sphere of activity corresponding to the civic cultures of the capitalist powers. In short, assessing claims about the quality of early twentieth-century community life requires understandings the historical field has fallen well short of achieving.

Regarding this question of community in republican China, the stakes were sky high. The notion of a void of civic morality became a key premise for Maoist social reconstruction. "The central theme of Maoism is that of a state alienated from its society, and a society destroying its own people," write David E. Apter and Tony Saich in their study of Maoist discourse at Yan'an.[29] State-society and communal relations were central to Maoist narratives. Responses to public distress are a measure of both. Our aim here is to trace how revolutionary culture made moments of distress, such as earthquakes and famine, "take on new meanings," in the words of Apter and Saich, "become coded, and serve as signifiers in a systematic and radical discursive practice."[30]

The social surveys, realist literature, civics textbooks and artistic production examined in this book give us just such a window onto how thinkers over the course of the twentieth century developed their understanding of public morality, and imagined its absence in China's interior. Why, in certain historical accounts, does communal relief crop up, and in other accounts of the same event, communal relief has no place at all? With the term revolutionary memory, *Modern Erasures* puts a name to this difference as it fleshes out the construction of shared memory of the recent past. In doing so, it makes no claims about the reality of Chinese rural life over the last century, of how things actually were, so to speak. Instead, it seeks to capture what Chinese and others have written about communal life in rural China, to identify and account for tensions within this varied body of writing, and locate it in the wider global experience of modernity.

Memory

This book examines perceptions of rural life through which understandings of the modern were constructed. For this, it uses the concept of cultural memory as defined by Jan Assmann – in short, the construction of identity through shared perceptions of the past through texts and other cultural forms.[31] It does this by isolating particular historical events to reveal the mechanics of cultural memory formation over the course of the

---

[29] David E. Apter and Tony Saich, *Revolutionary Discourse in Mao's Republic* (Cambridge, MA: Harvard University Press, 1994), 18.

[30] Ibid., xiii.

[31] Cultural memory here is distinct from the "collective memory" based on everyday interactions and communications conceived in the 1920s by Maurice Halbwachs. More recently, Aleida and Jan Assmann have proposed calling Halbwachs' notion "communicative memory" instead, so as to distinguish it from the more institutionally transmitted character of the Assmanns' understanding of cultural memory, itself a form of collective memory. Jan Assmann, "Communicative and Cultural Memory," in Astrid Erll and Ansgar Nünning, eds., *Cultural Memory Studies: An International and Interdisciplinary Handbook* (Berlin: De Gruyter, 2008), 109–18.

twentieth century. In doing so, it draws a distinction between two types of cultural memory. The first, what I call revolutionary memory, is character-istic of the cultural output of transformative political programs or regimes. The second, what I call communal memory, is the cultural production of any given community. Each term requires some explanation.

Revolutionary memory is revolutionary in the sense that it is transform-ative in aspiration, as easily evangelical or nationalist as it is socialist or communist in nature. It is a form of metanarrative populated with abstracted subjects and generalized ("typical") events. It is expansive in scale, encompassing units such as the nation, class or church. It positions past actors in positive or negative relations to an overarching goal, thereby establishing their worth. It offers an understanding of the past favorable to calls for social renewal.

Communal memory is a form of localized narrative, rooted in a community or social network, and populated with personalities and concrete ("unique") events. The meaning of community is by no means straightforward, and defining it "is a futile enterprise," in the words of Ildikó Bellér-Hann in a study of the Uyghurs of Xinjiang. Nonetheless, Bellér-Hann observes a general agreement among social scientists that it refers to "a social entity whose members are bound to each other by certain common traits and a multiplicity of social ties."[32] Geographically, community might encompass a social field covering a "marketing area" as defined by anthropologist G. William Skinner some time ago in his study of rural Sichuan.[33] Spatially, community can reach much further, of course, comprising a long-distance network of social connections within a native-place diaspora or other forms of association, which are equally unstable, overlapping and ill-defined as any given community.[34] What most clearly distinguishes communal from revolutionary memory is this difference in the scale of its constit-uency, however dynamic that might be. For communal memory, this scale involves proximity, even intimacy, regarding the events and peo-ple recounted.

---

[32] Ildikó Bellér-Hann, *Community Matters in Xinjiang, 1880–1949: Towards a Historical Anthropology of the Uyghur* (Leiden: Brill, 2008), 9–11.

[33] The scale of one's social field grew in size from those of ordinary farmers to local gentry elite and finally to scholar-officials. Skinner proposed that these spaces of interaction and exchange constituted the "culture bearing units" of rural China. Although challenged and revised over the years, his analysis remains classic. G. William Skinner, "Marketing and Social Structure in Rural China: Part I," *Journal of Asian Studies* 24/1 (November 1964), 32.

[34] On the dangers in essentializing social categories, and the idea of the social generally, see Bruno Latour, *Reassembling the Social: An Introduction to Actor-Network-Theory* (Oxford: Oxford University Press, 2005).

Unlike its revolutionary counterpart, communal memory need not entertain any telos. But, it is of course equally political, serving in many ways to reinforce the status quo. And it can convey the bad and the ugly in equal measure as the good. Sharing much with local history or legend, in communal memory instances of harmony may exist with those of discord, such as ethnic violence or tensions between rich and poor. And, like revolutionary memory, it assigns certain types of value, by transmitting standards and examples to later generations through which it upholds certain types of conduct.

Neither revolutionary nor communal memory, then, is any more "genuine" or "authentic" than the other in any absolute sense. In fact, they share a good deal. Both are cultural constructions joining the past to the present, and both are predominantly the preserve of those with the means to produce or stage media, which in the case of early twentieth-century China included printed texts, visual art, theater and monuments such as stone stele and grave epitaphs. Both therefore tend to reflect elite – or at least artist, priest or other "specialist"[35] – perspectives more, say, than what might be referred to as the communicative memory passed through everyday social interaction, as much as these forms of memory overlap in certain ways.

Lastly, despite sharing elite or specialist authorship, these two forms of memory often exist in tension with each other. Revolutionary memory is an external projection onto communities. When superimposed onto a locality, it is, at first, socially and culturally disruptive. It is introduced to localities by a range of outside activists, from reformists and missionaries to party cadres. It arrives in the form of storytelling, staged drama or pamphleteering, and as part of larger efforts to undermine and supplant existing forms of local authority. This, at root, is the most threatening aspect of revolutionary memory for local elites and, conversely for the marginalized of the same locality, its most empowering aspect. Nonetheless, over time, revolutionary memory acquires orthodox status as a legitimizing narrative for the exercise of state or party power in localities. But in doing so, it does not fully replace communal memory in any particular locality.

On a final note, I should explain why I have chosen the term memory, as opposed to history, for these contending treatments of the past. I do this because both communal and revolutionary memory include cultural forms beyond formal history writing; and, crucially, they each describe events and personalities recent enough to fall within living memory, which brings them into dialogue with communicative memory.[36] In this

---

[35] Assmann, "Communicative and Cultural Memory," 114.
[36] In this and other ways, this is a very different project than Rian Thum's excellent analysis of Uygur historical practices and engagement with a deeper past over the centuries. Rian Thum, *The Sacred Routes of Uyghur History* (Cambridge, MA: Harvard University Press, 2014).

and other ways, communal and revolutionary memory offer ways of viewing the past that coexist in an uneasy dynamic explored throughout this book. As a type of cultural practice, revolutionary memory is of course not unique to China and its revolutions. Conceptualizing it in relation to communal forms of cultural memory allows us to get past tired dichotomies used to examine the encounter between ("traditional") villagers and ("modern") outside forces or ideas. It does this by helping to break down distinctions, drawn or assumed, between subjective or moralist writing on the past, on the one hand, and its more objective academic, journalistic or realist modern form, on the other hand. In China's case, revolutionary memory was based as much on Chinese moral dialectics as on Marxist theoretical frameworks. Both communal and revolutionary memory offered competing moral rhetorics based on competing realities, but they each had elements that one might associate with tradition or modernity.

Our point of entry into these competing cultural forms is the question of civic action and mutual aid. By using the prism of resource exchange and other forms of assistance to chart discursive practices over the mid-twentieth century, I do not seek to fetishize the relief act, or ascribe to it any larger value in the offsetting of social injustices or inequalities in systems of ownership or other areas. Instead, I seek to isolate acts of relief in order to consider how, over time, their inclusion or exclusion from storytelling on the past or present – and on all scales of "us" versus the "other" – have borne on larger understandings of the world, and on how people have acted on those understandings. In other words, in this book I seize on the act of relief in order to chart how the telling of that act – or, contrarily, its erasure – has been used in the construction of identities and dichotomies both culturally (East and West, Confucian and Christian) and temporally (feudal and socialist, backward and modern). In this way, both revolutionary and communal forms of memory are practiced far beyond China. Communal memory transcends Confucianism or Han-Chinese contexts; revolutionary memory transcends Maoism or Communism. Each has served, in its own way, to shape the modern period in all its hybridities and contradictions.

Cultures of Violence

Chinese revolution and counterrevolution over the twentieth century went through numerous stages, producing a staggering amount of violence. The forces and motivations behind this bloodshed and destruction were extraordinarily varied. It would do no justice to events, ones that stretched over decades and spanned urban and rural contexts, to reduce political violence to any simple typology or agency.

But then certain aspects of mid-twentieth century violence beg for further explanation. What, for example, did radio broadcasts warning of "monsters" in their midst mean to 1960s youths, China's most educated generation to that point? To what extent was this education itself the foundation for their animus? What cultural conditioning was required for an "entire community," in Yang Su's words, to be "involved in the process of defining, or, to use a social-movement term, framing" victims of collective violence? How can we put substance to the "tensions" – identified by Richard Madsen in his study of the Cultural Revolution in a Guangdong village – "between the moral ideas of the Chinese peasantry and the dictates of official Communist ideology"?[37] Was the violence of the Great Proletarian Cultural Revolution a function of modern class war? Or was it more akin to the cultivated hatred and opportunism behind the mass murder of neighbors in Nazi-occupied Poland or 1990s Rwanda?[38]

In her work *A Continuous Revolution*, Barbara Mittler fleshes out in great detail how the Cultural Revolution did not, in fact, present a deviation in political culture. Instead, the late sixties saw a peak in the political use of song, comics, children's literature, such as character readers, and of iconoclasm and antireligion sentiment that had its origins in earlier periods. "The May Fourth Movement, which itself recycled many ideas developed during the late Qing," she writes, "became a crucial text machine in the making of a grammar of revolutionary culture in China, the application of which peaked during the Cultural Revolution."[39] The great achievement of her work is to capture the height of Maoism as a "lived experience" while making sense of how a hyperpolitical, menacing cultural moment could continue to have such widespread appeal for later generations.

That said, this monumental work on the popularity of the Cultural Revolution is notably bloodless. It does not reconcile the revolution's

[37] Richard Madsen, *Morality and Power in a Chinese Village* (Berkeley and Los Angeles: University of California Press, 1984), 8.
[38] See, for example, Jan Gross, *Neighbors: The Destruction of the Jewish Community in Jedwabne, Poland* (Princeton, NJ: Princeton University Press, 2001); and Scott Straus, *The Order of Genocide: Race, Power and War in Rwanda* (Ithaca, NY: Cornell University Press, 2006).
[39] Barbara Mittler, *A Continuous Revolution: Making Sense of Cultural Revolution Culture*, Harvard East Asian Monographs (Cambridge, MA: Harvard University Asia Center, 2016), 362; see also 30.

cultural grammar with its pervasive and ritualized violence, in places only referring in passing to "the many cruelties that accompanied this experience."[40] Arguably the most thorough study of 1960s red culture to date, Mittler's work avoids discussion of concrete messaging or content in its actual application to Chinese life and social realities. It is one thing for "MaoSpeak" to serve as a motivator for work and study, but how does it move people to murder their neighbors, and the elderly and children among them? It might be tempting to dismiss the political culture of the Cultural Revolution as crude propaganda, Mao worship, or high-stakes name-calling in a world of what Mittler calls "empty signifiers."[41] Doing so, though, underestimates its political potency in the moment. Introducing revolutionary memory to the Cultural Revolution helps account for the sheer "power of symbolic representations" at the time, in the words of Daniel Leese, while avoiding explanations for violence that easily attribute it to "brainwashing" and a "totalitarian concept of CCP rule."[42]

In the People's Republic, imperialism and its internal agents – real or perceived – continued to provide explanation for what held China back in poverty, galvanizing people for various movements (*yundong*), most famously the Great Leap Forward. American attacks just over the border in Korea during land reform and Vietnam during the Cultural Revolution only heightened the sense of a revolution under siege. Yet imperialism was much less central to the struggle sessions occurring in rural settings across the country. Speak bitterness sessions (as treated, say, in Gail Hershatter's remarkable oral history *Gender of Memory*) did give *communicative* memory a much-needed platform for what women or the poorest, or others close to them, had experienced in terms of debilitating debt and high rent, or hunger amid plenty, or thuggery, or sexual violence and predation over generations.[43] But the new terminology with which these experiences were voiced and framed – of evil gentry, landlords and black elements – sat atop decades of cultural memory, as explored in this book. The reasoning behind the systemic violence of the land reform era, in other words, was predicated on a specific understanding of the old society and its social dynamics; this understanding may have utilized Marxist terminology, but it was couched in dualities of good and evil, and rooted in constructed perceptions of the past.

---

[40] Ibid., 260.   [41] Ibid., 374.

[42] Daniel Leese, *Mao Cult: Rhetoric and Ritual in China's Cultural Revolution* (Cambridge: Cambridge University Press, 2013), 16.

[43] Gail Hershatter, *The Gender of Memory: Rural Women and China's Collective Past* (Berkeley: University of California Press, 2011).

So, how do we arrive at the logic driving the forms of killing that took place in sixties China? Philip Huang helps us get there. "The Cultural Revolution stands out in human history for the extreme disjunction between representational reality and objective reality," Huang has argued. "Between the Land Reform of 1946–1952 and the Cultural Revolution of 1966–1976, representational constructs of rural class struggle diverged increasingly from objective reality." In other words, at its peak the Maoist regime presided over a gross disconnect between two types of perceived realities: "objective" (or material) reality and "representational" (or symbolic) reality – the latter derived from Pierre Bourdieu's notion of "symbolic capital." Invoking Michel Foucault, Huang stressed how "representational constructs of rural class struggle" became in time "more *historically significant* than objective practice" by determining the course of events, including life and death. "By the end of land reform," he writes, "millions of intellectuals had participated in actions and thoughts that turned *class* from its material meaning in Marxist-Leninist theory into a symbolic-moral meaning in the dramatic struggle of good against evil within every village."[44] In this way, the Cultural Revolution involved a supercharged, if short-lived, triumph of representational forms of reality.

Scholars, then, have either traced the Cultural Revolution's bloodshed to the class war of land reform, or traced red youth culture further back to May Fourth but without adequately accounting for its violence.[45] Revolutionary memory helps us trace this explosive disjuncture of representative and objective realities to at least half a century earlier, to when Sun Yat-sen's Guomindang was confined to its Canton base and the Chinese Communist Party did not yet exist. It reinserts popular agency to the revolution and provides historical depth to the Maoist cultural repertoire nurtured at Yan'an. Revolutionary participants were not members of a blindfolded public dancing to the discordant tune of the Maoist wing of the party. They were rational actors informed by generations of cultural work on the past.

Of course, there was nothing inevitable about what transpired in communities across China in the late sixties, or in any period. The following chapters set out to isolate aspects of writing on communal life around

[44] Philip Huang, "Rural Class Struggle in the Chinese Revolution: Representational and Objective Realities from the Land Reform to the Cultural Revolution," *Modern China* 21/1, Symposium: Rethinking the Chinese Revolution. Paradigmatic Issues in Chinese Studies, IV (January 1995), 111; emphasis in original.
[45] See also Yang Su, *Collective Killings in Rural China*, 29; and Michael Schoenhals, "Demonising Discourse in Mao Zedong's China: People vs Non-People," *Totalitarian Movements and Political Religions* 8/3–4 (September–December 2007), 465–82.

May Fourth in order to chart their evolution to the height of Maoism. They do this not to establish a teleology, but instead to consider the political applications of cultural memory and the diverse pedigree of ideological practice under Mao.

Modernity

Modern identity has long been wrapped up in the idea of public welfare. Buttressing liberal democracies and authoritarian regimes alike, welfare is more fundamental to the modern sense of self than citizenship. In this way, the modern developmental state "secures legitimacy not by the participation of citizens in matters of state," explains Partha Chatterjee, "but by claiming to provide for the well-being of the population" through "governmental technologies that have promised to deliver more well-being to more people at less cost."[46]

For some scholars, this fundamental aspect to modernity can be traced to a time and place. In *Hunger: A Modern History*, James Vernon begins his work with the idea that "it was in imperial Britain over the past two centuries that the story of modernity became partially organized around the conquest of hunger, or at least its banishment to lands still awaiting 'development.'"[47] The use of the term conquest for the modern posture toward hunger is very apt, reflecting the use of modern science, technology and colonial experimentation that have empowered humanity to tap into new sources of energy and wealth, and more effectively command the natural systems on which humanity relies for its food.

But Vernon's story is much more than about changes in capabilities. It is about multiple firsts. "Imperial Britain," he argues, "played a formative role in changing the meaning of hunger and the systems of redressing it in the modern era." Not only did Britain produce Adam Smith and Thomas Malthus, the "first to establish the modern political economy of hunger," but "it was also in Britain" that the promarket, laissez-faire of classical economics "was first challenged, when hunger was discovered as a humanitarian issue and a social problem that measured the failure of the market to generate the wealth of nations, and of the state to protect its citizens from economic downturns over which they had no control."[48] *Hunger* seeks to establish, then, not what was new to the island of Britain in the modern era, but what was new to the human experience.

[46] Partha Chatterjee, "Community in the East," *Economic and Political Weekly* (February 7, 1998), 279.
[47] James Vernon, *Hunger: A Modern History* (Cambridge, MA: The Belknap Press of Harvard University Press, 2007), 4.
[48] Ibid., 3–4.

Establishing firsts in history is dangerous work, especially doing so in a universalist way. But then it is made easier when your immediate subject is a country with as rich, intact and accessible of a documentary record as Britain's, and you wish to extend your claims, explicitly or otherwise, onto other countries with varying degrees of survival to their historical record.[49] In this book I aim to demonstrate the nature of cultural erasure that enables universalist and modernist claims on humanitarian action to be made. In doing so, I aim to shed light on the intellectual and discursive mechanics behind what Alexander Woodside calls "those false forms of revolutionary fantasy that exaggerate the differences between 'traditional' worlds and 'modern' ones."[50] Woodside's *Lost Modernities* charts "the rise of embryonic bureaucracies" in a period of "precocious limited defeudalization" in the China, Korea and Vietnam of the late first millennium and second millennium CE.[51] One aspect of his study is the range of social welfare systems devised and implemented by civil bureaucrats in these three polities over the centuries. At times, these measures operated on assumptions associated with modern thought – for example that "poverty was politically created, rather than being eternal or inevitable."[52] At others, they employed strategies associated with modern state-society dynamics, in one case using the resources of rich households for "redistribution to famine-relief granaries and to the poor," endowing the rich "with a useful transformative power, rather like that of charitable foundations or NGOs: they were depicted as a state-directed asset, ready to supplement state power, rather than as an historic social class."[53] By recovering the "lost modernities" of these past political economies, Woodside seeks to "end uses of the singular term for the modern that merely camouflage one civilization's historical self-centeredness."[54]

This brings us back to Vernon's Britain. His benchmark for establishing the "novelty of our modern understanding of hunger" is a period "before it was imagined to be a problem."[55] "*Even in Europe*, a few centuries ago," he notes, "hunger was considered an inevitable part of the human condition, for it was sent as divine retribution for man's sinful ways."[56] In contrast, "the humanitarian discovery of hunger helped establish the right to subsistence, or at least the belief that it was morally

---

[49] In similarly sweeping fashion, Caroline Shaw's *Britannia's Embrace* asserts that "it was the British who first and most powerfully incorporated the provision of relief for persecuted foreigners into their national, and then imperial, raison d'être." Caroline Shaw, *Britannia's Embrace: Modern Humanitarianism and the Imperial Origins of Refugee Relief* (Oxford: Oxford University Press, 2015), 2.
[50] Alexander Woodside, *Lost Modernities: China, Vietnam, Korea, and the Hazards of World History* (Cambridge, MA: Harvard University Press, 2006), 3.
[51] Ibid., 6.   [52] Ibid., 59.   [53] Ibid., 67.   [54] Ibid., 9.
[55] Vernon, *Hunger: A Modern History*, 9.   [56] Ibid., 10; emphasis added.

wrong to allow another human being to starve to death."[57] In the under-standing of the premodern that informs *Hunger*'s thesis, the possibilities for interventions in the lives of the poor are remarkably narrow.[58] On closer inspection, Vernon's "story of modernity" is more about the stories the modern British have told themselves – what they "understood cultur-ally and politically," in his words – than about the world around them.[59]

Of course, most historians are quick to acknowledge the imperial con-texts in which international humanitarian systems were created in the eighteenth and nineteenth centuries.[60] Vernon does as well. It is hardly controversial to point out that imperial intervention and market integra-tion were intensely destabilizing for native communities in the colonial and semicolonial worlds. Official, missionary and academic study from the emerging disciplines of social science presumed to capture the essence of cultures amid these very transformations. They effectively took snap-shots of cultures at moments of crisis as communal fabrics frayed and social obligations broke down.

By way of example, when (over the course of the late nineteenth and early twentieth centuries and to China's immediate south) the French colonial enterprise made subsistence farmers into landless wage earners reliant on rubber and other plantation-based firms for survival, this change was accompanied by determinations on native industriousness and social relations. As Vietnamese were made to pay regressive taxes to finance new forms of administration and infrastructure that shifted politi-cal and market relations at the village level, new opportunities for profit-eering arose. In this context, French assessments were made on social values or associational life within the native population, which were then, in turn, used to justify further interventions by the colonial state. But most importantly, these assessments were internalized by "Vietnamese activists and writers" who in the 1920s "portrayed philanthropy and charity as new, modern, and Western" even as they "confirmed Confucian values and ideas" in embracing these activities, Van Nguyen-Marshall explains. The key difference was the end to which philanthropic and charitable activity was meant to be aimed: "national awareness and the acceptance

---

[57] Ibid., 40.

[58] For a window into the culture of disaster relief governance in China over the last millennium, see Pierre-Étienne Will, *Handbooks and Anthologies for Officials in Imperial China: A Descriptive and Critical Bibliography* (Leiden: Brill, 2020), in particular volume II; and Joanna Handlin Smith, *The Art of Doing Good: Charity in Late Ming China* (Berkeley: University of California Press, 2009).

[59] Vernon, *Hunger: A Modern History*, 7.

[60] Humanitarianism here can encompass a range of enterprises under the umbrella of "moral reform." See Ian Tyrell, *Reforming the World: The Creation of American's Moral Empire* (Princeton, NJ: Princeton University Press, 2010).

of one's responsibility towards the nation and one's compatriots" – in other words, the "foundation of a modern society."[61] Civic and humanitarian values, in other words, were couched in new terms, framed in new ways, and seen as an altogether new means of conducting oneself. Any similarity with indigenous values or legacies was not taken seriously.

This aspect of colonialism was only part of a larger process of the growth of capitalist structures and the cultural, political and social practices involved in their nineteenth-century expansion into other parts of the globe, what Gilles Deleuze and Félix Guattari termed deterritorialization/reterritorialization.[62] James Hevia, in turn, has applied this concept to the study of British penetration and undermining of the Qing imperial system more generally.[63] What I aim to do is demonstrate how these broader capitalist processes, and the various political and anticolonial responses to them, involved the articulation of humanitarian positions vis-à-vis the past, or "backward" communities that represented that past.

Chatterjee notes that in Western political theory "not all communities are worthy of approval in modern political life. In particular, attachments that seem to emphasize the inherited, the primordial, the parochial or the traditional are regarded by most theorists as smacking of conservative and intolerant practices and hence as inimical to the values of modern citizenship."[64] In a similar posture, writers on Chinese life over the course of the twentieth century participated in what I call the *deinscription* of civic value systems and practices from the cultural record – acts of narrative erasure that conjured up moral shortcomings and failures, which were used to justify social reprogramming – before the *reinscription* of a new moral order by party or other programs. In this way, May Fourth-era writing laid the cultural foundations for revolutionary memory, allowing an exaggerated sense of discontinuity with the past and a persisting pretension of modernity – its humanitarian awakening or enhanced valuation of human welfare – to take hold of historical narratives. This intellectual activity was in turn brought to bear on the wider population first through commercial media in the politically fractured 1920s, and then, with the consolidation of Guomindang power in the 1930s, through the

---

[61] Van Nguyen-Marshall, "The Ethics of Benevolence in French Colonial Vietnam: A Sino-Franco-Vietnamese Cultural Borderland," in Diana Lary, ed., *The Chinese State at the Borders* (Vancouver: University of British Columbia Press, 2007), 174–75.

[62] Gilles Deleuze and Félix Guattari, *Anti-Oedipus: Capitalism and Schizophrenia*, trans. Robert Hurley, Mark Seem and Helen R. Lane (New York: Viking Press, 1977), 222–40.

[63] James Hevia, *English Lessons: The Pedagogy of Imperialism in Nineteenth Century China* (Durham, NC: Duke University Press, 2003), 21–27, 128–42.

[64] Chatterjee, "Community in the East," 278.

pedagogical heft of the party-state. In the process, national construction involved a reduction of the rural to peasant culture – in other words, an understanding of the local as parochial and socially stunted, if not primitive and socially petrified. The civic values underpinning citizenship, and which served to heal the social ravages of capitalism in the individualist West, were absent, even impossible, in the local, and could only be injected through outside forces tethered to the nation-building project.

By probing into the workings of revolutionary memory a century ago, we can more easily unlock the vanity case of modernity: the notion that modern people got things done, for better or for worse, where their forebears did not bother. The revolutionary memory explored here is not uniquely Chinese. Similar treatments and uses of the past can be seen, for example, in the Russian experience of revolution.[65] Nor is it uniquely Communist. In China's case, revolutionary memory is a function of layers of cultural production by progressive activists around the fall of China's last dynasty, missionaries over the course of the nineteenth and twentieth centuries, Western journalists, poets and playwrights, and Guomindang and Communist Party propagandists. Looked at in this way, the Maoist evocation of the "old society" earmarked for destruction was only the more pointed end of a transnational conversation on "traditional" – in this case Chinese – culture and life. In this way, revolutionary memory should be seen more broadly than the Chinese or Maoist contexts as a form of modern erasure of the recent past.

——

Part I of this book ("Seeing and Not Seeing") sketches media outlets and the various social circles in China circa 1920 as a way of examining how phenomena in the countryside was seen, and not seen, by particular writers and activists at a watershed moment in the country's history. Chapter 1 charts four social channels leading into China's Northwest at the time of the great earthquake that struck remote Haiyuan, Gansu, in 1920: native Gansu networks, national (political and charitable) networks, foreign (missionary and other) networks, and scientific (geological) networks. The aim is to consider the ways in which crisis events in the early republic were responded to, commented on and remembered before the book follows threads of cultural formation over the ensuing decades. Chapter 2 turns to university circles in the nation's capital at the height of

---

[65] See, for example, Elizabeth Astrid Papazian, *Manufacturing Truth: The Documentary Moment in Early Soviet Culture* (Dekalb: Northern Illinois Press, 2009); and Igal Halfin, *From Darkness to Light: Class, Consciousness, and Salvation in Revolutionary Russia* (Pittsburgh, PA: University of Pittsburgh Press, 2000).

the May Fourth movement. It charts the intersection of the emerging discipline of sociology in China and the social survey movement with the great numbers of students who took up journalism in the 1920s as a way of capturing everyday life and diagnosing social ills with the aim of reformist or revolutionary transformation. After considering earthquake coverage by the New Culture movement journal *Xin Long* (New Gansu, *Long* being a secondary name for the province), the chapter steps back to view student reports on the broader crisis of famine over the year in order to compare it to memorialization of disaster within the same communities in the afflicted interior. Chapter 3 reveals the varied ways in which Western writers diagnosed Chinese deficiencies in the areas of governance, charity relief and the valuation of human life amid drought, famine and the earthquake around 1920. It then demonstrates the considerable amount of cross-fertilization of these ideas with Chinese intellectuals in the period as China's various revolutionary programs took shape over the 1920s.

Part II ("Revolutionary Memory in Republican China") charts cultural production over the 1920s and 1930s as a way of tracing the evolution of revolutionary memory. Chapter 4 examines children's magazines, history and civics textbooks, and vernacular Mandarin readers over the 1920s to show how detailed discussion of Chinese communities during famine and earthquake was left out of liberal and commercial narratives of republican history. Instead, pedagogical texts favored civic lessons and critical exposés of society in the Chinese interior by New Culture writers. Chapter 5 turns to the development of political theory and terminology over the 1920s by Guomindang and Communist strategists, most prominently Mao Zedong. It charts the development of the concept of evil gentry (*lieshen*) in party reports and Shanghai journals, and the co-option more generally by the Guomindang and Communists of New Culture and May Fourth encoding of rural life. Chapter 6 explores parallels in the 1930s between Guomindang sociology and international representations of rural China, focusing on the work of Pearl S. Buck. The chapter does this for what it says about convergences between artistic and academic writing on the nature of rural life, and the global conversations behind the reduction of complex communities into peasantries. Chapter 7 concerns the development of the woodcut (*muke*) in order to capture representations of rural life popularized by Communist-allied artists and accessible to the general population. It shows how the Chinese woodcut movement begun by Lu Xun and China's Leftwing Writer's League in the early 1930s shifted its focus over time from urban subjects and an emerging proletariat to, by the civil war (1945–49), what the chapter calls "forsaken subjects": people occupying rural landscapes of social distress devoid of community and civic values. Over the course of the 1940s, the woodcut evolved from portrayals of social desolation to affirmative messaging, one that assigned new codes, values and frames of reference to the life experience.

Part III ("Maoist Narratives in the Forties") turns to the border regions of the 1940s, examining the inculcation of Maoist morality through historical narrative in rural and urban settings. Chapter 8 considers the nature of Maoist storytelling in Yan'an before turning to the use of drama troupes in the surrounding border region as a way of enacting land reform and communicating new forms of Maoist morality to rural audiences. By the eve of the 1949 revolution, the scripts that Maoist drama troupes were performing, such as *Red Leaf River* (*Chi ye he*), not only dramatized the experience of famine in North China from the late 1920s to the late 1940s but also served in a sense as a stand-in for the history of society amid famine. Chapter 9 turns to the urban population under Communist control, and youth in particular, to consider the stories used to bring Maoist morality and party understandings of the past beyond Yan'an. It uses the example of Zhangjiakou's *Minzhu qingnian* (Democratic Youth) in the Jin Cha Ji border region, which formed part of the propaganda unit that would evolve into *Renmin ribao* in 1948. The aim is to demonstrate the central role that revolutionary memory of disasters such as famine played in party efforts to exhort and mobilize youth in rural China up to and through the 1949 revolution.

Part IV ("Politics of Oblivion in the People's Republic") explores tensions between communal and revolutionary memory of republican life as both forms of cultural memory evolved over the People's Republic. It does this first by returning to 1920 in Chapter 10 in order to revisit local records on the Gansu earthquake, and those of Guyuan in particular, southern Ningxia's regional hub. The aim is to piece together the process of local cultural production through the compilation of the republican and modern gazetteers at Guyuan, as well as innovations of the People's Republic – such as *wenshi ziliao* (Cultural and Historical Materials) – in order to compare them with revolutionary narratives and their political uses over the Maoist period, which is the focus of the remaining three chapters. Chapter 11 considers how perceptions of past village life were used during the land reform campaigns around the 1949 revolution before turning to the work of literary scholar Cai Xiang on the 1950s genre of cooperative movement fiction and the ways in which local narratives were subsumed into national ones by the end of the decade. Chapter 12 covers the reinforcement of revolutionary memory in the wake of the largely rural ravages of the Great Leap Forward famine around 1960. It considers how the ritualized consumption of revolutionary memory among the rank and file of the People's Liberation Army spread to the general population in various ways. It then covers classroom instruction, class-conflict exhibitions and the Socialist Education movement's Four Histories movement in southeast Shanxi's Jin district to consider how cultural memory was employed as a foil against which mass starvation under the New China was contrasted. Chapter 13 probes the extent to which tensions between communal and revolutionary perceptions of the past can help explain the continued potency of political labels two decades into the People's Republic. The chapter pursues these tensions for what they say about the relationship between epistemic and physical violence in Maoist ideology and practice by revisiting the extreme violence of the late sixties and collective killing in rural areas in particular. Finally, it considers the sixties in China in the broader context of state and civilian violence in the twentieth-century world and the civilizing mission of the colonial project.

Finally, the Conclusion considers the implications of the epistemic destruction of the twentieth century on general narratives and scholarly works on modern Chinese history. It then turns to the continued role of *wenshi ziliao* as a form of communal memory, the role of disaster commemoration in the political legitimacy of the Chinese Communist Party, and the continued political utility of revolutionary memory in the post-Mao People's Republic.

Part I

Seeing and Not Seeing

1   Networks into China's Northwest

Over the centuries, travelers heading from the populous valleys of Central China into Inner Asia have had the option of taking the high road over the Ordos Plateau. One of the less traveled of the trade routes later known collectively as the silk road, it offered its rewards, among them the great Buddhist statues and grottoes at Xumishan, before cutting west over the Liupanshan range. There it came under the watchful eyes of a Song-era garrison perched in the hills at Shoumaying as it descended onto the alkali flats and Tang-era salt mining community at Ganyanchi.[1] Moments before arriving at Ganyanchi's gates, travelers would have passed a patch of gravel beside the road. The spot was hardly worthy of a glance, until a wintry evening in 1920 when, in the space of minutes, a fault line several kilometers below the surface released the seismic equivalent of two hundred million tons of TNT into the surrounding landscape.[2]

The great Haiyuan earthquake of 1920 struck one of the most remote regions of China. Yet it also occurred at a watershed moment in Chinese history. The 8.5 magnitude earthquake would remain relatively obscure, despite its ferocity and destruction to the region. But the ways in which the event and events like it at the time were responded to, commented on and remembered reveals a good deal about the nature of changes wrought by the remaining century, about China's revolutions, and about the modern experience more generally. These responses came down to who people knew, what resources they had, and what, to them, was at stake in the world of 1920.

---

[1] Details on the region are based on a 2017 conversation in Yinchuan with the Ningxia historian and Guyuan native Xue Zhengchang. The Tang dynasty lasted from 618 to 907. The Northern Song dynasty lasted from 960 to 1127 – when the Song moved south of the Yangzi – until falling to the Mongols in 1279.
[2] Energy comparison is made in Zhang Siyuan, "Shisan shiji yi lai Guyuan diqu de ba ci zhongqiang dizhen," in *Guyuan wenshi ziliao* 1, 1987, 94.

Reports of the earthquake and life in its aftermath were transmitted to the wider national and global public via books and newsprint, consular and other official correspondence, and word of mouth in cities and towns across China and overseas. Chinese newsprint at the time took the form of hundreds of journals and newspapers: dailies and weeklies, tabloids and broadsheets. Some were state owned, such as Tianjin's *Da gongbao*, purchased in 1916 by the Beiyang government seated in Beijing.[3] But many were either sponsored by or affiliated with political factions and parties (presumably the case with the Beijing tabloid-sized daily *Xiao gongbao*) or stemmed from particular social or commercial networks. In the Gansu earthquake coverage examined below, these publications belonged to Buddhist associations, Christian missions, foreign interests (the *North China Herald* was British owned) and civic-minded collectives of journalists and activists – which appears to be the case for *Shihua* and *Zhongguo minbao*.

We begin this study by identifying four networks active in or connected to events in China's Northwest at the time of May Fourth: Gansu natives (and their outside contacts), national (such as state and charitable actors around the republic), foreign (missionaries and relief workers) and scientific (in this case, geological) networks. Like any social network, these were by no means discrete and overlapped to some degree. By sketching them, communication channels reveal themselves, along with the impacts certain social circles had on shaping the historical record at a particular time and place in modern history.

Native Networks

Night had fallen and typesetting was underway at a city daily in Shaanxi's Wei River valley when the quake struck, shaking the pillars and roof beams of the workroom and lowering the ceiling several meters toward the floor.[4] But no one on the premises was hurt, and so the staff continued their work preparing the Xi'an paper, unaware of the destruction that night in the rest of the great walled city, let alone in the uplands to the north, where downed lines cut off communications with Chinese Inner Asia. The following morning, as copies of *Guxin ribao* made their way around the provincial capital, the paper could only note the visitation of a great earthquake to the region.[5] The region's loss of life had, in fact,

---

[3] Wang Runze, *Zhang Liluan yu Da gongbao* (Beijing: Zhonghua shiju, 2008), 30.

[4] Some readers may like to note that Shaanxi (陝西) is distinct from Shanxi (山西), a neighboring province that also figures in developments in this book.

[5] *Guxin ribao*, December 17, 1920. Digital scans of this newspaper are available in the reading room of the Shaanxi Provincial Library.

been astronomical. But a broader picture of the unfolding disaster would come only with time.

Over the following week, a disjointed telegraph network pulsed with appeals to the country's coast for assistance. These cables landed on desks at government ministries seated in Beijing and Tianjin; at disaster relief charities and native-place associations for sojourners spread across the country; and at the editorial rooms of magazines and newspapers in major urban centers; in turn, they reached the wider public in news articles, editorial columns and relief appeals in whole or in excerpted fragments.

It made sense that the first news to reach the Beijing press came from the more populated Wei River valley around Xi'an, the largest city in the Northwest. There, county-level relief societies had already been in place to address the severe drought affecting the region, and their investigators were now assessing loss of life and damage in the surrounding areas. In Xi'an, at least, many residents were injured, but deaths were low.[6]

A week after the quake, one thing became clear: neighboring Gansu was its center, something that could be crudely deduced by comparing the duration of the tremors in each of the incoming cables. These had lasted five minutes in Taiyuan, the Shanxi governor reported, and twice that – a full ten minutes – in eastern Gansu. There, Lu Hongtao, the commander at the garrison town of Pingliang, reported that large numbers of people were crushed in their homes, and that Guyuan county to the north was especially hard hit. For the moment, communities in the area received 3,000 yuan from his purse in emergency relief, Lu reported, as he called on the finance ministry in Beijing and Gansu's provincial government in Lanzhou to release or raise more.[7]

It was not until the middle of January, a month after the earthquake, that more methodical, and far grimmer, county-by-county accounts reached coastal readers. Of twenty counties tallied in a mid-January report, two stood out, placed solemnly at the end of the list: Haiyuan, where "tremors lasted from 7pm on the sixteenth to midday on the eighteenth, destroying most of the buildings and crushing to death 50 percent to 60 percent of the people," Tianjin's *Da gongbao* explained.[8] And Guyuan, where "the entire [county seat] was leveled, and only one out of ten buildings spared. But the tremors had not even ceased by the eighteenth" when the report appears to have been filed. "There was no way of

[6] *Zhongguo minbao*, December 22, 1920; *Xiao gongbao*, December 23, 1920.
[7] *Shihua*, December 24, 1920.
[8] *Da gongbao*, January 13, 1921. The source states Ningxia but presumably refers to Haiyuan to its south since destruction in Ningxia town was relatively light.

determining how many people were buried in the rubble. The telegraph equipment was all ruined."[9]

Both counties were located in the foothills of eastern Gansu's Liupanshan, which stands between the Gobi desert and the northern reaches of the most expansive loess landscape on earth.[10] In eastern Gansu, cave houses made of loess were extremely common, like those found along the southern bank of the Yellow River in Henan province, a Beijing news daily explained to readers in its earthquake coverage.[11] A very fine yellowish earth, loess absorbs water easily without collapsing into mud, allowing it to be shaped into irrigation channels, terracing and building materials, while also being fertile for planting, despite appearing barren to the unfamiliar eye. The popularity of cave dwellings in Gansu was a function of both topography and poverty: they were cheap, requiring little more than tools to excavate thick deposits of loess soil plus limited timber for a facade. But cave homes also had practical benefits, among them protection from vermin and better insulation from Inner Asia's extremes of heat and cold than costly wooden structures – something foreign visitors to the region remarked on at the time.[12] Eastern Gansu's loess cave dwellings could also be unusually large, due to the area's richness in lime, which made the soil less prone to collapsing. The region around Liupanshan in fact hosted China's highest concentration of cave dwellings well into the modern period. But, located around depressions in the earth's crust (or grabens), it also sits atop a series of fault lines which, amid seismic activity, brought ceilings down onto living spaces and buried foodstuffs and livestock under great mounds of soil.[13]

For a month after the first tremors, news only trickled to unaffected parts of the country. Migrants from the region in Beijing received word from relatives by telegram of losses or miraculous escapes. But after four weeks the postal system had still not delivered Gansu's mail the thousand kilometers to Beijing.[14] Only toward the end of January did excerpted letters from the quake zone start appearing in the capital press – at times sent by local magistrates, the chief administrative official at the county level. In one case, the magistrate of eastern Gansu's Qingyang county

[9] Ibid.
[10] He Xiubin, Keli Tang and Xinbao Zhang, "Soil Erosion Dynamics on the Chinese Loess Plateau in the Last 10,000 Years," *Mountain Research and Development* 24/4 (2004), 342–43.
[11] *Xiao gongbao*, January 17, 1921.
[12] Myron Fuller and Frederick Clapp, "Loess and Rock Dwellings of Shensi, China," *Geographical Review* 14/2 (1924), 222.
[13] I wish to thank Barry Parsons for clarifying geological aspects of the region in our conversation in the summer of 2015.
[14] *Xiao gongbao*, January 17, 1921.

appealed to Gansu natives residing in Beijing through their native-place association (*tongxiang hui*), lamenting how even in his relatively lightly hit district relief was "like a cup of water [thrown on a bonfire], no help at all" considering the magnitude of the situation.[15]

This six weeks' worth of correspondence between remote corners of the loess plateau and centers of power in the Chinese republic reveals a few things. Authorities and community groups were working simultaneously to collect and disseminate data and generate appeals for help across their networks, nationally and overseas. These networks also overlapped considerably, operating both in tandem and parallel to each other. As they shaped perceptions of life in China's Northwest, earthquake cables and letters also served as a form of cultural legacy for communities and diasporas spread across the republic. Composed by Gansu residents and shared by recipients in Beijing and beyond, they were likely read aloud and shared in groups, at native-place lodges, workplaces and homes, as fresh news, as a way of mobilizing aid or as remembrance. Due to the monumental nature of the events described, these stories doubtless lived on in households as clippings or were passed down orally, eventually making their way, in the case of *Zhongguo minbao*'s uniquely comprehensive coverage of the earthquake, into poster displays at museums in Lanzhou and Haiyuan in the 2010s, nearly a century after the earthquake.

But then, one must not exaggerate the reach of these native networks and their publications. As historical events go, rarely has so much destruction fallen into such obscurity. The areas most affected by the great earthquake of 1920 were extremely remote, their communities on some of the furthest margins of national life (see Map 1). The record of the communities' appeals, falling as they did into the particular news organs of the time, shared the collective fate of much of prerevolutionary Chinese print media over the course of the tumultuous twentieth century: reduction to the faintest traces, surviving, in the luckiest cases, in semicomplete runs at a sole library collection in mainland China.[16]

The epistemological questions these varied documentary fates raise are the subject of this book. These questions are fundamentally about how accounts or stories from the recent past find channels to posterity while

---

[15] *Xiao gongbao*, January 26, 1921.

[16] The newspapers alluded to here appear in hard copy at Beijing University (*Shihua* and *Zhongguo minbao*), or on microfilm at the National Library in Beijing (*Xiao gongbao*) or the Shanghai Municipal Library (*Aiguo baihuabao*). In contrast, *Da gongbao* is found in bound reproductions at all three libraries. A tiny fraction of the period's newspapers has benefited from the digital age: of these papers, only *Da gongbao* appears in major online databases today.

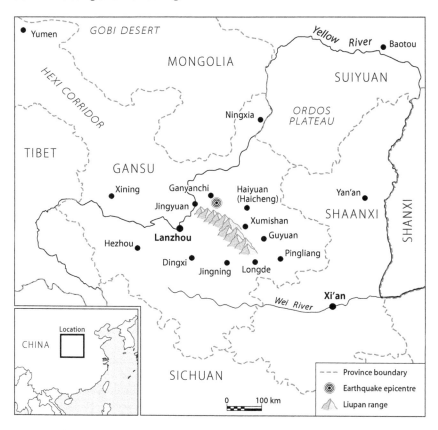

Map 1 Northwest China's Gansu and Shaanxi provinces, showing the 1920 earthquake epicenter and key locations and features mentioned in the text. Map created by Nick Scarle for the author.

others meet dead ends; about the ways surviving stories evolve over the course of their transcription and dissemination; and about the effects these evolutions have on broader public discourses on "how things used to be."

National Networks

On December 18, 1920, several thousand middle school and university students spread across China's major cities for a day of disaster relief appeals that verged on taking the form of public demonstrations. In

Beijing, where the event was jointly organized by an international relief committee and two Chinese Christian youth associations, male students paraded and appealed for funds on the streets and at shops and businesses while their female counterparts solicited donations at the homes of family and friends.[17] "What is today?" a student notice reminded readers of Beijing's *Chenbao* (a daily newspaper known in English as the *Morning Post*): "It's Drought Awareness Day."[18] In Xi'an, "charity relief donation boxes" were mounted around the city and publicized with great urgency in the city press.[19] Planned since November,[20] the national event was aimed at generating relief funds for residents of five northern provinces suffering from famine conditions since the summer, after a year's drought across much of the Yellow River basin. Few if anyone in the participating cities – residents of Xi'an excepted – were even aware that an earthquake had struck the country's Northwest just two nights before, leaving hundreds of thousands of survivors in search of food and exposed to the elements.

In the end, the brief national drive collected only 7,855 yuan in coppers and notes across the capital – enough to purchase a day's relief ration for roughly 157,000 people – a disappointing result explained, in part, by inclement weather including "ferocious winds" that drove students back to their campuses in the late afternoon.[21] Meanwhile, organizers estimated that some fifteen million people were in need of assistance across North China's drought-famine field.[22]

The students had aimed to invigorate a relief effort underway since late summer – decentralized and therefore hard to gauge in size and reach – carried out through the various channels linking state agencies and communities across the country. Various networks – among them county, prefectural and provincial governments, the military, native-place associations, charities, missions and international relief groups – had dispatched 182 million *jin* of relief grain to railheads across the stricken north over the month of December, enough to sustain around eleven million people on famine rations of half a *jin* per day until the

---

[17] *Da gongbao*, December 15, 1920.   [18] *Chenbao*, December 17 and 18, 1920.
[19] *Guxin ribao*, December 17, 1920.
[20] *Shihua*, December 2, 1920; *Yishibao*, December 2, 1920; *Minyi ribao*, December 19, 1920; *Zhongguo minbao*, December 19, 1920; *Xiao gongbao*, December 20, 1920.
[21] *Xiao gongbao*, December 23, 1920. The estimate is based on an average price of five coppers per *jin* (the price paid by relief societies for the predominant relief grain, millet) and a relief ration of half a *jin* per day (the prevailing ration used by major relief societies) over the year. For more on relief finances and logistics during this event, see Pierre Fuller, *Famine Relief in Warlord China*, Harvard East Asian Monographs (Cambridge, MA: Harvard University Asia Center, 2019).
[22] *Da gongbao*, December 15, 1920.

new year.[23] The December 18 student reminders of distress in the countryside were clearly addressed to those located outside these existing networks, to members of the country's urban centers cut off from what was a predominantly rural subsistence crisis.

Gansu played a part in this effort, however modest, having enjoyed a healthy harvest that autumn. Two months before the earthquake, the province designated a channel for charitable relief goods that went down the Yellow River and then by train via Baotou to the drought zone on the North China plain.[24] Struck by the quake just as famine to the east worsened over winter, Gansu was unlikely to attract the national attention it needed to relieve its communities and rebuild.

Moreover, politics in Lanzhou was in turmoil. Earlier in the summer, a 100-member strong meeting of the Gansu native-place association of Beijing, the association for officials, merchants and other Gansu natives residing in the capital, had put forward a motion to expel one of its most prominent members – the province's military governor since 1913, Zhang Guangjian – and to lobby central government authorities for his removal from office for "criminal misconduct."[25] A native of Anhui, the fifty-three-year-old Zhang had established his authority in the northwestern province through the patronage of former president Yuan Shikai, who died in 1916. Now Zhang's powerbase was further eroded by the changing fortunes of his Anhui political faction, which had been in control of the nation's capital until July 1920 when it was soundly defeated by its rival Zhili faction in a war fought in the environs of Beijing.

The governor's demise would, in turn, upset a delicate power arrangement in place within the province over his seven-year tenure. An enormous share of provincial revenue – some two-thirds – had gone to military expenditure under Zhang. The institution of the military that these monies financed, served to absorb elite ambitions within both of Gansu's main ethnic communities. Many of the province's Muslim elites originated in Hezhou, the center of Sino-Muslim culture in Gansu's southwest where families had the wherewithal to excel in the examination system, producing a formidable number of military officials.[26] In 1920, half of Gansu's

---

[23] *Zhengfu gongbao*, June 13, 1921.   [24] *Shihua*, October 16, 1920.

[25] *Zhongguo minbao*, August 16, 1920.

[26] Drawing from the work of Jonathan Lipman, I use the term Sino-Muslim (as opposed to Hui or Chinese Muslim) throughout this book to refer to the Chinese-speaking Muslim communities of Gansu in the republican period. The term Hui was officially employed as an ethnic (*minzu*) designation for Gansu's Chinese-speaking Muslims only in the People's Republic. In earlier periods, Hui was used by Chinese speakers as a general term for people and things associated with the Islamic faith. Han Dingshan, "Zhang Guangjian du Gan qi nian," *Gansu wenshi ziliao xuanji* 2 (1963), 17–27; Wang Jin and Yang Hongwei, *Gan Ning Qing minguo renwu* (Beijing: Zhongguo shehui kexue

eight military districts were commanded by Sino-Muslims, the other four by Han Chinese. The two sides vying to replace Zhang fell along this ethnic divide.

Eastern Gansu's two military commanders – one in charge of the northern gravel-covered half of the earthquake zone served by the Yellow River, the other its loess-covered southern half skirting the main national highways – were pitted against each other for the governership at the time the quake struck. A week before the earthquake, the Gansu native-place association of Shanghai had sent out a series of dispatches to organizations around the country urging Zhang's removal. Ma Fuxiang, defense commissioner of Ningxia and military officer there since 1912, telegraphed his support for the move, after which Gansu's Muslim military commanders voiced their support to Beijing for the forty-four-year-old Ma, a Hezhou native, to take Zhang's place.[27] In response, Lu Hongtao, defense commissioner of Pingliang district (and one of the first organizers of outside emergency relief for the hardest-hit communities as we have seen), cabled to Beijing his opposition to Ma's appointment. The fifty-four-year-old Lu was from Jiangsu but had served in military posts in Gansu for nearly thirty years, and won the support of Gansu officials and gentry in Beijing for his appointment to head the province. At the end of January, 1921, Lu was awarded the governorship in Lanzhou, while Ma was made military governor of neighboring Suiyuan province, a disagreeable result for Muslim separatists in Gansu, who were reportedly emboldened by it through the 1920s.[28]

In January, meanwhile, the unseated Zhang cabled details of his province's plight to Tianjin's *Da gongbao* newspaper, but he did so from the neighboring capital of Shaanxi, ostensibly because Gansu's telegram system remained crippled, but presumably also because of his loss of position at home.[29] Two weeks later, the newly formed Gansu Earthquake Relief Society (Gansu zhenzai jiuji hui) sounded an alarm over the paltry funding so far made available for relief, likening it to "a cup of water thrown onto a bonfire" (a stock phrase for extreme inadequacy) in a cable to the same state-owned news daily in coastal Tianjin.[30] Then, in February, aid organizers in Gansu appealed publicly to Lu Hongtao and Ma Fuxiang to recover the 1.5 million yuan in public monies Zhang

chubanshe, 2013), 1–9; Jonathan N. Lipman, "Hyphenated Chinese: Sino-Muslim Identity in Modern China," in Gail Hershatter, et al., eds., *Remapping China: Fissures in Historical Terrain* (Stanford, CA: Stanford University Press, 1996), 101.
[27] Wang and Yang, *Gan Ning Qing minguo renwu*, 118–20.
[28] Wei Shaowu, "Lu Hongtao du Gan shimo," *Gansu wenshi ziliao xuanji* 1 (1986), 58–60; Wang and Yang, *Gan Ning Qing minguo renwu*, 15–18.
[29] *Da gongbao*, January 11, 1921.   [30] *Da gongbao*, January 25, 1921.

was believed to have absconded with before his departure, and put it to earthquake relief.[31]

Two months after the initial quake, reports began to reach the coast more regularly through postal and telegraph channels. News outlets featured them in their spreads, serving as a public noticeboard on the distant, unfolding crisis. One of these was *Zhongguo minbao*, a Beijing broadsheet founded in 1920 that closely followed Gansu affairs.[32] Weeks of intensive coverage followed in its pages that finally shed light on the earthquake experience and aftermath. This included the first comprehensive count of human deaths in the earthquake to reach the reading public in the capital: more than three hundred thousand, albeit a figure based on tentative and clearly rounded sums pieced together from county reports and the paper's own correspondents in the field.[33]

Zhongguo minbao also announced major relief donations next to its front-page masthead, and condolences from military governors around the country inside, along with the news of relief fundraising drives in their constituencies.[34] In the domain of Manchurian marshal Zhang Zuolin, for example, collections of one or two yuan were taken at tax offices, telegraph bureau, local businesses, benefit shows and workplaces across the three eastern provinces of Fengtian, Jilin and Heilongjiang. Each of these collections for Gansu totaled several dozen to several hundred yuan from late winter into summer.[35] These small accumulating sums began reaching the Northwest at the start of March with the arrival of 10,000 yuan from Zhang's government via the Bank of China (in this case, designated for quake-hit areas of Shaanxi).[36]

One relief office set up by gentry in Gansu to manage relief funds from state and social networks around the country and overseas handled some 300,000 silver ounces over 1921, which was largely spent on free and work relief projects in ten of the worst-hit counties in three distributions in early and mid-spring and early autumn. In the case of Haiyuan, 1,500 silver ounces were distributed in March, 4,000 in May, and 4,000 in September; in Guyuan, 500 silver ounces in March, 4,000 in May, and 4,000 in September; and in Jingning, 500 silver ounces in March, 4,000 in May, and 4,000 in October, plus 3,000 silver ounces for the work relief overseen by Magistrate Zhou Tingyuan of clearing the river blockages

[31] *Zhonguo minbao*, February 23, 1921.
[32] Beijing shi difang zhi bianzuan weiyuan hui, *Beijing zhi: baoye tongxun she zhi* (Beijing: Beijing chuban she, 2005), 50.
[33] *Zhongguo minbao*, March 1–5, 1921.   [34] *Zhongguo minbao*, February 25, 1921.
[35] *Fengtian gongbao*, March 18, 20, 21 and 28, 1921; April 4, 17, 20 and 26, 1921; July 9, 10, 11, 18, 24 and 26, 1921; and August 10, 1921.
[36] *Guxin ribao*, March 1, 1921.

wrought by the landslides, to avoid flooding with the snowmelt of spring. With each county distribution, five to eight silver ounces each were allocated to 500 to 800 households in need, which had been identified through county registers of the poor and by canvassing. In a sign of the disorder in Guyuan and Haiyuan, the relief office spent around 150 yuan to cover the military escort accompanying its staff there.[37]

In light of other types of losses incurred in communities in eastern Gansu – sixty thousand cattle and sheep killed and 80 percent of buildings in ruins, in the case of Guyuan[38] – incoming aid was miniscule, and could only be used to prevent further loss of life to hunger and exposure. In comparison, native-place networks in Manchuria mobilized much more over the same winter for the Shandong and Zhili famine field, to where many Manchurian residents could trace their roots.[39]

But then, some of the quake's hardest-hit communities were at the center of a vast Islamic network linking adherents of the Jahriya (New Faith) from as disparate parts of Asia as Manchuria, Yunnan and Turkestan to the market town of Zhangjichuan in Longde county, Jingning's neighbor to the east.[40] Longde received 8,500 silver ounces in the gentry-led relief distributions touched on above, but there were presumably parallel channels of incoming assistance to the county's isolated valleys. Visiting Ma Yuanzhang a year before the Muslim figure's death in the earthquake, a Western journalist called Ma's home "a veritable clearinghouse for all charitable efforts" to the local poor via donations from pilgrims, students and the local rich.[41] There is no reason to think this network did not exercise this charitable culture in the aftermath of Zhangjichuan's sudden destruction, leaving traces elsewhere in the historical record.

As for English-language documentation of the Gansu earthquake and life in its aftermath, this was predominantly a product of missionary work. The output of this tiny community – minuscule in China's Northwest, and small anywhere in the republic relative to the population – is well worth including here for the outsized role it played in shaping perceptions of life in China for generations of non-Chinese. The record these missions left behind has become entwined with global conversations spanning the

---

[37] *Gansu zhenzai chouzhenchu diyiqi zhengxin lü* (n.p.: 1921), 1–25, Special Collections, Gansu Provincial Library; *Xinren zhenzai ji* (n.p.: n.d.), 1a–10a, Special Collections, Gansu Provincial Library.

[38] *Zhongguo minbao*, March 1, 1921.

[39] See Fuller, *Famine Relief in Warlord China*, 200–14.

[40] Jonathan Lipman, *Familiar Strangers: A History of Muslims in Northwest China* (Seattle: University of Washington Press, 1997), 114.

[41] Quoted in Anthony Garnaut, "The Shaykh of the Great Northwest: The Religious and Political Life of Ma Yuanzhang (1853–1920)" (PhD diss., Australia National University, 2010), 1.

Anglo-American, French and other imperial worlds with which Chinese of all kinds interacted to varying degrees over the course of the century.

Foreign Networks

Gansu, the republic's fourth-largest province, was especially unusual in shape, consisting of two bulges – one spilling west into Central Asia, the other east into "China Proper" – connected by the thin Hexi Corridor, a long fertile belt of oasis towns and orchards producing the region's famed fruit. Stretched in this way between the Tibetan plateau and the deserts and grasslands of Mongolia, Gansu stood at the crossroads of an extraordinary mix of cultures: between the mountain and steppe communities on its northern and southern edges ran the traffic of peoples, goods and religious thought over the main east–west trade routes that later became collectively known as the silk road.

At the time of the 1920 earthquake, the demographic arrangement of this territory was in large part a product of state social engineering fifty years earlier, in the wake of the Northwest's intercommunal wars of the 1870s. Back then, the Qing military endeavored to remove Muslims from more populated areas through the mass execution of thousands of people associated with the fighting, and through relocation of others into isolated but viable settlements selected by local officials for the purpose, away from highways and urban centers but with access to water, fertile land and other vital resources. The result was two concentrations of Muslims in Gansu: in the southwest around Hezhou at the foot of the Tibetan uplift, where thousands were moved from the Hexi Corridor in the 1870s; and in the area surrounding the Liupanshan range in the east, where families were relocated in similar numbers from Shaanxi's Wei River valley.[42] The mountain range forms a 300 kilometer-long barrier to east–west traffic, rerouting most travelers either onto the Yellow River as it skirts Mongolia or the main highways out of Xi'an to the south. Here, along the remote Liupanshan peaks, where Genghis Khan is thought to have died in the thirteenth century while on his final campaign against the Xi Xia Kingdom, the region's Muslim communities were, from the Qing perspective, safely placed out of the way.[43]

By the start of the next century, the Sino-Muslims of the Northwest had attracted the attention of Western missionaries who ventured into the

---

[42] Wen-Djang Chu, *The Moslem Rebellion in Northwest China, 1862–1878: A Study of Government Minority Policy* (Paris: Mouton, 1966, 151–53); Lipman, *Familiar Strangers*, 126, 128, 134.

[43] Leo de Hartog, *Genghis Khan: Conqueror of the World* (London: I. B. Tauris, 1989), 135–36; John Man, *Genghis Khan: Life, Death and Resurrection* (London: Bantam Press, 2004), 239.

region's isolated valleys where the area's highest concentrations of Sino-Muslims could be found. Much smaller in number than in the country's east, the missionaries to Gansu had nonetheless a relatively vocal presence, at least measured by the writing they produced from their stations, which remain easily accessible to the historian.

In the first few weeks of 1921, Ebenezer Mann recounted his experience of the December earthquake in a China Inland Mission periodical: it was "in the midst of prayer when the room shook," he wrote, for three minutes, with fifty aftershocks over the next twenty-four hours. "These Lanchow houses are very well constructed," he added, "with a strong framework of wood into which the walls are built so that they will stand a great strain and we all felt that very few English houses would have stood the test." Happily, for reasons of geography, topography and engineering, Gansu's capital city of Lanzhou, some 150 kilometers from the epicenter, got off relatively lightly with forty-two reported deaths.[44]

Twelve days after the initial tremors, a message arrived at the Borden Memorial Hospital in town asking Robert C. Parry, the sole foreign medical doctor in the province, to come tend to the 2,828 injured residents in Jingning county some 175 kilometers to the southeast. The hospital was the namesake of William Whiting Borden, who had bequeathed £250,000 to the China Inland Mission in 1913 after dying in Cairo while learning Arabic, so he could evangelize among Muslim communities in China's Northwest. Parry had only just taken over the hospital's operation the month before, when its founding physician returned to Britain on furlough.[45]

The doctor and an American companion began the trek by cart over the old imperial highway linking Gansu with Shaanxi's Wei River valley. Normally, travelers took four days to make the trip to Jingning, benefitting from the colonnades of towering trees that lined Gansu's highways – affording some refuge from the winter's driving winds and the beating sun of summer.[46] But, the men were forced to spend an additional two days on foot as their team negotiated a scarred wintry landscape that was almost completely reshaped by landslides, passing at one point a Russian general and his family, "Refugees from European Russia," who had been on the road for two years.

---

[44] Ebenezer J. Mann, "The Earthquake," *Links with China and Other Lands* 31 (April 1921), 331.
[45] "Will of William Whiting Borden, Leaving £250,000 to China Inland Mission in North America: To Be Proved in Chicago," 1913, CIM/01/04/3/95, China Inland Mission Archives, Special Collections, School of Oriental and African Studies, University of London.
[46] Eric Teichman, *Travels of a Consular Officer in North-west China* (Cambridge: Cambridge University Press, 1921), plate 24.

Soon after settling in at Jingning, Parry dispatched a letter to colleagues. In it, he explained that

the Magistrate had received no news of our coming, but welcomed [us] right royally. We are now in a comfortable tent in the same yard as himself. Quarters will be places [sic] at our disposal for dressings, and all injured will be urged to come. One thousand about have been buried since the earthquake. One is filled with admiration for the Magistrate here. When the earthquake came on he quickly ordered men to rush out and call the people from their homes. Then he retired to his own room and knelt down and prayed to Shang-Ti (God) to kill him, if it pleased him, but to spare the people. The walls of the house fell about him, even striking him, but he prayed on. Finally some one outside called him from without. Thinking his help was wanted he clambered out of the window as the door was jammed. On finding out however he was called out to save his own life, he knelt down in the yard and continued to cry to God to kill him but to spare the people. When the quake was over he went out to set the people to work at once and rescue the living who were prisoned in the debris. The next day when the people wanted shelter he sent out every one of the 70 or 80 tents in the Yamen [county offices], he himself sleeping on the ground with next to no cover over him. He has since given out a month's grain to those without food, from the granaries which he had built against the famine. He clothed the poor from the pawn shops. He has ordered and supervised the burial of the dead, including animals for prevention of diseases. For three days, he in addition to all the above work, fasted and wept for the people. He was evidently indispensable to the city and God spared his life. Now he says, 'I understand why God spared me. The people would have been completely disorganized if I had been killed.' He is really living for the people.[47]

Afterward, the doctor's letter reached the desk of a missionary stationed nearby at Qinzhou, who promptly placed extracts of it in a letter to the American vice consul in Hankou down on the Yangzi. From there, it was forwarded in early February to the office of the secretary of state in Washington.

A most vivid account of the earthquake's aftermath thus made its way overseas through Anglo-American channels, both through diplomatic channels and more public forums: periodicals published for parish readerships back home (excerpts of Parry's letter appear in Mann's article "The Earthquake" in the Lanzhou-based China Inland Mission quarterly *Links with China and Other Lands*); published travelogues and memoirs of service in the field (the letter is paraphrased extensively in *The Call of China's Great Northwest: or Kansu and Beyond*, written by a guest of the Manns in Lanzhou on the night of the quake and published two years later); and the "Outport" pages of newspapers in China's "treaty ports," where missionaries were a regular source of news from the country's interior (Parry's correspondence features in "Earthquake in North West

---

[47] J. Huston to Secretary of State, February 4, 1921, 2–3.

China: Terrible Loss of Life and Suffering" in *Celestial Empire*, an English-language weekly in Shanghai).[48]

In this way, the story of a Chinese magistrate named Zhou Tingyuan was passed down in time, preserved over the twentieth century in historical collections in Britain and America, finding its way into State Department files, into a magazine in the collections of the School of Oriental and African Studies in London, a memoir found on the shelves of the Strand bookstore in Manhattan, and microfilm of a weekly newspaper stored at the Library of Congress in Washington.[49]

Here, it must be noted that Parry's account of Magistrate Zhou is exceedingly rare, as are foreign accounts of upstanding public service in Chinese communities generally. Satirical treatments in contrast were popular, most notably *Letters from a Chinese Magistrate* and *Reminiscences of a Chinese Official: Revelations of Official Life Under the Manchus*, the latter serialized in the British-owned *Peking & Tientsin Times* over 1920–21 (a subject explored later in Chapter 3). Yet, there is no reason to doubt Parry's description of Zhou's exertions amid the ruins of his constituency: he remains very much singled out in local Jingning histories for numerous beneficial actions and initiatives he made as magistrate before, during and after the 1920 earthquake.[50]

Missionary attention to this one remotely stationed magistrate requires some consideration for what it says about missionary accounts more generally. American missionaries had set up Protestant evangelizing centers in Jingning in 1906 followed by Norwegians in 1919.[51] It would make sense for their workers to emphasize the vital nature of their enterprise to the cultures and communities in which they operated. An example of this was the wife of missionary Howard Taylor, who had toured the Gansu missions at the time of the quake. "As quickly as possible an Earthquake Relief Committee was organized with Mr. Mann as Chairman," she wrote under the name Mrs. Howard Taylor. "Then it was that the presence of missionaries was valued by all classes. They had been the first to see the situation, and to them the officials turned for counsel and help."[52]

---

[48] S. J. Garland, "Earthquake in North West China: Terrible Loss of Life and Suffering," *Celestial Empire*, February 5, 1921; it is worth noting that the byline reads Miss S. J. Garland.

[49] These are all the ways I came across English-language accounts of Zhou Tingyuan.

[50] *Jingning xianzhi* (1993), 616; Du Hongguang, "Zhou Tingyuan xingshi luyao," *Jingning wenshi ziliao xuanji*, vol. 2 (1992), 147–50.

[51] *Jingning xianzhi* (1993), 581.

[52] Mrs. Howard Taylor, *The Call of China's Great Northwest: Kansu and Beyond* (London, Philadelphia, Toronto, Melbourne and Shanghai: The China Inland Mission, circa 1923), 48.

Zhou's reputed faith – and by extension his indispensable role described in such detail – bolstered the sense of need for the Christian presence. "This official is known to be an exceptionally enlightened man, an 'almost persuaded' person, working entirely for the good of his people," Parry is quoted in a published version of his letter. Back in Lanzhou, Mann reckoned Zhou was merely "a professed Christian" who had not "yet got the real joy of believing." Regardless, Zhou was clearly in touch with Lanzhou's Christian community at the Borden Memorial Hospital to which he had reached out for assistance (authorities in nearby Guyuan had instead sent twenty-one carts of their gravely injured to the hospital in the garrison town of Pingliang).[53]

The incorporation of magistrate Zhou into multiple foreign accounts of the disaster in China's deep interior brought attention to a man who was by all accounts extraordinary; but attention to this one man also narrowed Jingning's wider social environment, its community, in subtle but important ways. For all its rich detail, Parry's report from a county with tens of thousands of survivors mentions one man alone in its relief – a man stationed, no less, far from his native Hunan, in the tradition of public service during the imperial era when, through the law of avoidance, magistrates served only outside their home provinces. Curiously, the missionary's description of Zhou, in fact, closely matches the Confucian ideal of the paternalistic administrator, the so-called father and mother official [fumuguan] to which district magistrates were expected to aspire in their dealings with the general population. But in doing so, Parry makes no mention of anyone beyond this outsider and his immediate family, of other crisis responders, or anything else holding the community together. In Parry's account, the communities of Jingning itself are invisible.

This invisibility extended to communal measures among the area's Muslims. In his journey there, Parry traveled between two distinct cultural poles: the region's political center at the Yellow River city of Lanzhou, where only some 10 percent of the population was Muslim, and which stood at the periphery of regional Islamic culture; and eastern Gansu, or Ningxia, which was one of the province's two main Muslim centers.[54] But then, even in the Jingning county seat, Parry would not have encountered Muslim residents in great numbers. In the districts artificially made into Islamic enclaves by Qing authorities over the previous half century, Muslim communities had been barred from settling

[53] Garland, "Earthquake in North West China"; Mann, "The Earthquake," 333.
[54] Lipman, "Hyphenated Chinese," 100–01; Lipman, *Familiar Strangers*, 20.

within city walls. So they had formed instead in the suburbs or in villages of cave dwellings dotting the region's hillsides and valleys.[55]

Gansu's Muslims then inhabited the geographic margins even within areas with Muslim majorities. So, not only had imperial relocation concentrated Sino-Muslim communities squarely onto the oval-shaped plateau of unstable terrain that hosted the earthquake epicenter on December 16, 1920. The more hilly and secluded character of their mostly cave-home communities heightened their exposure to the effects of the 1920 tremors. This included what scientists later tallied at 675 major landslides.[56] With hills covered with twenty to fifty meters of fine loess sediment blown in from the Mongolian steppes over the millennia, Jingning alone experienced 99 of these landslides, including one that traveled 3,350 meters across and then down a valley, blocking a river and resulting in the formation of a new five kilometer-long reservoir.[57] This would all help to explain the extraordinarily high toll the earthquake took on the region's Muslim residents, in particular.

In some crucial respects, though, Muslim communities were, in fact very much visible in local missionary accounts. Parry, Mann and Taylor all note the quake's heavy toll on Gansu's Muslim population, and that in contrast "generally Christians had been protected in the hour of peril," in Taylor's words, only suffering deaths at one location, in Qinzhou.[58] "A noted religious Mohammedan leader, Ma Shan-ren (馬山人), the leader of 'The New Sect' was at the time of the earthquake, at worship with his family," Parry notes in the excerpts forwarded to Washington. The doctor here referred to Ma Yuanzhang, who had been killed in Jingning's neighboring county of Longde. There, in "a long valley, mostly inhabited by Mohammedans [...] it is rumoured that about 10,000 of them were buried by the falling of the mountains on either side of the valley which have filled it up level." As for Haiyuan, he reports, "the Mohammedans" were said to have been "already looting the city" when the tremors began, leaving them "mostly buried alive." Parry continues:

This rumour is rather significant when we remember that Kansu has been on the verge of a Mohammedan rebellion during the last few months. It is reported they have lost some tens of thousands of their people. Hai-cheng [Haiyuan] is the center of a large Mohammedan population in the northwest of the province, and

---

[55] Lipman, *Familiar Strangers*, 22.

[56] Twenty-seven of these new lakes formed by the 1920 quake still existed in the 1990s. Li Tianchi, "Landslide Disasters and Human Responses in China," *Mountain Research and Development* 14/4 (1994), 342.

[57] Zhenzong Zhang and Lanmin Wang, "Geological Disasters in Loess Areas During the 1920 Haiyuan Earthquake, China," *GeoJournal* 36.2/3 (1995), 269–72.

[58] Taylor, *Call of China's Great Northwest*, 54–55; Mann, "The Earthquake," 333.

perhaps this place has suffered more than any other city during the earthquake shock.[59]

When Gansu's Muslim community did appear in missionary writing, the mention was primarily wrapped up in rumors of rebellion, looting and suggestions of divine retribution.

What Parry and his fellow missionaries were able to see, and not see, during their experience of the earthquake and its aftermath reveals a good deal about the social geography of the region, and about how certain local actors could serve as instruments for the missionary program and be highlighted in the historical record, while others were left out. It should be noted that only weeks after the December quake, the English-language *North China Herald* stressed to its readers the speed of relief measures by Gansu authorities. "The military officials were the first to render aid to the victims," a correspondent for the Shanghai-based paper reported from Pingliang. "Every one who sustained any loss of either relatives or of property is being helped by the military officials," the *Herald* added. "He [commander Lu Hongtao] is rushing tents, money, foodstuffs, and clothing to the stricken areas round about here."[60] In overlooking such examples of local relief, missionary reports said as much about the culture and aims of their producers as they did about the communities they endeavored to describe.

While missionaries comprised the bulk of foreign residents in rural China, they were by no means the only foreigners present over the course of the disastrous year. Joint foreign-Chinese "international" relief societies had formed in China's cities over the autumn of 1920 to help relieve the five-province famine just to the east of the earthquake zone. A considerable number of foreign residents took leave from their teaching, military or other posts in Tianjin, Shanghai and elsewhere for volunteer or paid work in their operations. Some published book-length accounts of their experience afterward.[61] Others produced letters, reports and articles that soon made it into private and more public circulation. The most prominent example of the latter involved a pair of Americans who were possibly the first outside investigators to visit the heart of the earthquake zone. In their reports, we see a more generous treatment of native relief, at least at first.

---

[59] J. Huston to Secretary of State, February 4, 1921, 3.
[60] *North China Herald*, January 15, 1921.
[61] For example, Harley Farnsworth MacNair, *With the White Cross in China: The Journal of a Famine Relief Worker with a Preliminary Essay by Way of Introduction* (Beijing: Henri Vetch, 1939); see also Fuller, *Famine Relief in Warlord China*, 221–28.

In early March of 1921, the writer Josef W. Hall and American Presbyterian Mission executive John D. Hayes traveled to Gansu on behalf of the Peking United International Famine Relief Committee, accompanied by a US colonel and a major attached to the American legation in Beijing. Arriving in Henan by train from the capital, they continued west on the old imperial highway, taking advantage of General Wu Peifu's "kind offer of horses and escort," they reported, "which enabled us to make a quicker and more satisfactory survey." The team would produce two reports for their Committee sponsors, one on conditions in the drought-famine zone along the Yellow and Wei River basins in Henan and Shaanxi, followed by one on the situation in Gansu.

There were any number of reasons why the men decided to open their first report by thanking General Wu, the chief strategist of the Zhili political faction in control of Beijing and victor in the Zhili-Anhui war the previous summer. For one, it reveals the diplomatic way their business was to be handled as the men ventured deep into Chinese territory. (A handwritten addendum at the report's end reads: "Note tone of report: had to protect those who were really trying by being polite about military governors." That said, Wu's assistance to the American team from his base in Baoding, Zhili, was covered in detail by the Xi'an press later in the month.[62]) Nonetheless, what follows in both American reports are notably laudatory accounts of what the team called the "energetic" relief they observed in communities along their way. "In passing through the hsien [districts] lying along the Sianfu [Xi'an] highway in Western Honan, it was most gratifying to see the excellent efforts the local officials and gentry were making to relieve the need of the [drought-famine] year," the men explained in their Shaanxi report. "The work in Ling Pao [Lingbao] Hsien impressed us in particular; for not only were they feeding and distributing in the country districts of their own hsien, but they were also taking in refugees from other hsien as well."[63]

Having assessed famine relief in Henan and Shaanxi, Hayes and Hall moved onto Gansu on April 2 via the road to Pingliang, leaving their companions from the US military behind. On the way, they were surprised to see "everywhere farm animals, chickens, fodder and fuel, and what is perhaps more striking long trains of cheap grain coming in from Kansu where the great loss of life had released large stores."[64] Ironically, the mass death brought overnight to the region's rattled highlands that

---

[62] *Guxin ribao*, March 14, 1921.
[63] John D. Hayes, "Report of the Shensi Investigation," typescript (n.p.: n.d.), RG127_001_005, Yale Divinity Archives, 1, 10.
[64] Ibid., 7.

winter appears to have served as a boon to the undersupplied grain market in its drought-hit lowlands to the east.

After covering the three days' journey from Pingliang, the team confirmed that the landslides were indeed most numerous in the area of Jingning. They also confirmed that further to the north, Guyuan was in "one of the most disturbed areas," and that death rates there were exponentially higher in the surrounding rural communities than in the county seat itself – a pattern observed around the earthquake zone. "Among the survivors of the original earthquake there are two main classes," they reported, "the maimed or injured, and the able-bodied. Of the former class a large proportion have succumbed to the bitter cold of that high plateau. The remainder have revived or survived through medical care by local officials or Missionaries and through the charity of their own kinsmen and townsfolk, leaving few now to require further attention or aid." To the investigators, the challenge, instead, appeared to be how to employ the able-bodied in constructive ways. But, even in this area the team determined that local efforts had been considerable already. After crossing the Ordos and reaching the Yellow River, where signs of the earthquake abruptly vanished, the team cabled Pingliang and Lanzhou. "Our wire was to the effect that the people were already making successful efforts at reconstruction throughout the area with the exception of the excavations in Chingning District," where the landslides had been most fierce and troublesome.[65]

The observations made by the Hayes-Hall Kansu Earthquake Relief Expedition reached a global audience in the form of a pictorial essay in the May 1922 issue of the *National Geographic Magazine*. "'Where the Mountains Walked': An Account of the Recent Earthquake in Kansu Province, China, Which Destroyed 100,000 Lives" appeared well over a year after the earthquake, when details of the disaster were still slowly reaching the outside world. Quite understandably, the most astonishing phenomena produced by the tremors dominate the magazine account, which Hall cowrote with China-based writer Elsie McCormick and signed using his pen name Upton Close. These phenomena included the displacement of whole mountains, the burial of entire villages (in scenes reminiscent of Roman tales "told of Pompeii," they wrote) and the journey of a row of poplar trees a kilometer and a half over a valley before the trees came to a rest entirely upright and intact.

Taking up almost the entirety of Hall and McCormick's twenty-page essay, these startling events are accompanied by no mention of what

---

[65] "The Kansu Report," typescript, unsigned (n.p.: addendum dates text to "late May" 1921), 2, RG127_001_005, Yale Divinity Archives.

locals were doing to alleviate conditions in their wake. "The native population was too stunned and the few foreign residents were too busy in relief work," the authors explain in the opening of their account, "to give any description of the dancing mountains and vanishing valleys" in the months that followed the initial tremors.[66] The only thing *National Geographic* readers learned about anything done to relieve the situation concerns measures taken by Hall's sponsors. "Several thousand men have been employed by the United International Famine Relief Society in releasing dammed streams and thus preventing disastrous overflows," the story reads. This, it adds, had followed on "pitiably insufficient efforts" by local authorities to do the same.[67]

So, how can one account for the discrepancies in these accounts, originating as they did from the same party of observers? How is that native efforts are recognized in the first two foreign accounts, only to disappear from the third? Some explanation might lie in the purpose behind each genre of writing. Part of Hall and Hayes' mandate was to verify the extent of distress in Shaanxi and Gansu. Their tour coincided with the release of a loan of four million yuan for famine and earthquake relief, a loan agreement struck between the Chinese central government and four international banks earlier in the year. Chinese aid organizers in Gansu had been successful in securing a modest portion of the sum, 80,000 yuan to be released that April.[68]

Where in Parry's and other missionary accounts from Gansu the invisibility of native mutual aid strengthened the sense of the indispensability of the missionary program, the reports by Hayes and Hall pointing out the existence of native relief measures evidently had a different purpose: reducing the pressure or demands that could be made on relief funds administered by the international society based in Beijing. What was at stake to the men, instead, and discussed at length in their two reports, was the issue of control over the expenditure of what was already scheduled for release that month. In Shaanxi, due to what they called a lack of "effectual Sino-foreign control," the team made the case for "more adequate international supervision in the actual distribution of funds" by the district committees.[69] In Gansu, they recommended that since *free* relief should continue to "rightly fall on the shoulders of the [local] wealthy," "The committee should confine its attentions to those forms of labor-giving relief" used in river works and other reconstruction efforts.[70]

[66] Upton Close and Elsie McCormick, "'Where the Mountains Walked': An Account of the Recent Earthquake in Kansu Province, China, Which Destroyed 100,000 Lives," *National Geographic Magazine*, May 1922, 445.
[67] Ibid., 451, 464.   [68] *Xiao gongbao*, January 17, 1921; *Guobao*, April 28, 1921.
[69] Hayes, "Report of the Shensi Investigation," 4, 6.   [70] "The Kansu Report," 2–3.

Native relief was, in this instance, reportable as intelligence for decision-making in Beijing on the question of fiscal control and accounting.

As a story told to a global audience well after the event, Hall's contribution to *National Geographic* served a different audience. In it, Gansu communities consist of hapless and helpless victims of nature, atomized and only relieved by outsiders. A brief exception to this is the article's mention of Zhou Tingyuan, which it introduces in a photographic caption as "the magistrate of Tsingning [who] lives in a tent on the site of his ruined yamen (court building). This official is codirector of the relief work in his district." Zhou is pictured beside his son and his wife, who is described as "an unusually progressive woman," with no further explanation (see Figure 1). Brief in its handling of Zhou and his family, and relief acts generally, the *National Geographic* piece does make room, however, for other social observations: in one instance, guests of a collapsed inn

THE MAGISTRATE OF TSINGNING LIVES IN A TENT ON THE SITE OF HIS RUINED
YAMEN (COURT BUILDING)

This official is codirector of the relief work in his district. His wife, an unusually progressive woman, and his son are also shown in the picture.

Figure 1 Magistrate Zhou Tingyuan and his family after the earthquake, 1921. Close and McCormick, "Where the Mountains Walked."

were unearthed alive "several days" after the earthquake, only to find that their "landlord [. . .] in spite of remonstrances, did not neglect to collect room rent for the full period of their stay."[71]

Holding up the reports of the Hayes-Hall Kansu Earthquake Relief Expedition against Hall's subsequent magazine writing reveals different ways of seeing and not seeing – different documentary progeny, so to speak – from the same sets of eyes. The different aims and audiences of these accounts led to different narrative emphases on who was doing what in the face of crisis. For its part, Parry's dramatic story from a region in crisis, however sympathetic to its subject – Zhou was "a man among ten thousand," he wrote, "whose chief fault is a tendency to self-satisfaction"[72] – exhibits two properties of missionary literature on China at the time: *invisibility* (of beneficial indigenous communal networks) and *indispensability* (of outside intervention, in this case the missionary program). These properties, as we will see, were not at all unique to evangelical storytelling on life in China's countryside. They, in fact, formed, in tandem, the discursive basis for a handful of competing ideologies underpinning the modernization project itself as it unfolded across early twentieth-century China.

But as much as *National Geographic* was a prominent platform to cover this remote corner of China at the time, on the whole, Gansu's stricken communities remained far from the national or international gaze. But this would briefly change in the spring of 1921 when attention to the area was kindled in another social network, and for altogether different reasons. Four months after the earthquake, the first team of Chinese geologists arrived in the region in search of oil, and the fortunes it could bring to the nation's destiny.

Scientific Networks

By 1920, China had experienced half a century of increased public interest in the value of minerals and other natural resources contained within its evolving borders. The fact that official and elite attention to coal deposits and other forms of energy reached back to the period of repeated defeat to Britain in the 1850s Arrow War was no coincidence.[73] The stakes were high. National salvation would become inextricably linked to the emerging world of modern science in China and the social circles forming around it.

[71] Close and McCormick, "Where the Mountains Walked," 449, 451, 452.
[72] J. Huston to Secretary of State, February 4, 1921, 3.
[73] Shellen Xiao Wu, *Empires of Coal: Fueling China's Entry into the Modern World Order, 1860–1920* (Stanford, CA: Stanford University Press, 2015).

It is more than a curiosity that the political awakening of the young Zhou Shuren, the future fiction writer and towering figure in the New Culture movement, Lu Xun, was triggered in large part by readings on geology. His "exposure to foreign studies of China alerted [him] to the link between geology and mining," Grace Yen Shen explains, "and shocked [him] into the realization that outsiders knew vastly more about Chinese territory than the Chinese did themselves." Three years before his famous departure from medical studies in Japan in 1906 to devote himself to a life of writing and activism, Zhou published a "Brief Outline of Chinese Geology" there, "the first work on Chinese geology written by a Chinese," in Shen's words. Other geological writings followed in which Zhou urged his compatriots to take up resource exploration and exploitation as a form of national defense.[74] It was not incongruous, then, to find men like Xiong Xiling, the former premier and most prominent philanthropist and disaster relief administrator of the early republic, in the news fifteen years later working to set up a joint-stock company with a British capital firm in order to develop oil and ore deposits in Xinjiang. In the intervening years, mining and exploration had become patriotic vocations (although, in Xiong's case, one might question his source of capital on nationalistic grounds).[75] The Gansu earthquake of 1920 came at a crucial moment in the exploitation of China's resource deposits. For this reason, earthquake investigations doubled as geological expeditions for the country's budding mining and drilling interests.

On April 15, teams of investigators from three central ministries departed Beijing for the Northwest. Following the foreign expedition by a little over a month, the Chinese academics took the northern route first by train to Baotou, and then up the Yellow River by boat to Lanzhou. There the geologists split into three parties: sent by the Ministry of Agriculture and Commerce, Xie Jiarong first went west to Qinghai and the oil fields at Yumen in west Gansu, before returning by way of Guyuan and Pingliang for earthquake investigations; his colleague Weng Wenhao, sent by the same ministry, went east in search of the epicenter, passing through Longde, Guyuan, Haiyuan and Pingliang; and Wang Lie, representing the Ministry of Education, covered the Qinling range of southern Shaanxi to the south together with the area of Haiyuan to the north as well. In addition to conducting their own field investigations, they gathered seismic, topographical and demographic data through survey forms

---

[74] Grace Yen Shen, *Unearthing the Nation: Modern Geology and Nationalism in Republican China* (Chicago: The University of Chicago Press, 2014), 42; see also Wu, *Empires of Coal*, 64.
[75] *Da gongbao*, December 18, 1921.

they left with magistrates to fill out and send to them upon their return to Beijing. From all this, the lead academics compiled numerous reports in the months and years that followed.[76]

One of the first of their reports to appear in print was the "Investigative Report of the Gansu Earthquake" ("Diaocha Gansu dizhen zhi baogao") by Wang Lie, then a geologist at Beijing University, which a group of Gansu students ran later that summer in a magazine they produced at the nearby campus of Qinghua. Having been dispatched by the Ministry of Education, it makes sense that Wang's report pays nearly as much attention to social and cultural matters (including relief) as it does to the geological and physical aspects of the disaster. After a discussion of certain features of the region's mountainous landscape that translated into devastation for communities there – and Haiyuan, in particular – amid the tremors, Wang provided a methodical run-through of relief measures (*zhenji zhi fa*) proposed, he said, by various camps in the region: work relief (*yi gong dai zhen*) to unclog the river systems, the approach most forcefully (*zuili*) supported, he explained, by foreigners working for the international relief society (Huayang yizhen hui *zhi waiguoren*); distribution of free relief monies to victims of the disaster, the approach most forcefully supported by the area's gentry (*ben di tushen*), due, in part, to the fact that disbursements to date had already exhausted available funds raised for relief; and finally the reconstruction of the county offices, jail, city walls and other public buildings, the approach most forcefully supported by officials. Wang then proposes a fourth concern: the superstition (*mixin*) of the people of Gansu (*Gan ren*) whose culture (*wenhua*), he explained, was "at a different level compared to that of the coastal provinces," some "fifty or sixty years behind," he specified, considering their use of caves as homes (*xuetu er ju*), the smoking rates among men (presumably of opium), and their approach to disease control and general hygiene (*weisheng*), among other things. He ends his report with a call for modernization of Gansu through railroad construction and industrial development (*fazhan*) in order to transform its culture.[77]

Wang's field report was consistent in notable ways with those of the Hayes-Hall Expedition made that same spring. Not only had Hayes and Hall also taken note of local relief efforts, they had made a point of distinguishing between the vocal preference for free relief among local gentry as opposed to the work relief measures proposed by foreigners on the scene. In both Wang's initial report and those of his American

---

[76] Li Xuetong, *Weng Wenhao nianpu* (Jinan: Shandong jiaoyu chubanshe, 2005), 32.
[77] Wang Lie, "Diaocha Gansu dizhen zhi baogao," *Xin Long zazhi* 2/1 (July 1921), 40–42.

counterparts, what distinguished outside versus local actors was not action versus inaction, but instead what *types* of action should be taken and what *conditions* should be made on giving aid. But, just as one sees with Hall's *National Geographic* article published the following year, subsequent reports on the Gansu earthquake become silent on the existence of native relief action, in any form.

Xie, who had only recently returned in 1920 from studies at Stanford University and the University of Wisconsin at Madison, worked closely with Wang and Weng, and his more extensive reports served as a form of composite report of each their findings.[78] In Xie's work, a good deal of data and detail on the series of tremors in China's Northwest can be found. For example, most counties recorded a 7 p.m. or 8 p.m. start to the December 16 earthquake – depending, it seems, on whether Beijing or local time was used – and in the southern, loess-covered sections of the quake zone it was accompanied by gale-force winds and dust storms that cast a swirling yellowish gloom across the region the following day. None reported any seismic activity before the main quake, only aftershocks, varying widely by place in duration and intensity.[79]

As for the human toll, Xie reported 234,117 deaths across fifty Gansu counties based on county door-to-door reports and official population rosters. Mortality, he found, was concentrated in a 20,000 square kilometer zone covering seven counties, each of which suffered between 10,000 and around 75,000 deaths. Nearly half of all deaths – 47 percent – was in two counties alone: Haiyuan (73,604) and Guyuan (36,176).[80] Compared to the several tens of thousands of deaths from recent seismic activity in Italy and Japan, Xie noted, Gansu's was the "world's greatest earthquake." Gansu also presented a paradox: its victims were overwhelmingly rural. Xie accounted for this by summarizing in great detail what made China's loess region distinct from much of the rest of the country. This included the popularity of cave homes (*yaodong*), the especially unstable nature of the terrain, and the acute scarcity of timber, which was used more commonly in the region's towns. But the much higher rural mortality also stemmed from the earthquake's timing: townsfolk were by and large still up and about in the evening when the first tremors struck and so were more likely to escape outside, Xie noted, while farming households had mostly settled in for a winter's night. And then rural residents who were fortunate enough to escape their crumbling homes found themselves spread widely across a vast area at night exposed

[78] Shen, *Unearthing the Nation*, 234.
[79] Xie Jiarong, "Minguo jiu nian shi'er yue shiliu ri Gansu ji qita ge sheng zhi dizhen qingxing," *Dixue zazhi* 13/6–7 (1922), 4.
[80] Ibid., 22.

to the elements, with little of the wooden wreckage of their homes that townsfolk could make do with as temporary shelter. "Afterwards, although counties dispatched emergency relief," he concluded, "communications were hampered and often it took days to arrive, which was too slow to save them."[81]

In Xie's accounting, local measures play no role in saving lives. Perhaps mortality was too monstrous in size for relief to appear worthy of mention. But then Xie does name outside interventions, specifically the 100,000 yuan spent by the joint Chinese-foreign (Huayang) relief society, branching out from its famine fighting efforts in neighboring Shaanxi and working closely with missionaries stationed in the Northwest. This had involved work relief over the year on river dredging and bridge and road works, employing workers from Jingning (where landslides were the worst), and secondarily, Guyuan and Haiyuan.[82]

In August, having completed their observations of the earthquake field, Xie and Weng journeyed west to Yumen, near the terminus of the Great Wall, to perform their second mission in the Northwest. This followed on a disappointing joint project formed eight years earlier between Standard Oil and the Beijing government to locate oil reserves in half a dozen Chinese provinces, for which work had been halted in 1915. What in part brought the geologists to western Gansu was that "Oil seepages had been recorded in the Yumen area for centuries," Shen writes, and so together the two men, attuned to this local knowledge, "conducted the first native Chinese petroleum reconnaissance there in 1921." It would be the basis for "China's first commercial oil field" in 1941 when the site became fully productive.[83]

In so much as the late nineteenth and early twentieth-century pursuit of natural resources was a product of intensifying competition among nations, it was, of course, tied to the mobilization of human resources, as well. Heightened concern and engagement with the natural world arose with parallel attention to the way people organized themselves, a subject that was increasingly viewed through a new term, society (*shehui*), which entered Chinese by way of Japanese. For this reason, even scientific journals like *Kexue* were concerned with the existence of civil society, in other words, indigenous institutions and practices that could be recognized and examined scientifically compared to Western models.[84] We saw this in the geologist Wang Lie's report from Haiyuan. The fact that he ended his earthquake survey with a cultural critique on superstition in Gansu was very much a reflection of the intellectual moment he was

[81] Ibid., 7.   [82] Ibid., 30.   [83] Shen, *Unearthing the Nation*, 166–67, 171.
[84] Zuoyue Wang, "Saving China Through Science: The Science Society in China, Scientific Nationalism, and Civil Society in Republican China," *Osiris* 17 (2002), 291–322.

writing. By one count, the earthquake and famine year of 1920–1921 saw a sharp peak in the use of *mixin* – superstition, literally "delusional beliefs" – in published writing in the stretch of time between the so-called Hundred Days' Reform of 1898 and the rise of the Guomindang to power in 1928.[85] Scientific surveys of China's disaster zones – whether due to earthquake or drought – would involve overlapping layers of investigation into natural and social phenomena.

As it took shape, China's scientific community cultivated a new work ethic among its members, one that prized fieldwork "in the outdoors, with an emphasis on exposure to the elements and physical labor," in Shen's words.[86] One of the drivers for this development was admiration for the initiative taken by Westerners to survey and exploit not only their own national dominions but also the lands under the control of other nations, like China. The fact that Westerners coupled geological exploration with investigations into disaster conditions in times of earthquake or famine only served to heighten the sense of newness to the study of disaster and its alleviation. Conversely, critiques of Chinese attitudes toward natural resource exploration and exploitation were coupled with perceptions of Chinese inaction in times of ecological crisis.

At the forefront of these developments was a new generation of young scholars enrolled in Xie, Wang and Weng's academic faculties in the capital. There, university budgets and staff time in 1920 did not allow for chaperoned trips to the field, a situation that irked particular students. In autumn of that year, "a group of seven friends led by Yang Zhongjian and Zhao Guobin rallied their classmates to establish a Geological Society" at Beijing University, Shen writes. Then in his second year at the nation's premier university, Yang had first arrived on campus only months after the mass student demonstrations of May 1919 over China's loss of Shandong province to the Japanese at the Treaty of Versailles. It is telling that, in establishing their new network, "The first meeting was held on October 10, 1920, in honor of National Day, and the Society saw its mission as a patriotic responsibility."[87] Students would immediately turn their attention to the series of ecological crises striking China's wider population that year.

Conclusion

Through the scattered fragments of writing that they left behind, social networks offered different and often contrasting ways of observing social

---

[85] Huang Ko-wu, "The Origin and Evolution of the Concept of *mixin* (superstition): A Review of May Fourth Scientific Views," *Chinese Studies in History* 49/2 (2016), 55.
[86] Shen, *Unearthing the Nation*, 48.   [87] Ibid., 83; see also 63.

responses to disaster nine years into the Chinese republic. Collectively, each network was concerned with mobilizing people and material resources for the challenges its members saw themselves, or others, facing in the wake of the great tremors that struck the Northwest in late 1920. In the process, however, their observations assumed an additional value beyond the immediate concerns of their immediate network. This value lay in the service of cultural memory as a political resource in the unfolding debates about the nature of China and the Chinese in the modern world. One key aspect of the cultural production of this period explored in this book is the invisibility it afforded certain historical actors and the indispensability it afforded others. The implications of these respective omissions and emphases would be far-reaching as they evolved in forms of writing and art over the remainder of the century.

Writing on the earthquake and wider famine fields of early republican China would reflect three increasingly conflated areas of intellectual activity around May Fourth: the valorization of science and the scientific method; commentary on China's ongoing transition to republican politics; and diagnostic exercises on the social and moral health of the nation, however that national body was drawn. This intermingling of the natural, the political and the ethical – a conflation, in other words, of scientific and moral discourse – would shape the theory and practice of modern Chinese political culture in the decades to come.[88]

---

[88] On this broader development, see Wang Hui, "The Fate of 'Mr. Science' in China: The Concept of Science and Its Application in Modern China Thought," *positions: east asia cultures critique* 3/1 (1995), 1–2; and Lu Ping, "Beyond Mr. Democracy and Mr. Science: The Introduction of Miss Moral and the Trend of Moral Revolution in the New Culture Movement," *Frontiers of History in China* 2/2 (2007), 254–57. On Communist Party cofounder Chen Duxiu's role in this development, see Charlotte Furth, *Ting Wen-chiang: Science and China's New Culture* (Cambridge, MA: Harvard University Press, 1970), 127.

2 New Culture Lenses onto Rural Life

As spring arrived in 1921, newsprint in the Chinese capital continued to transmit only scattered and sketchy reports of the earthquake that had struck the country's Northwest at the start of winter. How communities were coping in the wake of the devastating tremors was still very difficult to ascertain, due, in part, to Gansu's remoteness and the landslides blocking its limited communication outlets. The Hayes-Hall Kansu Earthquake Relief Expedition had reached the province only in March, and its pictorial report in the *National Geographic* would not hit newsstands until May the following year. The earthquake reports by China's leading geologists began appearing in various academic journals the following year as well. Only a couple of Beijing periodicals well connected to Gansu political circles were notable exceptions to a remarkably light media coverage in the capital of such an enormous event.

The striking scarcity of first-hand accounts of the Gansu earthquake – either by people who experienced it or those who promptly witnessed its aftermath – led the foreign expedition to call it "perhaps, the most poorly advertised calamity" of modern times.[1] On the face of it, this obscurity poses a challenge to the researcher. But it also provides an especially focused lens with which to isolate the historical record on a cataclysmic event, to probe its reproduction from one stage to the next and to identify journalistic practices at a pivotal moment in the history of twentieth-century revolutionary politics.

Nineteen months before the Haiyuan earthquake, a far better-known political tremor shook campuses and city squares across the Chinese republic. Triggered by deals brokered outside the French capital in the wake of the First World War, the May Fourth movement of 1919 took the initial form of marches and demonstrations in cities and towns across the country against the political faction running the government in Beijing and its failures at defending China's interests at Versailles. It

---

[1] Close and McCormick, "Where the Mountains Walked," 445.

would, in turn, be shaped by parallel intellectual trends through which its student energies would be channeled and articulated. The burgeoning print culture emanating from the republic's university campuses at May Fourth occurred several years into the New Culture movement and shared many of the latter's aims of cultural transformation. It also coincided with a parallel development in the intellectual life of the country, a proliferation in social data collection. This growth in surveys (*diaocha*), travel journals (*chaji*) and reports (*baogao*) over the course of the 1920s and 1930s – what historian Tong Lam has identified as the social survey movement (*shehui diaocha yundong*) – formed part of the wider adoption of new writing forms and methods aimed at transforming what was seen as an atomized population into a "legible" and viable body politic.[2]

Part and parcel of this fact-driven movement was the rise of sociology in China. Darwin's biological theories, having become fused with the notion of the social organism, had arrived in Chinese intellectual circles through Yan Fu's late nineteenth-century essays and translations of seminal English works on evolution and society, Huxley and Spencer's among them.[3] Foreign academics were at the forefront of the discipline in China, most notably the Princeton sociologist Sidney Gamble, who conducted a pioneering survey of Beijing in 1918–19.[4]

The starting point of much social science inquiry on China was that it was a social field in which facts were elusive or nonexistent, and the very existence of a society along the lines of the British, French or German body politic, as they were understood, did not yet exist. A loose "sheet of sand" was the way Guomindang leader Sun Yat-sen would famously describe his fellow Chinese as he campaigned to unify the republic in the 1920s.[5] Liang Qichao, the foundational thinker of modern China, had

---

[2] Tong Lam, *A Passion for Facts: Social Surveys and the Construction of the Chinese Nation State, 1900–1949* (Berkeley: University of California Press, 2011), 2. I use the term "legible" here in the sense employed by James C. Scott, *Seeing Like a State: How Certain Schemes to Improve the Human Condition Have Failed* (New Haven, CT: Yale University Press, 1998).

[3] Benjamin I. Schwartz, *In Search of Wealth and Power: Yen Fu and the West*, Harvard East Asian Series (Cambridge, MA: The Belknap Press of Harvard University Press, 1969).

[4] Sidney D. Gamble, *Peking: A Social Survey*, conducted under the auspices of the Princeton University Center in China and the Peking Young Men's Christian Association (New York: George H. Doran Co., 1921).

[5] David Strand, "Community, Society, and History in Sun Yat-sen's *Sanmin zhuyi*," in Theodore Huters, R. Bin Wong and Pauline Yu, *Culture and State in Chinese History: Conventions, Accommodations, and Critiques*, Irvine Studies in the Humanities (Stanford, CA: Stanford University Press, 1997), 329.

similarly lamented a country he saw devoid of "public morality" and divided into innumerable kinship and occupational units.[6]

May Fourth journalism would nurture such metaphors of a people beset by irrationalities and familial bonds and devoid of civic ethics, social impulse or initiative, and any of the traits underpinning a broader cohesive citizenry able to govern itself. May Fourth writing, in other words, appeared at the very moment when the Chinese social landscape itself "came into being" as a subject of study and activation. In this respect, developments in the Chinese republic paralleled the newfound stress in 1920s Japan on "society" and "social work" along European lines as distinct from indigenous relief and mutual-aid practices.[7] In the process, Lam explains, "social facts were constructed and mobilized to produce truth claims about the human world," setting into motion the transformation of modern China's political terrain.[8]

If Chinese society itself was coming into focus in the May Fourth era, so was the category of the student, a term signifying, as Fabio Lanza has argued, a self-assigned agent of political change and provocateur for Chinese modernity.[9] Student critique addressed a range of issues, from the institution of the family and the position of women to educational and governmental reforms. But another area presented student writers with an opportunity to question the customs and values underpinning everyday life. The series of ecological crises in the immediate wake of May Fourth presented dramatic opportunities to employ newfound journalistic methods and to practice what would develop over the 1920s into "a philosophy of the everyday," in the words of Rebecca Karl.[10] In December 1920, the relief and recovery demands of the Northwest earthquake were joined by those of an intensifying food crisis threatening more than twenty million destitute residents of the North China plain. These two separate crises unfolded in tandem. Student survey initiatives covered both, and in telling ways.

Social Surveys, May Fourth Omissions

Into the void of information on the Northwestern tremors stepped an upstart journal devoted to Gansu current affairs – a publication modest in

[6] Hao Chang, *Liang Ch'i-ch'ao and Intellectual Transition in China*, 1890–1907, Harvard East Asian Studies Series (Cambridge, MA: Harvard University Press, 1971), 155.

[7] Sheldon Garon, *Molding Japanese Minds: The State in Everyday Life* (Princeton, NJ: Princeton University Press, 1997), 49–59.

[8] Tong Lam, *A Passion for Facts*, 10–11.

[9] Fabio Lanza, *Behind the Gate: Inventing Students in Beijing* (New York: Columbia University Press, 2010).

[10] Rebecca Karl, "Journalism, Social Value, and a Philosophy of the Everyday in 1920s China," *positions: east asia cultures critique* 16/3 (2008), 539–67.

readership and resources, if not in its aims. Based on the campus of Qinghua University in Beijing, *Xin Long* had been founded a year earlier at a meeting of some forty Gansu students attending university in the nation's capital. The journal was part of an explosion of student-run publishing and reportage across China, one that injected political urgency into the reformist New Culture literary movement underway since the mid-1910s.[11] It joined several hundred reformist journals across the country, most prominently Shanghai's *Xin qingnian* (New Youth) and Beijing's *Xin chao* (New Tide).

The social circle out of which the *Xin Long* society emerged was closely involved with efforts to end female exclusion from higher education in China, one of the most significant, if hard fought, achievements of the May Fourth era. Central to the push for female schooling in Gansu was Deng Zong, an educational official who had encountered and embraced the republican ideals of Sun Yat-sen while studying at the capital's Daxuetang, the forerunner of Beijing University, in the final years of the Qing. Soon after returning to Lanzhou, Deng and colleagues established a Gansu provincial women's teacher's college in 1913. Three of his daughters soon matriculated. A week into the nationwide student demonstrations from May 4, 1919, one daughter, the twenty-two-year-old Deng Chunlan, learned of a speech supportive of coeducation by the newly appointed president of Beijing University, Cai Yuanpei. One of her brothers, two years her junior, was already a student at the national university, and a second brother was enrolled at Qinghua nearby. Chunlan mailed an appeal for permission to enroll herself. It was not, however, until after Chunlan and five other women traveled from Lanzhou to Beijing to make their case, and only following her advocacy for women's equality made it into Beijing's *Chenbao* newspaper, that Cai announced Beijing University's admission of women starting in early 1920. Chunlan's pioneering story became news across the republic.[12]

A few months later, in May, *Xin Long* was launched with Chunlan, a newly enrolled philosophy student, and her sister Deng Chunlin as contributing writers, while their brother Deng Chungao served as one of three assistant editors. Like much of the movement's writings, *Xin Long* published in the vernacular, which served both as a cultural statement against classical forms and a practical bid to communicate with the broader public. Copies were accessibly priced, at eight *fen* each, postage included, with production costs supported by donations from Gansu

[11] Timothy B. Weston, *The Power of Position: Beijing University, Intellectuals, and Chinese Political Culture, 1898–1929* (Berkeley: University of California Press, 2004), 190.
[12] Wang and Yang, *Gan Ning Qing minguo renwu*, 289–301; Weston, *Power of Position*, 197–200.

natives in Beijing and elsewhere (a fundraising task taken up by another sister, Deng Chunfen).[13]

The magazine's stated mission was to "introduce practical knowledge and studies" to Gansu, while according to its inaugural issue it would set out to "transmit [Gansu's] societal condition to the outside world so that its baseness or depravity [*beiwu*] is known to all countrymen [*guoren*] and remedied," in the unsparing words of its chief editor Wang Zizhi. "Afterwards it can be hoped the people of Gansu awaken [*juewu*] and act vigorously to bring reform to a filthy society [*wuzhuo shehui*]."[14] Already, May Fourth had had some immediate effect in Gansu, including the creation of an elementary school for girls in remote and particularly conservative corners of the province such as Guyuan. Inspired by events around the country, local women there had successfully pressed the county magistrate for its establishment. Within three months of the May demonstrations on the streets of Beijing, the Guyuan school opened in the distant loess plateau with sixty-eight students, including several Muslim girls after a special appeal was made to the Muslim community by its founding director.[15] Soon, amid this shifting cultural environment, *Xin Long* could be found at nine distribution points around the province, a publishing house in Lanzhou and teacher's colleges in eight towns, including Pingliang, the walled garrison city halfway between Xi'an and Lanzhou.

Although *Xin Long* started off with an ambitious monthly schedule, like many of its counterparts in the student press it appeared only sporadically. Its fourth issue was in April, 1921, four months into the series of tremors and aftershocks rattling Guyuan, Pingliang and surrounding districts. In the issue, the editors compiled a survey of the earthquake disaster, which included a compilation of county estimates totaling 314,092 human deaths and the loss of 808,270 crushed livestock across fifty-three counties; an appeal by three Buddhist monks writing for the Gansu Earthquake Relief Society; and a digest of seventeen other collated texts, ranging from official telegraph cables to eyewitness accounts sent by Gansu residents to friends, family and organizations in Beijing in the quake's immediate aftermath. *Xin Long*'s April issue most probably constituted the most comprehensive collection of news to date of the still-unfolding calamity.

[13] "Ben she jishi," *Xin Long zazhi* 1/1 (May 20, 1920), 31–32.
[14] Wang Zizhi, "Fa kan ci," *Xin Long zazhi* 1/1 (May 20, 1920), 3; Tse-tsung Chow, *The May Fourth Movement: Intellectual Revolution in Modern China*, Harvard East Asian Studies Series (Cambridge, MA: Harvard University Press, 1960), 71.
[15] Zhao Jinyun, "Guyuan diyi suo nüzi xuexiao de chengli," *Guyuan wenshi ziliao* 3 (September 1989), 221–32.

The survey opened with a telegram from Ma Fuxiang, the Sino-Muslim general in command of the eastern Gansu military district of Ningxia, which bordered Inner Mongolia on the northern edge of the earthquake zone:

On the evening of the sixteenth there was an earthquake lasting six to seven minutes. From then until now there have been dozens of aftershocks of varying duration in the eight counties under the jurisdiction of Ningxia. Homes have collapsed and people crushed to death ranging from several to several dozen to several hundred in each locality. Investigation into the countryside is underway and it appears that estimates of destruction vary in severity from light to severe. The initial quake cut the line running to the telegraph office at Guyuan and communication between Longdong [Eastern Gansu] and Lanzhou is down. Ma Guoming, the commanding officer at Baiyakou, and Huang Xueshi, the assistant commander at Ning'anbao, promptly dispatched mounted soldiers to fan out over the disaster zone and speed back reports. From these men have come word via Ning'anbao that at Haiyuan and Guyuan in Jingyuan prefecture the city walls, moat and government offices are ruined, and that the surrounding countryside was visited by a monumental calamity with seventy to eighty percent of the population killed or injured. Amid the flattened cave dwellings of Shagou [district], Ma Yuanzhang has met a tragic death. In the area of Pingliang and Jingning conditions are graver still, with no definite reports coming from the road to the southwest ... ... In Guyuan and Haiyuan, after the quake, the disaster-stricken who roamed about with nowhere to go, fled along the mountain paths. Those who died went unburied; those who lived on had nothing to eat, and they added to the ranks of bandits, forming crowds of them. Many were stirred up, and recently two hundred to three hundred of the disaster-stricken have arrived ... ... The telegraph line to Guyuan remains blocked and there is still no news coming in ... ...[16]

Xin Long followed with a second cable, this time from Lu Hongtao, the Han Chinese commander at Pingliang:

On the sixteenth of this month Pingliang and its surrounding countryside, as well as the ten counties in the district, were struck by a series of ten tremors, destroying homes and crushing to death countless people and livestock. The level of misery makes performing detailed recounting unbearable. Of the counties, Guyuan is especially hard-hit and the telegraph lines from all counties to the Gansu provincial seat are down.[17] No details of the situation are known.

Free from editorial commentary, the seven-page survey allowed existing materials to speak for themselves. And their sense of the complete abandonment of the people to their suffering makes for vivid, harrowing reading. But then an astute reader of the Beijing press that winter might

---

[16] "Gansu dizhen qizai zhi diaocha," *Xin Long zazhi* 1/4 (April 20, 1921), 28.
[17] No ellipses appear here although the original cable contains text in between these two sentences.

have noticed something amiss. Earlier versions of Ma and Lu's telegrams, printed a few months closer to the quake in the December 25 edition of a small Beijing tabloid, *Aiguo baihuabao* (Patriotic Colloquial News), were noticeably longer. The parts omitted from *Xin Long*'s digest are indicated by italics in the excerpts below:

In Guyuan and Haiyuan after the quake, the disaster-stricken who roamed about with nowhere to go fled along the mountain paths. Those who died went unburied; those who lived on had nothing to eat, and they added to the ranks of bandits, forming crowds of them. Many were stirred up, and recently two hundred to three hundred of the disaster-stricken have arrived. *Gentry [shenshi] have been collecting grain and clothing and are preparing it for distribution.*

   ... The telegraph line to Guyuan is now blocked and there is no news coming in. *With frequent visits to the disaster zone, mounted units stationed in Ningxia continue to spread out into the region to assess the situation. And soldiers have been sent to reassure the stricken, assembling along the borders of each district to protect the land. They have donated ten thousand yuan [silver dollars] from their pay and the military and civil officials and gentry have assembled to raise donations for emergency relief, and wait for further news.*

   The level of misery makes performing detailed recounting unbearable. Of the counties, Guyuan is especially hard-hit and the telegraph lines from all counties to the Gansu provincial seat are down. [Lu] *Hongtao has donated three thousand yuan and the merchant and education communities have donated two thousand strings of coppers. Staff have been dispatched with the monies to relieve the stricken people. Gansu province and all county lines remain down so* no details of the situation are known.[18]

Somewhere between the paper's publication of these cables nine days after the quake and their rendering at the campus offices of *Xin Long* four months later, all signs of local assistance and protection of the stricken of Gansu had disappeared. *Aiguo baihuabao* was a news daily founded within the capital's bannermen community in 1913 by Ma Taipu – a man about whom information is difficult to find – and edited by the Manchu writer Wang Lengfo.[19] Written in colloquial Chinese, or *baihua*, its focus on philanthropic affairs and the everyday hardships of common people appeared in a style of format and news coverage that was almost indistinguishable from other tabloid-sized dailies. These small newspapers appeared to be closely associated with the capital's military authorities given the volume of coverage in their columns of official affairs in the day-to-day running of the city. By printing these cables at such length, *Aiguo baihuabao* was extending its detailed coverage of Beijing poor relief to similar social concerns in distant Gansu.

[18] *Aiguo baihuabao*, December 25, 1920.
[19] Zhang Juling, "Qingmo minchu qiren de jinghua xiaoshuo," *Zhongguo wenhua yanjiu* 23 (Spring 1999), 105.

A similar disappearance occurs in a second entry in *Xin Long*'s digest: a letter from a Guyuan resident, surnamed Sun, to a man sojourning in Beijing, named Wang Hansan. It too had appeared earlier in a Beijing newspaper, *Zhongguo minbao* (Chinese Popular News). The letter (again with *Xin Long*'s deletions in italics) read:

The day after the quake the people cried out in terror and unease. That night a violent wind kicked up and scattered sand and stones alike. A panic developed over the threat of starvation and the bitter cold, which was truly difficult to bear. The sky grew dark, dogs howled and people wailed. At dawn the misery increased as people erected sheds for shelter and foraged for things to eat in the countryside. But the ranks of those without food swelled, and the hungry formed crowds similar to bandit gangs and multiple incidents of looting and pillaging occurred each day. *Initially, a gentleman named Yang Zhanshan who resides inside town to the east of the stone inscription to morality and prosperity, initiated the establishment of a soup kitchen, which Zhang Jichuan energetically supported with a donation of 1,200 jin of wheat flour and twenty shi of rice and beans to serve as emergency relief to the disaster-stricken for ten days. Afterwards, a cable arrived from Pingliang commander Lu [Hongtao] stating that he was donating 1,000 strings of coppers; that the body of soldiers at each garrison in Longdong [eastern Gansu] was donating 1,300 strings of coppers; and that the merchant association at Pingliang donated one thousand strings of coppers. The [Guyuan] county magistrate then used the household registers to identify the destitute and adults were provisioned with one dou of grain per month and children five sheng per month.*[20]

Identical to its handling of the generals' cables, *Xin Long*'s version cut off the moment the man's letter turned from banditry and violence to the provisioning of relief. It then resumed with the fact that "details have recently arrived of the greater severity of the quake in Haiyuan. There the city wall, moat and cave homes are all ruined. Afterwards, there was a major fire, and plundering to the point where the county seat has been reduced to a desert."[21]

The gaps in the texts form a pattern. Of the remaining fourteen documents featured in *Xin Long*'s digest – among them Governor Zhang Guangjian's cable to the central government, an appeal by the Pingliang Merchant Association and the letter from a Gansu resident to his brother in Beijing – editorial ellipses appear in all but three. Nowhere appears anything resembling care for the stricken.

[20] *Zhongguo minbao*, February 22, 1921. A *jin* at the time was equal to 600 grams and a *shi* anywhere from 100 to 160 *jin* depending on location, while a string of (normally one hundred) coppers also varied from a value of a silver yuan to considerably less. *Zhengfu gongbao*, June 13, 1921.
[21] *Zhongguo minbao*, February 22, 1921; "Gansu dizhen qizai zhi diaocha," *Xin Long zazhi* 1/4 (April 20, 1921), 30.

This makes for decidedly different readings of disaster. In the earlier, fuller, renderings printed in these dailies, the maelstrom of horror – wholesale destruction of the world around followed by exposure to wintry storms and predation – is tempered by instances of relief initiative, and in sufficient detail for readers to identify some method and agency in its source and allocation. In *Xin Long*'s version, after the sweep of an editor's redactive brush, the horror is everything.

May Fourth's Rural Voices

Although *Xin Long*'s staff came from a range of locations in Gansu, the network from which the society drew its support reflected only part of the diverse ethnic makeup of the borderland province. Of the fifty-three people listed as society members in its inaugural issue, only one bears the surname Ma – a common family name of the majority Sino-Muslim community in Gansu's quake-struck eastern highlands.[22] This fact held for the magazine's wider social network: among the twenty-two donors thanked in the magazine's fourth issue (for contributing 226 yuan toward the journal's overhead), there is also a striking absence of the surname.[23] This is surprising given that members of Gansu's Muslim community were active in political and educational circles in the capital as well. Hardship at home had recently led a group of young Muslim men in Gansu to seek support from Muslim clerics and commanders in the region so they could further their studies and pursue opportunities in Beijing. After their brief audience with Ma Yuanzhang in the spring of 1919 was cut short (apparently by the cleric's attendants preparing his sedan chair), the men succeeded in securing support from Ma Fuxiang. The Muslim general established an endowment of 5,500 yuan (later supplemented by a provincial tax on leather hides) raised from him and local official and merchant-gentry circles, for Sino-Muslim students to study in Beijing or overseas. In the fall of 1920, the first three of the fund's beneficiaries enrolled at Beijing's University of Law and Government and the Russian division of Beijing's Foreign Language University, followed by an additional fourteen students at various military and police schools in the nation's capital and the nearby Zhili garrison city of Baoding. Many of them would go on to high-level positions in the government of Ningxia.[24] Gansu's student sojourners were thus hardly a uniform grouping and were plugged into various patronage networks and social circles. Some made their way up the current power

---

[22] *Xin Long zazhi* 1/1 (May 20, 1920), 32.

[23] "*Xin Long zazhi* she tebie qishi," *Xin Long zazhi* 1/4 (April 20, 1921), back page.

[24] Ma Tingxiu, "Zaoqi Gansu huizu daxue sheng fu jing jiu xue gaishu," *Lanzhou Huizu yu Yisilan jiao: Lanzhou wenshi ziliao xuanji* 9 (1988), 189–93.

structure, while others occupied positions that were more marginal to immediate politics yet closer to the republic's centers of cultural production.

Gansu natives pushing for social and cultural change, such as those behind *Xin Long* magazine, did so from a fundamentally different position than their coastal, urban peers. These were rural sons and daughters communicating to cosmopolitan audiences about home. For much of the twentieth century, generations of scholars understood the student-led May Fourth movement as a coastal phenomenon, one that stemmed largely from Marxist and liberal contributions to the intellectual ferment experienced in the country's international enclaves along or near the coast. More recently, historians have reoriented May Fourth studies inland, revealing that many of the movement's most determined radicals heralded not, in fact, from China's cosmopolitan enclaves of Beijing and Shanghai, but rather from up-river cities such as Hangzhou and Wuhan and smaller provincial towns.[25] Much of the cultural iconoclasm of the period was not, then, a purely urban phenomenon, nor merely a product of urban perspectives on growing urban-rural divides along social, cultural or economic lines. Instead, the vigorous rejection of inherited ideologies and social practices of the May Fourth era was championed by sojourning students from the hinterland in conversation with their peers and the wider society back home.

Xin Long captures this very dialogue, engaged in by young men and women freshly arrived in Beijing from some of the republic's remotest communities. The Deng siblings and their colleagues were well-placed to undergo what one prominent historian of the period calls the "dialectical interaction between the quickening pace of change in urban centers and the petrifying weight of traditionalism in the agrarian heartland."[26] The Deng family, originating in Xining prefecture in the southwest reaches of Gansu (in today's Xunhua Salar Autonomous District of Qinghai province), moved to Lanzhou in the early 1900s for work and school. Other *Xin Long* founders were two students from quake-ravaged Jingyuan county, including chief editor and Beijing University student Wang Zizhi, and one from Haiyuan county itself, Feng Hanying, who was enrolled at Beijing Industrial University.[27]

Activists from hinterland communities were sufficiently familiar with rural life to be its sharpest critics. As one recent Gansu-based scholar explains, when the students behind *Xin Long* introduced the province's

---

[25] Wen-hsin Yeh, *Provincial Passages*; Rahav, *The Rise of Political Intellectuals in Modern China*.
[26] Wen-hsin Yeh, *Provincial Passages*, 194.
[27] *Haiyuan xianzhi* 40 *renwu zhi* (1999), 1084.

social situation to the outside world, and provided the material for school-children in Gansu to recognize the ills of their home districts and seek their communities' renewal, it was done with "impartiality in mind and a strict abidance to the facts." "In their writing on various aspects of Gansu's backwardness," Ma Yixin writes, "they mercilessly conducted, without hesitation, the severest of judgments" while targeting a range of phenomena inherited from the late imperial period, such as social and cultural institutions stemming from filial piety, from footbinding to arranged marriage and concubinage and their effects on female mobility and well-being.[28] May Fourth writers were, if anything, brutally frank or sincere to a fault.[29]

But have these social diagnoses been put to the test? Tong Lam's important study of the social survey movement begins with census taking during the New Policies of the late Qing (1901–11), only to skip to the Nanjing Decade (1928–37), when, he notes, survey conductors "produced social facts and manufactured truth claims" about Chinese society as part of the broader state-building project.[30] But what about the May Fourth generation in between? Did *Xin Long* and its counterparts identify – or did they conjure up – disjunctures between relief norms and practices in disaster governance? Did they identify, or imagine, a moral vacuum in which lessons were to be communicated – about personal conduct in times of calamity, or communal responses to suffering? Forming part of the structures of social relations and exchange – not to mention fundamental aspects of Confucian statecraft such as managing the state (*zhiguo*) and harmonizing the world (*pingtianxia*) – disaster governance stemmed from a range of indigenous codes and customs, mutual-aid practices, and religious doctrines and ideologies. How valid were reformist treatments of these and other areas of everyday life?

We can only get a sense of the refractive power of the lens through which May Fourth writers were viewing their world by reconstructing, as best we can, some of the immediate events they trained their sights on. To do this requires casting our investigative scope wider into the social field of ecological crises that year. *Xin Long*'s earthquake survey reached subscribers in the last few weeks of a long famine winter over much of the North. The spring harvest of May 1921 would come at the peak of drought-driven spikes in grain prices in Beijing and across some three

---

[28] Ma Yixin, "'Xin Long' zazhi yu Gansu jindai sixiang qimeng," *Lanzhou jiaoyu xueyuan xuebao* 30/9 (September 2014), 10.

[29] See, for example, Xiaoming Chen, *From the May Fourth Movement to Communist Revolution*, and Wen-hsin Yeh's chapter "Decry Filial Piety," in *Provincial Passages*, 174–96.

[30] Tong Lam, *A Passion for Facts*, 143.

hundred rural counties. How local communities, officialdom and regional networks across the nation responded to the needs of tens of millions of destitute and vulnerable inhabitants of the North and Northwest was an issue that spoke to the very heart of sociological investigation. By comparing published student letters with extant records on local disaster responses in their home districts, we get a sense of a different disjuncture, one between May Fourth representations of rural capacities and those offered by communal perspectives. Gazetteers, stone stele inscriptions and scattered press reports provide sufficient detail on two Zhili counties over 1920–21 for us to capture the nature of May Fourth representations of communities in crisis. In this wider conversation, *Xin Long*'s editorial choices take on added significance.

Students, National Disaster and the Media

Having embraced journalism with vigor in the aftermath of May 4, 1919, Beijing student circles soon populated the field of disaster coverage across the North. At the center of this phenomenon was Beijing University, which had recently become a fulcrum of New Culture intellectual life under the leadership of Cai Yuanpei, and where the many students working for newspapers would soon form their own union.[31] In mid-September, the Beijing Student Association added its own set of investigative teams to assess the famine conditions spreading across the region south of the capital. Working initially with a major relief society founded by philanthropist Xiong Xiling, a former premier of the republic, the association formed ten survey teams with four members each, charged with recording data, taking photographs and assessing hygienic conditions over three-week tours in a designated section of the disaster field (see Map 2).[32]

News of the student association's initiative spread beyond the capital and its campuses, and was picked up by Tianjin's *Yishibao* (*Social Welfare*) and the Guomindang's Shanghai-based *Minguo ribao* (*Republican Daily News*). Over the famine year, however, the most regular commercial host for student voices was the capital's *Chenbao*, a progressive highbrow broadsheet that regularly ran student contributions alongside transcriptions of lectures from Bertrand Russell's tour of the country over 1920–21

---

[31] Weston, *Power of Position*, 125, 190, 205.

[32] Beijing xuesheng lianhe hui, "Jing xuesheng diaocha zaiqing jihua," *Minguo ribao*, September 16, 1920; Beijing xuesheng lianhe hui, "Xuesheng hui jiuzai gongqi," *Yishibao*, September 20, 1920; "Xuesheng hui zaiqu diaocha yuan yi chufa," *Chenbao*, September 24, 1920.

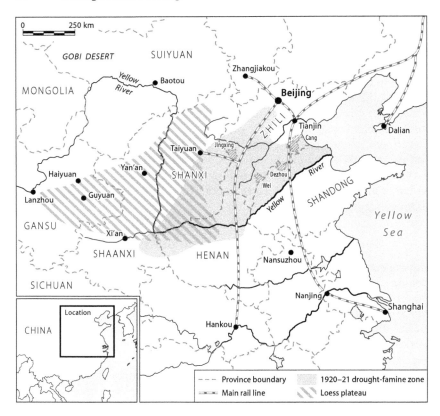

Map 2 North China, showing the 1920 earthquake region and drought-famine zone and key locations mentioned in the text. Map created by Nick Scarle for the author.

(which is covered in Chapter 3).[33] *Chenbao* was also a prominent platform for new journalistic voices, hiring female students as staff reporters at the same time that the paper published Deng Chunlan's appeals for entry into Beijing University for her and other women. Among the paper's hires was the Pingliang-born poet Wu Ruixia, who joined the paper as a news writer soon after enrolling in July 1919 at Beijing Women's Teachers' College, working for the paper during breaks to help cover the tuition fees her family back in Gansu increasingly struggled to afford.[34]

---

[33] *Chenbao*, November 7, 15 and 16, 1920.
[34] *Pingliang shizhi*, vol. 25, *renwu* (1996), 771.

In *Chenbao*, student journalists critiqued prevailing reporting practices; seeking to shape social surveying methodologies, they placed the investigation of relief methods specifically within the scope and mission of the social survey movement in which they aimed to take a leading role. In an early *Chenbao* essay, Beijing University geology student Yang Zhongjian, a native of Hua county in drought-struck eastern Shaanxi, set out guiding principles for disaster survey work – one that criticized the common practice of using stock phrases and vague estimations of mortality or refugee numbers in news reports and district gazetteers. Yang urged those surveying the famine field to "strive for numerical accuracy" and to base their conclusions on inductive methods only after interviewing a broad range of people in multiple locations. Ultimately, Yang added, famine surveyors should seize the opportunity to probe beyond the immediate subsistence crisis to broader, more entrenched social conditions.[35] Later that October, Miao Jinyuan followed with a *Chenbao* piece written on behalf of the student association. Framing the group's fact-finding forays into the famine districts as a form of social service grounded in the social survey movement, Miao reaffirmed Yang's stress on precision and methodology, stating that reports should be "unequivocal" and "clear and definite" in nature. Then, again echoing Yang, Miao stressed that the reports' ultimate purpose was to position them as the "vanguard of social reform [*gailiang shehui de ji xianfeng*]."[36]

Summer Break and Famine on the North China Plain

The first in a series of student contributions to *Chenbao* in autumn 1920 was a report by Yu Bingxiang, composed as he returned from summer break at home in Cang county, some sixty miles south of Tianjin. He was a Cang native himself, Yu explained, and everything he related about Cang's disastrous condition he had personally seen and felt. Households all over his native place had nothing left to eat after suffering cloudless skies for six months. He reckoned that on average each *mu* (or one sixth of an acre) under cultivation would, with luck, yield at best a *sheng* (or a pint) of edible matter. Although the northern section of the county had fared better, locusts emerged from low-lying, reed-covered land there to attack the winter wheat the moment it matured in spring, devouring much of it. Locusts again emerged to consume the sorghum as it ripened in the sun,

---

[35] Yang Zhongjian, "Bianji hanzai diaocha de suizhi," *Chenbao*, October 14, 1920; Xu Youchun, ed., *Minguo renwu da cidian* (Shijiazhuang: Hebei renmin chuban she, 2007), 1247.
[36] Miao Jinyuan, "Zen yang zuo hanzai diaocha de baogao," *Chenbao*, October 26, 1920.

this time leaving behind a "nearly bald" terrain, despite the desperate attempts of villagers to chase them off with bamboo poles. By the end of this second phase of locust attacks, the year's harvest was halfway over, and the crop appeared "swept clean." Then, just as the autumn wheat began to sprout, a third locust wave descended on the area.[37]

Yu then turns to accounts of banditry (*tufei*) in the district, which took the form of forty or fifty men "taking turns to harass communities, leaving them without rest," by posing (*jiazhuang*) as soldiers of Military Governor Cao Kun fleeing the nearby battlefields of the Zhili-Anhui July war, and then robbing village bourses "in broad daylight" (*minghuo*) of upward of 100 yuan each in the county's locust-hit northern sections. In Cang's southern sections, the men were even more brazen, seizing people for ransom and targeting certain households to demand money.[38] The report follows with drought and bandit conditions in neighboring counties – based in part on accounts from classmates with hometowns there – describing the destruction and dislocation wrought by drought and bandits in Nanpi; by drought and soldiers in Yanshan; by drought and bandits in Qingyun; and by drought and locusts in Qing.[39]

What is surprising is not what Yu's account vividly describes – the destruction of crops, violence and the dispossession of communities and wealthy households by desperate or opportunistic neighbors – but rather what it leaves out. Under the fallen Qing dynasty and in the years of the republic leading up to 1920, responses to disaster might have involved any number of measures taken by external (state or charitable) actors and/ or local (community) ones: emergency aid to the most vulnerable, loans or grants from granaries depending on levels of destitution, soup kitchens, and relief shipments of grain, cash and clothes from state agencies, native-place associations and outside charities.[40] Any sign of such practices are entirely missing from Yu's account.

Two stele (*bei*) erected in the wake of the famine year give a different window onto this same locality. Stele were stone tablets commissioned by members of a community to commemorate local events or figures and often placed in temple grounds or market squares – a practice dating back centuries. Hundreds of characters could be chiseled on a single marker, which meant they could relate a remarkable amount of detail to passersby. The medium also allowed for rubbings to be rather easily made of their contents, expanding their potential audience considerably. And, at times, their contents made their way into local histories or gazetteers, which is

---

[37] Yu Bingxiang, "Jin nan de hanzai huangzai bingzai feizai," *Chenbao*, September 28, 1920, 2.
[38] Ibid.   [39] Ibid.   [40] Fuller, *Famine Relief in Warlord China*, 125–73.

the case with the two stele examined below. When these stele accounts are held up to Yu's report, Cang reads like a different place. The first marker, a "Stele commissioned by the Cang County Disaster Relief Society to express thanks for relief by outside charities," produced in August 1921, details the social networks bringing in outside aid throughout the crisis.[41] The second, a "stele marking the disaster relief and benevolent governance [dezheng] of magistrate Wu," commissioned by a local member of the gentry identified only by the surname He, centers on a man who appears to have been the point man and facilitator of local relief throughout the crisis, the magistrate Wu Yong.[42]

The steles describe a region in desperation, with well over two hundred villages in Cang's eastern and southern sections especially struck by drought.[43] The same southeastern stretch had been inundated by a provincial flood just three years before, followed by consecutive years of weak harvests, after which residents sold for cash whatever livestock and work tools they had in order to buy food. Those with nothing left resorted to eating tree bark, leaves and other famine foods, and several thousand people a day, old and young, fled the region along the Grand Canal and other routes.[44] To stem the flight from villages and make grain prices more affordable, Wu had released 360,000 jin of grain from the county granary in July to help stabilize food prices, according to a Tianjin newspaper.[45] Afterward, his office sent agents to three locations in the lower Yangzi region to bring some 4,704,000 jin of sorghum and millet by rail for discount sale to the public, the paper later reported, which was enough to feed the entire county population of four hundred thousand for three weeks.[46] Poor residents were able to purchase these subsidized grains by producing earth salt for sale or by hawking mats made of woven bamboo and leaves, according to the district gazetteer.[47]

As the food crisis developed into full-fledged famine conditions, the Zhili governor, Cao Rui, sent in a sum of gold as seed money so that local gentry in Cang could form a county-relief society, along with 2,000 yuan in emergency relief meant to "jump-start" donations from the public. If meant to inspire largesse from those of means across the local area, these were disappointing amounts: 2,000 yuan was enough to give four coppers each to Cang's at that point estimated seventy thousand famine victims,

[41] Both stele were transcribed in the county gazetteer published the following decade. "Cangxian jiuzai xiejinhui ganxie ge cishan jiguan shizhen beiji," Cang xianzhi (1933), 13:59b–60a.
[42] "Suiru Wu xianzhang zhenzai dezheng beiji," Cang xianzhi (1933), 13:59ab.   [43] Ibid.
[44] Ibid.   [45] Da gongbao, July 21, 1920.
[46] My estimate is based on the famine ration of half a jin per person per day used by relief societies over the year. Da gongbao, November 9, 1920.
[47] Cang xianzhi (1933), 16:38b.

or barely enough for a *jin* of grain at grain discount offices – a point made later in the weekly journal of a leading Chinese aid group, the North China Relief Society, which had been founded in September by the former premier Liang Shiyi: the provincial contribution was "like dousing a cup of water on a burning cart of firewood," the group lamented.[48]

The governor's 2,000 yuan in seed money resulted in the creation of a countywide relief organization, which elected Magistrate Wu as its head, according to the stele commissioned later by the group, with a representative of a Shanghai-based Buddhist charity and a Catholic priest (presumably a Frenchman from the Order of Lazarists, which operated in the county) as assistant managers. These choices were presumably designed both to avoid communal favoritism and to open up the deep pockets of the foreign missionary and treaty-port communities. The stele goes on to explain that all matters passed before the review of Magistrate Wu, who had instructed that affairs be handled in a "public-spirited and just manner [*bi gong bi yun*]," checking on the famine stricken to "make sure that none were lost to hunger or to the cold" while "sparing them the hardship of beseeching help" by appealing himself to the state and outside agencies.[49] Wu kept in regular contact with various relief organizations in the region's big cities, and his society distributed relief on their behalf, such as shipments of grain and clothing from Shanghai's Guangrentang benevolent hall and the Zhili Righteous Relief Society (Zhili yizhen hui), a Chinese charity, along with smaller amounts of cash from the Japanese minister to China and sets of clothes from a group of Japanese students.

The largest group for which Wu's society acted as local agent was the North China Relief Society. Over the course of five months, the group's donations provisioned eighty-nine Cang villages with sacks of flour, cash and clothing.[50] Using the household registers maintained by the county to determine need, representatives of the group worked with Wu and local gentry to allocate relief rations to members of impoverished families at two distribution points: the county education bureau and Guandi temple.[51] Cart transport expenses totaling 5,000 yuan were covered by "capable" families in the villages.[52]

Agents from six other outside relief groups distributed aid directly to Cang communities: the Relief Society of China (Zhongguo yizhen hui) arrived over the year with clothing and sweet-potato biscuits; the Society

[48] Wan Zhaoji, "Cangxian sanzhen yuan Wan Zhaoji deng baogao," *Jiuzai zhoukan*, December 19, 1920.
[49] *Cang xianzhi* (1933), 13:59a–60a.   [50] *Cang xianzhi* (1933), 13:60a.
[51] *Jiuzai zhoukan*, December 19, 1920, and June 19 and August 21, 1921.
[52] *Jiuzai zhoukan*, August 21, 1921; see also *Cang xianzhi* (1933), 13:60a.

for Awakening Goodness (Wushanshe), the charitable arm of a Beijing-based religious sect, delivered millet and sorghum; the Drought Relief Society of Fengtian Province (Fengtian jiuji hanzai xiehui) provided grain and transportation; and Zhili Province's Shunzhi Disaster Relief Society (Shunzhi hanzai jiuji hui) contributed winter-wheat seed. Two independent relief operations were considerably larger than these: Tianjin's international joint foreign-Chinese relief society used resident Catholic officials to distribute an unspecified amount of rice, sorghum and peanuts "continuously" through the winter, spring and summer, including forty tons of dried sweet potatoes in the spring. And the Buddhist Foundling Relief Society of Shanghai (Fojiao jiaoying hui) sent in over 20,000 yuan in relief funds over eight months, which by March included support of eight thousand people in twenty-eight villages and the care of one thousand children through monthly cash payments to their families. Agents for the Buddhist society, which had been active in the area since the devastating Zhili floods of 1917, also distributed several thousand yuan in relief monies on behalf of the Shanghai-based Life Assistance Society of China (Zhongguo jisheng hui).[53]

In the end, the relief of Cang took on an overwhelmingly civic character, pieced together from a wide range of regional and national charitable efforts. (The central government's Relief Bureau sent in 250,000 *jin* of corn, millet and sorghum, along with five hundred sets of clothing; a poor showing compared to state relief in other Zhili counties that year, and one possibly explained by the fact that Cang had been initially categorized as a low priority compared to harder-hit districts nearby.)[54] Wu, a native of Anhui province, would be rewarded by the president of the republic, who reportedly composed a poem "commending him for serving as the father and mother of the people," using an expression common in the late imperial period to describe the paternalistic role that Confucian ethics enjoined local officials to take vis-à-vis the local population. "Although last year will be remembered as a cruel year for the people," the stele concluded, "from start to finish" the magistrate "shone throughout."[55]

What is striking about Cang's disaster response is the absence of more established institutions, such as the Chinese Red Cross, which could trace its origins to the Russo-Japanese War of 1904–05. The organization did

<hr>

[53] The foundling society was organized in the fall of 1920 by an older Buddhist relief group based in Shanghai, the Buddhist Compassion Society (Fojiao cibei hui), which had been formed in 1917 in response to the devastating floods hitting Zhili that year. *Shibao*, November 9 and December 11, 1920; Lingbo Yu, ed., *Xiandai Fojiao renwu cidian* (Sanzhong [Taibei]: Foguang chuban she, 2004), 927.

[54] *Cang xianzhi* (1933), 13:60a; *Da gongbao*, December 6, 1920; *Jiuzai zhoukan*, December 9, 1920, and March 27, 1921.

[55] *Cang xianzhi* (1933), 13:59a–60a.

not establish a subbranch in Cang until 1927; its overall role in 1920–21 was largely informational, producing reports of need from the field, while it contributed a total of 85,000 yuan and eight thousand items of clothing across the five-province famine zone.[56] Perhaps more surprisingly, neither does the Buddhist Red Swastika Society appear to have had a role in relieving Cang in 1920, despite being based in nearby Tianjin and having been active in Cang in the devastating floods of the 1910s, after which "charitable local gentry" had, according to a local history, established a Red Swastika Society subbranch.[57]

In the absence of such recognizable aid institutions, to outside observers in this rural district there was no clear agency leading the famine fighting, which was largely being done informally through a combination of networks bringing local and outside initiatives together, which would later disband at the end of the crisis. Yu's *Chenbao* piece gives no indication that any of this activity might exist, or that social networks existed that connected Cang officials and gentry with the republic's Buddhist, Christian and other confessional groups, its native-place associations, its military establishment and its benevolent halls.

Of course, Yu's appeal was made early on in the crisis, and in many ways served as a cry for help from the *Chenbao* readership, which may explain its focus on suffering and need. Would Yu have composed it any differently, say, midway through the famine? It is impossible to say. So we turn, then, to another special dispatch from the famine field, in this case some six months into famine across the North.

New Year and Famine along the Shanxi Foothills

Already in October of 1920, news reports estimated that half of Jingxing county's population of 250,000 was stricken by famine. Even affluent households had begun resorting to rice husks for food in the especially desperate, mountainous, northern section of the county, located some 100 miles southwest of Beijing on the provincial border with Shanxi. Moreover, similar to the experience in Cang, residents of Jingxing's southern reaches were suffering from robbery by soldiers roaming the area since their defeat on the plains to the east in July.[58]

Early in the new year, readers of the Beijing daily *Qunbao* (*Social Reports*) received an update on the situation in Jingxing. *Qunbao* offered a varied assortment of information spread over eight pages, including

---

[56] Zhang Jianqiu, *Zhongguo hongshizi hui chuqi fazhan zhi yanjiu* (Beijing: Zhonghua shuju, 2007), 6, 101.
[57] *Cang xianzhi* (1933), 8:187b, 16:40b.
[58] *Shuntian shibao*, October 14, 1920; "Da shi ji," *Jingxing xianzhi* (1934), 15:9b, 15:23a.

news wires on domestic and international events, train timetables, educational essays and serialized excerpts of foreign literature. In February, the daily printed a letter from an unnamed Beijing student returning home to Jingxing county for the New Year holiday. The student began by stating that conditions had worsened since the visits of numerous investigative teams, and that the report would serve both to ensure that all understood the current miserable condition (*canzhuang*) of the area's afflicted, and to draw the attention of philanthropists (*cishan jia*) who "valued doing good and took pleasure in giving away" (*leshan haoshi*), using an expression often used in gazetteer biographies.[59] The letter was clearly an appeal for help, and would have certainly registered with readers recalling the cataclysmic drought famine that had devastated the neighboring districts in Shanxi four decades before when consecutive years of drought and transport bottlenecks leading into the province, among other factors, led to the death of millions.

As in the letter from Cang, the student details a range of reasons for the subsistence crisis, which included mountainous terrain that provided limited arable land for a relatively large population, leaving many to cultivate steep slopes and rocky soil. Jingxing communities also had few wells, and their reliance on rainwater from nearby peaks meant, in times of drought and thinning mountain springs, longer trips to fetch drinking water, which sapped people further of energy. Sixty percent of county households could not carry on without aid, the student reported, a consequence, in part, of the effective closure of the area's eight major coal mines, which had employed twenty thousand workers. Nine out of ten coal miners had abruptly lost work and the remaining workers were receiving only half their previous daily pay, the writer explained, due to the "harsh measures of the capitalists [*zibenjia*]." Rather than "crouch down and die," the young and able-bodied had gone out thieving. In conversations in one village after another, the student learned that incidents of theft occurred nearly every day, along with suicides by hanging or poison and the selling of women and children. In a string of villages the student passed through, hundreds of starved hens lay frozen to death after a recent snowfall, while the main county road was dotted with the corpses of old and frail people perished from the cold.[60]

Here, again, the student leaves the reader with an impression of a region in complete abandon. Yet, despite the economic crisis among the county's coal-mining firms, the Jingxing magistrate had earlier

[59] "Zhili sheng Jingxing xian lü Jing xuesheng," *Qunbao*, February 21, 1921, 6. *Qunbao*'s masthead gives *Social Reports* as its English name.
[60] Ibid.

managed to raise 40,000 yuan in loans from the local coal industry by the end of October in order to finance the purchase of 600,000 *jin* of grain from Henan and Shanxi for discount sale to the county public.[61] Afterward, a month and a half before the student letter appeared in *Qunbao*, a group of Jingxing merchants and gentry had posted an announcement in *Yishibao*, a Tianjin broadsheet with a Beijing edition, thanking members of two charity organizations for recent visits to the district in the last few weeks of 1920: between them, six men and a monk from Beijing's Buddhist Relief Society (Fojiao chouzhen hui) and two men from Shanghai's Work Relief Association for the North (Beifang gongzhen xiehui) delivered 2.4 million *jin* of flour, 100,600 *jin* of hemp seed, 96,000 *jin* of millet, 2,800 items of clothing and 600,000 coppers – enough to purchase another 120,000 *jin* of grain at the county's discount grain centers. The donations had maintained forty thousand stricken residents, the announcement said, and both groups planned on returning in the spring.[62]

Both groups operated in the county through July 1921, and were joined by a relief society set up by the Shanghai Merchant Association to provide another five thousand people, totaling a fifth of Jingxing's population, with food over the remaining six months of famine conditions (see Figure 2).[63] The Buddhist group, founded at a Beijing temple the September before, had sent in monks conversant in the local dialect to preach the dharma to local residents, a dual relief and evangelism effort that devotees could read about in detail in the Buddhist periodical *Haichao yin*, published in Hangzhou.[64] The group, whose efforts prioritized widows, orphans and others without kin, also took in locally 550 children under the age of twelve while sending 350 others to a benevolent hall and a Buddhist shelter in Beijing.[65]

---

[61] *Jiuzai zhoukan*, October 31, 1920; *Shuntian shibao*, October 13, 1920; *Jiuzai zhoukan*, December 12, 1920.

[62] *Yishibao*, January 7, 1920. *Yishibao*'s masthead gives *Social Welfare* as its English name. Grain conversions varied by region; the volumes given here are based on converting *bao* at 160 *jin* each and *shi* at 120 *jin* each, conversion rates used by the Ministry of Communications in rail records for December 1920. The estimate of grain purchases at discount centers is based on a price of five coppers per *jin*. *Zhengfu gongbao*, June 13, 1921.

[63] This is based on the following calculation: 750,000 *jin* of grain, 155,350 *jin* of hemp seed, 18,358 *bao* of bran at 160 *jin* each (2,937,280 *jin*), and 1.2 million coppers purchasing 240,000 *jin* of subsidized grain totaled 4,082,630 *jin* or 8,165,260 daily famine rations of half a *jin*. (Hemp seed would have offered considerably more nutrition than the grains, but I do not factor this in here.) *Jingxing xianzhi* (1934), 15:23a–24a.

[64] Fojiao chouzhen hui, "Wei bei wu sheng zaimin gao ai," *Haichao yin* 12, December 1920; James H. Carter, *Heart of Buddha, Heart of China: The Life of Tanxu, a Twentieth-Century Monk* (Oxford: Oxford University Press, 2011), 92–93.

[65] *Jingxing xianzhi* (1934), 15:23ab; *Yishibao*, January 7, 1920.

Figure 2 "Spring relief distribution in Jingxing county by the Beijing Buddhist Relief Society and Shanghai Merchants Association Relief Society," March 1921. *Jingxing xianzhi* (1934). Republished in 1968 by Chengwen Publishing. Used with permission.

The activity of the Buddhist group and its partners in Jingxing was part of a larger field of outside agencies acknowledged in the 1934 gazetteer for delivering aid to the county over the year. The local annals recall 1920 as a year in which soldiers fleeing the Zhili-Anhui battlefield molested (*saorao*) many residents of the county's southern sections over the same period when the area saw "not a drop of rain" in the rainy season between May and September.[66] Similar to the case of Cang county, the Jingxing magistrate coordinated with outside agencies over the course of the crisis, according to relief society reports. In a December appeal to the work relief and well-drilling division of the Beijing-based North China Relief Society, he lamented the continued lack of adequate irrigation wells across the county.[67] The magistrate's appeal had followed the October delivery of some 8,330 *jin* of winter wheat seed from Beijing's Shunzhi

---

[66] "Da shi ji," *Jingxing xianzhi* (1934), 15:9b, 15:23ab–24a.
[67] *Jiuzai zhoukan*, October 31 and December 12, 1920; *Shuntian shibao*, October 13, 1920.

Drought Relief Society in a bid to sow a successful crop in spring. The North China Relief Society then arrived in January with 1,500 yuan in cash handouts to the population, followed by the Peking United International Famine Relief Committee (1,410,515 *jin* of grain, 15,085 yuan for various relief projects and a trainload of millet seed, along with bean cakes, quilts and clothing over the next seven months), the Zhili Charity Relief Society (8,439 yuan and 21,616 *jin* of sorghum and clothing), a Japanese student (two hundred sets of children's clothing), and Xiong Xiling's Beijing-based Relief Society of the Five Northern Provinces (7,000 yuan). Accompanying its accounting of this outside assistance, the gazetteer includes two photographs taken by the Buddhist Relief Society and Shanghai Merchant Association's relief group depicting several hundred people gathered at a spring grain distribution point in March 1921: one of a crowd posing in front of a distribution center, the other of clerks seated at tables in front of an official building with villagers lined in neat formation behind them, empty sacks over their shoulders.

So, where was local relief in all this? The 1934 gazetteer includes the biography of a man from the village of Dalongwo who was said to have been "thrifty and generous" with his earnings from his leather business in Beijing and Zhangjiakou, and in the famine year of 1920 he "helped those left bereft of anything, and many in the surrounding countryside benefited from his kindness."[68] Beyond such isolated acts, though, evidence of local relief in Jingxing is scant. Whether this means it did not materialize is another question. Across the provincial border in Pingding, a county with a similar profile to Jingxing's – mountainous, of limited fertility, yet highly populated – villages had convened in autumn to plan mutual-aid measures for the local poor; these measures had involved collecting a total of several hundred or a thousand yuan, depending on village size, from villagers deemed to have the means to contribute.[69] There is little social or cultural basis on which to assume that similar plans did not materialize, in some form or another, in neighboring Jingxing over the year.

Three days after its student report from Jingxing, *Yishibao* followed with an update on famine canvassing in the same area by the respective male and female investigative teams of Yanjing University. The update covered two Zhili counties, Xingtang and Lingshou, where the Buddhist Relief Society had expanded its famine relief operations in the last few weeks of 1920 – part of an effort that involved bringing in and distributing millions of *jin* to ten counties around the province in December. The

---

[68] *Jingxing xianzhi* (1934), 11:15b.   [69] Fuller, *Famine Relief in Warlord China*, 141–43.

students gave no indication of any Buddhist presence there at all.[70] In similar fashion, members of the Beijing Student Association survey effort reported only marauding soldiers, trampled crops and the afflictions of typhoid and other diseases in their autumn tour of southeast Zhili, asking of one county: "With local administration so naturally corrupt [*xingzheng ziran fubai*], how can it relieve disaster?" In eleven counties the team visited in Zhili and Shandong, it found a uniform scene of "the people [*renmin*] seated and waiting to die," ending with an appeal for "philanthropists [*cishan jia*] to heed their plight."[71]

Judging by what was appearing in *Chenbao* and other broadsheets at the time, student letters and surveys of the famine field gave next to no information on disaster mitigation taken at the local level. Students appeared as lacking in interest in local relief measures as they were informed of famine's horrors. If others criticized famine responses for being cups of water on a bonfire, students acted as if rural communities were just leaving the fire to burn.

Conclusion

The political watershed year of 1919 was followed by one of dismay over the specter of famine across North China, and a central government ill-equipped to respond. In its stead, community organizers, city-based charities, professional organizations and religious and native-place associations would together bear the brunt of maintaining tens of millions of destitute residents for half a year until international relief joined the effort in the spring of 1921. In an event that saw possibly one in twenty famine victims die of famine-related causes, and in another that would amount to one of the deadliest earthquakes of the century, May Fourth coverage could have accurately dismissed village mutual aid and civic activity as inadequate and overwhelmed. Doing so, however, would have acknowledged their very existence.

May Fourth coverage of communities in earthquake and famine zones conveyed what was meaningful to a new generation of activists. It also anticipated a journalistic innovation adopted later in the decade and central to Communist agitation in the 1930s. A form of literary nonfiction, *reportage* marked a move away from a novelistic focus on character

---

[70] "Yanjing daxue xuesheng zou zhi rexin kefeng," *Qunbao*, February 24, 1921. An account of Buddhist activity in these counties is given in *Haichao yin*, December 1920. See also Fuller, *Famine Relief in Warlord China*, 117–18, 127.

[71] Chen Zhengyu, "Zhi nan Lu xibei zaiqu de qingxing he jiuji fangfa," *Chenbao*, October 15, 1920. For examples of student reports on Henan and Shaanxi provinces, see *Chenbao*, October 16 and November 4, 1920, respectively.

toward description of events, locales or social phenomena. Crucially, the genre sought, as Charles Laughlin explains, to ascribe meaning to its subjects while remaining within the realm of factual objectivity.[72] Student handling of earthquake and famine in 1920–21 did not necessarily tinker with the timeline of events, or with "factuality" itself. Student messaging on the life experience in their native districts was encoded with meaning, instead, through a combination of emphasis, repetition and pointed absences.

Where were the authorities in all of this? The May Fourth movement did not, of course, occur in a political vacuum. Rather, it developed within a particular configuration of official regulation and influence over the Chinese print industry. The New Culture movement's emergence in 1915 had coincided with President Yuan Shikai's assumption of dictatorial powers soon after the republic had replaced the fallen Qing dynasty. But with Yuan's sudden death the following year, the grip he had placed on the republic's growing press was relaxed under Duan Qirui, the faction leader who succeeded him in the control of Beijing from 1916 to 1920. News dailies across the country, which had reduced dramatically in number during Yuan's tenure, rebounded to some five hundred by 1920.[73]

This does not mean that the Beiyang regime made no attempt at shaping China's cultural producers and broader public opinion. There was, in fact, a surprising alignment of the pedagogical goals of New Culture writers and Beiyang policymakers. Central government ministries joined in the scientific study of the commoner strata with the aim of shaping popular knowledge and molding a national citizenry. They just did so in less direct ways than Yuan and their Qing predecessors. Recognizing their weakened position in a context of increasingly autonomous regional governments and the extraterritoriality enjoyed by the treaty ports, Beiyang policymakers chose the tactics of persuasion over direct interference and prohibition. The regime purchased the Tianjin-based daily *Da gongbao* in 1916, acquiring a prominent platform in the increasingly intense field of competition for newsreaders.[74] And Beiyang policymakers attempted to influence the print industries located well beyond their northern powerbase. Through the creation of the Popular Education Research Society (Tongsu jiaoyu yanjiuhui), formalized by the Ministry of Education in 1915, the central government demonstrated

---

[72] Charles A. Laughlin, *Chinese Reportage: The Aesthetics of Historical Experience* (Durham, NC: Duke University Press, 2002), 9.

[73] Lin Yutang, *History of the Press and Public Opinion in China* (Shanghai: Kelly and Walsh, 1936), 117, 124.

[74] Wang Runze, *Zhang Liluan yu Da gongbao*, 30.

concerns more often associated with intellectuals at the time, as the historian Zhang Jing has demonstrated; this included keeping attuned to mass culture, and shaping the reading material available to the general public. As Zhang shows, this was done on the cheap, with a budget of 1,000 yuan from the ministry, which had the power to confirm but not nominate reviewers and censors recruited by the society from the ranks of educators and intellectuals. Many recruits came from New Culture movement circles, including the writer Lu Xun, who served the society for a year in the late 1910s. With limited resources and monitoring powers, the Beiyang regime thus positioned itself nationally as a cultural arbiter, but mostly indirectly, reaching the reading public through open letters and appeals in the country's major newspapers, written to single out what the society's reviewers deemed politically sensitive or scandalous literature. Trade groups such as the bookseller association in Shanghai were used by the ministry as intermediaries to enforce self-reporting systems among treaty port-based publishers that targeted what the society's reviewers deemed problematic works.[75]

But there was one crucial difference between the pedagogical goals of reformist intellectuals and the Beiyang regime. Officials continued a late imperial concern with private morality, which was seen as originating in the family and as providing the foundation for public life more broadly. For New Culture writers, the state of civic morality was of equal concern. Not only did they inveigh against neo-Confucian family ethics and its constraints on the individual, women especially, but they also reinvigorated an area of social critique spearheaded by reformist intellectuals in the late 1890s, one identifying a lack of public morality (*gongde*) in Chinese society; this was understood by the period's foremost thinker, Liang Qichao, as "those moral values which promote the cohesion of the group," in the words of his biographer, distinct from private morals (*side*), which "function to achieve moral perfection of individual personality."[76]

May Fourth disaster coverage involved politics played at a much deeper level, one that often spared specific officials or agencies from attack, lending student disaster coverage a measure of journalistic freedom – undetected by Beiyang censors seeking out literary or journalistic coverage of licentious scandal or political figures. Collectively, the movement imagined a "new social order," writes Shakhar Rahav, a nation-building mission that was to be achieved through moral transformation using print

[75] Zhang Jing, "Regulating Popular Political Knowledge: The Presence of a Central Government in the Late 1910s," *Twentieth-Century China* 47/1 (January 2022), 30–39.
[76] Hao Chang, *Liang Ch'i-ch'ao and Intellectual Transition in China*, 151.

media to "communicate moral lessons to others" at home.[77] For his part, within a year of *Xin Long*'s earthquake survey, coeditor Deng Chungao expounded on just this question of morality in a serialized essay in Gansu University's quarterly magazine.[78] With gentry or Buddhist initiative excised from accounts – deinscribing, in other words, these actors' significance from cultural memory – what remained in representations of rural life were cultures and communities in desperate need of rejuvenation. To students, nothing worthy of the name of public morality or civic values existed in the disaster field. These values were as lifeless as the surrounding fields they passed.

Yet the responses to earthquake and famine suffering recounted in communal records involved many of the key qualities civic textbooks would seek to instill, as we will see, in the next generation: a concern for others, one extending to the greater good; the initiative to act; and the organizational skills to intervene. But before we consider the prescriptions for the country's ills presented through the 1920s, the power of this idea of Chinese moral deficiencies needs to be fully accounted for. China's New Culture intellectuals were, of course, active and engaged with a wider global context. May Fourth social diagnoses and solutions to China's plight were remarkably similar to European and American ones. It is to these outside voices, those of Western missionaries, writers and thinkers resident in China over the earthquake and famine year of 1920–21, to which we now turn.

---

[77] Rahav, *Rise of Political Intellectuals*, 47.
[78] Deng Chungao, "Hewei daode?," *Gansu daxue zhoukan* 1/1 (1922), 23–29, and 1/2 (1922), 30–42.

3   Projections onto a "Chinese Screen"

The invisibility of social relief practices and institutions in surveys of rural Chinese life may have been characteristic of May Fourth journalism, but it was by no means unique to it. Foreign correspondents echoed student dismissals of the capacities of rural Chinese districts in times of crisis. "Chinese Resigned to Starvation," ran a representative November 1920 headline in the London *Times* just as indigenous mutual aid and relief programs were spreading across the famine field, "Death the Only Prospect," it continued.[1] Similarly, Josef Hall (aka Upton Close), coauthor of the *National Geographic* report on the Gansu earthquake based on his trip to the Northwest in late winter 1921, took no notice of medical aid, food distribution or any form of local disaster response in his report, describing only a scene of unfathomable destruction.[2]

Earlier that fall, Hall had traveled through the famine field with fellow American Eleanor Franklin Egan, correspondent for the *Saturday Evening Post*. Afterwards, his published travelogue made no mention of native relief of drought-famine victims, despite devoting nearly a dozen pages to their tour through northwest Shandong and south Zhili. Instead, Hall noted only "two courageous missionary women" working out of a Confucian temple under the inscription "the True Culture is Sympathy," words "most appropriate for the [relief] use to which representatives of another faith were putting the sage's sanctuary."[3] "If it were not for the missionaries there would be mighty little famine relief available for the interior multitudes of China to-day," Egan informed readers of the *Post* in the spring.[4]

---

[1] *Times* (London), November 16, 1920.

[2] Close and McCormack, "Where the Mountains Walked," 445–64.

[3] Upton Close (Josef Hall), *In the Land of the Laughing Buddha: The Adventures of an American Barbarian in China* (New York: G. P. Putnam's Sons, 1924), 145.

[4] It should be noted that Egan recognized the efforts of *urban* Chinese who, through what she called "all-Chinese famine-relief committees," received refugees in Beijing "long before the foreigners who live among them did anything." Eleanor Franklin Egan, "Fighting the Chinese Famine," *Saturday Evening Post*, April 9, 1921, 48.

Like proverbial ships passing in the night, native relief went unnoticed by unsuspecting foreign observers. This is perhaps not surprising, since the well-worn routes trod by foreigners in the interior provided only very limited exposure to the native population spread out along webs of paths connecting thousands of communities. Since the intensification of Protestant efforts in nineteenth-century China, Protestant communities were added to existing Catholic ones. Mission stations aiming to reach the country's common folk were found scattered along the cart paths and waterways that snaked inland from the treaty ports. The location of mission compounds channeled the flow of foreign movement in the interior, serving as relays for fellow nationals on holiday or business seeking familiar comforts and companionship. The wider social role played by the missionary community was facilitated by the availability of guidebooks to the national network of mission compounds, complete with suggested inland routes – something similar to today's *Rough Guides* or *Lonely Planets*.[5]

This goes some way in explaining the centrality of missions in foreign accounts of daily Chinese life, often at the expense of indigenous activity nearby. Before making her determinations on the indispensability of the missionary community in times of crisis, for example, Egan had spent two days in an American Board Mission compound in Dezhou, Shandong, one of the counties that had received part of a distribution of 5,000 tons of relief grain by provincial gentry just a few weeks before.[6] Afterwards, she and Close both traveled by cart through south Zhili's Wei county, where a handful of local men are credited in the county gazetteer for relieving their neighbors in 1920–21, and where in the village of Zhangjiazhuang – in an area where nine-tenths of the population was deemed affected by drought – a village-wide relief program carried its residents through the awful year, after which the villager initiating the program publicly burned all resulting notes of debt incurred as a "demonstration of charity."[7] Egan nonetheless concluded from her tour that "the mission stations, schools and colleges are supplying practically the entire working force in the outfields [sic] famine relief."[8]

Another reason for the prominence of missions was that they enjoyed a collective voice considerably out of proportion to their actual numbers on Chinese ground. Forming part of global networks of church parishes and organizations, French Catholic bishops or staff of the London

---

[5] Paul Hutchinson, ed., *A Guide to Important Mission Stations in Eastern China (Lying Along the Main Routes of Travel)* (Shanghai: The Mission Book Company, 1920).
[6] The full name of Egan's host is the American Board of Commissioners for Foreign Missions. Fuller, *Famine Relief in Warlord China*, 210.
[7] Ibid., 140.   [8] Egan, "Fighting the Chinese Famine," 48.

Missionary Society, for example, regularly contributed correspondence to the "Outport" (i.e., interior) sections of coastal news outlets based in Tianjin or Shanghai. When disaster struck, they also worked with major, high-profile city-based relief societies, serving on committees, gathering intelligence and facilitating relief movement and distribution.

Geography, modern media and social networks, though, are only part of the story of early twentieth-century missionary prominence. Another was the tone found in missionary treatments of Chinese society, which mirrored May Fourth writing in striking ways. For instance, if May Fourth student activists saw themselves constituting a "vanguard of social reform" descending on the famine field, missionaries could frame their endeavors in equally militant terms. "Comrades," began A. Mildred Cable and Francesca French in the opening to their 1925 volume for the Religious Tract Society of the China Inland Mission, "It is of no use for you to read dispatches from the front unless you have some idea of the line of battle to which they refer. Look at your map and locate LANCHOW, capital of the province of Kansu in North-West China."[9] Chances were good that any such map came from a monumental volume produced after the 1910 World Missionary Conference held in Edinburgh: a statistical atlas that partitioned China into discrete fields of Protestant missions, published in Shanghai as *The Christian Occupation of China: A General Survey of the Numerical Strength and Geographical Distribution of the Christian Forces in China*. In it, Gansu was shared by three mission groups – with large swaths of the province "unclaimed" by any mission and rendered pitch black, including the quake struck, predominantly Muslim region around Haiyuan and Guyuan.[10]

In addition to this martial quality, church writers and foreign visitors to church grounds added urgency to evangelical work by stressing its morally transformative purpose. Fundamental to the missionary enterprise, in other words, is the pursuit of change through exhortation. And this it shares with revolutionary agitation. "Yesterday our Chinese colleagues, after dispersing the crowds and getting a hasty meal themselves, set to work to prepare for to-day's distribution [...] with sleeves turned up, working side by side," Reverend J. D. Liddell wrote from Cang county, Zhili, in February 1921. "Only those who have lived in China will realize the utter abnegation of self which such actions implies, and must

---

[9] A. Mildred Cable and Francesca L. French, *Dispatches from North-West Kansu* (London: China Inland Mission, 1925), 1.

[10] Milton Stauffer, ed., *The Christian Occupation of China: A General Survey of the Numerical Strength and Geographical Distribution of the Christian Forces in China*, Special Committee on Survey and Occupation, 1918–1921 (Shanghai: China Continuation Committee, 1922), 106.

acknowledge that Christ has worked miracles in transforming lives and characters."[11] Chinese who acted for others in times of need could only be those shaped by newfound convictions: in Christ, or, alternatively, in the nation, in socialism, or, most broadly, in "modern man."

And then a third sentiment expressed alike by missionary and May Fourth writers was that tolerance of suffering – inaction in the face of need and callousness toward the suffering of strangers – was understood to be characteristic of Chinese culture. In this way, visitors to China and its missions came to perceive relief action, and inaction, in national, and at times racial, terms. "The French missionaries of Tchili must be given the first place among those who gave the alarm of the famine," Abel Bonnard remarked in his travelogue, *En Chine, 1920–1921*. The Frenchman's claims were made under similar circumstances to those of his American counterparts, coming after a tour by the bishop of Catholic mission grounds in severely afflicted Xian county. "Everything from his natural laziness to the profundity of his thoughts counsels the Chinaman to take no action."[12]

These representations of Chinese life were part of a broader body of ethnographic literature that had developed in conjunction with the growth of colonial projects in Africa and Asia over the 1800s. Travelers, benefitting from the increasing convenience of steamship travel at the turn of the century, could draw from a flourishing industry of guides to foreign lands and the social life and customs of their peoples – a central focus of this chapter. Much of this literature stemmed from a longstanding missionary practice of introducing home audiences to daily life in the distant mission fields, where generations of missionaries served as pioneers in linguistic and ethnographic study.

Visitors to the East consequently arrived with a fair amount of preconditioning through which they viewed and processed events around them. And this conditioning was by no means limited to evangelical material. On asserting the primacy of Western beneficence and valuation of life, missionaries were joined by more secular and celebrated writers, including Bertrand Russell, Somerset Maugham, Sidney Gamble and Alexis Leger (aka St.-John Perse). All four men were in China around the country's series of ecological disasters in 1920–21. Through their writings, the travel essay, sociological study, poetic verse and vignette, each offered readers windows onto alien social and cultural worlds to hold up against their own, either as armchair travelers or while treading foreign

[11] J. D. Liddell, "On the Edge of the Famine: Tsangchow [Cangzhou] February 8 and 9, 1921," *The Chronicle of the London Missionary Society* 29 (June 1921), 138.
[12] Abel Bonnard, *En Chine, 1920–1921*, trans. Veronica Lucas (London: George Routledge & Sons, 1926), 127–28.

paths themselves. In the broader logic of colonialism and the civilizing mission, the idea that benevolence was practiced or not, or suffering alleviated or not, became a key criterion with which cultures and peoples were categorized in the hierarchy of nations, an understanding of the world encapsulated in Rudyard Kipling's poem "The White Man's Burden," which had urged Americans to "Fill full the mouth of Famine," among other things, as they subjugated the Philippines at the turn of the century.[13]

This does not, however, mean that national, racial or civilizational dualities of charity and callousness, or action and inaction, were merely imposed on China from outside. May Fourth-era writers embraced and internalized such dichotomies in a form of coproduction that is another focus of this chapter. In the paradigm to which many reformist writers subscribed, Chinese culture was configured to preclude the very idea of assisting strangers or of mitigating social ills in any meaningful way. Here we capture this paradigm by reviewing the literary diet offered to foreign visitors to China during the May Fourth period.

Finally, it might be noted that what follows here is not an attempt to seek out the chauvinism or ugliness of early twentieth-century foreign writing on Chinese life. By and large, what follows is a review of works available to read in the reading rooms of the British Library at St. Pancras and the Library of Congress in Washington. And many of the people behind these writings positioned themselves as sympathetic to China and "endeavoured to write as a friend of the Far East," in the words of one review in 1920.[14] Rather, the aim is to identify a disconnect between the observations made here by a range of outside writers on issues of charitable initiative and human welfare in China and what Chinese communal records say. The significance of this disconnect is what it reveals about the level of conditioning the reading public had before and during visits to China regarding particular areas of Chinese life, and the ways in which this foreign cultural production seeped into Chinese intellectual circles as well.

Reading China

Since the missionary movement's pivot away from Chinese elites toward the country's poor and marginalized over the course of the nineteenth century, social programs went hand in hand with evangelical work.

---

[13] Rudyard Kipling, "The White Man's Burden – An Address to the United States," *Times* (London), February 4, 1899.

[14] P. Pelliot, "Émile Hovelaque, *Les Peuples d'Extrême-Orient. La Chine*," *T'oung Pao* 20/2 (March 1920–March 1921), 157.

Missionary interventions in the lives of the poor were similar to those made by church parishes in industrializing cities back home, including the creation of orphanages, schooling – especially for females – and food and medical relief in times of calamity. Attention to the unfortunate was stressed by virtue of the gospel teachings, but missions also needed to justify the formidable expense of their presence overseas to parish sponsors back home. This made the health of social ethics among native peoples a central topic for missionary literature.

Preparation for missionary work depended in part on where in the hierarchy of cultures one's destination country stood. "The difference between sailing south for the Congo and east for China or India," reads the biography of a medical missionary to China's Northwest, was "the difference between the simple and the complex." The missionary arriving in the Congo found the "ground comparatively speaking clear [...] 'clear' because the social or religious innovator proceeding to Congo has no such ancient civilisation as that of India or China to face; no articulated system of religion such as that of the Hindu, Confucian or the Neo-Buddhist." When in the 1910s the Scotsman's assignment was Shaanxi province, his "preparation for the East had included a certain amount of reading upon the religious and social systems at work in China."[15] His peers presumably did the same. A *Manual for Young Missionaries to China* deemed it "an excellent plan always to have on hand some good book on China."[16]

These books covered a range of topics, but on the subject of Chinese beneficence their dismissals were markedly uniform: diplomat-turned-Yale Sinologist S. Wells Williams' *Middle Kingdom* of 1848, revised and enlarged in 1883 (charity "thrives poorly in the selfish soil of heathenism" and only when "higher teachings have been engrafted into the public mind" would these even "badly managed establishments [...] promise something better");[17] Justus Doolittle's *Social Life of the Chinese* of 1865 (charity is performed "oftentimes in consequence of a vow made before some idol for the promotion of selfish ends [...] more than because the donors desire [...] to benefit [...] the recipients");[18] *China and the Chinese* (1869) of upstate-New Yorker Rev. John L. Nevius (the existence of Christian charity is "due mainly to high moral principle, and a sense of duty and responsibility" while the "principal ingredient" in its Chinese

---

[15] John Charles Keyte, *Andrew Young of Shensi: Adventure in Medical Missions* (London: The Carey Press, 1924), 111–12.

[16] Arthur H. Smith, ed., *A Manual for Young Missionaries to China*, 2nd ed. (Shanghai: The Christian Literature Society, 1924), 26–29, 33.

[17] S. Wells Williams, *The Middle Kingdom* (New York: C. Scribner's sons, 1883), 265–66.

[18] Justus Doolittle, *Social Life of the Chinese*, vol. 2. (Cheng Wen Publishing Company, 1966), 174–76, 196; first published 1865.

counterpart is "selfishness" – the "false religions of China" reward "meritorious actions" for "selfish ends");[19] the Hong Kong archdeacon John Henry Gray's *China* of 1878 (the "truth" was that, "as a rule," the Chinese had "little or no sympathy" for those destined to have infirmities due to past acts "against the gods" – charitable acts were "of course regarded as a work of merit");[20] and, lastly, New England-native Arthur Smith's *Chinese Characteristics* of 1894 ("in all" the charitable acts listed by the author "it will be observed that the object in view is by no means the benefit of the person upon whom the 'benevolence' terminates, but the extraction from the benefit conferred").[21] Charitable Chinese evidently met calamities with alms in one hand, karmic abacus in the other.

Before departure for the East, readings could be complemented by coursework on comparative ethics. The Chinese "body politic" has "for generations" been "flaccid, torpid, semi-comatose," Professor William Edward Soothill related in a 1923 lecture at Oxford designed, according to its printed edition, expressly for "students designated for mission work in China." While the "ancient Chinese" were in fact "religious" possessors of "a clear recognition of the value of virtue," for a thousand years the country had "no moral and spiritual renascence and lived in the depressing atmosphere of a false and enervating natural philosophy." Buddhism's moral contribution in the early years of the first millennium was "chiefly" a "doubtful form of mercy toward animals" only adding some "weight to the quality of mercy already advocated by Confucius and other sages."[22]

Soothill's distinction between an ethical ancient past in China and its present moral malaise was nothing new, even to Chinese themselves. Soothill, the former principal of the Shanxi Imperial University, was instead invoking influential revisionist readings of the Chinese classics by one of his Victorian predecessors at Oxford, James Legge, whose translations had located monotheistic kinship between Christianity and ancient Confucianism, which was now ripe for reunion and rejuvenation through missionary vigor. The Almighty was not out to "destroy the Philosophy of the East, but will 'fulfill' it," Soothill remarks in his 1906 edition of the *Analects*, "transforming what is worthy from vain adulatory approval into a concrete

---

[19] John L. Nevius, *China and the Chinese* (New York: Harper and Brothers, 1869), 213–14.
[20] John H. Gray, *China: A History of the Laws, Manners, and Customs of the People* (London: Macmillan, 1878), 46, 56–58.
[21] Smith, *Chinese Characteristics*, 12–14, 186–93. First published in 1890 Shanghai by the North China Herald Office, Smith's work appeared in a 1930s French translation, *Moeurs Curieuses des Chinois*, by a Parisian publishing house in a series that also included W. E. Soothill's lectures *Les trois Religions de la Chine*.
[22] William Edward Soothill, *The Three Religions of China: Lectures Delivered at Oxford* (London: Oxford University Press, 1923), preface and 186, 195, 206–7.

asset in the nation [sic] life and character." In the figure of Confucius, his Western reader would "see distinction and dignity" in the "aspirations" of this "multitudinous race [...] where before a swamp of mental and moral stagnation may have seemed to be his sole environment." The "renascence has now occurred" for the Chinese, his lecture explained, "brought by agencies either directly Christian or allied with Christian forces."[23]

None of this is to deny that a notion of moral credit had currency for centuries in China – particularly in popular culture (a tradition examined by Cynthia Brokaw[24]) – only that to Protestant observers a profit motive lay behind merciful acts performed within indigenous communities. The possibility of a more complex combination of motivations – ethical, emotional, social or otherwise – to Chinese charitable endeavors was rarely entertained.

And then Protestant fixation on a profit motive behind charity stemmed from what was as much a conflict within Western Christianity as it was one between Christians and nonbelievers in Christ. Spiritual self-interest was a driving force behind one of the largest and longest-lasting missionary presences in China, the Holy Childhood Association. Soliciting small donations from European children to sponsor the adoption of Chinese babies and their baptism in Catholic foundling homes (with extraordinarily high death rates), the group saw the "souls of the Chinese infants" becoming "intercessors with God on behalf of those who had sent them to heaven," in the words of Henrietta Harrison. One 1870s poem, recorded in the organization's *Annales*, has a dying French child speak of his "brothers the little Chinese" who were "to crown me with a wreath of gold. And put on my white wings."[25] A pioneer in international aid, the group sought, through the baptism of so many Chinese babies, a greater mass of angelic advocates for the salvation of children at home. Martin Luther's vision for the reformation of the medieval Church had lain in rejecting, arguably more than anything else, any such combination of faith and meritorious acts, leaving salvation to faith in Christ's grace alone, that is, "justification." Such dismissal of merit as a means of salvation courted execution across papal Christendom in Luther's time;

[23] Norman J. Girardot, *The Victorian Translation of China: James Legge's Oriental Pilgrimage* (Berkeley: University of California Press, 2002), 252–53, 268; Soothill, *Three Religions of China*, 186; William Edward Soothill, *Analects of Confucius* (Yokohama: W.E. Soothill, 1910), i–v.

[24] Cynthia Brokaw, *The Ledgers of Merit & Demerit: Social Change and Moral Order in Late Imperial China* (Princeton, NJ: Princeton University Press, 1991). See also Kathryn Edgerton-Tarpley, *Tears from Iron: Cultural Responses to Famine in Nineteenth-Century China* (Berkeley: University of California Press, 2008), 58–59.

[25] Henrietta Harrison, "'A Penny for the Little Chinese': The French Holy Childhood Association in China, 1843–1951," *American Historical Review* 113/1 (2008), 78–80.

the cooling of Catholic-Protestant relations on this matter has also been remarkably recent, largely a development of the 1960s Second Vatican Council.[26]

It follows then that Catholic dismissals of Chinese benevolence as a merit-accumulating enterprise were far rarer than Protestant ones; instead, Catholic writers tended to condemn the degeneracy of a generic "paganism." Based at Daming in the plains of south Zhili – the center of the drought-famine in 1920 – the French priest Pierre Mertens introduced his home audience that year to his "Oasis de la Charité Catholique." There, he explained, "superstition, barbarism and pagan selfishness" had filled the Saint Enfance nurseries and orphanages with hundreds of children.[27] Similarly, in a volume later published by Vichy's Maison du Missionaire, the Académie Française laureate and Lazarist Henry Watthé explained that, "Whoever says paganism says rapid decadence of conscience and mores, and an irremediable return to barbarism." The Chinese, Watthé continued elsewhere in the volume, "does not stop, unless he's a Christian (if a pagan, it's an exceptional rarity!), to study the morality of his schemes or his actions. He sees but the end: money, honor, pleasure." "In fact," Watthé continued rhetorically,

is not the *chef-d'œuvre* of Christian education this *Petite Sœur des Pauvres chinoises*, and this *Fille de la Charité chinoise* who, part of a very inferior race (in the point of view of moral conscience, mind you), can raise themselves to the level of their elders in charity and generosity, namely the disciples who [seventeenth century Lazarist order founder] Saint Vincent de Paul breathed life into all over France and in our Occidental countries.[28]

As the audience of many of these missives and reports were parishioners in the home country sponsoring the very existence of these missions, members of the latter could go to great lengths to stir the hearts of potential pledgers at home. The Lazarists of the French Province of Champagne hosted a *collège français* and a towering stone cathedral on their mission grounds at Daming in south Zhili. Raising and maintaining

---

[26] The origins of Christian and Chinese notions of salvation through merit are also surprisingly similar in their eclecticism. One Protestant theologian cites half a dozen Greek and Judaic origins to its Christian forms, while in China the supernatural retribution of the early classics (*Spring and Autumn Annals, Classic of Changes*, etc.) mixed with later esoteric tenets of both Buddhism and Daoism to produce a hybrid and somewhat Confucianized popular merit system from the Ming onward. Heinz, *Justification and Merit*, 1–3, 13–14, 97; Brokaw, *Ledgers*, 40, 53–55.

[27] Pierre Mertens, S. J., ed., *La Légende Dorée en Chine: Scènes de la vie de Missions au Tche-li Sud-est* (Lille: Societé Saint-Augustin, Desclée de Brouwer et Compagnie, 1920), 58.

[28] Henry Watthé, *La Belle Vie du Missionaire en Chine: Récits et croquis* (Vichy: Maison du Missionaire, 1930), vol. 1, xi; vol. 2, 109, 115.

such a facility must have required appeals for considerable funds from Champagne and beyond. In a 1920 essay published in the northern French city of Lille, mission priest P. M. Cannepin asked the "little children of France" whether they "all, in France" don't "adore the little Chinese!" But "the adults," he went on, "are connivers, liars, hypocrites, that's for sure!" Cannepin recounted how a "good woman back home" had expressed horror over the idea that the priest was off to live among the Chinese. "They'll put you in the cangue, cut you into little pieces," she cried. "Yes," Cannepin responded rhetorically, "the adults with their almond eyes and their ebony braids serve as scarecrows repelling the good people at home! But 'Little Chinese' you adore them without even knowing them – and you're right."[29]

On the eve of the feast of the Epiphany in early January 1920, Bishop S. G. Monseigneur Henri Lécroart, head of this same south Zhili mission, prefaced a book on mission life with the question, "What is true of China, is it not equally valid – more or less – for all Catholic Missions in infidel lands? What does the missionary find in his new country of adoption? He finds the pagan [...] above all the lettered pagan who inhabits a pride from a thousand years of inertia." No distinction was necessary, Lécroart explained, between the "Chinese, the Hindu, the Hottentot" – rather the bishop "simply spoke of the pagan, that is man degraded, congealed, mummified in his errors; the pagan for whom justice, discretion, generosity are words meant only to hide his vices. Fortunately," Lécroart concluded, "there is still the poor, the peasant, the child."[30]

Reaching China's young, and females generally, involved the efforts of women, both foreign and Chinese, from all denominations, resulting in a subgenre of missionary literature for their benefit. In the Protestant mission field, women in fact formed a majority of foreign workers – and single women nearly a third[31] – and for their needs the Massachusetts-based Central Committee on the United Study of Foreign Missions put out a "simple, more concrete study book for use in meetings and in the study classes for young women" destined for the mission field. *Ming-Kwong: "City of Morning Light,"* a "text-book" of a "composite city" of "Central China," advises its readers that "philanthropy of a certain kind was not new to the Chinese [...] Their charities, however, were spasmodic, accompanied with graft and carried on chiefly for the purpose of storing up merit for themselves in the next world." The upshot, these

[29] P. M. Cannepin, "Les Poupées Vivantes," 293, in Mertens, *La Légende Dorée en Chine*; emphasis in the original.
[30] Henri Lécroart, preface to *La Légende Dorée en Chine*, by Mertens, v.
[31] Jane Hunter, *The Gospel of Gentility: American Women Missionaries in Turn-of-the-Century China* (New Haven, CT: Yale University Press, 1984), xv, 11, 277.

China-bound students learned, was that the rising "Morning Light" of "Christian social service attracted them. They responded to it" and with "surprising [. . .] swiftness the idea spread and expressed itself in practical ways [. . .] and [they have given] generously to famine relief."[32]

Part of this female framing of mission work were books on "pagan" women the world over, a genre that included the London Missionary Society's *Women of the North China Plain* from its World Womanhood Series. Based on the author's time in "Siao Chang," a mission district "twice as large as Wales" in south Zhili, the work's section "A Typical Life-Story" asked of its reader to

> imagine yourself to be one of these Chinese sisters [. . .]. First of all, there is a tremendous subtraction sum to be done [. . .] take away prayers by your mother's knee; take away walks by your father's side, when he answers your eager childish questions about the stars and the sea [. . .] though your heart and soul are very much the same as the young hearts and souls in England, your surrounding atmosphere is so different that you develop differently. The conversation you hear is often sordid and soiled, full of jealousies and evil gossip, cunningness and superstition. The women tell lies to shield the children they love, the men use craft and bullying to gain their own way.[33]

Such a setting was hardly conducive to human fellowship or to random acts of kindness.

Nor was this necessarily a reader's first opportunity to consume such bleak takes on the Chinese life experience. London's Great Missionary Exhibition of 1909 involved hundreds of costumed missionaries recreating Chinese (along with African and Indian) "daily life," a touring spectacle that also visited Liverpool, Birmingham, Macclesfield, Limerick and Cork.[34] Churches offered similar recreations on a more regular basis. The London Missionary Society was in 1920 advertising that its Livingstone Bookstore in Westminster "caters for all the needs of the Sunday School Teacher and Missionary Worker," a service that included Chinese-style sets and costume rental for both adult and children's stage dramas. Selections included *Blind Chang: A Missionary Drama*, which opens with two Chinese robbers preparing to pounce on the blind hero who has "heard that the white doctor" in the Manchurian capital of Mukden "can give him back his sight" while Boxers threaten to torture a compatriot foolish enough to lavish hope on the "foreign devil"; *Bao's*

---

[32] Mary Ninde Gamewell, *Ming-Kwong: "City of Morning Light"* (West Medford, MA: Central Committee on the United Study of Foreign Missions, 1924), 9, 176–77.

[33] Ethel S. Livens, *Women of the North China Plain* (London: London Missionary Society, 1920), 12–14.

[34] Eric Reinders, *Borrowed Gods and Foreign Bodies: Christian Missionaries Imagine Chinese Religion* (Berkeley: University of California Press, 2004), 1–7.

Adventure: A Chinese Play in Two Acts, which contrasts the avaricious and useless Chinese "priest-doctor" with a "Dr. Hope" and a "Nurse Well" (the latter prescribing prayer for Bao's maimed leg); and *The Way of the Merciful: A Chinese Play in Three Acts*, which again contrasts mercenary native doctors with white doctors laurelled with lines like "our wonderful foreigner [...] the beloved physician at Tsang Chou" (or Cang county, whose famine relief operations were explored in Chapter 2). As transparent as these caricatures may appear, one wonders what effect they may have had on the British parishioners who, while rising during each performance to sing "certain appropriate hymns between the Acts," as the script booklet suggested they do, also might have attended the preperformance "talks or discussions on the subject [each play] presents."[35]

The inclusion of children in the discussion of Chinese failings, many of whom would soon come of age in the crises of the twentieth century, was a task often taken up by maternal figures in the mission field. One such author, credited for her 1892 work simply as "a Missionary's Wife," composed *China and Its People: A Book for Young Readers* in the form of a lesson for her nephew "E. H." back home and his little "brothers and sisters" – one that framed the wider world in similar hierarchies to those taught adults heading into the field. "The Chinese, you know, are not a barbarous people, like the natives of Central Africa or Australia," this "Aunt Helen" explained. While she was "sorry to tell" her young audience that the Chinese were "too often hard-hearted of the sick and poor," promise lay in the fact that "they have not heard from their childhood the 'sweet story' of Him who went about doing good."[36]

The *True Tales About a Chinese Boy and His Friends* appeared in 1918, a book whose "main effect," according to its introduction by a faculty member of Columbia University's Teacher's College, was "to impress one with the limitless possibilities for good, if proper help could be extended to the Chinese." Among these Chinese was a photographed "granny" (the author had "found hundreds like her. In all their lives they had never heard a single beautiful song, nor had one happy day") and a begging blind man fearing the "Beggar Chief would beat him" for returning with his day's meager collection of coppers just before "a silver

[35] Phyllis M. Higgs, *Blind Chang: A Missionary Drama* (Westminster, UK: London Missionary Society, 1920), 3, 13; Harold D. Cotton, *Bao's Adventure: A Chinese Play in Two Acts and Six Scenes* (Westminster, UK: London Missionary Society, circa 1920), 1, 14; Vera E. Walker, *The Way of the Merciful: A Chinese Play in Three Acts* (Westminster, UK: London Missionary Society, circa 1920), 2, 8.
[36] "A Missionary's Wife" ("Aunt Helen"), *China and Its People: A Book for Young Readers* (London: James Nisbet and Co., 1892), iii, 14, 20–21.

dime" drops into his can, "one hundred cash all at once!" followed by the sound of "queer English speech."[37]

French and English-language books lining library shelves or the trunks of arriving missionaries circa 1920 presented readers with a remarkably limited range of possibilities for the practice of Chinese ethical life, ones that placed foreign largesse front and center. These Christian voices, though, were hardly alone. They were joined by others over the earthquake and famine year, those of writers whose artistic representations of life in China proved, in their moral messaging, little different.

Dust, Diplomacy and a Nobel

As significant as the missionary community was to mainstream thought in early twentieth-century understandings of foreign cultures, the broader discursive climate of the time is perhaps best captured by the writings of a Frenchman then posted at his country's legation in Beijing. Alexis Leger had arrived in 1916 as the twenty-nine-year-old third secretary on his first overseas assignment for the diplomatic service. In letters home to France, Leger deplored the "cocoon-like mode of life" led by the diplomatic corps in their Beijing quarter and the "snobbery of its inhabitants" whose lives remained "totally unrelated to China." Leger ventured beyond the narrow confines of these circles, making, he grandly put it, "direct contact with much of the real China" during evenings over chess with the Chinese leadership and extended excursions from the capital. This included renting space in a small Buddhist temple on a "rocky eminence" at the northwestern outskirts of Beijing, keeping in touch with the legation through a mounted messenger.[38]

"Out here the nights are immense and empty," Leger wrote from his refuge, a "compelling pervasiveness of absence and void," which allowed him to "dream until dawn" – while his "old chief boy" from the legation prepared his meals. Flooded valleys were at times below his perch, at others a shriveled river soon to "disappear beneath the sand" beside a "tiny rural community" that was "dying out." At "eye-level" stood the "first massive ranges" of the "Mongolian uplift" and the "pale yellow line of the first camel-routes" leading into Inner Asia. There, high above the expanse, Leger found "immense peace for the spirit," even the urge to "take up my pen again, in spite of all my longstanding resolutions to the

---

[37] Evelyn Worthley Sites, *Mook: True Tales About a Chinese Boy and His Friends* with an introduction by F. M. McMurry (West Medford, MA: The Central Committee on the United Study of Foreign Missions, 1918), 11–12, 52–70.

[38] St.-John Perse (Alexis Leger), *Letters*, ed. and trans. Arthur J. Knodel (Princeton, NJ: Princeton University Press, 1979), xii, 258, 286, 312.

contrary." These "desert expanses," he wrote his mother, have "exerted a hold on my thoughts, a fascination that approaches hallucination."[39]

"The whole of China is nothing but dust," the young French sojourner concluded, taking his gaze over Beijing's surrounds and the Gobi desert beyond for the entirety of a country awesome in size and variation. "China is nothing but dust," he wrote to another correspondent, a "land worn down to the bone of age." And elsewhere, "What other image can I pick from all this heathen dust for you?" he asked his mother.[40] It was as though, to an imagination held hostage by this alien landscape, metaphoric skeletons unearthed by Gobi winds could, as we will see, be taken for Chinese self-worth and the national condition itself.

In March 1921, Leger laced his conclusions into a suggestive letter to an unnamed "European Lady," advising her against coming to swap the "good + sign of Europe for the – sign of Asia." It was a "question of breed, race, and blood," he explained, a "loyalty in all things to the fine onward movement" that drives "us men and women" of the West. In contrast, "negation, apathy, or amnesia – the real name of which is resignation or desertion" and "all-pervasive neutrality" comprised the spirit of the East for which this Western woman was "too strong." "No, dear friend," Leger continued, "the amnesiac stare that China turns on us really has nothing invigorating." Looking out to a parched landscape, Leger mused to her that "China, like its women, has hips too narrow ever to conceive anything ample in life."[41] There, around the moment famine raged across the North China plain, Alexis Leger penned a poem for a 1924 edition of *La Nouvelle Revue Française* under the *nom de plume* St.-John Perse, a work that would lead to a Nobel Prize for Literature in 1960.

There is little need here to quote at length from *Anabasis*. What matters is the "total effect" the work produces, as T. S. Eliot wrote in the preface to his 1930 translation, of "one intense impression of barbaric civilization."[42] The validity of what transpired from these self-described moments of "hallucination" was unquestioned by its enthusiastic American translator: Leger was an "authority on the Far East," Eliot explained, simply because "he has lived there, as well as in the tropics." Militant praise came from other critics: *Eloges*, an earlier poem by the Frenchman, had "already" captured "the seas and islands of the tropics," the preface to the 1926 Russian edition proclaimed. "Now, with *Anabasis*, he achieves the conquest of Asia, the vast roof of the world." To the critics, this "conquest" was Leger's encapsulation of the Asian mind: the

---

[39] Ibid., 312, 357.   [40] Ibid., 296, 366, 372.   [41] Ibid., 372–73.
[42] St.-John Perse (Alexis Leger), *Anabasis*, trans. T. S. Eliot (New York: Harcourt, Brace & Company, 1949), 10; translation first published in 1930.

poem "could be understood better by an Asian than by a Westerner," in the words of the poet's official Nobel biography.[43] For this, Leger "marshals for his conquest" not the sword but the "tongue" of Ronsard, La Fontaine and Racine in a work brimming with "beauty and strength," the 1929 German edition read, capturing the "spirit of our day, that alert and heroic spirit" bearing France a "new colonial empire before its southern gates" – these "gates" presumably Marseille and other ports shuttling ships to the African possessions and beyond.[44]

Anabasis, written with China in mind, sits comfortably then with the colonial works of its day. Early in 1921, Leger returned to the theme of desolation in a letter to *Heart of Darkness* author Joseph Conrad. Here, Leger appears to be consciously conceiving of a desert counterpart to Conrad's seafaring literary canvas, most famously his 1901 tale of an Englishman's trek up the Congo to find a colleague driven to madness by the "Dark Continent." "The whole of China is nothing but dust, an ocean of wind-blown dust," Leger wrote, a "poor imitation" of the "sea itself." The "boundless earth" of Zhili and inner Mongolia was to Leger a "most perfect imaginable simulacrum of the seas – a mirror image, like the very ghost of the sea [...] the sea turned inside out." China had nothing of "interest" for Conrad, Leger advised, other than perhaps a "few fine specimens of the European adventurer; and beautiful adventuresses as well, transplanted from America or White Russia." The rest was a "vast human community, perfectly anonymous and uniform, and infinitely gregarious – an undifferentiated mass forever impervious to individualism's happiest mutations."[45]

Leger could just as well have been reading out of a fellow countryman's book on "Far-Eastern" peoples reissued a year before his *Anabasis*.

The Chinese hive is, in its own way, as perfect as a hive of bees [Émile Hovelaque explained]. But in our societies made of mixed races and influences, the European, richer in individual variation, betrays less visibly this common character of fixedness and fatalism that shines forth from this China, one in civilization and in blood, and which makes the Chinese a being in all resemblance to an insect or a plant determined by its invariable species.[46]

But it is the focus of the preface to the poem's 1931 Italian edition that strikes closest to the matter of indigenous initiative during crisis and the valuation of human life. The "genius of the poet" seized for his "fantasy"

[43] Ibid., 12, 104; Horst Frenz, ed., *Literature, 1901–1967: Nobel Lectures, Including Presentations, Speeches and Laureates' Biographies* (Amsterdam: Nobel Foundation/ Elsevier, 1969), 560.
[44] Perse, *Anabasis*, 104–7.   [45] Perse, *Letters*, 366–68.
[46] Émile Hovelaque, *Les Peuples d'Extrême-Orient. La Chine* (Paris: Ernest Flammarion, 1923), 264–65.

two required elements of the epic story, the critic explained: vast space and, quoting from the poem itself, men *"of little weight in the memory of these lands."* Man, in the China of Alexis Leger-cum-St.-John Perse, was "at the mercy of the elements rather than of his own works." It was a land where "history matters, not people." In short, again quoting the poem, *"The Stranger has laid his finger on the mouth of the Dead."*[47]

Strangers were also in China to feed the living, according to Leger's correspondence, only to be frustrated by native intransigence. "Nothing [is] more atavistic than the fatalism of these people," he wrote his mother in April 1918 amid an outbreak of pulmonary plague when foreign loans to Beijing for the crisis were "guaranteed," he continued, without specifying the conditions imposed on the Chinese side. "Human life counts so little to them"; they set nature "free" to "solve the demographic problem." Leger had apparently gleaned this idea from a meeting between the dean of the collective body of treaty-port powers, then the British minister, and an unnamed Chinese statesman in which an "offer of financial assistance" by the "Great Powers" for flood-famine relief was rebuffed by a Chinese content to respect the "higher laws of natural harmony" and the "demographic equilibrium." "The poor British Minister," Leger recounted, "couldn't get over [the statesman's] placidity."[48] (Leger might have been surprised to hear one of his American counterparts, the US vice consul in Hankou, advise his superiors in Washington in April of 1921 that the "free gift of food by the foreigner" for North China's afflicted was like "trying to dam a river with human hands. It is malicious interference with natural laws"; or to hear a fellow Frenchman touring the famine zone in 1920 wonder if "restoring a happy medium" in China's population was not preferable to any future crowding the "nervous sensibility of the Occident" might generate by relief.)[49]

What is striking is the extent to which Leger's experience paralleled those of his diplomatic peers. In the spring of 1921, the newly arrived American envoy Joseph W. Stilwell "had been in Peking only six months," Barbara Tuchman relates in *Sand Against the Wind: Stilwell and the American Experience in China*, "when he found an opportunity to break away from Legation life and become acquainted with China on a working level." For four months, the young Stilwell supervised the road construction in Shanxi province by an international relief committee, "working daily with Chinese officials … playing the game of 'face,' learning Chinese habits and characteristics and interrelations" while "the wind whirled clouds of yellow dust over deserted homes." Later,

[47] Perse, *Anabasis*, 108–9; emphasis in the original.   [48] Perse, *Letters*, 328.
[49] J. Huston to Secretary of State, April 18, 1921; Bonnard, *En Chine, 1920–1921*, 127.

"in the time between picnics and tennis with other foreign families," the future Allied commander in China during World War Two "pursued his habit of writing short stories and sketches of foreign life as he had seen it," earning $100 from *Asia* magazine for an article on his 1921 relief experience. "The Chinese government did not make a habit of relief projects," Tuchman concludes from her subject's experience. "Emergency distribution of food stores, if undertaken at all, was never done in time to prevent mass starvation. Accustomed to the Western impulse to 'do something,' China let the foreign activists do what they could but the Oriental attitude did not insist on man conquering his circumstances."[50]

"On a Chinese Screen"

After two tours of the country in 1920–21, W. Somerset Maugham published a series of character vignettes of Chinese and resident foreigners in China. In 1922, *On a Chinese Screen* joined Sidney D. Gamble's *Peking: A Social Survey*, which had appeared just the year before, on the list of the New York publishing house George H. Doran Company. These two very different works reveal notable convergences between sociological inquiry at the time and literature, in this case a tourist's impressions of life in Beijing and elsewhere.

Both works suggest the degree to which social knowledge and observation are limited to one's social contacts and available resources. Gamble's ambitious work was groundbreaking in its data-driven analysis of the Chinese capital. Based on fieldwork conducted from 1918 to 1919, it covers the conditions of daily life and the institutions governing it, from household income levels and the gender and ethnic breakdowns of neighborhoods to the penal system and the city's legions of rickshaw pullers. The book's chapter "Poverty and Philanthropy" is extensive and remarkable in its detail and data on destitution and forms of official relief, largely through the police, with the exception of a short, three-sentence section entitled "Shan T'ang" or "private charitable associations." Here it falls silent. These groups, sometimes translated as benevolent halls, were an integral part of efforts to stabilize the food supply and house, clothe and feed the hundreds of thousands of city poor and incoming refugees over the famine year 1920–21, extending their activities into the famine districts in the environs of the city.[51] But Gamble's team, working just the year before, found it "impossible to secure any detailed report of the

---

[50] Barbara W. Tuchman, *Sand Against the Wind: Stilwell and the American Experience in China: 1911–45* (London: Macmillan, 1971), 88–94.
[51] On this see Fuller, *Famine Relief in Warlord China*.

work of these associations, but from appearances they were not very active and the work of one or two of them seemed to have been taken over by the police."[52] His survey goes on to cover at length the creation of a Community Service Group in one of the city's districts. This pilot group consisted of Chinese and resident foreigners, many of whom stemmed from local branches of the Young Men's and Young Women's Christian Associations, under whose auspices Gamble's survey had been conducted. One of the group's first endeavors was in poor relief, and Gamble provides a description of the group's efforts to canvass the local poor using rosters of the needy provided by authorities, and providing those found on "the verge of starvation" with support and "padded winter clothes." The fact that such an approach to alleviate local suffering was already the practice of the charitable and community-minded in the area appears to have been lost on his team of surveyors.[53]

Maugham's *On a Chinese Screen* is a markedly different read, rendering its observations in the form of character sketches in a motley collection of vignettes. In its fifth sketch, "The Chinese Minister," Maugham writes of his subject's "thin, elegant hands," of his "gold-rimmed spectacles," of the fact that "he had the look of a dreamer. His smile was very sweet," of his "exquisite courtesy," of the way he held a vase "with a charming tenderness, his melancholy eyes caress(ing) it as they looked" with lips "slightly parted as though with a sigh of desire." "But," the narrator continues,

to me the most charming part of it was that I knew all the time that he was a rascal. Corrupt, inefficient and unscrupulous, he let nothing stand in his way. He was a master of the squeeze. He had acquired a large fortune by the most abominable methods. He was dishonest, cruel, vindictive and venal. He had certainly had a share in reducing China to the desperate plight which he so sincerely lamented.[54]

Maugham's travelogue follows with two missionaries, an Englishman and a Frenchman, who "had certainly one admirable thing in common, goodness," along with another thing, "humility" – the Englishman being a "man whose purse was always open to the indigent and whose time was always at the service of those who wanted it" (namely, "The Servants of God"). Maugham continues with a woman whose "charity was above all things competent and you were certain that she ran the obvious goodness of her heart on thoroughly business lines" ("The Missionary Lady"); a "conscientious" British man "untiring in his efforts

[52] Gamble, *Peking: A Social Survey*, 283.   [53] Ibid., 395.
[54] W. Somerset Maugham, *On a Chinese Screen* (New York: George H. Doran Co., 1922), 23–26.

to suppress the opium traffic" ("The Consul"); and the Spanish nun who was "a very picture of charity" in her crowded orphanage. "I marveled when I saw the love that filled her kind eyes and the affectionate sweetness of her smile."[55]

This is not to say that Maugham was particularly enamored of his "own people" resident in the East. He expressed scepticism, for instance, of the formulaic nature of missionary commentary on the native population. "Mrs. Wingrove said the same things about them [the Chinese] that I had already heard so many missionaries say," he noted after an evening in a mission home on a "little hill just outside the gates of a populous city." "They were a lying people, untrustworthy, cruel, and dirty, but a faint light was visible in the East."[56]

Nonetheless, the cast of characters presented by his *On a Chinese Screen* continues with a man who "was upright, honest, and virtuous" despite having "neither passion in him nor enthusiasm [. . .] there is no doubt that he would have done everything in his power to serve you" ("The Seventh Day Adventist"); or the American who, after presiding with a Chinese judge over an execution, regretfully reflected "how terrible it was to make an end of life deliberately" ("The Vice-Consul"); or the Englishman who "when the hat was passed around for some charitable object he could always be counted on to give as much as anyone else" (the chief executive at Jardine, Matheson & Co., once a major opium dealer in China). Their idiosyncrasies and philistine tastes aside, China's caring and conscientious were Western bred, no matter if Maugham could find little else in them to admire. Responding to criticism of the misanthropic tendencies of his art, he once protested that "I do not think I have done this. All I have done is to bring into prominence certain traits that many writers shut their eyes to."[57] What is especially telling is that, when the Chinese social landscape was the subject, the takeaway from Maugham's ethical summations matched those of Sunday school dramas back home.

This raises the question of the basis on which both of these men composed their works. Gamble's approach was scientific, using questionnaires and other methods to gather data from across an ethnically diverse city of more than one million residents. But on closer inspection, the limits of his social reach are apparent. He acknowledges "the students of the Peking (Union) University who helped in the study of the philanthropic institutions of the city," a university with a total of eighty-five male students, and one Gamble categorizes as a Protestant mission school. He

---

[55] Ibid., 35–39, 47–54, 145–46, 159, 169, 212, 229.   [56] Ibid., 37–41.
[57] Quoted in Michael Wood, introduction to *On a Chinese Screen*, by W. Somerset Maugham (New York: Arno Press, 1977).

also thanks the city chief of police, General Wu Bingxiang, for sharing police reports, which goes some way to accounting for the almost singular attention Gamble's work gives to official, as opposed to charitable, poor relief.[58] And then there is the issue of language and how accessible Beijing's vibrant Chinese news industry was to Gamble. "A personal study of the Chinese documents was impossible because of the language barrier," he writes, explaining that, instead, his work relied on books and newspapers in English and French such as the Supplement of the Peking *Leader* for background on Beijing life, guilds and other institutions.[59]

For his part, Maugham was, foremost, a storyteller and a prolific playwright, with several plays running simultaneously in early 1920s London – one of them set in Beijing. Still, one might ask how anyone can capture the moral fiber of strangers over a cup of tea or a round of billiards, as Maugham took liberty to do. "You cannot tell what are the lives of these thousands who surge about you," Maugham wrote in a moment of particular candor a few pages from the end of *On a Chinese Screen*. He continued,

Upon your own people sympathy and knowledge give you a hold; you can enter into their lives, at least imaginatively, and in a way really possess them [...]. But these are as strange to you as you are strange to them [...] you might as well look at a brick wall. You have nothing to go upon, you do not know the first thing about them, and your imagination is baffled.[60]

In Maugham's case, one might ask how a visitor alighting onto the station platform or docks of a Chinese city might acquire intimate understandings of Chinese ministers, or of the "baffling" market crowds. On this one can only speculate, of course, but the newsstands of Beijing's Legation Quarter or treaty port settlements offered a good deal of reading material on current affairs and translations of Chinese literature and political commentary. This included *Letters from a Chinese Magistrate* and *Reminiscences of a Chinese Official: Revelations of Official Life Under the Manchus*, both of which were part of a well-established genre satirizing Chinese officialdom that had been freely printed in the relative safety of the foreign concessions since the late Qing period. And both appeared in the English-language press around the time of Leger and Maugham's stay.

This genre of writing was, by design, ambiguous in authorship. The sale of these translations then fed Western understandings of Chinese governance and ethical life, further enhancing the cross-fertilization of ideas that marked this period. One gets the thrust of *Letters from a Chinese*

---

[58] Gamble, *Peking: A Social Survey*, xvii, 136.   [59] Ibid., xv.
[60] Maugham, *On a Chinese Screen* (1922), 234.

Magistrate from its opening line: "During the now defunct Ching regime," it begins, "I hated more than anything the corrupt and money-loving officials who never had any regard for the welfare of the country and the people."[61] As for *Reminiscences*, it had been compiled between 1901 and 1905 by Li Boyuan while cloistered in Shanghai editing tabloids heavy with coverage of the city's notorious entertainment scene. Li had no experience with the country's river works or any other official administrative concern. "The tales collected [by Li] were current gossip about official circles strung together into a novel, but without much variety," the writer and critic Lu Xun later commented, and "it was only the general interest in the subject" of state corruption and collapse "at the time that made this novel famous overnight."[62]

The historian Owen Lattimore worked briefly as a copy editor and proofreader at the *Peking & Tientsin Times*, which published both *Letters* and *Reminiscences* over the years 1920–22, before he headed into Inner Asia to conduct his well-known fieldwork. "[*Reminiscences*] was an amalgamation of translations from several Chinese novels of a well-known type, picaresque and scurrilous," Lattimore wrote later in his unpublished memoirs.

With youthful irresponsibility I made a ghost-rewrite hash of it, missing the point of what every Chinese knew, that it was a political lampoon, of a genre important in the eighteenth and nineteenth centuries, in which Chinese authors subversively attacked their Manchu rulers, blaming them for the corruption of Chinese officialdom (and having a good time doing it). Old Woodhead, my editor, was delighted, however. As a diehard opponent of any revision of the Unequal Treaties, he relished any "proof" that the Chinese were "racially" incapable of honest administration, justice in the law-courts, and all the rest of it.[63]

"How to Get Rich through Relief Work" and other chapters from the Shanghai novel were thereby passed off as news in the North China mouthpiece of H. G. W. Woodhead, "a last-ditch defender of the crumbling walls of foreign privilege," in the words of Lattimore.[64] As the *Times* explained to its readers, many of whom were members of the country's diplomatic community, "it is the belief of the Editor that the *Reminiscences* will be found to contain a graphic, interesting, and not overdrawn account

[61] Anonymous, *Letters from a Chinese Magistrate* (Tianjin: Tientsin Press, March 1920), 3; reprinted from the *Peking & Tientsin Times*.
[62] Lu Xun, *A Brief History of Chinese Fiction* (Beijing: Foreign Languages Press, 1959), 375–79.
[63] Owen Lattimore, "Happiness Is among Strangers," 90, manuscript dated 1970, MSS80712, box 59, folder 19, Owen Lattimore Papers, 1907–1997, Library of Congress Manuscript Division.
[64] Ibid., 83.

of the tortuous methods of Chinese officialdom in the latter portion of the nineteenth century" and that "there has been no marked improvement in the competence or integrity of local officials under the Republic."[65]

The appearance of *Letters from a Chinese Magistrate* in 1920, and *Reminiscences of a Chinese Official* in 1922 might help explain how an American traveling the following year in North China could so confidently inform his readers that "for centuries the 'squeeze' connected with the building of the dikes, or even their maintenance, has been one of the richest perquisites of certain official positions." The visitor's solution was no less surprising. "Perhaps this is why the latest task of wrestling the Yellow River," he continued, "has been given to an American firm established in China."[66]

Setting internal differences aside – Catholic versus Protestant, reportage versus art – the Western writing consumed or composed over the disastrous year formed part of what historian James Hevia has called a "sociology of the Chinese,"[67] a genre presuming to identify defects possessed by a national collective before prescribing a corresponding corrective action: callousness or a semicomatose body politic called for mission work, graft or avarice called for foreign control over Chinese finances, and so on. China was "wise enough – unlike all other countries – to entrust certain branches of her administration to foreigners until she is capable of taking over control," Emily Georgina Kemp, a longtime British resident, explained in her 1921 study, *Chinese Mettle*. In the meantime, China's "vital need" was for "honest, incorruptible, educated Chinese" to step up and "save their country," which was "steadily *moving forward*," with the "mettle of the race" – its "temperamental characteristics," undergoing "as great a change as the social fabric."[68]

The notion of national character flowered with the rise of nationalism in Europe and the expansion of Western colonialism over the course of the nineteenth century. As with any idea, its proponents cited observable truths: corruption was no fiction at all in Chinese government during the republic, nor had it been under the Qing. But any idea of national character involves a process of seeing, and not seeing, and the distillation of selective observation into essential, ahistorical qualities. By the time of the May Fourth movement, the national characterization reflected in

---

[65] Anonymous, *Reminiscences of a Chinese Official: Revelations of Official Life under the Manchus* (Tianjin: Tientsin Press, 1922); reprinted from the *Peking Gazette* and the *China Illustrated Review*.
[66] Harry A. Franck, *Wandering in Northern China* (New York: The Century Company, 1923), 305.
[67] Hevia, *English Lessons*, 60, 178, 273.
[68] Emily Georgina Kemp, *Chinese Mettle* (London: Hodder and Stoughton, 1921), 12; emphasis in the original.

Western writing had been internalized by Chinese intellectuals, becoming a practice of potent ideological and political utility, one that transcended national divides.

"The Problem of China"

It would be difficult to overstate the attention given by the Chinese press to Bertrand Russell's extended visit to China in 1920–21. Local reception of the British mathematician and philosopher's lecture tour, organized and financially supported by Liang Qichao,[69] ranged from news photographs (rare in mainland papers at the time), full-page portraits in New Culture magazines and news updates on his troubled health (stricken, as he was during his stay, with pneumonia) to nearly daily translations of his lectures in Beijing's *Chenbao*. Fearing the rationalism torchbearer's words might be taken for gospel, the Beijing Christian Association even saw to shadowing his tour with a series of critical essays in its journal *Shengming* (Life).[70]

Upon conclusion of his stay, Russell lent his voice to the wider genre of national characterization. "The callousness of the Chinese is bound to strike every Anglo-Saxon," he expounded in an end-of-tour piece "Some Traits in the Chinese Character" printed in the December 1921 issue of Boston's *Atlantic Monthly*. "They have none of that humanitarian impulse which leads us to devote one per cent of our energy to mitigating the evils wrought by the other ninety per cent," while the Chinese would "not have had the energy to starve the Viennese" – using an example from the recent Great War – "or the philanthropy to keep some of them alive." Russell was hardly a harsh critic of China, determining elsewhere that "the Chinese" were "in many respects more civilized than ourselves and at a higher ethical level" before the arrival of Europeans.[71] He nonetheless concluded that "much was done by white men to relieve the [1920–21] famine, but very little by the Chinese, and that little vitiated by corruption."[72]

More than run-of-the-mill "China" material for foreign consumption, though, to the readers of the country's most established news magazine of

---

[69] Vera Schwarcz, *Time for Telling Truth is Running Out: Conversations with Zhang Shenfu* (New Haven, CT: Yale University Press, 1992), 127.

[70] Lectures appeared in *Chenbao* throughout the autumn of 1920 and a feature ran in *Xin Long* on June 20, 1920. *Shengming*'s critical essays appeared on February 15 and March 15, 1921.

[71] Bertrand Russell, preface to "The YMCA Government of China," by Rachel Brooks, 1934?, typescript 394, box 185, Manuscript Collection, New York Public Library.

[72] Bertrand Russell, "Some Traits in the Chinese Character," *Atlantic Monthly*, December 1921, 776.

the time, Shanghai's *Dongfang zazhi* (or *Eastern Miscellany*), the Briton's words offered a way for reformist-minded Chinese to view themselves, or at least to perceive their fellow nationals. Editors at *Dongfang zazhi* wasted little time – less than a month – in printing "Zhongguo minguo xing de jige tedian" (Some Traits in the Chinese Character) for the *Dongfang zazhi*'s first issue of 1922, effectively reducing what would be a fifteen-chapter post-visit reflection (Russell's essay became a chapter in his *The Problem of China* monograph of 1922) down to a brief analysis in which "avarice, cowardice, and callousness" are laid out as the "chief defects" of the Chinese. Significantly, in its translation, Russell's use of the collective "us," presumably referring to his reference to "Anglo-Saxons," is rendered as "*women Ouzhouren*," that is, "*We Europeans* use one percent of our energies" – an exponential expansion of the original racial generalization.[73] This, its *Dongfang zazhi* translator advised his readers/countrymen, was a lesson (*jiaoxun*) from the Briton to which "it seems all Chinese should give a careful reading."[74]

This idea of a new humanitarianism open to adoption by the Chinese helped shape the ideological climate for China's looming modernization drives. It joined other dimensions to modernization programs such as a "hygienic modernity" that, as Ruth Rogaski has shown, sprang from competing Western and Japanese health administrations in the treaty ports to envelop, and provide definition to, China's new cosmopolitan elite vis-à-vis their poorer, "backward" countrymen.[75] The *Dongfang zazhi* served as a leading platform for this fast-developing transcultural conversation concerned with the cultivation of the Chinese *Volksgeist*. Here, this broader conversation intersected with more targeted coverage of the disasters striking Chinese communities at the time. For this, editors at *Dongfang zazhi* turned to the talented student and political activist Yang Zhongjian, whose efforts to mobilize student surveyors of the famine field we touched on in the previous chapter.

In the summer of 1920, Yang had spent over two months on the road between his hometown in Shaanxi's Hua county and Beijing, where he was enrolled as a geology student at Beijing University. Scorched fields lined his path, with the roads filled with those in flight, the young, the old and females in general begging along the way. Yang took detours to avoid reported bandit gangs on the route ahead, bands that swelled with idle and increasingly desperate able-bodied men. For the readers of *Dongfang*

---

[73] Bertrand Russell (Luo Su), "Zhongguo minguo xing de jige tedian," *Dongfang zazhi*, January 10, 1922, 30; emphasis added.
[74] Ibid., 29, 33.
[75] Ruth Rogaski, *Hygienic Modernity: Meanings of Health and Disease in Treaty-Port China* (Berkeley: University of California Press, 2004), 229.

zazhi, Yang made a compelling case for the root causes of the food crisis and rising violence afflicting the faltering Chinese republic in 1920. He first revisited the statistical and methodological challenges he raised in his *Chenbao* piece published the week before (and discussed in Chapter 2), especially the lack of any concrete numbers on China's population and therefore the difficulty in estimating the numbers of famine victims, without which effective relief is impossible. He then argued that increasing local tax levies are the primary factor behind the intensity of the drought disaster (*hanhuang*), followed by pressures on the grain supply by increasing nonfood cash-crop production in the affected provinces, along with a recent downward trend in successful harvests generally.

The picture Yang offered of rural governance and social relations across four provinces, however, is of a different order. He was most pointed in his critique of local disaster responses in his native Shaanxi and neighboring Henan. After describing the devastation brought by drought to his home district, the only community response he noted in the province is what he called the ridiculous (*kexiao*) policy of the governor and Hua county magistrate to join rural residents (*xiangren*) in their daily prayers for rain. In Henan, he observed people merely sighing at the skies (*dui tian jietan*) and a local magistrate spending public (or literally the people's) funds (*mincai*) on the staging of an opera to thank the heavens for a recent spell of rain. By contrast, in sections of neighboring Shanxi he acknowledged how irrigation had mitigated the effects of drought; there the question was whether or not grain stabilization and other relief measures (*pingtiao zhenji deng*) drawn up by the authorities were to prove merely empty words (*kong wen*), as he put it, and have no effect. As for the establishment of famine relief measures in the hardest-hit sections of south Zhili through which he passed on his return to Beijing, Yang mentioned nothing.[76]

Bleak across the board, the magazine's only field report from what was the country's greatest humanitarian crisis in half a century found nothing resembling disaster responses among the country's rural majority. One of republican China's most prominent current event platforms made strikingly similar determinations to missionary and other non-Chinese accounts of the famine field that same year, conditioning its readership for the gloomy "lesson" on Chinese "callousness" presented by one Bertrand Russell.

---

[76] Yang Zhongjian, "Bei si sheng zaiqu shichaji," *Dongfang zazhi*, October 10, 1920, 24–28.

Conclusion

Street-side observations diagnosed social ills with the broadest of brush-strokes, reaching to the environs of the Haiyuan earthquake zone. Observing a lone girl begging in the streets "was one of those occasions when the missionary burns with indignation," A. Mildred Cable and Francesca French wrote from 1920s Gansu, "at the unrighteous legislation of a country which admits of no appeal for the redress of the wrongs to the helpless."[77] Alexander Hosie, former UK consul-general at Tianjin, came to a similar conclusion about racial flaws when he heard women wailing at the door of his inn in Lanzhou and imagined a great commotion unfolding, only to be told that it was over a death in a family. "So flippantly was the information vouchsafed, that I again turned in with thoughts of the callousness of the Chinese race."[78]

For members of societies reeling from the horrors of the Great War, Western writers were surprisingly quick to find other cultures lacking in their valuation of human life. The strength of these ideas, despite their contradictions, stemmed in part from their utility to the pedagogical programs of the colonial, evangelical and revolutionary regimes of the early twentieth century. May Fourth-era handling of rural society during times of disaster was thus part of a much broader nation-building project, one involving goals of state-strengthening and revolutionary change yet pursued by a broad spectrum of intellectual contributors.

Every change of political regime brings with it new ways with which to view the recent and distant past. The nation-building project in China has shaped historical understandings in several ways. This includes the curation of the historical record; in other words, what out of the massive corpus of imperial and republican archival and media documentation was retained, and what was lost – sold casually for its paper-pulp value or other purposes – or simply destroyed. What remains, when compiled and interpreted by the wide spectrum of those active in historical writing, from scholars and journalists to party publicists, can acquire powerful, sometimes hegemonic, grips on overall perceptions of the past.

Henrietta Harrison has shown how scholarship over the course of the twentieth century shaped surviving records and interpretations of key events in Sino-British relations, while fostering the broadest of generalizations about value differences between East and West. A decade before the earthquake and famine of 1920–21, a pair of British writers published a history of the Qing based on documents of the Qing Court, selected and

---

[77] Cable and French, *Dispatches from North-West Kansu*, 32.
[78] Alexander Hosie, *On the Trail of the Opium Poppy: A Narrative of Travel in the Chief Opium-Producing Provinces in China* (London: G. Philip & Son, 1914), 137.

translated in ways that served to justify the use of British force in the Opium Wars. The historians in effect reduced a range of strategic and political concerns of the Qing state over the British presence down to an obsession with the kowtow and other forms of ritual observance. Their history of the Qing, translated within the year into Chinese, informed a generation of republican scholars, who, in turn, curated their own archival compendia for publication in the 1920s, also winnowing down hundreds of Qing files on the British threat into a handful of documents suiting revisionist narratives of the imperial past.[79] Working in a period of liberal scholarship in China, prior to the dominance of the Guomindang or Communist Party state, these historians were moved by a surge in Han Chinese nationalism and a desire to reimagine the Manchu Qing as "ignorant and passive in the face of the rising power of the West" – in Harrison's words – while "using cultural differences to explain disparities of power."[80]

Whether through the lens of May Fourth-era social surveys of recent events or through Western writing on the Chinese, explanations for Western power over the Chinese was reduced to questions of culture and day-to-day values. If a change of culture was the overriding answer to national weakness in the face of imperialist pressures, then, in the eyes of many May Fourth-era writers, mass dissemination and popularization of a transformative social vision was essential. The production of cultural memory and understandings of the recent past in support of such a vision is a subject we turn to next.

---

[79] Edmund Trelawney Backhouse and John Otway Percy Bland, *Annals and Memoirs of the Court of Peking (from the 16th to the 20th Century)* (London: W. Heinemann, 1914). Cited in Henrietta Harrison, "The Qianlong Emperor's Letter to George III and the Early-Twentieth Century Origins of Ideas about Traditional China's Foreign Relations," *American Historical Review* 122/3 (2017), 680, 691–92.

[80] Ibid., 696.

Part II

Revolutionary Memory in Republican China

4   Civics Lessons

Reports from the disaster zones of early twentieth-century China presented an incongruous set of representations, as discordant as the politics of the time. Anyone reading in *Qunbao* of abject suffering and lack of assistance to the starving in mountainous Jingxing county, as we saw in Chapter 2, could have easily spotted mentions of cash and clothes distribution to the poor of rural Zhili by a Chinese charity in the same issue – inches away on the same page, in fact.[1] New Culture or May Fourth movement voices appeared with those of relief society staffers, professional journalists, magistrates or other residents of the disaster zone and stringers for China's news wires. The volume of reporting on communities in crisis added up to a diverse and heterogeneous field of social coverage, a sort of cognitive dissonance that formed part of what Tong Lam aptly calls a "Babel of Facts" produced by the republic's myriad journalistic and social survey endeavors.[2] The fact that May Fourth writing on China's ills shared anything with prominent Western writers did not, then, mean their opinions or methods had a firm grip on wider public opinion; that would come with time, and with the pedagogical power of the party state. Despite being overwhelmingly city based, there was still a great range of perspectives in the Chinese press with connection to a range of social networks reaching deep into the countryside.

Within this cacophony, however, the fundamentals of a revolutionary platform were taking root as reformist views on rural life found ready vehicles in the most prominent cultural platforms of the day. What is significant about the documentary moment of 1920 is not, then, the overall volume of attention paid to rural, indigenous acts of poor relief

[1] "Zhengjihui sanfang Dongling jizhen," *Qunbao*, February 21, 1921, 6. In a similar way, the same student report from Jingxing county that appeared in *Qunbao* appeared again a few weeks later in the journal of the North China Relief Society, *Jiuzai zhoukan* (*Famine Relief Weekly*), beside dozens of pages of detailed coverage of native aid activity across the famine zone. "Zaiqing baogao: hanzai: Jingxing lü Jing xuesheng nianjiazhong diaocha ben xian min zhuangkuang," *Jiuzai zhoukan*, March 6, 1921, 20–21.
[2] Tong Lam, *A Passion for Facts*, 16.

on the one hand and outsider, urban or foreign acts on the other hand. Instead, what is significant is the subtle act of erasure shared by a range of writers at the time. And this is shown by the lengths to which writers and editors in reformist publications distinguished between acts of disaster alleviation, validating some, discrediting others, while overlooking still others entirely. In their treatments of rural life in times of crisis, certain actors and practices were given center stage while others disappeared from view.

A 1921 essay in *Shengming*, the magazine of the Beijing Christian Educational Press, most explicitly captures this practice. Buddhist-led parades of child refugees were especially commonplace during the famine and earthquake winter of 1920–21, visible on the streets of Beijing and in its press. As temperatures warmed in late February 1921, 160 children were led by a handful of monks out of the Shanguo temple on a fundraising march to the city's Central Park before being hosted at the city's Dafo temple for lunch.[3] Six hundred young charges of the Buddhist Relief Society were seen walking around the eastern section of the city on foot a few days later,[4] followed by another two hundred children sheltered inside the North City's Fucheng gate, touring the western suburbs in a bid to "liven up the kids' spirits."[5]

During the same winter month as this very public Buddhist activity occurred – and, as it happens, the same issue in which the magazine covered Bertrand Russell's lecture tour of the country – *Shengming* set out to contrast, point by point, shelters managed by the Christian community with what it called "Chinese methods." Eight of ten residents of Christian facilities were trained in weaving, rug making and other crafts, *Shengming* estimated, while the majority of boys they took in were schooled in some way. By contrast, the magazine asserted that their Chinese counterparts assigned no work "in the least" and provided "absolutely no education." Meanwhile, it explained, children and adults were afforded "peace and comfort" and "sanitary conditions" in Christian shelters while in Chinese ones filth and "extreme misery" prevailed.[6] To substantiate its claims, *Shengming* used the example of an inspection of the Buddhist Relief Society's shelter in famine-struck Zhengding county, Zhili, which the group had opened the previous fall.[7]

---

[3] *Qunbao*, February 21, 1921.   [4] *Chenbao*, February 26, 1921.
[5] *Fengsheng*, February 28, 1921. The same story ran in *Xiao minbao*, February 28, 1921. Another example appears in *Guobao*, March 11, 1921.
[6] Lin Hongfei, "Hanzai zhong de jidujiao Fojiao he guanliao zhengke," *Shengming*, February 15, 1921.
[7] *Shihua*, October 21, 1920.

On one level, the magazine's exposé merely reflected the intense competition among faith groups in a period of great religious diversity and activity. And its claims ran up against reports in other news sources. Earlier in September, *Zhongguo minbao* had reported the planning of a range of classes at the Buddhist group's facilities in the famine field, from assorted handicrafts to basic medical skills and midwifery.[8] Repeated monk-led walks around the city by the refugee children staying in temple shelters, as spring approached, were hardly suggestive of indifference to the well-being of their charges. And if spartan conditions prevailed at these shelters, it was hardly surprising as some accommodated as many as five thousand people at a time.

On another more profound level, the exposé signaled the existence of a wider set of pedagogical practices, extending much further than the city's Christian community. What was evidently playing out in both missionary and mainstream Chinese media over the course of the 1920–21 disaster year were efforts to identify qualitative differences between cultures of poor relief. In this exercise, only certain relief activities qualified as worthy of mention in disaster reporting, while others were dismissed or were simply dropped from view. The basis for the Christian magazine's treatment of Buddhist relief operations was, revealingly, an article published previously in *Chenbao* by a twenty-three-year-old graduate of a Beijing state medical school, Chen Wanli – a Jiangsu native as well as a non-Christian, *Shengming* made a point of noting.[9] Through the eyes of Chinese Christians and the country's more secular reformists, the correct methods of poor relief provisioning formed part of the developing idea of modernity: its methods either reflected a progressive departure from the past (a defining characteristic of modernity) – in which case they were held up as models of civic behavior – or were quaint or backward vestiges of an outdated order, regardless of how efficacious they may have been in sustaining lives at the time.

Of course, Chinese Christians and reformist-minded Chinese represented a range of political stances and viewpoints and by no means spoke in unison, even if many educated Chinese at the time, females especially, had been trained in mission schools. But their stances toward rural communal capacities in times of crisis revealed a convergence of ideas on what rural communities were capable of, and not. Even the most radical of May Fourth-era writers were, by and large, not yet fully equipped to apply the Marxist frameworks that would be in fashion among intellectuals later in the 1920s. Casting rural communities in ways that echoed the writings of Marx – static and backward, as petrified

---

[8] *Zhongguo minbao*, September 30, 1920.   [9] Xu Youchun, *Minguo renwu*, 1460.

as jade museum pieces – May Fourth-era activist writers worked largely from a preparty position, serving an earlier stage of the epistemic demolition that would accompany subsequent revolutionary programs.

The effect of May Fourth disaster coverage (examined in Chapter 2) had been to contribute to the deinscription of Buddhist or Confucian culture from its place in local politics, stripping elites of symbolic stature and moral authority in the day-to-day leadership of community affairs. The social welfare measures associated with "tradition" served as a benchmark of dysfunction and disarray against which those of reformist or revolutionary figures could be presented. In this chapter we examine a subsequent process undertaken over the 1920s by Chinese educators: the reinscription of China's political sphere. This involved ascribing new meaning to historical events, to social phenomena and to localities, both rural and urban, placing them squarely within the nation-building project. We examine this first through the early 1920s, a period when liberal perspectives and commercial operations dominated the production of reading materials consumed by China's youth – magazines and schoolbooks. We will pursue particular threads of collective forgetting and reinforcement in the broader development of cultural memory in the wake of the May Fourth movement. This involved the development of social frameworks and terminology with which revolutionary memory would be constructed. Together, these cultural practices provide a window onto how May Fourth social paradigms were passed onto generations of audiences well beyond the country's intensely politicized intelligentsia.

Progressive Pedagogy

The social and cultural questioning of the May Fourth era spread into the school curriculum of the 1920s. This resulted in a movement in literature and education for the young that paralleled and interacted with wider political movements.[10] The Commercial Press was early twentieth-century China's most established publishing house. Founded in Shanghai in the late Qing period and still in the republic a leading purveyor of knowledge for all ages, the Press produced a catalogue of teaching materials that shaped a new generation of Chinese in the wake of May Fourth, starting with youth magazines and textbooks.

One way to picture these changes is to imagine a young reader's intellectual growth at the time, perhaps a child born to a somewhat

---

[10] Chang-tai Hung, *Going to the People: Chinese Intellectuals and Folk Literature, 1918–1937* (Cambridge, MA: Council on East Asian Studies, Harvard University, 1985), 107–34.

prosperous family in, say, Hankou, in 1911 – the moment the Xinhai revolution broke out in the river city. Our reader could have resided in most any large town in China, considering the Commercial Press's distributional prowess, but let us picture "Meiqing" at home along the Yangzi, where on her ninth birthday in 1920 her father might have bought her a year's subscription to *Shaonian zazhi* (Youth Magazine) for one yuan, after he spotted an advertisement in his copy of *Dongfang zazhi* (another Commercial Press publication), promoting *Shaonian zazhi* as a magazine designed to "foster the mind and spirit" of young students.

Shaonian zazhi first touched on the subject of Gansu's plight in its current events section two months after the quake struck, amid pages of science experiments, arts and crafts, and other educational games and activities. The brief story, which appeared with phonetic symbols and exaggerated punctuation between each of its 133 characters to assist readers, relates how the tremors – felt in many parts of the world on the sixteenth of December – were affecting seven provinces, with Shaanxi, Gansu and the district of Ningxia particularly struck. "More than ten consecutive tremors leveled buildings" in the region, "injuring and killing many people," the story explains, giving the example of Tongzhou, in Shaanxi, "where over a stretch of one *li* the town lay in ruins and entire streets of residents lost their lives." It then ends with a note on the extent of loss and "How terrible! How cruel!" it truly was.[11]

Later in 1921, *Shaonian zazhi* followed with a story of roughly equal length entitled the "Earthquake in Guyuan, Gansu." The piece notes the great losses suffered in the Northwest in December, together with a series of aftershocks that struck Guyuan later in July, which "ruined much livestock and farming equipment, destroying hope for a successful harvest." "There are many Protestant foreigners [*haoduo Xinyejiao de waiguoren*] who are surveying afflicted households and relieving them with donations," the story continues, referring, one assumes, to the foreign-run Earthquake Relief Committee. "We must express due gratitude," it adds, before noting that "relief monies are limited and not enough to go around. Though we are all Chinese, still we are not heeding calls to raise relief money for our Gansu compatriots [*tongbao*]!"[12]

On their own, there is little that raises eyebrows in these briefest of sketches, aside perhaps from the exclusive mention of foreign relief initiative in one, and its implicit message of national shame. What is more noteworthy is how Meiqing's magazine handled a similar event across the Eurasian landmass at the same time. Over two days in September of 1920,

[11] "Shishi hua: Da dizhen," *Shaonian zazhi* 11/2 (1921), 1–2.
[12] "Shishi hua: Gansu Guyuan dizhen," *Shaonian zazhi* 11/9 (1921), 1–2.

an earthquake "killed and injured countless people and led to immeasurable loss of property" in Italy's north, *Shaonian zazhi* explained. "Disaster victims there still sleep on the streets, wailing and waiting to be fed," the story continued. "It is said the Italian government has already sent soldiers who are doing their utmost to offer aid and protection. Truly this is the right [*yingdangde*] thing to do!"[13]

Over 1920–21, *Shaonian zazhi* impressed its young readers with the enormity of suffering at the base of the Italian Alps and atop Gansu's loess plateau. Remarkably, though, the very same phenomenon that Gansu's leading May Fourth journal scrubbed from reports on China's Northwest, as we saw in Chapter 2 – first responders in the form of mounted soldiers at Ningxia and Pingliang, and caravans of garrison tents and provisions – was singled out for praise to *Shaonian zazhi*'s readers taking in events in Tuscany and Lombardy. In all of *Shaonian zazhi*'s stories, anyone doing anything at all in events of this kind was foreign.

This holds true for the children magazine's coverage of famine, which ran in the October 1920 issue that covered the Italian earthquake. In the same month that Yang Zhongjian's survey of the famine field ran in her father's issue of *Dongfang zazhi* (a story covered in Chapter 3), *Shaonian zazhi* depicted for Meiqing the range of disasters afflicting the country so far in the year: marauding soldiers were distressing residents already suffering the drought-famine conditions that prevailed across five northern provinces, which had followed a year of rainless skies that had left a parched earth, failed crops and empty grain stocks. "Now tree bark, stubble and roots have been eaten up!" the story reads. "Children and women have all been sold away!" With twenty million stricken residents of a massive disaster field facing the coming months of winter, it was "truly an exceptional calamity to behold." "Now the charitable rush to set up emergency relief," it continued, "even foreigners [*jiushi waiguoren*] are heading to the disaster zone one after another to dispense aid. Youthful gentlemen with minds set on charity, you too find a way, pull together and come to the rescue!"[14]

Meiqing's first exposure to the experience of earthquake in the Northwest would, then, have stressed foreign action. Her next exposure to the event could well have been in the classroom, considering the marginality of Gansu to national affairs, and in this lesson there would be no mention of earthquake responses at all. The textbook *Gansu sheng yi pie* (Gansu Province in a Glance) appeared in 1926 as part of the

[13] "Yiguo da dizhen," *Shaonian zazhi* 10/10 (1920), 3.
[14] "Beifang da hanzai," *Shaonian zazhi* 10/10 (1920), 4–5.

Commercial Press's Young Men's Historical and Geographical Series. In it, the disaster is not central, but appears instead in the form of a noteworthy aside, a terrifying curiosity. The text takes the reader on a westward tour of Gansu, covering cultural sites, social and topographical characteristics, and local products starting with the eastern region of Ningxia. Soon arriving in Longde county, the narrator notes the poor soil and poverty of the people, and the area's lack of enough work or trade, before pausing its virtual tour to say, "There is something that must, by the way, be mentioned, and that is the great Gansu earthquake of the ninth year of the republic."[15]

The text describes the moment the quake struck at eight in the evening of the sixteenth, listing the string of counties within its reach, and how it hit Haiyuan and Guyuan most intensely.

Right at the moment of the tremors there was a roar of thunder and great winds kicked up a fog of dust. Over about twenty minutes of tremors, town walls fell apart, buildings collapsed, and innumerable people and livestock were buried under earth that burst forth over several miles. Giant mounds formed, blocking the river channels and destroying the roads. Investigators determined that in this quake alone more than 200,000 people had died in Gansu, plus over a thousand in Shaanxi. Truly an unprecedented calamity!

In ten provinces, as far away as Hubei, the quake could be felt, the text notes – an area it puts at more than 1.7 million square kilometers. Then, continuing on its way west from the Longde valley, it leaves the great Gansu quake behind. By Meiqing's midteens, the earthquake's proportions had assumed the qualities of a legend. Beyond the marvel of its immensity, all the reader is left with to ponder are the dead.[16]

The Republic in Histories and Fiction

As the 1920–21 famine and earthquake disappeared from headlines and conversations kept pace with events and the steadily turning pages of the calendar, the various humanitarian crises of the early republic receded into notable obscurity for events of their scale. It is unlikely that Meiqing would have encountered much at all on the experience of either the 1920 famine or quake. In its place, schoolbooks offered historical grand narratives and broad social critiques.

History and geography schoolbooks at the time generally did not mention natural disaster, or social life generally. Beyond political matters and

---

[15] Chen Bowen, *Gansu sheng yi pie* (Shanghai: Shangwu yinshuguan, 1926), 9. *Young Men's Historical and Geographical Series* is the formal English name of the series.
[16] Ibid., 9–10.

international relations, histories tended to focus on ideas of racial origin and the republic's various ethnicities, especially as they related to the question of Chinese territory and its boundaries.[17] This held for the catalogue of republican histories at the Commercial Press, which remained the predominant producer and distributor of Chinese school-books through the 1920s, offering an array of textbook series that students were often assigned or read in succession through the course of their studies.[18] An established firm that had been one of the first to appear and quickly lead the textbook market at the beginning of the century, by May Fourth the Press was stocked with liberal, reformist editors from the New Culture movement, such as the Vassar College and University of Chicago-trained editor and textbook writer Chen Hengzhe, who had taught history at Beijing University in 1920 before she worked at the Press from 1922 to 1924, and the Princeton University-trained editor He Bingsong, who worked there from 1924 to 1932.[19] In the Press's publications, treatment of the republican period consisted entirely of political events, or at most covered broader social and cultural movements with immediate political significance, such as May Fourth itself.[20]

A representative example of the preoccupations of republican histories is the 1924 collaboration between two of the period's most preeminent scholars, the historian Gu Jiegang and New Culture thinker and essayist Hu Shi. *Our Country's History: A Modern Primary and Middle School Textbook* covers, in its second volume, diplomacy, war, rebellion and religious groups, and political change during the late Qing. After the 1911 revolution, the text focuses on matters of religion and ethnicity, and events pertaining to the integrity of Chinese territory and national identity itself, such as Mongolian and Tibetan affairs and the North-South split of 1917, which precipitated civil war through the 1920s. Matters of interest through 1920–21 are the Zhili-Anhui war and activity nationwide over the organization of national and regional assemblies.[21]

[17] Robert Culp, *Articulating Citizenship: Civic Education and Student Politics in Southeastern China: 1912–1940*, Harvard East Asian Monographs (Cambridge, MA: Harvard University Asia Center, 2007), 72–84.

[18] Peter Zarrow, *Educating China: Knowledge, Society and Textbooks in a Modernizing World, 1902–1937* (Cambridge: Cambridge University Press, 2017), 17–18.

[19] Robert J. Culp, "'Weak and Small Peoples' in a 'Europeanizing World:' World History Textbooks and Chinese Intellectuals," in Robert Culp and Tze-ki Hon, eds., *The Politics of Historical Production in Late Qing and Republican China* (Leiden: Brill, 2007), 218.

[20] Commercial Press examples from 1927 and 1928, respectively, include: Lü Simian, *Xin xuezhi gaoji zhongxue jiaokeshu: ben guo shi* (Shanghai: Shangwu yinshuguan, 1927); and Chen Gongfu, *Zhongguo zuijin sanshi nian shi* (Shanghai: Shangwu yinshuguan, 1928).

[21] Gu Jiegang and Wang Zhongqi, *Xiandai chuzhong jiaokeshu: ben guo shi* (Shanghai: Shangwu yinshuguan, 1924–25), 132–33. Hu Shi is credited as a critical contributor to the volume.

In the early 1930s, when Meiqing was in her early twenties, Gansu affairs did crop up in unusual detail in *A Colloquial History of the Country*, part of a second textbook series written by historian Lü Simian for the Commercial Press. After a run-through of republican government and finance, and relations with Moscow (regarding Mongolia), with London (regarding Tibet) and with Tokyo (regarding Manchuria), the text explores affairs at the provincial level, including Yan Xishan's reforms to Shanxi's administration. It then turns to Gansu politics, touching upon the political tussle played out over December 1920 between the outgoing military governor, Zhang Guangjian, and those bidding to succeed him, the generals Ma Fuxiang and Lu Hongtao, but without any mention of the quake that leveled the province that same month.[22]

If students took in the experience of rural life from the printed page, it was most likely from literature. In her early to midteens, Meiqing would have had two main literary access points: on the one hand, the short stories, poems, memoirs and novels serialized in newspapers and magazines of all types, and, on the other hand, Mandarin readers at school.

The New Culture movement's embrace of the vernacular of course greatly expanded the reach of those taking up the pen. And similar to May Fourth activists, many Chinese writers of the first half of the twentieth century were in fact the children of gentry in small towns and villages. Lu Xun was merely the most famous of numerous writers who were torn in their work between hometown affinities and newfound urban identities. "Hometown" (Guxiang), for example, written in January 1921 and first published in *Xin qingnian* later that May, recounted a visit Lu Xun made to his native Shaoxing, a town around a hundred miles southwest of Shanghai, to retrieve his mother and complete the sale of their family compound before returning to Beijing. The story relates how "scattered across the distant horizon," the "towns and villages" coming into view upon approach were "drab, desolate, devoid of any semblance of life." A childhood playmate Lu Xun had longed to see again, a farm boy bursting with energy and know-how decades before, was now a "lifeless wooden figure" – losing more from his crops than he was ever taking in – worn down and broken by "too many children, famine, harsh taxes, soldiers, bandits, officials, gentryfolk," and now pitifully deferential to his cosmopolitan friend.[23] Upon leaving, the story concludes,

---

[22] Lü Simian, *Baihua ben guo shi: ce 5: xiandai shi* (Shanghai: Shangwu yinshuguan, 1933), 204.
[23] Lu Xun, "Hometown," in William Lyell, trans., *Diary of a Madman and Other Stories* (Honolulu: University of Hawai'i Press, 1990), 89, 97.

My hometown receded ever farther into the distance and the familiar landscapes of the surrounding countryside gradually disappeared too. Strange to say, there was not a shred of regret in my heart. I only felt that there was a high and invisible wall all around me that isolated me from my fellow human beings.[24]

Later in the year, Lu Xun followed with "Ah Q – The Real Story," his satire of rural life centered on a country bumpkin who – proud, paranoid and self-destructive – stood in, one could say, for China itself at the time. Serialized in *Chenbao* over five weeks in late 1921 and early 1922, the story would become one of the most written about and performed works of modern Chinese fiction.[25]

The two stories, written in the same year, capture the range of Lu Xun's treatment of rural life: at times humane and heartfelt, at others tragicomic. Collectively, fiction writers in the early republic represented the diversity of personalities, practices and experiences of rural communities. As Tao Tao Liu notes, for each story at the time opening with characters bitterly "pulling out even the roots" of native-place sentiment – as in the case of Feng Yuanjun's 1926 story "Pillage" ("Jiehui") – there was another recounting villagers of steadfast character, members of the struggling poor who were generous to a fault toward strangers in calamitous times, such as Feng Wenbing's "Laundry Mother" ("Wanyi mu") from 1923.[26]

Mandarin textbook readers, in contrast to the more varied literature of the 1920s, were curated in ways that provided students with high concentrations of social criticism. Designed to expose a new generation of Chinese to the standardized national vernacular in which they were composed from 1920, Mandarin readers served an additional function, supercharging cultural change by exposing students to commentary and critique by leading figures of the New Culture movement.[27] One prominent example is another Commercial Press collaboration between Gu Jiegang and Hu Shi, a collection of readings for lower middle-school students that included essays by Beijing University president Cai Yuanpei on the "new lifestyle" (*xin shenghuo*), stories on Mencius and Abraham Lincoln's childhoods, the tales of Hans Christian Anderson, translations by Lu Xun of Russian stories and by Yan Fu of Thomas

---

[24] Ibid., 99.
[25] Lu Xun, "Ah Q – The Real Story," in Lyell, trans., *Diary of a Madman and Other Stories*, 101–72.
[26] Tao Tao Liu, "Perceptions of City and Country in Modern Chinese Fiction in the Early Republican Era," in David Faure and Tao Tao Liu, eds., *Town and Country in China: Identity and Perception* (Basingstoke, UK: Palgrave, 2002), 210, 215.
[27] Cyrus H. Peake, *Nationalism and Education in Modern China* (New York: Columbia University Press, 1932), 112.

Henry Huxley's *Evolution and Ethics*, and a lesson by Cai on "science and superstition."[28] This hybrid, miscellaneous nature placed Mandarin readers somewhere between social studies and morality guides.

Significantly, in 1922, the Guomindang joined the Commercial Press and other publishers in shaping adolescent education more broadly. Six years before the party's seizure of central government control, the Guomindang established a Shanghai-based publishing arm, the Minzhi shuju (Popular Wisdom Book Company).[29] The following year, around the time Meiqing would have graduated from primary school, two middle-school teachers in Shanghai's neighboring town of Wusong compiled material for a Mandarin reader for distribution by the Guomindang publishing house. Among essays by Liang Qichao and Hu Shi and by editors at New Culture magazines such as Li Dazhao and Zhou Zuoren (the brother of Lu Xun) at *Xin qingnian* and *Xin chao*, respectively, the volume included reprints of essays on cultural practice and social conditions in the interior. In these, writers grappled with the question of native place, exploring issues that led to extended reflection on the growing chasm between urban and rural life. These reflections regularly drew distinctions between East and West, between superstition and science, or between traditional treatments of ailments and modern medicine. By association with the first side of these divides, the efficacy of any aspect of rural culture and organization came into question.

A prime example is Fu Yuan's essay "Notes from a Southern Tour" ("Nanxing zaji"), which first ran in the Guomindang newspaper *Minguo ribao* before appearing in the Mandarin reader published by the party's Popular Wisdom press. In it, the author recounts a visit home to see a mother left half-paralyzed by an illness. Fu struggles with the question of whether communities in the interior possessed the know-how to preserve and protect human life due to continued faith in what were seen as false cures, popular resignation to fate and reliance on divine intervention. Such modes of thought could be all too real. But their emphasis in narratives of rural life cast communities as generally incapable in other vital ways. Efficacious relief and the will to act were incongruous with popular belief in fate and prayers for rain. Understanding of rural capacities was subsumed, in other words, within a fast-developing duality of old and new. In this duality, those consciously allied with science could alone save lives, and, by contrast,

[28] Gu Jiegang, *Chu ji zhong xue jiaoke shu: Guoyu bianji dayi* (Shanghai: Shangwu yinshuguan, 1929).
[29] Culp, *Articulating Citizenship*, 140.

the old society, as it came to be understood, was devoid of effective interventions or solutions to social ills.[30]

Civics and New Moralities

As the republic fell further victim to imperial encroachment and internal wars, the national curriculum adjusted to meet new teaching needs. But it was not at all evident how curricular development in such a large and diverse country should proceed. At the National Educational Association Conference in 1919, there was extensive debate over whether textbooks should focus on local issues, or on national ones. The conference's resolution on the matter was ambiguous, resulting in mixed messages conveyed to publishers on the balance and nature of local or regional versus national coverage by schoolbooks.[31]

One decision, however, was more widely shared: civics readers (*gong-min xueke*) would replace the self-cultivation (*xiu shen*) curriculum adopted by the Qing in 1902 following the Boxer Uprising. The conference resolved that civics readers train students in the four areas of hygiene, morality, law and economics.[32] In one sense, this was merely a further modernization of the self-cultivation curriculum of the late Qing. Promoted by a faltering imperial house on the cusp of constitutional reforms, the classically based self-cultivation curriculum had been modeled on that of Imperial Japan, where Meiji schoolbooks stressed filial piety, discipline, devotion and respect for those in authority, and other neotraditional values seen as fostering a national polity.[33]

But, around 1920, new civics readers were built on a new set of assumptions – particularly in the lower grades of school – that included the assumption of a Chinese cultural deficit in concern for human welfare, especially toward the less fortunate. By 1923, upper middle-school students studied complex but concrete issues relating to family life – early or arranged marriage, concubinage and divorce among them – as well as poverty, criminality and other subjects of study in the developing field of sociology.[34] As for Meiqing, aged twelve that year, her civics teachers would have had a more challenging task: conveying what was called civics' "minimal essentials" at the primary and lower middle-school levels. This delicate balance of rich but simple content, of rigorous but straightforward methodology was noted by Liang Qichao in a preface he contributed

[30] Hen Gong and Zhong Jiu, eds., *Chu ji zhong xue: Guoyu wendu ben* vol. 1 (Shanghai: Minzhi shuju, 1923), 51–57; reprinted 1928.
[31] Peake, *Nationalism and Education in Modern China*, 109.
[32] Quoted in ibid., 107. See also Zarrow, *Educating China*, 82, 86, 101.
[33] Zarrow, *Educating China*, 81–83.   [34] Ibid., 87.

to a manual issued by the Commercial Press that same year. In it, he defined civics as teaching people of all ages to grasp their interconnections in order to "create a modern society and livelihood."[35]

To meet this challenge, three of Liang's colleagues at the Nanjing Higher Normal School (today's Nanjing University) produced the *Gongmin xue kecheng dawang* (Elementary Principles of Civics), a volume of structured lessons for primary and lower middle-school teachers on self-comportment within modern structures of society and the economy. The first lesson on social organization (*renqun*) considered the student in the household with the goal of "fostering practical morality [*daode*]," health and fitness, and a sense of patriotism. Proposed class material for fostering this civic morality (*gongmin daode*) were lessons on punctuality, obedience, honesty, cleanliness, tidiness, frugality and, finally, charity toward both people and animals. Students were encouraged to exercise these traits by promoting good health and physique, helping in the family garden, organizing civic youth groups to serve one's school and society, and performing an act of charity each day.[36]

This training in moral excellence (*meide*) would in turn develop a "national spirit" and support the building of the country – the goal of the text's chapter on the Chinese republic. Here, the opening lesson encouraged students to "recognize the importance of humanitarian [*rendao zhuyi*] services to the nation," while the second lesson had them "analyze the natural qualities [*xingzhi*] of the Chinese people in order to help in their training in civic morality." This training could take several forms and aims, among them "mutual aid among humanity, true righteousness towards human life, and humanitarian service [*renlei huzhu rensheng zhenyi ji rendao fuwu*]."[37]

The *Elementary Principles of Civics* was very much a product of its time and place. First drawn up by a special committee formed at the first annual conference of the Chinese Society for the Advancement of Education, its compilers for the Commercial Press explain that its content was based on civics texts published in various American states, while it clearly incorporated principles of character development from late Qing self-cultivation schoolbooks, which in turn were built on Confucian ideals of moral cultivation and virtuous conduct. Its purpose, however, reflected political urgency, offering training that was urgently needed, the editors explained, because of the country's chaotic transition so far from a monarchy to a democratic system. "The system has not suited the

---

[35] Liang Qichao, preface to *Gongmin xue kecheng dawang*, by Zhou Zhigan, Yang Zongming and Lu Duanyi (Shanghai: Shangwu yinshuguan, 1923), 1–2.
[36] Zhou, Yang and Lu, *Gongmin xue kecheng dawang*, 42–47.   [37] Ibid., 71–73.

people, or the people have not suited the system," they wrote; "either way, at the heart of it is an issue of incompatibility."[38]

"Formerly men cherished the family and racial viewpoint," read the 1919 conference resolution on the proposed aims and content of civics texts, "but now men should cherish the social and world viewpoint."[39] Chinese educators thus sought more explicitly to mold a citizenry for participatory government and national service. More radical reformers, such as Chen Duxiu, added to this the need to practice social and economic democracy by breaking down gender and class barriers.[40] Chen, like many of his peers, was influenced by John Dewey, who gave a series of lectures in China in 1919 and 1920 promoting educational reform and the cultivation of social traits underpinning democratic systems. "The best way to develop intellectually," the American philosopher said in a lecture at Beijing University, "is to take the social welfare as our major concern, and think about ways of developing our abilities so that we can serve the common good."[41]

Meanwhile, the mass education movement underway from the late 1920s broadened the reach of the Commercial Press's academic list beyond the pupils of the modern school system taking shape in cities and towns across the republic. Literacy programs championed by educational reformers brought intellectual views on Chinese shortcomings to the rural commoner. In their character exercises and drills, farmer's Mandarin readers issued by the Press expressly aimed to instill a sense of community responsibility and cooperation in villagers (although, pointedly, lessons on national duty were largely limited to the company's urban textbooks).[42]

Part of the larger nation-building project, civics was closely aligned with the aims of the social survey movement; it was in many ways a pedagogical response to it, developing in parallel to it and within the school system. Yet, despite this alignment with a movement dedicated to the empirical analysis and understanding of Chinese society, civics lessons rarely offered a record or a sense of how communities, rural or urban, had responded to recent humanitarian challenges. This was something civics shared with history textbooks, which by and large avoided mention of specific social institutions or events from the recent past. While sociologists of course did produce studies of particular social problems,

[38] Zhou, Yang and Lu, foreword to *Gongmin xue kecheng dawang*, 1.
[39] Quoted in Peake, *Nationalism and Education in Modern China*, 107. See also Zarrow, *Educating China*, 82, 86, 101.
[40] Culp, *Articulating Citizenship*, 99.   [41] Quoted in ibid., 106.
[42] Kate Merkel-Hess, *The Rural Modern: Reconstructing the Self and State in Republican China* (Chicago: University of Chicago Press, 2016), 39.

schoolbook treatments of Chinese society more generally remained strikingly abstract, leaving students with a blank screen on which overarching social depictions might, in time, be cast.

Conclusion

If disaster events played a part in modern China's national narratives, it was in a generic form, devoid of specificity or elaboration. Touched on purely as signs of extreme poverty, social disorganization and inept governance, they played, at most, supportive roles in calls for social transformation. Temple-based charitable activity or native work-relief projects would have little or no place in them. Nor would other forms of indigenous relief forming part of city and country life.

The commemoration of disaster, no matter of what scale, was instead the preserve of communal memory. While communal memory is treated in more detail in Chapter 10, for the moment it should be pointed out that communal records provided examples of recent disaster responses to emulate. In contrast, republican schoolbooks gave moral instruction by suggesting the nonexistence of native humanitarian practice in disaster events of the recent past. Communal records, then, could be as morally normative as the ethics books that were a part of the school curriculum, with the vital difference that schoolbooks were culturally negative in their approach, while communal records were, by and large, culturally affirmative.

Fundamentally, communal records present glimpses of lives intersecting with others in the wider community during shared events, both joyous and disastrous. And they regularly note that in times of great need, there were neighbors who stepped up. The communal records that passed down descriptions of past times of strife – stone stele erected in temple courtyards or transcribed in district gazetteers – did not merely relate how magistrates, gentry, merchants or farmers acted during past calamities but also how people *should* act in such times.

Some local biographies mention little else beyond charitable acts of their subjects. In doing so, they demonstrate most clearly the potentially pedagogical role of communal memory. Take, for example, the following entry from the biographical section of an official history of Gansu's capital, Lanzhou:

Chai Yingcang, whose year of birth is uncertain, was a man from Renhe village in Pingfan county in the Qing period, which is in today's Honggu district. He was filial towards others, a man of many good deeds. Grateful for the achievements of his forebears, he cherished every fragment of written material. In times of drought he distributed grain and subscribed to relief funds over and over again, saving multitudes of people.[43]

Chai's biography ends there. What little detail it offers suggests that this Gansu native was from a family of some accomplishment, and that he harbored a Confucian respect for ancestry and the written word. But it gives no indication of his social standing, of any official position or degree he may have had, of his occupation, of any particular disaster in which he acted or even of the specific period in the Qing dynasty in which he lived.

There are numerous possible reasons for why a biography such as this might have been produced (and reproduced). When local histories identified and extoled those who acted humanely in the past, they brought prestige to particular households. They also served as reference guides for incoming officials – suggesting to newly assigned magistrates, for example, which families they might go to for relief underwriting or oversight in times of crisis. But such an incomplete biography as Chai's would barely have served such purposes. In this most basic form, it served a more fundamental role as a model for community conduct. It also fit into a larger field of communal records such as gravestone epitaphs, biographical sketches and songs of lament that could both commemorate the suffering wrought by episodes of strife and provide lessons in community membership: civics at the most local level.

By contrast, for a republic frequently struck by calamity, its students were taught remarkably little about the experience of earthquakes and famines – even though such events tested the same civic and humanitarian capacities the *Elementary Principles of Civics* and other texts sought to instill in students at the time. So why were surviving legacies of civic organization and humanitarian action in times of calamity left out of national narratives, and from classroom materials on republican life? The New Culture magazine on Gansu examined in Chapter 2 might go some way in explaining this.

Xin Long ran a feature story on the Boy Scouts (Tongzijun) in its inaugural issue of May 1920. The Boy Scout phenomenon was one shared by all the world's powerful countries, the story explains, yet the movement was not aimed at a country's military qualities but rather the quality of its ordinary citizens (*putong guomin de xingzhi*). Scouts in towns and villages across the United States had raised funds to provision their troops in the Great European War, it explains, while English scouts had followed their nation's army to the front, providing

[43] *Lanzhou shizhi* (2013), 423.

first aid to the dead and wounded. Scout acts could be of any scale, the article explained, "from saving someone from flood waters to handing a beggar a copper dollar or giving him a way of support himself."

Elsewhere, the article explains that

in a narrow sense one can say these acts set the standard for saving life; in a broader sense one can say they set the standard for patriotism [aiguo]. Saving a life, loving one's country, are these not things that a citizen must do? [44]

On one level, there is little difference in the messaging here by this May Fourth journal of Gansu natives and a later local history of the Gansu provincial capital: one concerns the ethic of a civic movement, the other concerns those of an obscure Qing subject from Lanzhou. Xin Long's editors were surely aware that, just beyond their campus offices at Qinghua University, passersby pulled the poor to safety from icy canals after suicide attempts or handed out cash so the poor could carry on without selling their children. These acts were regularly reported in city newspapers over the famine year in which Xin Long was launched. [45]

Evidently, the difference between communal ethical instruction and that exemplified by the scout movement was this: humanitarian acts that kept communities together without engagement with international or national-level actors, ones that were initiated by village elders, monastic networks, garrison officers or individuals without reference to any facet of the national project, were dated in their mindset and social origin, and were therefore disqualified from observation, dropping from the national gaze.

National pride, or shame, as a motivator for relief action was not new, having played a role in greater Shanghai's mobilization of famine aid for the North as far back as the 1870s. [46] What came to the fore in the 1920s, instead, was a conflation of humanitarian values with national destiny, one that began to shape cultural memory and the historical record itself, engendering the idea that when disaster struck in republican China's vast interior, people there did nothing of note. In the representational framework presented collectively by May Fourth-era disaster surveys, national magazines for both adults and children, school readers, histories and civics texts, mentions of natural disaster assumed a different message: China's failure was a moral one.

In this way, education in 1920s China mirrored the official pedagogical campaigns that formed part of the broader social management strategies

---

[44] Zhao Zongjin, "Tongzijun," Xin Long zazhi 1/1 (May 1920), 27, 29.
[45] See Fuller, Famine Relief in Warlord China, 54, 101–5.
[46] Edgerton-Tarpley, Tears from Iron.

of the state in neighboring Japan, as examined by Sheldon Garon. There, over the course of the 1920s, state ministries oversaw the formation of "'moral suasion groups' [*kyōka dantai*] that would 'spiritually guide the people's sentiments and elevate and improve public morals'" in both the city and countryside. Central to these moral-reform campaigns were questions of mutual-assistance practices and poor relief.[47] As similar pedagogical tendencies took shape in republican China as part of the nation-building project, the country's varied social landscape was flattened into a field of enlightened and backward aspects, action and passivity, wakefulness and slumber, even good and evil. It was a field ripe for the interventions of the party program.

[47] Garon, *Molding Japanese Minds*, 11; see also 8–15, 40–59.

5   Party Discipline

May Fourth-era social surveying and agitation served as a form of discursive demolition of scholar-gentry standing in Chinese society, both culturally and socially. The movements' voices largely emanated, as we have seen, from what one might call preparty positions, their words readily finding their way beyond campuses into the country's commercial news outlets. Guomindang and Communist efforts over the remainder of the decade would see to the taming of May Fourth energies, allying the student movement to party-led worker and peasant movements, and tethering them to the evolving organs of state power. May Fourth activist journalism had coincided with the appearance of China's first Leninist-style single-party state in the form of Sun Yat-sen's republican experiment in Guangdong province, along with the inaugural meeting of the Chinese Communist Party in Shanghai in June 1921. With the formation of the United Front between the two parties three years later, May Fourth's political groundwork would give way to an era of formal revolutionary construction (*jianshe*) when perceptions of rural society would crystallize within a revolutionary program, invigorated by the mass workers' mobilization in the May Thirtieth movement of 1925.

At the Guomindang's Second National Conference held in Canton the following year, party strategists resolved to harness student activism into a party-led youth movement (*qingnian yundong*) down to the county and school levels. "Students and youths should be guided to become social workers and not become a privileged intellectual class," the congress stipulated, while "education was to serve to revolutionize and make commoners [*pingminhua*] of students." To do so, party branches were to create special youth publications designed to "refute reactionary thoughts and build revolutionary culture."[1] By 1928 party sponsorship of civics texts, language readers and other schoolbooks further tightened

---

[1] "Qingnian yundong jueyi an," in Zhongyang zhixing weiyuan hui, *Zhongguo Guomindang di er ci quanguo daibiao da hui: Yiyan ji jueyi an* (N.p.: February 1926), 58–59, Peking University Library Collections.

controls on speech and intellectual activity.[2] In April of that year, a commentator in *Chenbao*, the prominent platform for an earlier generation of student journalists, would lament that "schools are becoming party branches, students are turning into tools."[3]

Party tutelage of student affairs, however, did not necessarily mean radical changes to the methods of social critique and mobilization used by an earlier generation of student activists. The appropriation of popular culture, a key revolutionary practice, had been proposed in earlier May Fourth discussions. By way of example, Miao Jinyuan – who had urged in *Chenbao* in 1920 that students use social surveys in order to serve as the "vanguard of social reform," as we saw in Chapter 2 – had also suggested to fellow students that they politicize widespread cultural practices such as the rhymed couplets families across China placed on front doors at the New Year. His proposed alternatives – "Always maintain a youthful spirit," read one and another, "Never become enslaved to people with old values" – were harbingers of party incorporation of mass culture and the glorification of youth by the state in the years to come.[4]

One crucial difference between intellectual activity during May Fourth and the Nanjing Decade (1928–37), though, was the added muscle and teeth brought to political doctrine and mobilization later in the twenties. In the revolution's early stages, this took the form of party cadres preparing village ground for the arrival of Guomindang forces sweeping through toward Beijing in the Northern Expedition to unify the country in 1926–28. Originating in shared communications offices in Canton during the United Front, Guomindang and Communist Party doctrine on the nature of Chinese society developed in tandem. After Sun's death in early 1925, the doctrine of both parties would take shape in part under the figure of Mao Zedong after he was appointed to run the Guomindang Central Propaganda Bureau in October[5] and soon afterward the Guomindang's Peasant Movement Training Institute.[6]

Picking up where we left off in our last chapter, here we move from the treatment of civics and republican history by Chinese educators in the New Culture period to the formation of political doctrine on the nature of rural communities during the First United Front (1924–27). We do this for what it says about shared aspects of Guomindang and Communist dogma before the violent rupture of the party alliance in 1927, and what it reveals about the social frameworks and terminology with which

[2] Culp, *Articulating Citizenship*, 133.
[3] Quoted in Lü Fangshang, *Cong xuesheng yundong dao yundong xuesheng* 1919–1929 (Taipei: Zhongying yanjiuyuan jindaishi yanjiusuo, 1994), 304.
[4] Quoted in Weston, *Power of Position*, 203.   [5] Fitzgerald, *Awakening China*, 233.
[6] Apter and Saich, *Revolutionary Discourse in Mao's Republic*, 103.

revolutionary memory would be constructed over the following decades of civil and anti-Japanese war.

Maoist Diagnoses

Only four years before assuming his role in the Guomindang propaganda bureau at Canton, Mao had formally applied to join the Young China Association in a letter to the chair of its board of directors, Yang Zhongjian.[7] In that brief, mundane formality, one can see a baton, so to speak, passed from May Fourth activists to the agents of formal revolution. Yang himself had joined several Marxist study groups since his arrival in Beijing in 1917, and joined the Guomindang in 1922. But as famine conditions eased in the spring of 1921, and the Chinese Communist Party convened for the first time in Shanghai, he and other participants in the May Fourth social survey endeavor prepared for study overseas. *Xin Long* coeditor Deng Chungao enrolled in Stanford University's philosophy program in 1922 (and after that the University of Chicago), while the magazine's Haiyuan-born cofounder, Feng Hanying, expelled from the Beijing Industrial University for allegedly subversive activities, pursued chemistry at the University of Paris in 1923.[8] As for the especially prolific Yang, who promoted the social survey movement and critiqued famine responses in the *Dongfang zazhi*, *Chenbao* and elsewhere (as we have seen), he moved to the University of Munich in 1923 to pursue a doctorate in philosophy.[9]

Mao, in many ways, would pick up where his May Fourth peers left off in their analysis of rural social dynamics. Within weeks of his appointment in Canton, he produced the first in his series of reports breaking down Chinese society into various interest groups. The first strategy document – published at the beginning of December 1925 in *Geming* (Revolution), a semimonthly publication of the Guomindang – placed Chinese society within a capitalist framework, albeit in a "backward" condition. To Mao, five class categories constituted Chinese society, based on material position and political interests. The division between class "enemies" and "friends" lay at the line distinguishing the "big" from the "petty" bourgeoisie and landlord class. Mao thus at first drew the revolutionary battle somewhere within

---

[7] Mao Zedong, "Letter to Yang Zhongjian," in Stuart R. Schram, ed., *National Revolution and Social Revolution, December 1920–June 1927*, vol. 2 of *Mao's Road to Power: Revolutionary Writings 1912–1949* (Armonk, NY: M. E. Sharpe, 1992), 99.
[8] Wang and Yang, *Gan Ning Qing minguo renwu*, 298; *Haiyuan xianzhi* (1999), 1084.
[9] Xu Youchun, *Minguo renwu*, 2173.

the capitalist classes, which, based on his calculations, positioned 395 million people against 5 million.[10]

In the space of a few months, Mao's formulations of Chinese society would rapidly evolve. A month later, in the January 1926 issue of *Zhongguo nongmin* (The Chinese Peasant) issued by the Guomindang Peasant Department, Mao's analytical language and framework changed, no longer placing Chinese communities in a strict capitalist structure. Now, China's big landlords, defined as those owning more than 500 *mu*, constituted the "only secure bulwark of feudal and patriarchal society" and the "deadly enemies of the Chinese peasantry." The question was where the battle line should be drawn within the peasantry: in other words, whether the struggling land-owning peasants, who numbered sixty million people within China's "petty bourgeoisie," would join the revolutionary struggle or not. Although "they curse the foreigners as 'devils,' the warlords as 'money-grabbing commanders,' the local bullies and evil gentry as 'the heartless rich,'" Mao reported, struggling owner-peasants might be too cautious to throw their lot behind the revolution. What it came down to in this analysis was the extent of exploitative practices in any particular locality. "In special circumstances," he concluded, "when we encounter the most reactionary and vicious local bullies and evil gentry who exploit the people savagely, as in Haifeng and Guangning, they must be overthrown completely," and in these cases struggling landowning peasants would presumably come on board.[11]

Here, Mao's analysis of rural China in early 1926 drew from debates underway since the late nineteenth century about the feudal (*fengjian*) nature of Chinese political culture. These debates took several forms. In the late Qing period, Kang Youwei and Liang Qichao, among others, had identified periods of local self-rule (*zizhi*) in the ancient past as a counterbalance to centralized or despotic rule, and saw in self-rule the basis for constitutional or federalized government in the modern period. For thinkers around May Fourth, such as Chen Duxiu and Qu Qiubai, feudalism was instead a system of gentry and patriarchal or clan power that marked China's "backward and uncivilized" stage of "social development," in the words of Lidong Zhao.[12]

---

[10] Mao Zedong, "Analysis of All the Classes in Chinese Society," in Schram, ed., vol. 2 of *Mao's Road to Power*, 250, 260–61.

[11] Mao Zedong, "Zhongguo nongmin zhong ge jieji de fenxi ji qi duiyu geming de taidu," *Zhongguo nongmin* 1 (1926), 14, 17, 20. Translations are from Mao Zedong, "An Analysis of the Various Classes among the Chinese Peasantry and Their Attitudes toward the Revolution," in Schram, ed., vol. 2 of *Mao's Road to Power*, 304, 306, 309.

[12] Lidong Zhao, "Feudal and Feudalism in Modern China," *Journal of Modern Chinese History* 6/2 (2012), 206; see also 200.

By using a term, feudal, already used by intellectuals in this diagnosis of rural China's social ills, then, Mao both asserted the country's backwardness and, in more subtle ways, identified the revolutionary promise of political participation at the grassroots. In the process, however, he employed another expression that was already more widely used in newspapers and gazetteers at the time to describe especially exploitative actors at the local level: *tuhao lieshen*, or "local bullies and evil gentry" (variously translated as "local tyrants and bad gentry"). It should be noted that in this text from January 1926 Mao uses the expression sparingly. In the first instance, he described the exasperation of a particular class of middling farmers toward the more powerful "local bullies and evil gentry" dominating their community; in the second, he uses the expression to capture the acute social tensions that lay behind uprisings in Guangdong earlier in the decade.

Soon, however, what began essentially as rhetorical devices in Mao's essays on revolutionary strategy over 1926 crystallized into class designations projected over the entirety of Chinese history. In the summer of 1926, Mao composed a follow-up piece in *Nongmin yundong* (The Peasant Movement), the periodical of the Peasant Department of the Guomindang Central Executive Committee. A "feudal class" was now positioned as "the greatest adversary of revolution in an economically backward semicolony." Moreover, the counterrevolutionary interests and dominance of rural affairs by "local bullies and bad gentry" "had crushed the peasants for several thousand years."[13] Rather than reflecting the historical moment and its particular dynamics, Mao now cast rural problems as existing since the classical period.

Presented as a timeless picture, Mao's socioeconomic sketch was, in fact, a vivid reflection of his political moment. The mid-1920s was particularly tumultuous within the Guomindang, from the struggle for power between its leftist and rightist wings after Sun's sudden death in March 1925 to the massacre of Communists and their allies by forces loyal to Chiang Kai-shek in April 1927 that put an end to the United Front. Failing in the aftermath to secure an urban position at Changsha, Mao was driven into the mountainous border region of Jiangxi and Hunan, where he and others formed the guerilla force that would grow into the red army.[14]

Mao's political coming of age amid internal purges and guerilla warfare goes some way in explaining his conceptualization of social relations and

[13] Mao Zedong, "The National Revolution and the Peasant Movement," in Schram, ed., vol. 2 of *Mao's Road to Power*, 388–90, 392.
[14] Apter and Saich, *Revolutionary Discourse in Mao's Republic*, 103.

mass movements and its pronounced mixture of military with political strategies. "It was significant," John Fitzgerald writes, that Mao's "first major analysis of classes in society should have proceeded from an analysis of political tension within the Nationalist Party."[15] Or, as David Apter and Tony Saich put it in their study of Maoist discourse, "In short, Mao's power is first military, and his texts are military instructions, which gradually he converts into a theory of peasant revolution."[16]

By the end of 1926, the term gentry (*shen*) no longer appeared in Mao's social analyses without moral qualification (i.e., *lie* [bad or evil]). When contributing in this way to the conversion of the term evil gentry into an official social category for use in class war, Mao added a moral quality to a materialist analysis, and did so using a mixture of feudal and Marxist categories.

This discursive practice would fully emerge in one of Mao's best-known political writings, his "Report on an Investigation of the Peasant Movement in Hunan" from early 1927. Composed after a month's visit to five counties in the province, the essay opened with the prediction that the peasant movements spreading across the country would "sweep all the imperialists, warlords, greedy officials and corrupt bureaucrats, local bullies and evil gentry into their graves." In the six pages that followed, the term *lieshen* appeared some sixty-two times.[17] Evil gentry had taken the form of a mantra.

It is important to stress that these methods used by Mao to capture "social reality" had broader application than the realm of political mobilization. They would also serve as the basis for statistical work in the future People's Republic, as Arunabh Ghosh has noted. Competing against other statistical methods based on census taking and on random sampling and probability theory, Mao's "ethnographic" approach was, "from the perspective of PRC statisticians, the most indigenous among these approaches," Ghosh writes, "because it could be traced to Mao's 1927 *Report on an Investigation of the Peasant Movement in Hunan* as well as to his later essays, such as 'On Book Worship' and 'On Practice.'"[18]

In Mao's ethnographic approach one can detect echoes of the rationale for May Fourth student investigations in the countryside earlier in the decade (discussed in Chapter 2). Mao very self-consciously rejected bookish learning, placing "himself squarely in the middle of the investigation," Ghosh writes, describing his own approaches in his Hunan

---

[15] Fitzgerald, *Awakening China*, 256.
[16] Apter and Saich, *Revolutionary Discourse in Mao's Republic*, 104; see also 81–85.
[17] Mao Zedong, "Hunan nongmin yundong kaocha baogao," *Xiangdao* 191 (1927), 8–13.
[18] Arunabh Ghosh, *Making It Count: Statistics and Statecraft in the Early People's Republic of China* (Princeton, NJ: Princeton University Press, 2020), 5.

report as holding "*fact-finding conferences* in villages and county towns," and by "*listen*[ing] *attentively*" both to "experienced peasants" and to "a good deal of *gossip*."[19] Resulting in a kind of qualitative sampling, Mao's investigations produced a "'typical' or 'paradigmatic' understanding [that] could then be extrapolated to produce wider, more comprehensive knowledge of social, economic or cultural trends."[20]

It would take some time, though, for Mao's writings to acquire seminal status in much of Chinese intellectual life. More immediately, the terminology and tone used by Mao's propaganda office during his brief tenure there in the mid-1920s were shared by party resolutions on the peasant movement, including those made at the Guomindang's Second National Conference in January 1926 in Canton. Estimating that the peasantry comprised more than 80 percent of the population, the conference resolved that the aim of the national revolution was "above all to liberate the peasantry." In economic terms, this involved: concrete measures to relieve burdens, end predatory practices and create opportunities for poverty reduction among the working poor, including a ban on high interest rates; rent ceilings and floors for prices of agricultural goods; lower work hours and increased pay for farmworkers; peasant banks and cooperatives; distributing to the jobless and poor farmers the proceeds from cutting official waste; an end to the monopoly of trade by "unscrupulous" merchants; and relief measures for peasants in times of need.

As for how this economic program would be implemented, the political program drawn up at the 1926 conference offered little beyond slogans based on ill-defined, yet morally infused social categories, as expressed in the resolve to "eliminate groups harmful to peasant interests: warlords, compradors, corrupt officials, evil gentry and local bullies." At the most local level, this would involve "putting an end to the monopoly of village government by local bullies and evil gentry."[21] A key tactic for this was the peasant uprising.

It is important to step back for a moment to consider what type of person was initiating and overseeing armed actions by poor farmers and laborers, and how they fit into the intellectual developments over the previous decade. Many of the cadres advancing with the National Revolutionary Army to incite rural agitation in South and Central China in the wake of the Northern Expedition, and afterward in the northern base areas, had rural origins themselves. Some four-fifths of the leaders of the more than fifty Communist uprisings from 1927 to

[19] Mao, quoted in ibid., 50; emphasis in Ghosh's translation.   [20] Ibid., 5.
[21] "Nongmin yundong jueyi an," in Zhongyang zhixing weiyuan hui, *Zhongguo Guomindang di er ci quanguo daibiao da hui: Yiyan ji jueyi an* (February 1926), 51–53, Peking University Library Collections.

1929 were village born, like Mao. And most, like Mao, had at least a middle-school education.[22]

Party cadres were, then, similar in many respects to their May Fourth predecessors. Relatively well-educated, they sprang from a generation of school children raised in a curriculum that dealt with republican social history in the vaguest of terms. Rural in origin, they built revolution on the foundations of a student movement that had grown from core concerns of political, educational and family reform to campaigning for the moral rehabilitation of rural communities. Nationalist in mindset, social revolution was, to many, a vehicle for national salvation.

Although modern peasant uprisings had occurred as early as 1922 with Peng Pai's organizing efforts in Guangdong, the peasant movement more broadly, and under party tutelage, took off only after the May Thirtieth movement of 1925, and most vigorously after the rupturing of the United Front in 1927. This time line applied as well to the more reformist mass education movements led by such figures as the liberal James Yen and the Confucian Liang Shuming, which did not shift to rural Hebei and Shandong until 1926.

The rural gaze of both reformist and revolutionary intellectuals took hold, in other words, only after the terminology of evil gentry had been incorporated into a series of "established points of a comprehensive political program" with which "cadres were to become fully conversant" – in the words of Marcia Ristaino.[23] "During the early phase of the Northern Expedition," writes Patricia Thornton, "the combined Nationalist and Communist forces labeled local notables who opposed the advancing [National Revolutionary Army] troops as 'local bullies', 'evil gentry', or counter-revolutionaries and accused them of acts detrimental to the nation and injurious to the people."[24]

A key point to note here is that the party-led peasant movement was not based on uniquely revolutionary premises. Rather, it sprang from broadly shared understandings of Chinese society, also embraced by intellectuals from both liberal and Confucian camps, as well as missionaries. The mass literacy movement, spearheaded by James Yen and Zhu Qihui – the philanthropist and wife of former premier Xiong Xiling –[25] sought to

[22] Han Xiaorong, *Chinese Discourses on the Peasant, 1900–1949* (Albany: State University of New York Press, 2005), 126; see also 122–25, 133.
[23] Marcia R. Ristaino, *China's Art of Revolution: The Art of Mobilization of Discontent, 1927 and 1928* (Durham, NC: Duke University Press, 1987), 1.
[24] Patricia M. Thornton, *Disciplining the State: Virtue, Violence, and State-Making in Modern China*, Harvard East Asian Monographs (Cambridge, MA: Harvard University Asia Center, 2007), 105.
[25] Shi Xia, *At Home in the World: Women and Charity in Late Qing and Early Republican China* (New York: Columbia University Press, 2018), 86–92.

inculcate in commoners this intellectual consensus espoused in Commercial Press publications for schoolchildren. Textbooks and readers aimed at farmers and laborers, based largely on American pedagogical methods, characterized China's countryside as socially disorganized and morally deficient, which required redressal through lessons in moral and social rejuvenation.[26] The joint Guomindang and Communist attack on the northern regional regimes in 1926, together with the village mobilization that went along with it, could be seen as a militarized counterpart to the broader rural reconstruction movement launched in the mid-1920s – one carried out in various forms across the political spectrum over the same period.

Intellectual Reworkings of Rural life

The period of recentralization of power under the Guomindang regime from 1928 coincided with a litany of severe crises, from drought-famine across much of the North and Northwest to continued civil war with remaining regional armies, the local effects of the Great Depression, and heightened interventions by the Japanese army, including the assassination of Zhang Zuolin in Manchuria. It is not surprising that the first few years of Guomindang rule saw a dizzying flurry of debate over the appropriate analytical frameworks with which to comprehend the country's afflictions. Much of this debate was conducted by party theoreticians resident in Shanghai, mainly Stalinist-style Communists, Trotskyites or members of the left wing of the Guomindang. Participation was mostly limited to those employing, or at least familiar with, Marxist theories mixed with elements of feudalism – a social system that was often invoked by participants without being clearly defined, one that was made to match in some way or another local conditions and the evolution of Chinese society generally. Non-Marxists such as Hu Shi, Liang Shuming and Fei Xiaotong were of course also involved in the debate. Interpreting feudalism as a social structure of medieval Europe that did not apply to imperial or modern China, non-Marxist scholars were more likely to work toward village solidarity rather than class struggle, through schooling and other aspects of the rural reconstruction movement of the 1930s.

Whether or not participants in the rural debate embraced feudalism as an analytical tool, the period saw the disappearance of the farmer as an occupation in favor of a political category and subject – the peasant – now

---

[26] Merkel-Hess, *Rural Modern*, 43, 80–81; Guy Alitto, *The Last Confucian: Liang Shuming and the Chinese Dilemma of Modernity* (Berkeley: University of California Press, 1979), 150, 175.

seen to constitute nearly the entire rural social and cultural field (a subject discussed at greater length in our next chapter).[27] For now, it should be noted that the co-option of social-scientific study by movements for political mobilization resulted in reductionist frameworks for understanding rural life: one that pitted a moribund or evil gentry against a peasantry. The winnowing down of a complex and in certain respects sophisticated field of rural social actors into simplistic analytical models allowed rural society to be cast with the broadest of brushstrokes.

Guomin gonglun (The Citizens' Opinion) was one of numerous short-lived journals founded at the establishment of the Nanjing regime in 1928 that participated in the debate about the nature of Chinese society. These publications represented a range of revolutionary positions both under the Guomindang umbrella – such as *Xinshengming* (New Life), *Qianjin* (Forward) and *Geming pinglun* (Revolutionary Review) – and outside the ruling party, such as the Communist *Xinsichao* (New Thought) and the Trotskyite *Dongli* (Driving Force). By 1930, most of them would be banned by the Guomindang regime.

Less clearly allied with any particular faction, *Guomin gonglun* in many ways captures the development of mainstream reformist thought on rural society and the political solutions proposed at the moment of consolidation of Guomindang power. First published when our imagined Meiqing would have been seventeen and at university age, the inaugural issue of *Guomin gonglun* was introduced with an editorial by the journal's president:

Today's is a dog-eat-dog society [Yu Guanbin begins]. Justice and truth, these words are hard to come by [. . .]. Only selfishness, profit, falsehood, and stubbornness fill people's heads [. . .]. Military men are like this, so warlords proliferate; officials are like this, so corruption blossoms; students are like this, so academic trickery thrives; village gentry are like this, so local bullies and evil gentry proliferate; ordinary people are like this, so banditry and robbery proliferate.

The new journal, Yu explains, was "dedicated to bringing justice and truth back to life," and it aimed to do this by "capturing the spirit of the masses, with utmost equanimity, utmost uprightness, utmost reliability, and utmost frankness."[28]

One way the journal did this was to cover the rising scourge of banditry. Banditry had of course long existed as a general term for organized robbery, and the poor, mobile males associated with its practice were long viewed as a threat to the imperial state and to local elites, in

---

[27] Myron Cohen, "Cultural and Political Inventions in Modern China: The Case of the Chinese "Peasant," *Daedalus* 122/2 (Spring 1993), 151–70.
[28] Yu Guanbin, "Chuangkan ci," *Guomin gonglun* 1 (1928), 2.

particular. This was not only for reasons of violence and theft from communities, but also because teams of single males living beyond the limits of the patriarchal household posed a threat to the Confucian social and moral order. Bandits were therefore considered "beyond the pale" and punished – like rebels – especially harshly in the imperial period.

With the fall of the Qing and its bureaucratic controls, republican politics and brinkmanship within the local self-government movement of the 1910s gave elites considerably more room to pursue their political and financial interests, particularly at the local level, creating opportunities for local gentry to abuse newfound powers. The extent to which communities suffered overbearing policies by large landowners and other elites of course varied over time and place. But the escalating war and civil strife of the mid-1920s doubtless exacerbated antagonistic social relations in the countryside, making it considerably more difficult for communities to benefit from mutual aid or to rebound from disaster. At the same time, changes to the penal code in the beginning years of the republic further strengthened the hand of local officials in the policing of banditry, empowering them with extrajudicial legal authority to execute on the spot those deemed to be bandits – without appeal.[29]

The fact that the bandit enjoyed a reversal of fortunes of sorts, in social and ideological terms, over the 1920s is especially noteworthy. When *Guomin gonglun* covered banditry it did so in ways that humanized those that joined its ranks. The journal's fifth issue ran "A Sociological Investigation into Banditry" ("Tufei zhi shehui xue de kaocha") in which the writer, Shen Yanjun, grappled with the disintegration of rural communities stemming from "bad governance since the turn of the century."[30] In this, Shen was echoing the position of many liberal or conservative thinkers at the time, who saw the immiseration of the Chinese countryside deepening around 1900 amid heightened outside interventions in Chinese economic and political life, including foreign patronage of China's increasingly warring militarists. Writing in 1928 – a year that saw numerous wars during the final stages of the Northern Expedition, and drought-famine spreading from Shandong across the North to Inner Mongolia and Gansu – Shen writes how "the nation had completely lost the ability to protect the people."[31]

At the root of the crisis of banditry was the "subjugation of morality [*daode*]." In social terms, Shen argues, banditry stemmed from the "division of society by feudal influences," which led to capital flight to the

---

[29] Xu Xiaoqun, "The Rule of Law without Due Process: Punishing Robbers and Bandits in Early-Twentieth Century China," *Modern China* 33/2 (2007), 230–57.

[30] Shen Yanjun, "Tufei zhi shehui xue de kaocha," *Guomin gonglun* 1/5 (1928), 9–11.

[31] Ibid., 10.

cities, the proliferation of "warlords," the impoverishment of farming communities and the collapse of rural education. Ordinary people then resorted to plundering wealthy households, holding people hostage for ransom and highway robbery. Their reason to take such extreme measures of course varied, he writes, but could be summed up in the "seeking equality of economic livelihood among the impoverished, who can no longer endure the oppression of the local bullies and evil gentry."[32]

By seeing banditry as a form of class conflict, the writer took those participating in acts of banditry into the fold of the proletariat. Robbery, he explains, is "compelled by hunger and cold," it is not for pleasure-seeking. Although led by a headman, bandit gangs, he continues, were nonhierarchical and "similar to joint-stock companies" in how they distributed their spoils. And although gangs respected no moral codes toward outsiders, their internal discipline respected "righteousness" (*renyi*).[33]

In the inaugural issue, the president of *Guomin gonglun* had explained that the journal aimed to "smash the false, evil, shameful old society, and begin building a genuine, good, splendid new society," and that only after a "revolution in thought and lifestyle cleanses [society] to the very bottom, only then can a new society and culture be created."[34] A journal that humanized those driven to violent extremes in a climate of social breakdown and competition also associated the old with evil and the new with goodness, while advancing a moral classification of society that originated in the propaganda unit of the National Revolutionary Army. Moreover, the article succinctly captured the stages of revolution to that point: the dismantling of older social forms and practices, before reconstruction with the social and cultural values of the rival revolutionary regimes.

Conclusion

Over three years, *lieshen* (bad or evil gentry), a compound at first employed by the joint propaganda offices of the Guomindang and Communists for instances of inhumanity and abuse of power by local elites, had grown into an umbrella term for political enemies shared by both revolutionary parties. Moral language originally used for social and economic injustices was refashioned as a tool for policing party discipline. The culture of the party state was supercharged with a conflation of moral with political behavior.

Seen from a broader perspective, in his capacities as propaganda officer, Mao Zedong had followed his May Fourth peers into the

[32] Ibid., 10.   [33] Ibid., 11.   [34] Yu Guanbin, "Chuangkan ci," 2.

countryside, in his case in search of social conflict instead of earthquake and famine conditions. In the wake of the deinscription of rural gentry and their communal roles from the disaster reports of an earlier generation of student investigators, Mao's reports used operative terms like evil gentry to reinscribe class positions onto village life.

These political labels had immediate application in the civil war that followed the end of the United Front in 1927. Guomindang use of the term evil gentry for a broadly defined and therefore elastic segment of the population continued, becoming state policy under the Nanjing regime; only now the Guomindang grouped their erstwhile political allies in with the series of social and political types targeted for elimination as threats to the consolidation of party control and the advancing of the state agenda. "In May 1927, Guomindang branches at the county level were ordered to eliminate all 'Communists, local bullies, and evil gentry, corrupt officials and venal underlings, and reactionary, opportunists, corrupt, and evil elements' from their ranks," writes Patricia Thornton. "On August 18, 1927, the Nationalists amended the penal code by mandating the punishment of 'local bullies and evil gentry' in order to 'develop the spirit of party rule and safeguard the public interest.'"[35] Evil gentry had joined banditry as an ill-defined category in the republican criminal code.

In early 1928, the Guomindang's *Minguo ribao* spelled out who in fact qualified as local bullies and evil gentry, breaking the criteria into two categories. The first category of eight types of criminal behavior "concerned those with feudal thoughts and morality," Qi Tai wrote in the party's Shanghai-based news daily. Transgressors included those who slandered official policies of the Guomindang state, those who lured friends and relatives astray from the revolutionary program, those that forbade the younger generation to enter the party or practice patriotism and those that did not invest available funds into their children's education or allow adult children to exercise their "right to marry freely." A second category of local bullies and evil gentry "concerned those committing personal crimes," and listed nine examples. This included people colluding with corrupt officials, those facilitating human trafficking and those harming party cadres. "Local bullies and evil gentry were not permitted into the party" in any capacity, as formal members or in supporting roles, and those with "unchanging thoughts" were to be admitted into "re-education centers for local bullies and evil gentry" (*tuhao lieshen chenghuayuan*).[36]

---

[35] Thornton, *Disciplining the State*, 106.
[36] Qi Tai, "Jinzhi tuhao lieshen huodong zhi biyao," *Minguo ribao xingqi pinglun* February 16, 1928, 4–5.

Of course a lexicon shared by Communists and Guomindang was not necessarily used for uniform ends. Once in power, the Guomindang leadership tempered its hostility toward local power holders, putting the discursive tools at its disposal in the service of state strengthening and fiscal goals rather than fomenting social revolution. For the Communists, now hunted and flushed into some of the remotest sections of the country – first the highlands of Central China, and soon the Northwest – revolutionary terms were used to secure popular support through continued social agitation and the destabilization of local power structures.

Nonetheless, for both Leninist-style parties straddling the political spectrum, the struggle against evil gentry marked the reinscription of China's political terrain after the intellectual and cultural shocks of the May Fourth era. In the case of the Guomindang, this took the form of neotraditional values of discipline, devotion and sacrifice, disseminated through the Guomindang's New Life movement of the mid-1930s. Either way, party doctrine and social categorization had become tools for testing loyalty, identifying foes and exacting personal sacrifice for the larger cause of the party. Having focused here on the place of the notion of evil gentry in the formative years of Guomindang and Communist doctrine, we turn next to the development of the other pole in the political dynamic of Chinese revolutionary politics: the peasantry.

6   The Emergence of the Peasantry

In the wake of May Fourth, a markedly uniform treatment of village life began to take hold of school curricula, of coverage in leading newsstand magazines and of party orthodoxy. Over the course of the 1920s this had involved an unusual alignment of commercial publishing with revolutionary messaging, and of liberal, progressive and missionary ideas with Communist and Guomindang political platforms. The broader transmission of rural representations would involve their incorporation into forms of media and art with vastly larger public exposure. If Chapter 5 bridged May Fourth social writing with party orthodoxy later in the 1920s, here we explore parallels in the 1930s between Guomindang pedagogy and international representations of rural China, focusing on the influential work of the American writer Pearl S. Buck. We do this for what it says about convergences between artistic and academic writing on the nature of rural life, and the global conversations behind the reduction of complex communities into peasantries.

Literary Convergences

In 1933, the Guomindang's Popular Wisdom Book Company issued a textbook, *Shehui xue ji shehui wenti* (Sociology and Social Issues), for advanced students. In it, its author Mao Qijun broke the subject down into five thematic chapters on issues concerning race, family, cities, labor and, lastly, the peasantry (*nongmin*).[1] In doing so, the Guomindang text reduced the countryside – a social sphere in which the vast majority of Chinese still resided – into the theater of a relatively new political subject, the peasant. (Folded into Mao's chapter on the peasantry was the figure of the landlord. Politically distinct from the peasant, by 1933 the landlord had evolved from the inert, petrified gentry of May Fourth-New Culture writing and in turn from the evil gentry of joint Guomindang and

[1] Mao Qijun, *Shehui xue ji shehui wenti* (Shanghai: Minzhi shuju, 1933), 4–5.

Communist Party literature during the First United Front.) On one level, this was simply a practical way of devising a school lesson plan. On another level, the text signaled a broader shift in the intellectual treatment of residents of rural China, understandings of the challenges they faced and the contrast they posed to modernizing urban communities.[2]

Sociology and Social Issues accounted for China's rural immiseration through two main sets of factors. Economically, the bankruptcy of agricultural communities stemmed, it explained, from oppression under exploitative landlords, primitive transportation and onerous taxation. This was a compelling account of developments in the countryside, one also observable from the vantage point of the city: with the growth of cities in the preceding half century, which often involved the flight of village elites to urban areas, absentee landlordism and armed debt collection by urban agencies – and their deleterious effect on communal bonds – became more widespread;[3] the country's rutted roads were generally impossibly slow going, and rail lines increasingly paralyzed or taken over for war, with catastrophic consequences in times of dearth, especially;[4] and then proliferating taxes over the course of the 1920s put debilitating burdens on the general population in many places – taxes created by increasingly autonomous regional governments intent on state strengthening and waging civil war, not least the newly installed Nanjing regime itself.[5]

But then *Sociology and Social Issues'* handling of rural culture and its social capabilities was of an entirely different order, treating them in the most generalized terms. Rural poverty, it reads, was due to three "characteristic features" of village life: "superstition [*mixin*]," "conservatism [*baoshou*]," and "lack of organization [*wu zuzhi*]." No structures existed beyond the clan or household for collective decision-making, risk sharing, crisis mitigation, or anything resembling duty or service to the community. "When disaster [*tianzai*] occurs," students were instructed, "there is no knowledge on how to guard against it, and then no knowledge on how to relieve it [*bu zhi jiuji*]. Consequently, the only way to live free from

[2] On this, see Cohen, "Cultural and Political Inventions in Modern China" and Hayford, "The Storm Over the Peasant."

[3] Jeremy Brown, "Rebels, Rent, and Tai Xu: Local Elite Identity and Conflict during and after the Tai Ping Occupation of Jiangnan, 1860–84," *Late Imperial China* 30/2 (December 2009).

[4] François Godement, "La famine de 1928 à 1930 en Chine du Nord et du Centre" (Master's thesis, Université Paris VII, 1970), microfiche, 90–93.

[5] Prasenjit Duara, *Culture, Power and the State: Rural North China, 1900–1942* (Stanford, CA: Stanford University Press, 1988), 217; Li Huaiyin, *Village Governance in North China, 1875–1936* (Stanford, CA: Stanford University Press, 2005), 37.

worry is to beseech heaven and appeal to the Buddha [*zhi you qiutian bai Fo*]."[6]

With the publication of *The Good Earth* in 1931, Pearl Buck, the daughter of American missionaries to China, provided an intimate portrait of the struggles and rising fortunes of a Chinese farming family, yet one that echoed, in subtle yet significant ways, Mao Qijun's sociological text. The novel, based largely on the time Buck spent with her husband, the agronomist J. Lossing Buck, from 1917 to 1919 in the town of Nansuzhou on Anhui's section of the North China Plain,[7] follows the formation of a humble farming household before its flight south during drought-famine, and its experience of flood and locust infestation in its prosperous years of landownership after its return home. In Wang Lung, an earnest, illiterate man of inexhaustible industriousness, Buck created a simple hero of all-too-real contradictions, caught up and complicit in many of the social vices of the day, eschewing some, embracing others. At times incorruptible, Wang is disgusted by his relatives' profligacy, and lashes out at his thieving son even as they suffer hunger as refugees, only to scoop up land and exact high interest from struggling neighbors upon their return home. Embodying male privilege, Wang purchases a woman as a concubine while neglecting the tireless wife who bore him many sons; yet all the while he remains steadfast in his care and affection for his mentally disabled daughter.

For a work that made a monumental mark on the Western imagination – "It can almost be said that for a whole generation of Americans she [Buck] 'created' the Chinese," Harold R. Isaacs found in a series of interviews he conducted in the 1950s[8] – *The Good Earth*'s nuanced style differed profoundly from the stiff categorization of contemporary political tracts. Through pluck and good fortune, its hero reflected the often cruel but potentially rewarding fluidity of Chinese society. Passing through numerous socioeconomic positions over the course of his life, Wang Lung could have been pinned to any one of the numerous political categories – poor peasant, laborer, rich peasant, landlord – developed at the time.

But then, beyond Wang's family unit, an entire field of social institutions is, in Buck's hands, invisible; community is remarkably vacant. Step-by-step, Wang's survival strategies in times of disaster are of a family abandoned by a lack of community to the whims of fate. "Even

---

[6] Mao Qijun, *Shehui xue ji shehui wenti*, 223.
[7] Peter J. Conn, *Pearl S. Buck: A Cultural Biography* (Cambridge: Cambridge University Press, 2002), 68.
[8] Harold R. Isaacs, *Scratches on Our Minds: American Images of China and India* (New York: John Day, 1958), 155.

money would do little good now," Buck's narrator explains when drought-famine struck Wang's region, "for there was no food to buy." Elsewhere it relates how the south of the country "was not as it was in their own land [to the north], where even silver could not buy food because there was none." And then, further on, "Wang Lung and his family had come from a country where if men starve it is because there is no food, since the land cannot bear under a relentless heaven. Silver in the hand was worth little because it could buy nothing where nothing was."[9] Yet in the summer and autumn of 1920 – a few months after the Bucks moved from their North China home of nearly three years to Nanjing – hundreds of millions of *jin* of grain were brought in by train and cart to the North China plain from Manchuria, Inner Mongolia and the Yangzi River basin, expressly for discount sale to residents with available cash at price stabilization centers – enough to provision millions of people across the famine zone.[10]

In the novel, Wang and his family flee the drought districts by train, first purchasing rail tickets to do so with precious cash that could have been spent on food. Yet, in 1920, during the beginning months of famine, the hundreds of thousands of refugees fleeing south on the rail lines to the Yangzi, or north to Inner Mongolia or Manchuria, could do so for free on the state rail system, overseen and financed by the Ministry of Communications.[11]

Once amid the bounty of the South, Wang Lung's family buys congee with the little cash they beg, and work at "public kitchens" – institutions opened by the city's gentry and rich residents.[12] These public kitchens, variously called *gonggong shitang* or *pingmin shitang* in news reports at the time, existed in Chinese cities, where philanthropists sold subsidized food so that the modest earnings of laborers, peddlers and others among the working poor could be stretched that much further.[13] *Free* relief, however, has no place in Buck's story. As we have seen, soup kitchens (*zhouchang*), for the destitute to obtain small portions of porridge free of charge, existed as well, and in far greater overall number than public kitchens, especially in times of disaster. In major crises, soup kitchens might operate from late autumn through to spring, both in rural districts across the famine field, and in cities around the country for the resident poor and refugees.[14]

In the novel, Wang Lung and other refugees spend coppers on reed mats for constructing makeshift shelters along the walls and lanes of town.

---

[9] Pearl S. Buck, *The Good Earth* (Cleveland and New York: The World Publishing Company, 1947), 73, 86, 93.
[10] Fuller, *Famine Relief in Warlord China*, 153–56.   [11] Ibid., 177, 182–83.
[12] Buck, *The Good Earth*, 82, 84, 86.   [13] Fuller, *Famine Relief in Warlord China*, 96.
[14] Ibid., 54–60, 157–62, 179–80, 194.

This was a common practice of displaced Chinese as they waited out harsh or hostile conditions back at home. But then shelter systems existed as well, organized in various ways by a combination of authorities and charities in towns adjacent to and distant from disaster zones. Such systems might use temples, disused factories and the cavernous spaces of old mines to house families for the duration of a crisis, and included heating facilities fueled by donated coal to help destitute foragers survive the winter.[15]

Finally, when floods and locusts visit their compound in later years, the Wang family merely shut its gates to the starving outside. Throughout Buck's novel, the idea that households might organize or sponsor assistance to carry fellow villagers, let alone passing strangers, through crisis times is entertained by no one. Beyond the family, there is little sign of any social affinities or obligations that might resemble community. Yet, in fact, depending on time and place, village meetings were held in disaster districts to raise resources for the resident destitute, often with contributions that were scaled progressively on household land ownership and wherewithal. And, at times, local relief in both urban settings and in remote villages was initiated and overseen by individual households.[16]

So what is one to make of this? Although based on her experience living in China's North around 1920, *The Good Earth* in fact more closely resembles the region's experience of famine at the novel's release ten years later. From 1928 to 1930, North China, and in particular Inner Mongolia and the loess region of Gansu and Shaanxi, was struck by one of the deadliest famines of the modern age, one that would have been fresh in the minds of Western news readers at the time Buck's novel topped bestseller lists in 1931–1932.[17] Provincial governments and the new Guomindang regime had failed spectacularly to divert public attention and resources to relief from the numerous civil wars across the country in the late 1920s, from anti-imperialist efforts aimed at thwarting Japanese moves in Manchuria and from state-strengthening projects.

Yet nowhere does Buck's novel mention a regime, or a year. Only fleeting revolutionary fervor and the locomotive place the story vaguely in the early twentieth century. Only a single mention of Anhui province places it in a particular locale, somewhere in the country's northern reaches. Buck's achievements in portraying the worldview of a humble farmer, a man caught up in the swirl of events around him yet fixated on the soil throughout, both contributes to the story's power and at the same time conjures up a place in which the passage of events is immaterial.

[15] Ibid., 52–53, 100.　[16] Ibid., 103–5, 137–43.　[17] Conn, *Pearl S. Buck*, 123.

By presenting Chinese life in this way, by giving no clear anchor in time, *The Good Earth* gives the impression that it taps into China's essence. It relates that assistance to the poor is essentially trade based in Chinese society, an extension of everyday economic activity: No charitable impulse or initiative exists of any significance. Chinese communities are depicted as essentially lacking the social chemistry to organize: No civic sector exists, none of the layers of coordination and networking – village, district, regional, empire or nationwide – behind disaster mitigation.

Yet, in fact, the various interventions used by communities and officials to mitigate disaster required considerable planning and a good deal of logistical know-how: the setting up of grain discount centers in disaster districts, which involved, at the very least, the creation of public bonds or other types of fundraising; the procurement of grain from distant regions; the issuance of tax-free passports from the state for its transportation; the mobilization of carts from merchants and capable local families for the restocking of remote granaries; and the safeguarding of grain until families acquired a set amount, depending on stocks at the time of sale. Soup kitchens involved much of the same tasks, plus the canvassing of homes to determine levels of need and generating a system of ticketing for admittance – often performed by local gentry. A system of stamp duties and railway surcharges collected at stations across the network often lay behind free refugee travel, while shelters involved a creative series of ad-hoc property conversions. All of this took time, energy and resources, not to mention coordination within and between communities, many far flung.

Most importantly, in Buck's telling, Chinese life is less a function of circumstance, of fluctuations in investment, in initiative, in innovation – in short, the very dynamic of historical change – than it is of hard-wired cultural traits. In other words, if, like in her story, relief practices fail to materialize, it is not because of a social or political failure at any point in time (and there are countless instances of relief failures in Chinese history), but because of a cultural impossibility to conjure up the very idea, and deliver on it. Just as in the text *Sociology and Social Issues*, the only indigenous force standing between life and death for a rural Chinese family was the "small, imperturbable god" in the village "temple of the earth," which Wang visited amid extreme drought to spit and gnash his teeth at.[18]

In short, Buck's great achievement with *The Good Earth* is that the ugliness that did exist at times in Chinese communities – infanticide, human trafficking, hoarding and predatory lending, cannibalism and

---

[18] Buck, *The Good Earth*, 68; see also 191.

other depraved acts of desperation – appears in her work in a most sympathetic family portrait that somehow humanizes and demystifies elements of the Chinese experience. At the same time, however, her work shared a key literary element of the missionary culture in which she grew up: the invisibility of indigenous civic practices and institutions and the most rudimentary of relief intervention strategies. *The Good Earth* advanced this invisibility into the 1930s and, no less, to a global audience, quickly selling in more than two million copies and converted into a film seen by some sixty-five million people around the world.[19] Crucially, though, the story left out a second key element of missionary literature: the indispensability of the Christian program to China's condition. Instead, it left China's ills open to other remedies. For this, Buck's work transcended Christian literature, while earning the ire of former colleagues in the global missionary movement.

The Peasantry Emerges

In 1938, the Nobel committee awarded Buck the Nobel Prize in Literature, citing "her rich and truly epic descriptions of peasant life in China."[20] Crucially, nowhere in *The Good Earth* does the term peasant appear. To Buck, her protagonist was a farmer, an earnest if quaint "country bumpkin" to those around him.[21] The Nobel committee merely used a term for Buck's work that had become part of the standard discourse in references to rural China over the intervening years since the novel's appearance. The peasant framework with which to understand China was, by the 1930s, fast becoming commonplace, shared across the political spectrum, both within the country and overseas.

As Buck's case shows, a writer did not have to embrace any particular politics or school of thought to compose narratives of rural China as an arena of peasants, at once socially primitive and timeless – narratives that shared, in other words, the qualities of revolutionary memory. (Whether or not Buck consciously wrote these social qualities into her descriptions, she had evidently internalized them. Five years after the novel's publication, Buck contributed an introduction to Lin Yutang's book-length study *My Country and My People*, of which the sixth chapter, "Social and Political Life," opens with a section on the "Absence of the Social Mind." In it, Lin, a Harvard-trained graduate of the University of Leipzig and one of the foremost writers of his generation on Chinese subjects in English, explains that "'public spirit' is a new term, so is 'civic

---

[19] Isaacs, *Scratches on Our Minds*, 156.   [20] Frenz, *Literature, 1901–1967*, 560.
[21] Buck, *The Good Earth*, 145.

consciousness,' and so is 'social service.' There are no such commodities in China."[22] "It is, I think, the truest, the most profound, the most complete, the most important book yet written about China," Buck commented.[23]) Since the May Fourth movement was sparked a dozen years earlier, student dispatches from the earthquake and famine field and schoolbooks issued by the country's commercial and political presses served, as we have seen, to deinscribe the textual presence of China's rural social and cultural authorities, and to thereby undermine their actual and symbolic power. In spite of its sympathetic portrayals, Buck's *Good Earth* joined in diagnosing the shortcomings of Chinese public life by overlooking a range of its existing institutions.

As Buck's work grew in stature over the course of the 1930s, revolutionary discourse would impose new symbols and subjects for the construction of a new political order. If rural networks had no capacity for mutual aid or civic life, now, from this diagnosis was posited an agent of change: the revolutionary party. "The peasantry's inferior position is due to an ignorance of how to work together," *Sociology and Social Issues* explained. "Because they don't know how to work together, there is nothing to arouse social awareness."[24] "By 1935, a [Guomindang] government publication would baldly state that the work of rural reconstruction boiled down to improving 'rural organization,'" Kate Merkel-Hess notes in her study of rural modernization in the republic, and "some reformers adopted a term for their efforts to use village social life to mobilize and order rural people: 'social education' (*shehui jiaoyu*)."[25]

Nation building of course broadened the field of political and labor actors, and did so in the service of productive and fiscal goals across both capitalist and communist systems. This brought marginalized sections of society – women, the young, the poor, ethnic minorities – into the fold of the national project and destiny. Estimating and harnessing human and material resources on such a scale required the standardization of nearly every aspect of life: from measurements and workers' habits for mechanized manufacturing to dialects, customs and gender roles for developing a coherent citizenry, and the homogenization of farming practices and land husbandry for the purposes of resource extraction and centralized economic planning. Similarly, national political programs involved the flattening of social complexity into the "legibility" required by state and corporate planners and strategists, to use James C. Scott's term.[26] Among these constructions was the party-led peasantry, one somehow at the

[22] Lin Yutang, *My Country and My People* (London: W. Heinemann, 1939), 164.
[23] Pearl S. Buck, introduction to *My Country and My People*, by Lin Yutang, xii.
[24] Mao Qijun, *Shehui xue ji shehui wenti*, 223.   [25] Merkel-Hess, *Rural Modern*, 80.
[26] On this modern phenomenon globally, see Scott, *Seeing Like a State*, 87–102, 181–92.

same time both politically explosive and passive – both revolutionary subject and victim.

The twentieth-century appearance in Chinese political language of the peasant – agriculturalists as a social group or class (*nongmin*) as opposed to an individual who chooses for a variety of reasons to cultivate the land (*nongfu*, *nongren* or *nongding*) – was no minor semantic development. For one, its introduction helped drive the creation of two distinct political fields in China, the urban and the rural, with which the modern state would manage economic activity and set controls on mobility – despite the existence of a fluid relationship in matters of social relations and trade and governance between city and countryside in Chinese history to that point.[27] In this way, modern Chinese political thought projected feudal economic structures onto China's past, conditioning society over time, for the neofeudal controls on production and population movement of the state-strengthening project. These controls would peak in the People's Republic but had clear ideological foundations earlier in the twentieth century.

When Guomindang publications invoked popular experience of disaster, it was with broad brushstrokes and with social mobilization and other state goals in mind. Party publishing left more empirical study of China's ecological crises to foreign investigators such as Walter H. Mallory, a foreign-relief administrator in 1920–21 whose *China: Land of Famine* was issued in Chinese by the party's Popular Wisdom Book Company three years after its publication by the American Geographical Society in 1926.[28] Instead, disaster narratives favored generalization, serving as stark examples of social ills to be targeted for party interventions: village inertia and social predation.

Conclusion

Buck's work appeared at a time when Chinese literature came to share many of the aims and practices of the social survey movement, which had exploded in size in the preceding few years. "Between 1917 and 1927 only 80 social surveys had been published, but between 1927 and 1935 social surveys were so in vogue that 9,000 projects were completed in different parts of China," notes Tao Tao Liu, with rural surveys outnumbering urban ones after 1932. "The vogue for social science rubbed off on the writers of literature, who had just as strong a desire for national salvation,

---

[27] On this, see Cohen, "Cultural and Political Inventions in Modern China."
[28] Walter H. Mallory, *Jihuang de Zhongguo* (Shanghai: Minzhi shuju, 1929); Walter H. Mallory, *China: Land of Famine* (New York: American Geographical Society, 1926).

and who were influenced by the language and style of social surveys and the 'scientific' dissection of social phenomena."[29]

Somewhere in between social scientists and fiction writers were historians seeking to piece together the story of the still-emerging Chinese nation. Among them, "two [rival] master narratives shaped the representations of Chinese history in the late Qing and Republican period," Huaiyin Li writes: a modernization narrative, which positioned the country as "backward," and a revolutionary narrative, which positioned it moving from "late feudalism" to capitalism.[30] Both were predicated on the existence of a peasantry.

Arguably the most prominent academic writing on Chinese rural life at the time was the young sociologist Fei Xiaotong, who embarked on his first major fieldwork project in Guangxi in 1935, followed by research in 1936 in Kaixianggong village in his native county of Wujiang, Jiangsu. Trained under the anthropologists Sergei Mikhailovich Shirokogoroff at Qinghua University and Bronislaw Malinowski at the London School of Economics, Fei too was interested in rural life and culture, but was critical of social surveys for their general reliance on inexperienced assistants for data collection and the often-detached relationship scholars had to their subject areas, devising their questionnaires and responses from afar. Nor did he reference historical records like local gazetteers in his work, which to him offered only elite perspectives. Instead, Fei developed what he termed community studies (*shequ yanjiu*), spending close to two months conducting the Kaixianggong fieldwork, which resulted in an English-language book, *Peasant Life in China*, that at its publication in 1939 made him a global "pioneer in the application of anthropological field techniques to complex societies," notes biographer David Arkush.[31] Other English-language works in the field of Chinese community studies followed, such as Martin C. Yang's *A Chinese Village: Taitou, Shantung Province*, which Yang completed in 1945 after conducting research of his home village under the supervision of an anthropologist at Columbia University.[32]

But there were limits to Fei's influence and that of the field of community studies he had initiated. His non-Marxist, functionalist approach had

---

[29] Liu Tao Tao, "Perceptions of City and Country in Modern Chinese Fiction in the Early Republican Era," in David Faure and Liu Tao Tao, eds., *Town and Country in China: Identity and Perception* (Basingstoke, UK: Palgrave, 2002), 220.

[30] Huaiyin Li, *Reinventing Modern China: Imagination and Authenticity in Chinese Historical Writing* (Honolulu: University of Hawai'i Press, 2013), 14.

[31] David R. Arkush, *Fei Xiaotong and Sociology in Revolutionary China* (Cambridge, MA: Council on East Asian Studies, Harvard University Press, 1981), 93; see also 58, 85, 92.

[32] Martin C. Yang, *A Chinese Village: Taitou, Shantung Province* (London: Kegan Paul, Trench, Trubner & Co, 1947).

not involved class conflict in its analysis of rural society, which placed him against the political and intellectual currents of the time. "Except for a very preliminary series of articles in the *Yi-shi bao* in 1936," Arkush notes, the approach taken in *Peasant Life in China* would be better known in the Anglophone and Japanese worlds, appearing in Chinese versions only toward the end of the twentieth century.[33] In the 1930s, "a tiny minority" was "interested in this kind of research in China," Arkush adds.[34]

It was not until the eve of Communist victory that Fei's work captured a sizable Chinese readership. And by that time his approach had taken a more accessible style, one that spoke in more general and conceptual terms than his earlier empirical studies of village life. *Xiangtu Zhongguo* (issued later as a book entitled *From the Soil: The Foundations of Chinese Society*) was serialized in a Shanghai journal in 1947 and 1948 and then quickly sold out as a book in a series of reprints from April 1948 until January 1949.[35]

Significantly, Fei, too, sought to identify essential differences in social organization between China and Western or modern societies. To him, "the Chinese system of organization" was egocentric, best visualized as a "pattern of discrete circles" emanating from each person – what he termed the *chaxugeju*, translated somewhat awkwardly as the "differential mode of association." No matter how far one's network reached – to the community, the nation, all of humanity – "one's self is still at the center."[36] This stood in contrast to what Fei saw as the organizational makeup of Western societies based on clearly defined boundaries and membership. Here, Fei provocatively cast Chinese as more individualist than their Western counterparts. In this respect, Fei's pioneering contributions to the study of Chinese life shared both the dualist frameworks of much Western sociologist work to that point and the calls to reform the "selfishness" of Chinese and country folk, in particular, that had been driving rural reconstruction efforts since the 1920s.

But then, as important as the growth of the social sciences was – in the form of social canvassing and analysis, and anthropological or sociological fieldwork – its influence on the general population of China was limited. Crucially, the growth of the social sciences over the 1930s and 1940s coincided with a coming together of journalism with literature and art in the pursuit of similar goals: namely, truth claims about social life.

[33] Arkush, *Fei Xiaotong and Sociology in Revolutionary China*, 89.   [34] Ibid., 59.
[35] Ibid., 141.
[36] Fei Xiaotong, *From the Soil: The Foundations of Chinese Society* [*Xiangtu Zhongguo*], trans. Gary G. Hamilton and Wang Zheng (Berkeley: University of California Press, 1992), 67.

This was most evidently marked by the formal adoption of reportage in China after the genre's appearance in German Communist circles over the 1920s. "Reportage authors attempt to make actual historical experience *meaningful*," Charles A. Laughlin writes, "to rescue the truth of actual events from the hollowing, reifying effects of journalistic objectivity." Although Laughlin traces the roots of Chinese reportage back to late Qing travel writing, only in the 1930s, he writes, did the "socially effective literature" advocated earlier by Liang Qichao at the turn of the century come into being with its attention to "the broader, collective experience of contemporary social life."[37]

The shaping of popular ideas involved the incorporation of popular art forms into political work and the adoption and development of new artistic genres and techniques such as the woodcut (*muke*), an increasingly prominent genre in the representation of social life. Woodcut artists joined writers of fiction and reportage in this broader creative shift toward revelatory art, one that sprang from a moment of epistemological ferment, or what Xiaobing Tang, in his study of the woodcut movement, calls a "grave discourse on truthfully representing social and historical reality."[38] Fundamental to this cultural movement, Tang explains, was the verb *biaoxian*:

Literally meaning "to bring to the surface" or "to externalize and manifest," *biaoxian*, during this period [c. 1930], was often used to mean "to express" and "to represent." When followed by the terms for "social life" or "Zeitgeist," the verb described the act of representing or manifesting social reality or the truth about the current age [. . . ;] for a writer or artist to represent or express social life artistically as well as truthfully, he or she could not be satisfied with representing what there was to see, but rather had to demonstrate how social life should be seen. Indicating more than a mechanical and naturalistic "reflection" or "depiction," *biaoxian* acknowledged the necessity of unifying subjective understanding and objective truth, which in turn translated into a determination to render reality through a revelatory artistic vision.[39]

In the next chapter we chart the emergence of visual art forms and their exchange at market squares in the interior over the 1940s, bringing revolutionary memory to bear on social interaction in the countryside. From 1935, national woodcut exhibitions broadened interest in the form beyond an initial circle of printmakers, while traveling exhibitions and dedicated newspaper supplements created networks and exposure for the movement in major cities along the country's

---

[37] Laughlin, *Chinese Reportage*, 9–10; emphasis added.
[38] Xiaobing Tang, *Origins of the Chinese Avant-Garde: The Modern Woodcut Movement* (Berkeley and Los Angeles: University of California Press, 2008), 217.
[39] Ibid.

coast.[40] Before long, however, the Japanese seizure of Shanghai in 1937 flushed the woodcut movement's first generation from the cosmopolitan center to inland cities such as Hankou and Chongqing, and eventually to Communist base areas in the deep interior – an area of cultural work to which we next turn.[41]

[40] Ibid., 173, 196.   [41] Ibid., 210.

7   Woodcuts and Forsaken Subjects

At the turn of the 1930s, the author and critic Lu Xun had been actively exploring expressive forms beyond the written word, among them the comic and the woodcut, appreciative of their potential for mass accessibility and appeal.[1] While the cartoon was conveyed to the reading public in newspapers and magazines, the woodcut would eventually reach well into the largely illiterate countryside, adorning the gates of village compounds and changing hands at temple fairs. Bold black-and-white graphics reminiscent of woodblock prints had been characteristic of certain Chinese publications of the 1920s. But the woodcut form did not fully take hold in China's avant-garde artistic circles until Lu Xun, a towering figure in the literary world, promoted foreign woodcuts among local Chinese artists in 1929.[2] While resident in Shanghai, he had worked with local publishers to reproduce Japanese and Soviet studies and criticism of modern art, with a particular interest in the use of graphic art to capture human experience amid the emerging industrial cityscapes of the modern world.[3] The graphic power and political potency of the woodcut form had arguably come of age with Belgian artist Frans Masereel's 1918 work *The Passion of One Man*, a series of prints fleshing out the travails of a labor activist in Europe, which Lu Xun would introduce to a Chinese readership in a magazine in 1932.[4] A year later, Chinese presses were producing black-and-white print volumes by the thousands, and the form was fast becoming, in the words of Xiaobing Tang, a "cosmopolitan visual art that best captured the raw forces and fantasies of the modern age."[5] But its exchange soon moved beyond urban settings, bringing modern techniques to folk art and becoming "an easily recognizable

---

[1] Mittler, *A Continuous Revolution*, 363.
[2] Xiaobing Tang, *Origins of the Chinese Avant-Garde*, 99.
[3] Elizabeth Emrich, "Modernity through Experimentation: Lu Xun and the Modern Chinese Woodcut Movement," in Pei-Yin Lin and Weipin Tsai, eds., *Print, Profit, and Perception: Ideas, Information and Knowledge in Chinese Societies, 1895–1949* (Leiden: Brill, 2014), 71.
[4] Xiaobing Tang, *Origins of the Chinese Avant-Garde*, 146.   [5] Ibid., 148; see also 147.

visual vocabulary for the general populace," in the words of Elizabeth Emrich.[6] Constituting "the most consequential art movement in modern China," Tang writes, the woodcut's accessibility across cultural and class lines made it the "visual Esperanto of the modern age."[7]

The rise of the woodcut coincided with a concerted shift in goals set by members of China's literary and artistic worlds. At the end of the 1920s, with the violent break of the Guomindang-Communist alliance, Chinese art took on heightened urgency, one that led to a conscious sense of mission behind a range of cultural forms. Leftist intellectuals closed ranks behind a tighter political program in the wake of Guomindang suppression in 1927, which was swiftly followed by more aggressive moves by Japan on Chinese territory. The 1928 assassination of Zhang Zuolin, the main power holder in Manchuria, was followed by Japanese invasion of his former domains three years later and fighting between Chinese and Japanese forces in Shanghai in 1932, stoking patriotism and fear over China's survival as a nation. Amid this climate, and following directives from the leadership of the Chinese Communist Party, the League of Left-Wing Writers was formed in Shanghai in late winter 1930 out of two literary groups, together with the circle of young artists around Lu Xun.[8] Out of these circles arose much of the artistic talent and political energy that was combined in the emerging medium of the Chinese woodcut.

In this striking visual form, one can observe a narrative subject integral to revolutionary memory: if revolutionary memory is a form of overarching metanarrative joining the past to the present, something that I call *forsaken subjects* populate its landscapes. In the woodcut form, forsaken subjects personified the popular experience of what became known as the old society. They inhabited a social space of predatory relations, one marked by a vacuum of civic values and impervious to change, and so backward and "feudal." In some cases, the revolutionary memory conveyed through woodcut narratives disembedded relationships from clear historical time lines or community settings, conferring on them a timeless quality; in others, these relationships were planted squarely in time or in village scenes, but ones devoid of beneficial social ties or institutions or recourse in times of need. What remained of human interaction was violent in nature – predatory or vengeful – reducing communal relations

---

[6] Emrich, "Modernity through Experimentation," 73.
[7] Xiaobing Tang, *Origins of the Chinese Avant-Garde*, 1, 218.
[8] Lawrence Wang-chi Wong, "A Literary Organization with a Clear Political Agenda: The Chinese League of Left-Wing Writers, 1930–1936," in Kirk A. Denton and Michel Hockx, eds., *Literary Societies of Republican China* (Lanham, MD: Lexington Books, 2008), 313, 316.

in the past to a severely limited range of possibilities. Over the course of war with Japan and its aftermath of civil war, the woodcut would evolve from such portrayals of social desolation – of moral impasse and cultural failures – to affirmative messaging by the end of the 1940s, which assigned new codes, values and frames of reference to the workings of daily life.

Woodcuts: Imagining the Marginalized

The woodcut movement cut its teeth with depictions of humanity set in industrializing scenes. But it soon followed the mid-1930s reorientation that scholarship and theorists undertook – from generalized debate on the overall nature and history of Chinese society, favored in the first few years of the Nanjing Decade, to a focus on the rural by 1935.[9] Woodcut representations of the downtrodden and calamity generally followed a similar time line.

From the late 1920s to the mid-1930s, the Chinese woodcut appeared in left-leaning magazines, special issues of art journals and exhibitions, demonstrating a keen sensitivity to the suffering and travails of ordinary folk. In this first phase, which is the focus of Xiaobing Tang's study, woodcuts presented the underclass in mostly urban landscapes, struggling amid the architectural and technological signs of modernity in places like Guangzhou, or in ambiguous surroundings in which the jobless languished, wasting away – leaning against a wagon for support in Hu Yichuan's early piece *The Hungry* from 1931, for example, or collapsed on the ground in Wozha's *Drought* from circa 1935.[10] Several series of woodcuts offered narratives of social ills, political awakening and action, such as Zheng Yefu's *Flood* from 1933 and Lai Shaoqi's *Unemployment* from 1935.[11] Li Ping's *Laborers* from 1936 depicted a couple with the woman holding a child's hand and the man beside her looking back, off frame, holding up a giant, sinewy fist in defiance.[12] Such works captured, in their raw simplicity, the spirit of an emerging proletariat.

At this pivotal point for modern China, on the eve of the total war brought on by Japan's 1937 invasion of Beijing and much of the country, we might revisit our imagined reader, Meiqing, whose education over the course of the 1920s and early 1930s we tracked in Chapter 4. In this way we might more easily picture the way the woodcut intersected with other art forms and might have spoken to an educated member of her

[9] Xiaorong Han, *Chinese Discourses*, 75.
[10] Xiaobing Tang, *Origins of the Chinese Avant-Garde*, 105, 158. English titles for these works are from Tang's text.
[11] Ibid., 147, 191.   [12] *Shenghuo manhua*, vol. 2 (May 1936), 34.

generation. Meiqing would have been twenty-five years old and perhaps a few years into her first full-time job as a middle-school teacher in, say, the Shanxi border town of Datong. That same year of 1936, the volume *Zhongguo de yi ri* (One Day in China) was released, a literary project led by Mao Dun and the Literature Society based on an idea introduced by the Russian writer Maxim Gorky two years earlier "at the First Congress of Soviet Writers (the same conference in which he coined the term 'socialist realism') as a device for stimulating collective writing."[13] In Meiqing's copy of *One Day in China*, perhaps borrowed from a library in town to show her students in class, she would have found a panoramic woodcut reproduced in the inside front and back covers entitled *A Record of Major National Events* by Tang Yingwei, the editor of a cartoon monthly magazine. The work consists of a chaotic spread of overlapping vignettes depicting political demonstrators, scuffles and arrests in city streets and Japanese forces engaging with Guomindang troops at the Great Wall. Its great detail includes a man rushing between the scenes holding a banner scrawled with the words "Dispense porridge [*shizhou*]." Elsewhere, a second man gazes at the viewer beneath a banner reading "Lingshan disaster relief [Lingshan *zhenzai*]" as people collapse to the earth around him.[14]

Who knows what a person of Meiqing's profile would have made of these prominent details. Her understanding of the experience of disaster and responses to it over the intervening years would have been mediated, in part, by the news dailies and weekly journals in the library of her teacher's college or subscribed to and shared among her colleagues. When she was a child, these articles had expressed the diverse range of voices and social circles of Chinese republican society. Maybe in her formative teenage years she had been a reader of the major Tianjin newspaper *Da gongbao* and its various editions, which had followed the greatest famine of the Guomindang period – the North and Northwest famine of 1928–30 – with impassioned coverage. Or maybe she had read Shanghai's established daily *Shenbao* instead, which had practically ignored the famine.[15] More recently, since the rise of the Guomindang, news outlets had shrunk in number and news coverage narrowed in scope, in line with Sun Yat-sen's Three Principles and other official party

[13] Sherman Cochran and Andrew C. K. Hsieh with Janis Cochran, eds. and trans., *One Day in China: May 21, 1936* (New Haven, CT: Yale University Press, 1983), xiv. Originally published as *Zhongguo de yi ri*.
[14] Xiaobing Tang, *Origins of the Chinese Avant-Garde*, 179, 200 and plate 9.
[15] For an insightful discussion of this contrast, see Andrea Janku, "From Natural to National Disaster: The Chinese Famine of 1928–1930," in Andrea Janku, Gerrit J. Schenk and Franz Mauelshagen, eds., *Historical Disasters in Context: Science, Religion and Politics* (New York: Routledge, 2012), 227–60.

doctrine generally and the framing of events in terms of anti-imperialism and national salvation. Disaster coverage was losing out to conversations over nation building and fighting the Japanese since their establishment of Manchukuo out of China's three northeastern provinces in 1932.

More fundamentally, the way Meiqing approached her reading of events was likely shaped, in part, by the homework and classroom conversations she had been immersed in since primary school. The issues of *Shaonian zazhi* (Youth Magazine) given to her by her father at the time of the Gansu earthquake and northern famine of 1920–21, had, as we have seen, mentioned nothing of anyone helping anyone within China's afflicted communities over that year. Nor was it likely that her middle school or university civics texts had mentioned anything of rural capacities for mutual aid, nor her readers produced by the Guomindang publishing house. In her teachers college library, the few books devoted to the study of modern Chinese disasters would likely have been Mallory's *China: Land of Famine*, or reports issued by international relief societies in Chinese and English versions, and printed by the Commercial Press.[16] And so when Mao Dun's *One Day in China* prominently displayed a woodcut with calls for effective relief, there was little evidence of such relief offered in Meiqing's generation's education. The idea of effective relief measures appeared modern, its study appeared to be the preserve of foreign figures such as Mallory, and it was increasingly associated with the political currents of nationalism and socialism.

As for the artist, it is uncertain what he had in mind when depicting explicit demands for relief measures in this monumental work. A leading voice at the time for the Modern Prints Society, it made sense, though, that he contributed to Mao Dun's project. In the society's journal a year earlier, Tang had called on his peers in the woodcut industry to "represent the complex formations of human society" through which the viewing public could "experience a shock more distinct and more poignant than from real life."[17] "It is only appropriate," he also wrote, "for us to use woodcuts as a tool to awaken the national consciousness of the people of the country."[18]

---

[16] For example, Beijing guoji tongyi jiuzai zonghui, *Beijing guoji tongyi jiuzai zonghui baogao shu* (Beijing: Beijing guoji tongyi jiuzai zonghui, 1922); Dwight W. Edwards, ed., *The North China Famine of 1920–1921, with Special Reference to the West Chihli Area: Being the Report of the Peking United International Famine Relief Committee* (Beijing: Peking United International Famine Relief Committee, 1922).

[17] Quoted in Xiaobing Tang, *Origins of the Chinese Avant-Garde*, 188.

[18] Quoted in ibid., 197.

Social Desolation: Deinscription in Prints

Throughout the 1930s – a decade of unfolding disasters and economic crisis, Japanese aggression and the buildup toward all-out war – woodcuts increasingly reflected a society in heightened despair and disarray. This period would see a shift in the form's focus from the social dislocation brought by war, to a state of social destitution more generally: human relations reduced to the struggle for self-preservation.

This second phase of the movement, from the mid-1930s to the mid-1940s, is evident in a major bilingual compilation of works published by the Chinese Woodcutters' Association in the aftermath of the war with Japan. The volume, dedicated to Lu Xun ten years after the writer's death in 1936, includes Li Hua's *Fleeing Refugees*, in which an older woman with three children in tow walks amid ruins, and, ahead, a man in Western dress is carried in a sedan chair; Sha Qingquan's *Calamity*, a portrait of a farmer looking to the sky as locusts devour the stalks around him; Cai Pozhi's *Refugees Flocking to Kweilin Station*, which depicts a great mass of people hoisting children and bundles of belongings onto the roof of a train; Mai Gan's *Starvation*, a depiction of a jumble of contorted bodies, big and small, mashed up against a wall, gripping empty buckets and pans; and Ge Kejian's *Refugees*, which presents a dark, shadowed close-up of five sullen adults.[19]

Shared by multiple works over the course of the war was the potent symbol of the empty bowl held up in desperate appeals. To whom these appeals were made is often left to the imagination: relief workers and passersby? Wider society? Humanity at large? The heavens? It is noteworthy that for the cover image of its wartime volume, the Woodcutters' Association selected Yang Newei's *Refugee Children*, a print of four ragged, emaciated children holding empty pans. Back in 1936, on the eve of all-out war, similar woodcuts by Zhang Wang had appeared in Shanghai's *Shenghuo manhua* (Life Cartoons): *Image of a Starving Child*, a close-up of a boy's face, holding an empty bowl to a person off frame,[20] and *Panic*, a shadowy close-up of two parents with a child and baby, the child clutching chopsticks as the father holds up an empty bowl.[21]

Depictions of cannibalism presented the most desperate depths of deprivation. Such imagery had precedent in Chinese artistic commentary in times of famine – for example, in the series of woodblock prints

---

[19] Zhonghua quanguo muke xiehui, ed., *Kangzhan ba nian muke xuanji*, or *Woodcuts of War-Time China, 1937–1945* (Shanghai: Kaiming shudian, 1946), 4, 10, 26, 52, 94. English translations of the works are provided by the source.
[20] *Shenghuo manhua*, vol. 2 (May 1936), 42.
[21] *Shenghuo manhua*, vol. 3 (June 1936), 36.

commissioned to draw attention to the plight of famine victims in North China during the 1870s.[22] Again, amid total war with Japan and civil war, woodcut depictions of cannibalism captured the utter social devastation of the period. In 1936, *Shenghuo manhua* had printed *Cooking a Son*, a cartoon by Chen Huiling depicting a skeletal couple, the man with tears streaming down his face, the woman covering hers with her hands, with between them a boy's body cooking in a steaming pot.[23] By the early 1940s, well-known woodcut artists also addressed the grisly subject, including Ren Feng, whose *The Market of Human Meat* showed shadowy figures appearing to be making transactions in a barren landscape of ruined structures and bare trees,[24] and Liu Xian, whose *Fighting to Eat* from 1947 pictured a group of adults and children on a hillside hunched over a butchered human corpse, chewing on its entrails, with a lone bare tree in the distance.[25]

Stripped trees in arid, almost lunar landscapes reflected the extreme measures residents took in times of crisis, foraging for tree bark, leaves and other famine foods. But these sparse trees also marked the general ecological degradation of large sections of North China's denuded and overworked terrain, a condition further exacerbated in times of drought, flood or war. Woodcuts captured human effort to overcome such circumstances, perhaps most powerfully Gu Yuan's depiction of seven men, their bodies nearly horizontal, tugging together at a rope from a well under a blazing sun in *Struggle against Famine and Drought* from 1945.[26]

But by the end of the war with Japan, prominent woodcut artists evoked a second, equally grave condition: the nearly complete loss of anything resembling community. An early example of this sense of desolation is Luo Gongliu's *Disaster Victims*, a small woodcut that appeared in an issue of the magazine *Qingnian liangyou* (Companion Pictorial) in 1941. In it, two women huddle in front of a bare horizon, one holding an infant to her chest, the other crouched beside a child, her head buried in her hands.[27] Gu Yuan's *Starvation* from 1943 offers a similar scene of mother and child in a denuded landscape, though here they are near to a dead body that is gathering the attention of crows (see Figure 3). Similarly, *Starved to Death*, a scene cut four years later by Liu Xian, presents a woman, child and infant together standing

[22] Edgerton-Tarpley, *Tears from Iron*, 218–20.
[23] *Shenghuo manhua*, vol. 2 (May 1936), 36.
[24] Wang Renfeng, *Ren Feng muke ji* (Shanghai: Kaiming shudian, 1948), 30.
[25] Liu Xian, *Liu Xian muke xuanji* (Beijing: Xinhua shudian, 1984), 79.
[26] Xin yishu she, ed., *Muke xuanji* (N.p.: Lianhe shudian, 1946). English title from the original.
[27] *Qingnian liangyou*, vol. 2, no. 6–7 (1941), 32. English name of periodical appears on the cover of the source.

Figure 3 Gu Yuan, *Starvation*, 1943. Peter Townsend Collection, National Gallery of Australia. Used with permission.

before a sun-beaten horizon dotted with stripped trees and huddled and collapsed bodies.[28]

This pervasive sense of social desolation, however, is most palpable in *Renmin de shounan* (The Afflictions of the People), a series of thirteen pieces cut by Ren Feng in the early 1940s based on the suffering of farmers (which he had witnessed) hit by major flooding of the Huai River and other effects of the war in Anhui and elsewhere. In *He's Given Up All Hope*, a man steps over a body in an open field while gazing at the horizon, a limp child in his arms, trailed by a skeletal dog. In *Who Can Save Them?*, a mass of bodies, mouths agape, are swallowed in rising waters, from which an arm reaches for the heavens. And in *Is This Destiny?*, a ghostly, half-clothed skeleton hovers in the air over a huddle of languishing and emaciated bodies, its bony arm reaching down to snatch a child from its parent's arms.[29]

---

[28] Liu Xian, *Liu Xian muke xuanji*, 78.
[29] Wang Renfeng, *Ren Feng muke ji*, 21, 20, 25.

As Ren Feng explained in a compilation of his work published after the war, the question Is this destiny? (*zhe shi mingyun ma?*) had come to him as his eyes met those of a group of disaster victims in Anhui who were huddled by the ruins of a bombed-out temple, apparently breathing their last – a vision that remained with him. Detailing faces of dread with exceptionally intricate line work, his prints captured the intensity of despair created by year after year of total war. But this driving question behind Ren Feng's series, of a people left to the dictates of fate, could have just as easily been asked by Pearl Buck, who lived and wrote about life on the same section of the North China plain thirty years earlier. Or by the earthquake and famine investigators of the May Fourth era: as mountains crumbled and drought hit, as flood waters rose or soldiers pillaged, where were gentry or neighbors of means in times of need? Nowhere to be found. By the late 1940s, there was hardly much at all in the cultural memory of the emerging nation – in elite and popular art, in educational texts, in media commentary on society and civil strife – that said otherwise.

After attending an exhibition of Ren Feng's work in 1945, the author Mao Dun noted that *The Afflictions of the People* gave a resounding response to the question that came to his mind as he viewed the artist's work: "Is it possible for the people to forever have the wool pulled over their eyes [*bei qipian*], to forever be enslaved [*bei nuyi*]? No way!" In his 1945 postscript to Ren Feng's volume, Mao, soon to serve as the People's Republic's first minister of culture from 1949 to 1965, added that "the purgatory of afflictions [*shounan de lianyu*] the people face" in Ren Feng's work "will forge their combat skills, and incite their yearning for liberation."[30]

Assigning New Values: Reinscription in Prints

Depictions of the struggle for subsistence intensified in tone as war with Japan climaxed in the 1940s, heralding a third phase of the woodcut movement, one charged with fierce social conflict between clearly defined class positions. In other words, while woodcut negations of rural culture over the course of the war with Japan served to reinforce intellectual trends underway since May Fourth, it was not until the latter half of the 1940s that the form would clearly take up affirmative, explicitly political messaging. This began with anti-Guomindang imagery, and swiftly moved into depictions of class positions and Chinese Communist Party policies such as land reform.

---

[30] Mao Dun, "Kanle Wang Renfeng de zuopin zhan," signed "last day in 1945," in Wang Renfeng, *Ren Feng muke ji*.

With the resumption of civil war following Japan's defeat, Guomindang control or outright seizure of food supplies became a pronounced wood-cut theme. During the war with Japan, state welfare provisioning had already been the subject of satirical pieces, such as Ren Feng's *Relief*, which shows old women and children collecting gruel from the steaming vat of a military relief station as a bespectacled, smug officer looks on, seated on a wicker chair.[31] After Japan's surrender, though, the Chinese military became the scourge in woodcut scenes. Guomindang soldiers walk out of a home tugging a goat and carrying baskets of grain in Li Hua's *After the Grain-Tax Is Taken* from 1946, leaving behind a woman and an old man with empty baskets, and a pleading child. Li's *Refusal of Grain* from the following year shows a barefoot body collapsed at the feet of a suited man and soldier standing beside overflowing baskets of grain as a mob stirs in the distance. In Li's *The Starving Line Up* from 1948, a soldier in silhouette looks on as a woman with a wailing child clutching her chest holds out an empty bowl.[32]

Accompanying these more targeted depictions of the Guomindang were general images of hunger and the struggle to survive. For example, Yan Han's *The Struggle for Foods* (1943 or 1944) depicts men attacking a vigorously defended grain cart;[33] Zhao Yannian's *Scramble for Rice* (1947) depicts a crowd storming a grain shop;[34] and Ke Tian's *Hunger*, which appeared in a Chinese Woodcutters' Association volume from 1948, depicts a cluster of anguished adults, and a stooped man in front, clutching a bowl and grimacing at something off frame.[35] In such ways, the powerful image of the outstretched empty vessel resonated into the civil war period.

This brings us to the question of audience, and how this new world of images was brought to the public. An art form originating in China's avant-garde circles would not necessarily speak to the general rural popu-lation without considerable effort and modification. As early as 1936, the Modern Prints Society had held successful woodcut shows attended by thousands in the countryside around Guangzhou.[36] But reaching and resonating with residents of more remote and culturally isolated sections of the country posed a considerable challenge, especially during the struggle against Japan.

---

[31] Wang Renfeng, *Ren Feng muke ji*, 23.
[32] Li Hua, *Li Hua muke xuanji* (Beijing: Xinhua shudian, 1958), 17, 21, 41.
[33] Xin yishu she, ed., *Muke xuanji*.
[34] Zhonghua quanguo muke xiehui, ed., *Zhongguo banhua ji* (Shanghai: Chenguang chuban gongsi, 1948), 97. English title from the original.
[35] Ibid., 64.   [36] Xiaobing Tang, *Origins of the Chinese Avant-Garde*, 191.

In 1938, the Jiangsu native Yan Han moved to northern Shaanxi, where he studied woodcut techniques for three months at Yan'an's Lu Xun Academy before forming a woodcut troupe with colleagues. Four years followed with the Eighth Route Army in southeastern Shanxi and later further afield in northern and western China where the troupe was tasked with galvanizing residents into resisting the Japanese. There in the interior, the artists discovered that the woodcuts they carried from recent national exhibitions were readily rejected by the population, especially the use of light in their Western samples. Locals particularly disliked the designs incised into the cuts to capture tonal changes, dismissing the works as overdone "'yin-yang faces'."[37] Residents in the interior advised sojourning artists "that it was not necessary to render everything one could see," Yan Geng explains, "and preferred the single outlines of folk art," encouraging them to minimize line cuts and clarify the definition of shadowy faces and other elements.[38]

Adding urgency to the troupe's mission was the Japanese enemy's success in marrying political symbolism with folk-art forms, such as agricultural calendars and *manhua* cartoon posters in various sizes – in one case, reworking a Buddhist "Judges of Hell" *nianhua* print with pro-Japanese messaging.[39] In response to reports made to the Lu Xun Academy by Red Army commanders on these Japanese propaganda feats in the field, party propagandists focused on the lunar New Year for their outreach activities. Areas of Shanxi squeezed by Japanese blockades were short of materials at a time when the walls and gates of villages were normally awash with customary forms of art. In early 1940, the roving academy troupe were quickly tutored in the use of watercolor by local *nianhua* creators, and cut eight new variations on the traditional New Year *nianhua* print along with posters, flyers and serialized scenes of the troupe's woodcuts. But, rather than merely hand their prints away, the troupe decided to hawk them cheaply at rural markets – in one case, at one *jiao* for eight prints – as a way of both testing their popular appeal and ascribing to them a sense of value beyond items of free propaganda. After a favorable response to the troupe's new-style *nianhua*, a print run of ten thousand sold in its entirety.[40] Through such efforts, the work of prominent artists Hu Yichuan, Luo Gongliu and Yan Han reached into homes across the

[37] Quoted in Zhou Aimin, "Matisse and the Modernity of Yan'an Woodcuts," trans. Matt A. Hale, *Inter-Asia Cultural Studies* 7/3 (2006), 516.
[38] Yan Geng, *Mao's Images: Artists and China's 1949 Transition* (Wiesbaden: J. B. Metzler, 2018), 112–13.
[39] James A. Flath, *The Cult of Happiness: Nianhua, Art and History in Rural North China* (Vancouver: University of British Columbia Press, 2014), 138.
[40] Zhou Aimin, "Matisse and the Modernity of Yan'an Woodcuts," 514–16.

northern borderlands.[41] In places, woodcut themes were introduced to communities via travelling shows, an area of cultural dissemination depicted by Huang Rongcan's *Woodcut Exhibition in a Village* from around 1945 (see Figure 4).

A decided shift from European to native styling in the modern woodcut form, however, did not occur until after Mao Zedong's 1942 Yan'an talks on the political role of culture. At this time the form also acquired an emphasis on affirmative themes that presented the benefits of the revolution to rural life, at times executed with the juxtaposition of the old and new China.[42] A most vivid example is Gu Yuan's *A Comparison*, a two-part piece that appeared in the Communist Party's *Jiefang ribao* (Liberation Daily) in the summer of 1943. In the left frame, a Henanese woman reaches for the last bunch of leaves on a bare tree, precariously

Figure 4 Huang Rongcan, *Woodcut Exhibition in a Village*, circa 1945. Collection of Picker Art Gallery, Colgate University. English title provided by the source. Used with permission.

[41] Flath, *Cult of Happiness*, 138.   [42] Yan Geng, *Mao's Images*, 99.

stretched over a skeletal child with a distended stomach below. Behind them, the horizon is defined by a dead body and a dog picking at a corpse and, in the distance, a farmstead. In the right frame, in contrast, a farmer heads home with a hoe over his shoulder, past a woman at a spinning wheel, children with school satchels, grazing livestock and stalks of corn and cabbage. The couple's *yaodong* cave dwelling and its brick and carved timber façade place the scene in the Northwest border region where the Communist Party had made its base at Yan'an since 1936.[43]

The slow replacement of desolate scenes with affirmative ones heralded the revolution's reinscription of the rural order to make way for the construction of a new China. This involved the mid-1940s appearance of the landlord (*dizhu*) as a target of political action. The landlord as a subject was not new. It had been used and represented earlier in more satirical or sober depictions. One example is a cartoon by Huang Shiying, editor of a magazine of social commentary and satire launched in the spring of 1936. In *Patrol of the Big Landlord*, a crowd of thin farm hands watch a couple – their robes stretched around their rotund physiques – as they are pulled past in a cart, both as fat as the giant sullen hog tugging their cart through the fields.[44] Later in 1941, in the middle of the war with Japan, Gu Yuan's woodcut *Refugee Landlords Returning* pictured a solemn family on horseback and two loaded oxen led by a stooped man – the woman of the family wearing a conspicuous crucifix around her neck – passing before a series of *yaodong* cave dwellings dug into the hillside.[45]

But what increasingly marked the woodcut form in the mid-forties was the depiction of revolutionary acts in the settings of landlord homes. This occurred as major woodcut artists began to formally incorporate party policy into their work. In 1942, Yan Han returned to Yan'an's Lu Xun Academy to work at its research department for three years, making studies of the people's livelihood in the border region comprising Shaanxi, Gansu and Ningxia. With Japan's surrender, and as a staff teacher at the academy, he traveled in the Communist held areas of North China observing land reform, a movement through which "the peasantry was liberating itself [*fanshen*] on a spectacular scale" – in the words of the foreword to a 1949 collection of his works – casting off the yoke of "several thousand years of feudal exploitation."[46]

Soon, Yan's woodcuts presented elaborate scenes of revolutionary acts endorsed by the party. *Distributing Loose Objects* from 1945 depicts

[43] *Jiefang ribao*, July 17, 1943, reprinted in Chang-Tai Hung, "Two Images of Socialism: Woodcuts in Chinese Communist Politics," *Comparative Studies in Society and History* 39/1 (January 1997), plate 11.

[44] *Shenghuo manhua*, 2 (May 1936), 21.   [45] Xin yishu she, ed., *Muke xuanji*, 20.

[46] Anonymous, foreword to *Yan Han muke xuanji* (1949), 9.

a collection of men and women leisurely going through fabrics, chests, cupboards and bird cages beneath the trees and foliage outside what appears to be a wealthy family home. Two years later, his *Distributing the Grain* shows women and men peaceably hauling sacks of grain down the stairs from the ornate entrance of a compound. *Settling Accounts with the Landlord* from 1947 is a dark-toned depiction of a fat man, terrified, smoking pipe in hand, his wife huddled behind him, confronted by villagers – male and female – their heads in knotted kerchiefs, who are poring over contracts and deeds spread on the floor and tables in a lavish interior of hanging works of art, clocks and potted plants. And *The Interrogation* from 1948 pictures a man in the cap and gown of the gentry stooped in submission before a table of accusing villagers, their heads in knotted kerchiefs while two men sit in the background with rifles slung ominously over their shoulders.[47] On the eve of Communist victory, publishers were issuing compilations of these and other works by Yan and his peers in formidable numbers: three thousand copies in the case of his April 1949 book from the Northeast Art Publishing House. This did not introduce his images of rural life to the public – already his work with the Lu Xun Academy woodcut troupe had changed hands in rural markets across the North and West – but certainly raised them, and the art form more generally, in stature.[48]

These years also saw the publication of images with heightened aggressive tones, many with ambiguous targets, appearing to rechannel the emotions of anti-Japanese resistance into revolutionary fervor. A Chinese Woodcutters' Association volume from 1948 included a piece consisting of men, freed from loosened ropes that dangle from their bodies, poised to throw stones off frame (*Revenge*, by Chen Yanqiao) and another of a swarm of figures scrambling over a hill, spears and rifles in hand, mouths agape, pointing at targets that are again off frame (*Flood of Wrath* by Li Hua).[49]

But then subjects were soon clearly identified: in Yan Han's *Speaking Bitterness* from 1947 (republished in 1954) a ragged man stands amid the ruins of a home, pressing his forearm to his face, as a subdued crowd listens.[50] In Liu Xian's *Struggling against an Evil Tyrant* from 1950 (republished in 1984), a man, head bowed with a placard reading "Evil Tyrant" (*e'ba*) around his neck, kneels on a stage at the feet of two soldiers, while another man raises his arm toward a jeering crowd of hundreds.[51] And in Li Hua's color print *Struggling with the Landlord*

[47] Yan Han, *Yan Han muke xuanji* (Beijing: Beijing huabao she, 1949).   [48] Ibid.
[49] Zhonghua quanguo muke xiehui, *Zhongguo banhua ji*, 69, 49.
[50] Yan Han, *Yan Han muke xuanji* (1949), 19.   [51] Liu Xian, *Liu Xian muke xuanji*, 28.

from 1951 (republished in 1958), an older man stands being judged before a desk of cadres, encircled by villagers raising fists and spears in the air as they denounce him.[52]

Conclusion

The Chinese woodcut rose to prominence on a surge of social and ethnographic interest among Chinese artists, serving to speak for the voiceless and downtrodden. But the form was subjected to a series of compromises that parallel what had occurred in May Fourth and New Culture journalism a decade earlier. As we have seen, student calls to embrace empirical analysis and analytical complexity in disaster coverage came up against the demands of political exigency. The result was a tendency toward typecasting and social effacement in activist treatments of rural life.

Later on, with the founding of the League of Left-Wing Writers in the wake of the first United Front's collapse its planners issued a series of instructions at what was described as "a seminar of the participants of the modern literary movement in Shanghai" in 1930. "Three roles were assigned to writers," explains Lawrence Wang-chi Wong: "Destruction of the old society and all its ways of thought," "Propagation and promotion of the ideals of a new society," and "Establishment of new literary theories," which included the adoption of what the committee called "scientific methods" in literary criticism.[53] This politicization of art was not without controversy. As much as the famed author and advocate of popular art wished to see major changes to his country, Lu Xun had expressed ambivalence at the time about the relationship between literature and politics, and especially the revolutionary uses of the art form. But this ambivalence was largely to the dismay of his younger peers.[54]

By the time of Communist victory in 1949, the woodcut had facilitated the removal of particularity and circumstance from social narratives. It had helped to bring the rural masses into public consciousness, but did so in part by positioning them in a gallery of social types, assigning them subjectivities that were inserted into metanarratives of national suffering. The woodcut, in short, offered a visual analog to May Fourth-New Culture depictions of communal life a quarter of a century earlier. Total war and its chaotic aftermath through the 1930s and 1940s brought enormous suffering to the general population. Yet cultural memory over

---

[52] Li Hua, *Li Hua muke xuanji*, 46.
[53] Wong, "The Chinese League of Left-Wing Writers," 316–17.
[54] Emrich, "Modernity through Experimentation," 68; Xiaobing Tang, *Origins of the Chinese Avant-Garde*, 77–78.

the intervening time flattened recent history into a singular, unchanging experience, giving credence to Mao's 1926 report of invariably toxic dynamics at the village level. If the woodcut form was a measure of rural social health, the possibilities for human ethics and interaction in the Chinese village had become remarkably narrow. Rural community appeared to be beyond the pale.

Whether in the hands of an illiterate farmhand or a gallery owner, whether standing alone or in juxtaposition, the woodcut as revolutionary art was inscribed with at least two layers of meaning: immediate, circumstantial truths (people *were* starving along the roadsides as soldiers marched on; stricken farmers *were* press-ganged into the army or molested by armed rent agents; children of debt-ridden parents *were* dying of curable illnesses) and essential truths about society generally (this is how things are and have always been). In doing so, the woodcut appeared to tap into China's essence in ways that echoed Pearl Buck's *Good Earth* – in print or on the silver screen – and its representation of rural Chinese life over roughly the same stretch of the twentieth century. And in important ways, these perceptions of Chinese community were compatible with the interpretation of Chinese society and its foundations offered by *Xiangtu Zhongguo* (From the Soil) in 1948 by Fei Xiaotong, whose search for essential differences with Western societies had found Chinese wanting in their ability to pursue the greater good.

Of course, the visual arts constituted only part of a range of cultural forms representing the present and recent past, transcending particularity and taking on essential "truths" as they did so. As we have seen, in urban culture this involved May Fourth-New Culture journalism, Commercial Press or Popular Wisdom texts and party publications more generally. Or this could take the form of village culture, such as storytelling and stage drama, subjects to which we turn next.

Part III

Maoist Narratives in the Forties

8   Village Drama

The 1920s and 30s saw the figure of Mao Zedong ascend from political activist to architect of a radical social experiment. Over the two decades leading into the 1940s, the one-time member of the Young China Association had gone from Guomindang propagandist in Canton to fugitive and guerilla-band commander, followed by his emergence as leader of a remote border state of a country at total war with Japan. Isolated and limited in resources, Mao's Yan'an experiment would in many ways be conducted through the power of ideas.

Although it was most clearly articulated during the Yan'an years, the Maoist approach to culture drew from techniques developed in earlier phases of the party. Communist efforts to successfully negotiate between the party agenda, on the one hand, and local concerns and tastes, on the other, had begun in the late 1920s following the formation of the Red Army. It was then, at 1929's Gutian Conference, that Mao and other proponents of political – as opposed to purely military – warfare put their stamp on a blueprint for propaganda techniques employed across the movement. The proposals included targeted messaging – in other words, messaging to specific social groups, occupational groups and age groups – rather than generic campaigns to the population at large, and the use of a range of media to convey such messaging through visualization in prints, dramatization in song and costume, and as news posted on pamphlets and village walls.[1]

But, more importantly, party strategists made a point of rolling out party messaging in two distinct registers. As David Holm explains, "Propaganda work, in order to be effective, had to be articulated both temporally and geographically. In the words of the Gutian resolution, effective propaganda has 'time quality' (*shijianxing*) and 'local quality' (*difangxing*)."[2] *Local* quality messaging involved both particularity

---

[1] David Holm, *Art and Ideology in Revolutionary China* (Oxford: Clarendon Press, 1991), 19, 21.
[2] Ibid., 20.

(targeting specific local matters and local figures) and accessibility (framing matters in ways that would resonate with the unseasoned or unedu-
cated). Local quality messaging, in other words, was the party's entry
point into localities.

By contrast, "time quality" messaging – insomuch as it involved the
audience's subjectivity within evolving power structures and events over
time – required a certain amount of preconditioning, historical understanding and familiarity with terminology to be fully understood and
appreciated. In other words, time quality messaging was a locality's vehicle into the broader revolutionary movement. Once the material conditions underpinning local tensions were eased – say, with land or marriage
reform – local quality messaging was supplanted by time quality messaging. In this way, time quality-cum-revolutionary messaging could outlast
material conditions and social realities, eventually forming the ideological
base for continuous revolution into the People's Republic.

Put another way, around the same time of 1930, Communist Party
strategists had made a point of distinguishing between the "movement
slogan" and the "propaganda slogan." The movement slogan was "to be
developed specifically to suit certain local conditions," Marcia Ristaino
explains, "aimed at fulfilling the more obvious requirements of a specific
target group. For example, the working conditions at a particular factory
or within a certain village." In contrast, "the so-called propaganda slogan
was characteristically broad and theoretical in content." Conveying party
goals or orthodoxy at any one time, propaganda slogans "were to be used
internally to enhance the spirit of the organization, or, in places where the
Communists enjoyed considerable strength, they might be disseminated
publicly, often through such media as wall posters, theatrical performances, posted cartoons, and publications."[3] In other words, if the
movement slogan was aimed at immediate and tangible goals, the propaganda slogan instilled discipline and dedication, laying the ideological
groundwork for the long game.

The Chinese Communist project in the country's Northwest was
brought to the world's attention in its earliest stages with the publication
of Edgar Snow's *Red Star over China*, based on the young Missouri
journalist's stay in Shaanbei, or northern Shaanxi, in 1936 immediately
after the Communists' circuitous arrival there from Central China by way
of the Long March.[4] This Communist project in the Northwest involved
the creation of peasant associations, women's leagues, cooperatives and
other forms of political organization, mass education and institution

---

[3] Ristaino, *China's Art of Revolution*, 153.
[4] Edgar Snow, *Red Star over China* (London: Victor Gollancz, 1937).

building – what would become known in 1970s scholarship as "The Yenan Way."[5]

Since then, scholars have added a focus on the role of language and representation in human behavior and formal power structures. "As a first step toward constructing" the ideological structures at Yan'an, write David E. Apter and Tony Saich in their study of Maoist discourse, "Mao used his newly realized power to change his role from a predominantly military figure to a storyteller, creating a master narrative of the revolution." From storyteller, they explain, he soon assumed the position of "cosmocrat," setting China's revolutionary goals while providing the metrics to measure its progress toward them. To achieve this, Maoist discourse provided a constellation of signs through which people would navigate and reconfigure the social world up to and through the Cultural Revolution of the 1960s.[6]

Mao achieved this while based a couple of hundred miles east of the 1920 earthquake epicenter at Haiyuan. There, Yan'an would become the fulcrum of a revolutionary movement that formed in the Shaan Gan Ning border region, an area stretched over the central sections of the loess plateau. Part III of this book considers Maoist narratives of the past in theatrical and textual form in light of May Fourth, missionary and Guomindang-era precedents before them. In other words, it connects aspects of Maoist discourse and social mobilization already recognized by scholars with preceding generations of republican-era cultural conditioning that underpinned its power, as charted over our previous seven chapters. We consider Yan'an storytelling through Apter and Saich's interview-based studies and Gang Yue's work on revolutionary fiction, followed by village stage drama in surrounding communities, drawing from the works of David Holm and Brian James DeMare on Maoist theater. Finally, in Chapter 9 we consider how youth were reached in the urban sphere through special magazines in townships and cities as the movement vied for ideological control over the northern landscape in the final years of civil war. As we will see, in each case – whether an operatic plot line, a magazine feature or a lecture-hall story by Mao himself – Maoist narrative resonated on two levels: "The first time as myth and the second as logic," in the words of Apter and Saich, "once as retrieval" of a dead-end past, "then as projection" onto a pathway of redemption.[7] In the process, an old society was created, a past shaped into a foil to bring out the brilliance of the revolutionary change to come.

[5] Mark Selden, *The Yenan Way in Revolutionary China* (Cambridge, MA: Harvard University Press, 1974).
[6] Apter and Saich, *Revolutionary Discourse in Mao's Republic*, 67.   [7] Ibid., 15.

Maoist Morality for Rural Audiences

In dialogue with Yan'anites while huddled at meeting halls cut into the terraced hills of Shaanbei, Mao established his reputation as a master story-teller. After their first voicing from raised platforms or huddled benches, these narratives were set to paper and formalized by him, often at feverish pace deep into the night, becoming textual orthodoxy as they were transmitted more widely. Mao's repertoire both drew from the Chinese classical canon and offered accounts of life in what was to be known as the old society. From the existing canon, he gave renewed life to ancient stories such as the tale of the "foolish old man" who moved a pair of mountains blocking the sun from his farm. Originally from the fifth century BCE and forming part of the Daoist canon a millennium later, "The story was told by Mao as part of his final speech at the Seventh National Congress meeting of the CCP on June 11, 1945, in Yan'an," Barbara Mittler explains, just as the Second United Front was falling apart.[8] "Today, two big mountains lie like a dead weight on the Chinese people," said Mao, "one is imperialism, the other is feudalism. The Chinese Communist Party has long made up its mind to dig them up."[9] In this way, Mao's iconoclastic vision was very much rooted in fundamental aspects of Chinese culture, constructed with select elements of China's inheritance that would somehow escape the fate of the "feudal heritage," while lending an authority to his speech with timeless, all-encompassing tales of social ordering in the style of the sages, most prominently that of Confucius.[10]

At the same time, Mao composed stories that bore on China's more immediate history, stories that conveyed the extreme sense of uncertainty, randomness and helplessness brought by decades of war, civil strife and social dislocation. "In Yan'an three stories were constructed," Apter and Saich observe, "each representing a different aspect of loss: displacement of the peasant from land and community; the decentering of China and its replacement by outside forces; dismemberment and loss of imperial control."[11]

While the latter two types of narrative concern national strength and integrity, the first concerns conduct within communities. "Here is a characteristic tale recounted in one form or another by many of those interviewed," Apter and Saich write:

The second or third son or a daughter of a poor peasant household has been deprived of the family's plot of land because of death, indebtedness, or natural catastrophe and the lack of support from the landlord or the

---

[8] Mittler, *A Continuous Revolution*, 196.   [9] Quoted in ibid., 197.   [10] Ibid., 199.
[11] Apter and Saich, *Revolutionary Discourse in Mao's Republic*, 72. Their findings are based on interviews with former Yan'anites they conducted in China from 1986 to 1989.

community. The teller describes the decline of the family, the failure of the uncle to help out, and the negative effect of such circumstances on the teller's own personal situation. The starting point then is ground zero: no land; absolute poverty; minimal opportunity; the death of the lineage, which will rupture the worship of ancestors. The story is first about sheer survival: leaving home, being bonded or sold. It personalizes such predicaments: the uncle who steals the widow's little bit of money, how Landlord Han confiscates the last bit of rice while his own family is provided with luxuries and his eldest daughter is sent away to school. The children of Landlord Han do not work; the children of widow Li work for nothing and starve.[12]

"In Mao's hands," they explain, composite pictures of the past were constructed out of individual, deeply relatable tales. "Widow Li and Landlord Han are generalized surrogates for a great many individual experiences" and become "surrogates of a total history."[13] In this way, stories flattened past lived experience to bolster the promise of future transformations. "Mao's speeches and writings retrieve and rework time," they explain. "The past is both a golden age and a patrimony lost, a negative pole leading to a time of chaos and an overcoming project. Retrievals established the point of departure for a redeeming narrative, the platform on which to project and construct a millennial end – in short, a logic."[14]

The narrative model constructed according to this logic was not unique to Mao's personal style. It became characteristic of the era, manifesting for instance in the "narrative closure" described in Gang Yue's study of revolutionary fiction. Taking as an example Liu Qing's short story "Son of the Earth" ("Tudide erzi") from 1945, Yue writes:

> Like many works of this period, the story tells about hunger in the old society and the fulfillment of hunger in the new. In the old society, the peasant Li Laosan was deprived of his land and forced at times to pick discarded rotten cabbage leaves for food . . . . After several years of hard work [and government help and advice], Li has saved enough money, bought a small farm of his own, and become a son of the earth once again.[15]

Revolutionary fiction promised to empower and enable individuals – the downtrodden, the destitute, women generally – to participate and live in dignity in their communities. At the same time, it denied the past viability of those same communities, gutting them of any collective or cooperative history. "Recalling [past] bitterness and thinking over [present] sweetness (yiku sitan)" became, in Yue's

[12] Ibid., 76   [13] Ibid.   [14] Ibid., 88.
[15] Gang Yue, The Mouth that Begs: Hunger, Cannibalism, and the Politics of Eating in Modern China (Durham, NC: Duke University Press, 1999), 161–62.

words, an exercise central to "class education based on the historical contrast between the old and new society."[16]

The Maoist metanarrative – Mao's total history – was a logical destination of May Fourth-New Culture narratives of deinscription. Mao's stories did not just "retrieve" a deep "mythic past" but also an immediate history. Building on the corpus from which revolutionary memory of the recent past had been constructed – social surveys, missionary sociologies, Commercial Press and Popular Wisdom pedagogies, woodcut prints of communities during times of crisis and disaster – Mao's social prototypes at Yan'an could lock into place as self-evident truths. Casting China amid disintegration and social chaos, Chinese culture and society, in Maoist discourse, were calcified, "a kind of linguistic and symbolic prison composed of dead or obsolete political languages" – Confucian or Buddhist values that were vacant or irrelevant to current affairs.[17] Drawing from the Marxist lexicon, Maoist sociology in other words marked the culmination of decades of claims about Chinese social and cultural incapacity for meaningful action toward solidarity and alleviation – claims that served to sweep away aspects of the country's patrimony, and make way for a new regimen for personal and public conduct. In short, revolutionary memory provided historical depth and validation to Maoist discourse and moral authority.

The question remains: what, from its inception at Yan'an, gave Maoism its teeth, its cultural and political predominance over contending visions of socialist revolution at the time? How did it prevail locally in the Northwest, and, over time, in the pockets of Chinese revolutionary activity elsewhere in the 1940s? Two main reasons, among many, may be entertained here: the revelatory experience Mao's vision offered, one which gave it almost a spiritual quality – and fear.

The fear behind Maoism's consolidation of ideological power stemmed from Mao's adeptness at outmaneuvering his rivals, together with his success at forestalling broader intellectual activity that could pose a challenge to his goals. At once a seasoned guerilla and a political operative, he fused political goals with military ones – as he had done as Guomindang theorist in Canton in the mid-1920s – climbing the ranks in both uniform and civilian dress. In early 1938, as he successfully jockeyed for party dominance at the sixth plenum of the Chinese Communist Party, Mao also argued for a more indigenous, Chinese-grounded form of Marxism.[18] This could bring greater accessibility and popularity to the movement, but also sideline Mao's more theoretically

[16] Ibid., 165.   [17] Apter and Saich, *Revolutionary Discourse in Mao's Republic*, 13.
[18] Selden, *Yenan Way*, 191.

adept, Moscow-trained rivals. A party ideologue of rural Hunan origin, he composed enormous volumes of texts while remaining positioned as a man of the people, set apart from urbane, bookish rivals bent on abstractions and orthodox theory. Four years later, at the 1942 Yan'an Forum on Literature and Art, Mao famously called for the restriction of cultural production to vaguely defined "popular" forms, effectively stripping authors and artists of creative autonomy and harnessing culture to the needs of the party-state.[19] This was swiftly followed by two years of intensive cadre education and criticism sessions called the "rectification movement." Launched by speeches condemning formalist Marxism (it was less useful than shit, to paraphrase Mao – a point that made real sense to audiences composed of farmers) and comparing unorthodox thoughts to a sickness to be cured, the movement culminated in a period described by Apter and Saich as one of "forced confession and the enactment of false guilt" during "a moment of vindictive retribution called the Rescue Campaign" of 1943.[20]

At the same time, Mao's stories were received with exhilaration. Speaking of their interviewees, Apter and Saich write, "For them, word and text, far from being oppressive, became a form of unique knowledge and understanding. So what seemed to be polar opposites, the liberation of the individual and the collectivization of the self, instead of working against each other became complementary."[21] How was this achieved? "Another answer is that they were indoctrinated. Of course this is the case, but indoctrination implies a kind of resentful passivity or at least an abdication of judgment. But interviewees described a quickening of intelligence, a sense of self-worth and accomplishment, something 'oceanic' or like Barthes's *jouissance*."[22]

For the thousands of idealists and activists who journeyed to Yan'an, grasping social truths unfolding before them was evidently a revelatory experience. While the collective was reconstituted through storytelling and machination, revelation and discipline, revolutionary memory provided the conditioning for the ready reception of its shared insights. This Communist collective would of course spread, encompassing the Shaan Gan Ning border region and beyond. Over the same stretch of time as Mao's consolidation of power at Yan'an in the early 1940s, new cultural forms were coming of age: the woodcut, as we have seen, and *yange* village drama, an older, already familiar form that would be given explicitly new content.

[19] Flath, *Cult of Happiness*, 139.
[20] Apter and Saich, *Revolutionary Discourse in Mao's Republic*, 25, 73; Selden, *Yenan Way*, 188–200.
[21] Apter and Saich, *Revolutionary Discourse in Mao's Republic*, 21.   [22] Ibid., 22.

Beyond Yan'an

Maoist instruction reached the broader population via many of the same pedagogical tools – from school history texts to Mandarin primers for children and adults – used by rival political movements and generations of Chinese educators. By way of example, Mao headed a team of Yan'an writers in composing a short, two-chapter history schoolbook in 1939. Its opening chapter, "Chinese Society," covers geographic territory, ethnicity and ancient Chinese technological innovation in a similar fashion as its Commercial Press or Popular Wisdom counterparts. It frames premodern history as an extended prelude to the present revolution: "Chinese society remained feudal for 3,000 years," it explains, during which "the principal contradiction in feudal society was between the peasantry and the landlord class." China's modern period is defined by imperial shocks, bringing a shift to "semi-colonial and semi-feudal" status since the first Opium War, and finally "colonial, semi-colonial and semi-feudal" status since Japanese seizure of Manchuria in 1931. A list of rebellions over the millennia establishes the revolutionary potential of the peasantry, setting up chapter two, "The Chinese Revolution," which, apparently composed by Mao alone, provides a blueprint for the struggle ahead.[23]

The movement also turned to character primers, most famously the *Three Character Classic*, a type of manual for children and new readers with origins in the thirteenth century, if not earlier, that had long combined character drilling with moral instruction, and evolved over time as regimes and social mores changed. The *Emancipation Three Character Classic* appeared in 1947 during the Land Reform movement. To the original's opening line, "Men at their birth were basically all equal, but later they would be divided into different classes," the Maoist version adds, "From this moment onwards, people began to bully each other, and landlords to oppress peasants."[24]

Shared strategies with other educational efforts, past and present, extended to the use of village song and stage and other areas of "folk" culture. New Culture-era socialist activists, such as Peng Pai in early 1920s Guangzhou, had innovated the use of local culture for agitation, injecting revolutionary messaging into folk songs and theatrical performances.[25] Around the same time, young scholars based at Beijing University, inspired by the historian Gu Jiegang, had embarked on folk

---

[23] Mao Zedong, "The Chinese Revolution and the Chinese Communist Party," 308–09, in Schram, ed., vol. 7 of *Mao's Road to Power*.
[24] Quoted in Mittler, *A Continuous Revolution*, 153.
[25] Robert Marks, *Rural Revolution in South China: Peasants and the Making of History in Haifeng County, 1570–1930* (Madison: University of Wisconsin Press, 1984), 181–82.

song collection in rural districts across the country.[26] By the 1930s, Hebei's Ding county to the south of Beijing became the focus of intense script collection, and drama reform and training by what Kate Merkel-Hess describes as "a loose coalition of reform-minded elites who sought to create a rural alternative to urban modernity [...] around the idea of 'rural reconstruction' (*xiangcun jianshe*)."[27] More prone to narrative than the "show-style mélange of dancing and singing" elsewhere in the North, Ding county plays were brought to prominence with the 1933 publication of forty-eight scripts in Li Jinghan and Zhang Shiwen's *A Selection of Dingxian Yangge Plays*.[28] "Less violent and more participatory" than its Maoist variant in Yan'an,[29] the rural reform movement – appearing at the peak of social surveys across China – formed its own modern theater troupes motivated by similar concerns over rural shortcomings, and explored how organization and civic action could lead to village, and therefore national, strength.[30]

Communist interest in the dramatic form followed a time line similar to that of academia or social reformists. Party cultural workers were already performing for troops in the Jiangxi soviets in 1927 – following the bloody rift with Chiang Kai-shek's Guomindang and the creation of the Red Army – the same year that Mao began advocating cultural work, and performance specifically, as part of party strategy.[31] With the northward shift of Communist activity after the Long March, rural propaganda efforts centered on the *yangge*, "the name given to the motley collection of songs, dances, and folk plays traditionally performed in north China from the New Year until the Lantern Festival," explains David Holm.[32] "Of all the forms of *yangge*, the folk play was clearly the genre most highly regarded by the CCP, partly at least because of their bias towards 'content'."[33]

Over the course of the war with Japan, the embrace of *yangge*-style plays and music by party theater teams positioned them favorably against profit-driven competitors, such as *xibanzi* opera troupes. "By the land reform era," Brian James DeMare writes, "dramatists had developed *yangge* further, crafting *geju* operas, a mixture of Western spoken drama, local opera, and dance."[34] A drama troupe might consist of a dozen musicians and three times that number of actors, both male and female,

[26] Holm, *Art and Ideology in Revolutionary China*, 118.
[27] Merkel-Hess, *Rural Modern*, 3.
[28] Holm, *Art and Ideology in Revolutionary China*, 119.
[29] Merkel-Hess, *Rural Modern*, 3.   [30] Ibid., 80.
[31] Brian James DeMare, *Mao's Cultural Army: Drama Troupes in China's Rural Revolution* (Cambridge: Cambridge University Press, 2017), 28.
[32] Holm, *Art and Ideology in Revolutionary China*, 115.   [33] Ibid., 299.
[34] DeMare, *Mao's Cultural Army*, 113–14.

who would march many miles to a targeted village to perform for an audience of thousands or several dozen.[35]

Yet local appeal for party productions was by no means assured. Land reform-era audiences, weary of seemingly ceaseless war, often preferred entertainment over politics. At times, government mandates prioritizing modern *geju* operas were defied locally, and touring drama corps, who often worked closely with Red Army units, were successfully pressured by audiences to revert to traditional playbills and schedules.[36] Only after considerable adjustment to local habits and tastes did party dramatists make serious inroads into rural cultural life.[37] These successes were part of a concerted, and much broader, effort to tailor party communications in order to penetrate and win over rural communities.

New Opera

Although party cultural workers consciously based their *geju* style of village opera on the *yangge* repertoire of song, dance and acting, its introduction marked a departure from prevailing theatrical forms in the countryside. Viewing this new genre's hybrid composition of traditional and modern elements with spoken word quickly became an initiation into Communist life. "For villagers [living by the front lines], and for refugees from Henan and elsewhere in the Kuomingtang sectors," Holm writes, "being taken to a performance of 'White Haired Girl' was often their first introduction to life under the CCP."[38] This reach of the *yangge/geju* movement in the 1940s Communist zone, and the sheer depth of that reach, can hardly be exaggerated, something Holm makes clear:

It is not for nothing that Mao Zedong referred to the Shaan-Gan-Ning Border Region as 'one big *yangge* troupe'. Indeed, because of the peculiarities of the regional Shaanxi dialect, even the term for 'socialism' seems to have become inextricably entangled in the popular mind with the performance of *shehuo* ['another name for what is generally known as *yangge* in north China']. This was particularly the case in East Gansu and the southern counties of Guanzhong and the Yan'an subregion, where -*uo* finals are pronounced as *ui* and the words *shehui* ('social') and *shehuo* thus sound nearly identical. Such metaphors and confusions generate a whole complex of associations: of revolution as a festival (together with its ritual reversal of status hierarchies, its turning the world upside-down); of a revolution as a performance (a real-people and real-events drama, with a coherent story-line leading from the old society to the 'great reunion' of the new society); of revolution as a celebration (a celebration, that is, of the restoration of legitimate authority, and the imminent arrival of an era of Great Peace); and of the

---

[35] Ibid., 101.   [36] Ibid., 138.   [37] Ibid., 6, 8.
[38] Holm, *Art and Ideology in Revolutionary China*, 323.

Border Region as a spiritual militia armed against incursions by demonic hordes
from outside the boundaries of a civilized (Chinese) world.[39]

First drafted in 1944 and one of the first land reform dramas, *The
White Haired Girl* (*Bai mao nü*) served two main aims of cultural
workers at Yan'an: reinforcing new understandings of the old and
new China, and transmitting party policy and practice to the general
population. Written by a team of dramatists at the Lu Xun Academy
and based on a story from northern Hebei, "The White-Haired
Female Immortal," it had at its center a young heroine – a feature of
many land reform-era dramas. Set in an unnamed county of Hebei in
1935, the play revolves around seventeen-year-old Xi'er, the village
beauty and daughter of a tenant farmer. Coveted by the thirty-year-old
Huang Shiren, from whom her father rents their land, Xi'er is purchased by Huang as a household servant, and is then raped by him.
Pregnant, Xi'er flees to the mountains, her hair turning white with
stress, returning a year later with the arrival of the Red Army to take
on her former scourge. "Huang Shiren oh Huang Shiren, you murder-
ous devil [*sharen de mowang*], you man-eating wild beast [*chiren de
yeshou*]," the multitudes (*zhong*) join Xi'er in singing before Huang's
public trial (*gongshen*) – the newly introduced community forum with
which the play concludes. "Your thousand years of old feudalism [*jiu
fengjian*]," the people chant in the play's final lines, "Today are dug up
and gone [*duangen*, literally cured]! Your ten thousand years of iron
chains, smash with you to pieces [*da de ni sui fenfen*]!"[40]

Bringing raw intensity to the village stage, the play's plot introduced
colloquial shorthand for essential differences between pre and postlibera-
tion society. Based on the fact that the youthful Xi'er was considered to be
a ghost by villagers due to her shock of white hair, a couplet was "first used
to interpret *The White-Haired Girl*, and later to describe almost all works
produced on this model," Gang Yue explains: "The old society turned
humans into ghosts; The new society turned ghosts into humans" (*jiushe-
hui shiren biancheng gui; xinshehui shigui biancheng ren*).[41]

White Haired Girl was also a way of introducing class labels into everyday speech. The play opens with Huang referred to as *caizhu* (which could
translate colloquially as "money bags" or more formally as "capitalist"
depending on the context) or addressed as young master (*shao dongjia*) by
villagers; only after the appearance of the Communists in the last part of
the play, as DeMare notes, does the term landlord (*dizhu*) surface in

[39] Ibid., 26, 333.
[40] He Jingzhi and Ding Yi, *Bai mao nü* (Beijing: Xinhua shudian, 1951), 121.
[41] Gang Yue, *Mouth That Begs*, 162.

village dialogue.[42] Who qualified as a landlord? The status had been formally defined by Mao a decade earlier in an effort to standardize its application and use in rural areas. "Warlords, officials, local tyrants and evil gentry are political representatives and exceptionally ruthless members of the landlord class," he explained in 1933. At heart, though, the landlord was someone whose "principal form of exploitation" was the "exaction of land rent from the peasants," in contrast to the rich peasant, whose "main form of exploitation is the hiring of labour." But Mao's categorical net grew still wider. "The administration of ancestral temples [i.e., communal land, which often included school land] is also a type of exploitation through land rent," Mao continued, and the class position of landlord could apply even more broadly to usurers and "persons who assist landlords in collecting rent and managing property."[43]

With *White Haired Girl*, the writing team sought to "show the difference between two societies as well as demonstrate the *fanshen* of the people," in the words of one of its members, referring to the revolutionary process of transformation and the term with which the play literally ends: "We – must – *fan – shen* (*Women – yao – fan – shen*)!!!"[44] Instrumental in this transformation was the subjectivity that came with the internalization of landlord, various levels of the peasant and other class positions.

But the *geju* opera did more than inject the archetype of the landlord into a new cultural form. Evolved in Mao's writings from the vague "evil gentry" of the 1920s to a defined political position in the early 1930s, the figure of the landlord in *The White Haired Girl* took on added layers of hypocrisy and menace. At times the names of *geju* characters are "ironic or contain 'feudal' thought," Barbara Mittler points out, "the rich landlord who mistreats the white-haired girl, for example, is called Huang Shiren 黃世仁 (one who has practiced the Confucian virtue of humanity for generations)." In other instances, villain's names incorporate *de* (virtuous) or *zhong* (loyal) in this way.[45] Meanwhile, Huang and other chief villains of land reform dramas are made to personify patriarchal privilege and its claims over the female body. It does this in ways designed to resonate with audiences at a visceral level, through sexual violence and the monopoly of women by the monied, through concubinage and other forms of commodification. Staging such scenes had the potential to reach the humblest of audience members: female servants recognized personal injustices they had suffered, and poor male farmhands were reminded of

---

[42] He and Ding, *Bai mao nü*, 2, 16, 25, 42; DeMare, *Mao's Cultural Army*, 130.
[43] Mao Zedong, "How to Differentiate the Classes in the Rural Areas," 137–38, in Schram, ed., *Mao's Road to Power*.
[44] Quoted in DeMare, *Mao's Cultural Army*, 117; He and Ding, *Bai mao nü*, 120.
[45] Mittler, *A Continuous Revolution*, 58.

their struggle to form families of their own – as eligible females were taken as concubines by men of means – and the indignity they faced of dying alone.

The White Haired Girl premiered in Yan'an in the spring of 1944 with the party elite in attendance before touring the northern base areas with cultural work teams. Three years later, "Jack Belden became one of the few Westerners to observe Mao's cultural army in the field" when he sat for a showing attended by two thousand villagers during a freezing night in North China. During the trial's enactment the time came for Huang's fate to be decided; "At this juncture, to my utter surprise, many members of the audience stood up in great excitement," Belden recounted, "shouting 'Sha! Sha! Kill him! Kill him!' while women wiped their eyes and wept at other points."[46] That same year, the play's themes were reproduced on colored prints by a workshop in the Hebei county of Wuqiang, along with a series of *nianhua* based on land reform themes, resulting in 10,979 *White Haired Girl* prints being distributed through the Xinhua bookstore.[47] As the play made its way through villages across the North, live and in print, one of its main writers "noted how villagers called the show's actors by their stage names, while young children even cursed the actors playing villainous roles."[48]

With the resumption of civil war over the course of the 1940s, each of the liberated areas soon had its counterpart to The White Haired Girl, land reform works of operatic fusion bringing together local and modern Western styles, and mostly composed by teams of dramatists.[49] Some *geju* operas, though, were single efforts, growing out of their author's impressions of village life while operating in the field. Such was the case with Red Leaf River (Chi ye he), written by a party activist after he had performed political work in the final weeks of the war with Japan in a Shanxi village of the same name. There, in the mountain range running along the eastern edge of the loess plateau, Ruan Zhangjing had resolved to address the prevalent notion of fate among the poor, especially how fate was seen to determine fortunes such as landed wealth. In the process, Ruan sought to capture the travails of an "old peasant" he had encountered there, DeMare explains, "who had told him a sorrowful tale of landlord oppression that had torn his family asunder."[50] First drafted and staged in 1947,[51] Ruan's Red Leaf River became the leading land reform opera in the Communist-held sections of the Jin Cha Ji border area, namely Shanxi, Inner Mongolia and Hebei.

Red Leaf River shares a good deal with its famous counterpart. It, too, revolves around a young female role, Xi Yan'er, a nineteen-year-old

---

[46] Quoted in DeMare, *Mao's Cultural Army*, 113; see also 118.
[47] Flath, *Cult of Happiness*, 142.   [48] DeMare, *Mao's Cultural Army*, 118.
[49] Holm, *Art and Ideology in Revolutionary China*, 323.
[50] DeMare, *Mao's Cultural Army*, 123.   [51] Ibid., 123.

married into a family of tenant farmers, the Wangs. And in the play names are also suggestive. In a bitter irony, her family name is the character for happiness, something she shares with Xi'er, the white haired girl. As for its main villain, Lü Chengshu, at whose hands the Wang household suffers repeatedly, his given name translates roughly as "one who inherits and undertakes the reading and writing of books," tying him to the literati, or at least the gentry elite. And Lü is also a sexual predator, assaulting Yan'er halfway into the play, and, in similar fashion to *The White Haired Girl*, the play brings together sexual violence with class antagonism, while casting villainy in animalist terms. "Lü Chengshu, man-eating tiger, black-livered capitalist dog [*gou caizhu*]!" Yan'er exclaims before she takes her own life by casting herself into the Red Leaf River.[52]

But then there are features that distinguish *Red Leaf River* from its counterpart. The play is structured around famine events, reaching back to the early years of Guomindang rule. Act 1 opens in the middle of 1930 amid the distress of three years of drought and famine across the North and Northwest. (The famine menaced communities in Shaanxi, Gansu and Inner Mongolia most severely, touching areas that would form part of the Jin Cha Ji border area.) In act 2, the following year, "famine [*jihuang*] continues without end," in the words of the Wang family head, and the general suffering acted out and voiced provides the sense of calamity to the drama.[53] Equally significant is *Red Leaf River*'s uniquely drawn out portrayal of land redistribution in its fourth act, set in 1943 after the Communist Eighth Route Army had swept through the area during the war against Japan. In the play's final scene, a people's court (*renmin fating*) is formed to try Lü, who is denounced and beaten to roars of the crowd's approval, and the recently formed poor person's association (*qiong ren hui*) is instructed to "most equitably and fairly divide up [*gonggong daodao de fen*]" the residence, land and possessions of Lü's household.[54] The play then ends with the multitudes singing: "Landlords are dying out [*dizhu sijue*], feudalism is swept away [*fengjian saowan*]!"[55]

In this way, *Red Leaf River*'s land reform scenes served as a dramatic "how-to" demonstration of the process for activists in their communities carrying out these policies just as the play was first appearing on stage in 1947. Visiting Shanxi in 1948, *Fanshen* author William Hinton offers a window onto a performance that spring in the Lucheng county

---

[52] Ruan Zhangjing, *Chi ye he* (Shexian, Henan: Taixing qunzhong shudian, February 1948), 56.
[53] Ibid., 36.   [54] Ibid., 97.   [55] Ibid., 98.

village of Long Bow. Land reform had been underway for two years already in the village when a visiting drama troupe of fifty players put on a four-hour-long staging of *Red Leaf River* one night after delivering a day of one-act comedies. Before them sat several thousand people on bricks or stools brought with them from home, comprising a broad spectrum, presumably, of Long Bow residents. (Half of Long Bow villagers were poor peasants, according to Hinton, who together owned roughly a quarter of the land. Seven percent of the village were classified as landlords or rich peasants and owned roughly a third, while the remaining 45 percent of land was owned by middle peasants.[56]) "The women around me wept openly and unashamedly," Hinton recalled. "No one sobbed, no one cried out, but all wept together in silence." Soon the men joined in shedding tears, their faces lit by "a makeshift stage of pine poles set under an enormous vaulted sky," the surrounding landscape pitch black except for a single kerosene lamp lighting the action and elaborate scenery onstage.[57]

Script revisions were continuous, in part to keep up with intense audience reactions to the heinous crimes committed by the stage villains. "As the crowd broke up" in Long Bow, Hinton recalled that "they preferred the optimistic final half, the battle and the victory. The only fault they found with the final part was that no one beat the landlord" who was instead "turned over to the People's Court instead of punished on the spot."[58] The original 1944 version of *The White Haired Girl* had ended in the same way with a public struggle session that spared Huang Shiren corporal punishment before he was handed over to a government office. Holm relates the work's evolution from there: When the writers tried it out on staff and students at the Lu Xun Academy, the play was met with unease afterwards over Huang's light treatment, most colorfully by a cook in the canteen who insisted that the evil villain be shot. Still, the academy leadership held firm: "At the time we still felt that basically one should still work for solidarity with the landlord class," the academy's drama head explained. "If he were to be shot, that would certainly have gone against government policy. So we didn't change it."[59]

Things did change soon afterwards at the play's premiere before a party congress, staged in the auditorium of the nearby Central Party School, with Mao, Zhou Enlai, Zhu De, Liu Shaoqi and other party delegates in attendance. The following day the Central Party Office dispatched a message to the academy with the following three points: "First, the

---

[56] William Hinton, *Fanshen: A Documentary of Revolution in a Chinese Village* (New York: Monthly Review, 1966), ix, 28.
[57] Ibid., 25, 31.   [58] Ibid., 31.
[59] Quoted in Holm, *Art and Ideology in Revolutionary China*, 322.

play was exceptionally timely. Secondly, it was successful artistically. And finally, Huang Shiren should be shot."[60]

In spite of such directives from the top, the nature of landlord depictions and levels of violence onstage were not without controversy within the party. Major party publications such as *Jiefang ribao*, founded in Yan'an in 1941, consistently issued conflicting statements on the revolution's need for cooperation between classes, on the one hand, and the submission of the rural elite through relentless class struggle, on the other.[61] At times, county governments criticized *Red Leaf River* and other plays for "being out of touch with current policies that called for the elimination of landlords as an economic class," DeMare explains, "but not the physical extermination of landlords."[62]

On landlord criminality, plays nonetheless displayed little ambiguity, an approach to characterization at times written into dramatic instruction. The 1949 script of *Nine Items of Clothes* (*Jiu jian yi*), an opera written in Manchuria after the liberation of the three northeastern provinces, opens with the following guidance to actors taking on the role of the play's chief villain: "Hua Zifang – 50 years old. Possesses a lot of land and property, so he is called Half the City Hua [Hua Bancheng]. Another alias is Jupiter Hua [Hua Hua Taisui]. A man of extreme viciousness, he's also known as a true to life-Hades [Yan Wang]. One big evil tyrant [*e'ba*], there is no evil he does not commit."[63] Hua's given name, meanwhile, roughly translates as "one considering himself excellent or virtuous."

Party-sponsored art, then, stirred public passions that, in turn, were used as grounds for further validation of violence in party messaging. As the Central Secretariat explained in its directive to ramp up the retribution in *White Haired Girl*: "Huang Shiren is a character so steeped in evil that it would not be right not to have him shot. The broad masses will definitely not tolerate that."[64] In this way, party plot lines kept one step ahead of party policy.

Party-sponsored mass culture also provided the language, the ritual and the political cover for public acts of violence. This was *geju*'s most tangible contribution. Artistically "a form of bricolage," in Holm's words, doubling the number of characters in older stories, stitching new passages into others, *geju*'s "really new aspect" was "its use as a weapon in the

[60] Ibid.; see also DeMare, *Mao's Cultural Army*, 118, 124–25.
[61] Dagfinn Gatu, *Village China at War: the Impact of Resistance to Japan, 1937–1945* (Copenhagen: Nordic Institute for Asian Studies, 2008), xiv.
[62] DeMare, *Mao's Cultural Army*, 139.
[63] Song Zhide, Tie Fu, Dong Chuan and Jin Ren, *Jiu jian yi* (Shanghai: Shanghai zazhi gongsuo, 1949), 1.
[64] Quoted in Holm, *Art and Ideology in Revolutionary China*, 322.

hands of village activists, and as a vehicle through which they could produce a dramatic re-enactment of contemporary events and their own role in the revolutionary movement."[65]

This feedback loop between audience and artist in the party's cultural realm paralleled a spiral of political violence within communities themselves. As Deng Xiaoping said of land reform operations in western Anhui:

> The masses would hate a few landlords and want them killed, so according to the wishes of the masses we would have these landlords killed. Afterwards, the masses would fear reprisals from those who had ties to those we had just killed, and would draw up an even bigger list of names [. . .]. We kept on killing, and the masses felt more and more insecure [because of reprisals . . .]. The result was that over two hundred people were killed, and work in twelve administrative villages was ruined.[66]

The extent to which cultural production fueled animus and helped identify its targets is of course difficult if not impossible to gauge. What is clearer is the role stage dramas had in introducing the terms and framing of communal violence. And then regardless of whether communal bloodshed was self-defeating or in fact favorable to party aims, the intense atmosphere it created served, in turn, to enhance the logic and appeal of the Maoist view of the world. Apter and Saich explain that, in times of civil war,

> violence offers ample opportunity for the genesis of storytelling. It generates despair and yearning. People come to believe that only drastic solutions will work, that any authority is better than none, and that the *available would-be leaders are wanting* – they succumb to corruption; they kill too many people; they demand too much and deliver too little. Such conditions are, on the whole, propitious for totalizing cosmocrats, whether political, religious, or both, who, in a context of high uncertainty, retrieve myths of a golden past and project the logic of a millennial future. When a politics of yearning rapidly goes from despair to redemption it exorcizes cynicism, opening the way for the kind of innocence that favors extremism. These circumstances prevailed when Mao took command of the CCP. In this context his extremism sounded reasonable.[67]

Harsh measures also acquired the weight of reason when the moral failings of the community was assumed, something for which cultural conditioning in the form of revolutionary memory was instrumental. Drawing dramatic distinctions between bogus feudal beneficence and its genuine revolutionary counterpart could only fully resonate on the basis of decades of cultural production on society in the recent past,

---

[65] Ibid., 313.   [66] Quoted in DeMare, *Mao's Cultural Army*, 102.
[67] Apter and Saich, *Revolutionary Discourse in Mao's Republic*, 72; emphasis added.

a body of educational and artistic work that pointed to little to nothing in the way of civic leadership at the communal level.

Conclusion

At its most fundamental level, Maoist politics stemmed from two types of messaging: one that drew from the level of communal memory, designed to address particular grievances and tensions in a particular locality, for example; and one that drew from revolutionary memory, designed to engender ideological positioning or subjectivity. Each type had its strengths and weaknesses as a tool for political mobilization.

Concrete and specific to a locality, and so operating on the level of communal memory, "local quality" messaging and "movement slogans" easily resonated within a community. At the same time, this type of messaging was time sensitive, at risk of losing its political efficacy once local conditions and personalities changed. In contrast, "time quality" messaging and "propaganda slogans" operated on the level of revolutionary memory. Suspended in abstraction, they were age and context resistant and thus more useful over the long term. Once the party's pedagogical apparatus was in place in any particular locality, and once revolutionary memory became the politically dominant prism onto the past, time quality messaging and propaganda slogans would serve as mobilizing devices in the myriad campaigns under Communist rule.

Village theater was one of the first entry points for Maoist messaging into rural life. Through it, village politics were cast into new frames, models of village activism and trials were showcased and power relations based on education, gender and other factors were overturned in performative ways. Print media provided the means for still more complex ideas to be brought to the public, complex ideas that were still combined with the symbols and style of storytelling brought to the opera stage. For this aspect of Maoist narrative we turn to the party's media unit in the border region to the east of Yan'an, where, at Zhangjiakou along the Great Wall, the party developed periodicals aimed at a broader range of education levels.

9   Reaching Urban Youth

For much of the war with Japan, the Maoist stronghold at Yan'an was separated by many miles of mountainous terrain from Japanese forces. This meant Maoist communication reached two main types of audiences as it took shape in party media over the course of the forties: one consisted of Yan'anites and residents of the wider Shaan Gan Ning border region, where Mao's decade-long social and political experiment was created amid relative insulation from attack. The other was the population of other border regions, who were concentrated along the country's rail lines, in its main cities and towns and on its most productive farmland – vastly greater in number yet more precariously situated near areas under Japanese occupation or Guomindang control. [1]

The closest of these more exposed Communist-held areas was the Jin Cha Ji border region, which served as a buffer between Yan'an and the Japanese front, consisting of sections of Shanxi, Chahar (Inner Mongolia) and Hebei. Party messaging in Jin Cha Ji had to strike a delicate balance between anti-Japanese resistance and political agitation, while also appealing to the more literate audiences found in the region's towns and small cities. At Zhangjiakou (Kalgan), a trade entrepôt along the Great Wall between the North China plain and Mongolia, the party set up one of its more sophisticated press bases. [2]

Prominent in this area of Communist media work was Deng Tuo, a Fujian native who became vice-head of the Central Party Propaganda Department for the Jin Cha Ji region in the immediate wake of Tokyo's surrender in 1945. With the resumption of civil war, party messaging was transmitted over a series of regional platforms that refined communication strategies adopted in the early years of the party. This included newspapers such as *Jin Cha Ji ribao* (Jin Cha Ji Daily) – of which Deng had been appointed editor-in-chief in 1944, and where he held editorial

---

[1] On this wartime dynamic, see Gatu, *Village China at War*.
[2] Timothy Cheek, *Propaganda and Culture in Mao's China: Deng Tuo and the Intelligentsia* (Oxford: Clarendon Press, 2011), 71.

and managerial positions on and off for the remainder of the decade[3] – and platforms with more ambiguous ties to the party, such as "gray" periodicals that inveighed against the Guomindang and advocated for public welfare policies while withholding any clear Communist affiliation. Then there was the "mosquito newspaper," a more targeted medium published periodically or as commemorative or festival editions "in response to actual needs in a particular area," Marcia Ristaino writes.[4]

The distinction drawn here between these different types of publications is important since they could serve different cultural strategies. The mosquito paper was in the spirit of the "movement slogan," Ristaino explains, often incorporating local forms of storytelling and illustration into its messaging, and thus grafted onto existing communal forms, including communal memory, that were specific to a locality.[5] In contrast, publications designed for a wider audience were less tied to local conditions and freer to frame content along the more abstract or theoretical lines of the "propaganda slogan," producing material more akin to revolutionary memory.

The focus of this chapter are party efforts to reach the more formally educated segment of the population in its zones of control. Our example is the work of the division of the Jin Cha Ji Daily Press that published the magazine of the regional youth association, *Minzhu qingnian* (Democratic Youth). More urban in its reach, the magazine presents Maoist literature consumed by a generation coming of age with the resumption of civil war over the control and direction of the country. Distributed by Xinhua bookstores, the monthly reached into homes and schools in towns and cities across the three-province border region, at a distance from the Land Reform movement underway in surrounding rural districts. Beneath the intense imagery of a red and black cartoon cover, its pages are a window onto Maoist communication to readers for whom agrarian land tenure and reform were largely abstractions. Distinct from the local orientation of the mosquito newspaper, the magazine served as a vehicle for the broader, more theoretical tenor of the propaganda slogan through which new political frameworks were popularized. The children and adolescents reading *Minzhu qingnian* most likely had some degree of formal education and resided in regional hubs like Datong, in northern Shanxi, where a decade earlier middle-school history lessons had been given by Meiqing, the young reader-turned-middle-school teacher we followed in previous chapters. With the resumption of civil war in the mid-forties, at the time of the flowering of the woodcut form and of land reform theater, Meiqing's students would have been in their

---

[3] Ibid., 106.   [4] Ristaino, *China's Art of Revolution*, 154.   [5] Ibid.

revolutionary prime, exposed to offshoots of *Jin Cha Ji ribao* if not the broadsheet itself, which, judging by its final issue of June 14, 1948, reached print runs of fifty thousand.[6]

Here we consider three types of texts that conveyed revolutionary messaging in three different ways: through stories, through numbers and through ideas. These texts appeared in the first of four years of civil war between the Japanese surrender and the founding of the People's Republic. In a way, through them, we come full circle: we started with student surveys of disaster-struck rural communities over the same stretch of time that Chinese Communist cells slowly began taking shape in Beijing, Shanghai and other cities over the autumn of 1920 before convening formally as a party in Shanghai in June 1921.[7] Here, with *Minzhu qingnian*, we arrive a quarter century later at the revolutionary platform created by the party for a new generation. Compiled by the youth association in a key border region, it was an outgrowth of a media bureau that would prove formative in the cultural and communications administration of the People's Republic. The magazine allows us to complete in some ways our charting of the pedigree of Maoist sociology on the eve of revolution. Famine, as we will see, remained central to the stories and essays communicated to China's urban youth on the eve of the revolution. It served both as a material phenomenon to account for in Chinese history and an illustrative tool for the diagnosis of moral and social ills.

A Narrative Piece

Storytelling served as a window onto social conditions in the countryside for readers of all education levels. When committed to paper, stories were formalized as they traveled widely over time and place in magazines and other forms of print media. Popular stories included profiles of revolutionary actors large and small, providing audiences with new role models while bringing women, laborers and others among the previously marginalized into the revolutionary fold. At times, social survey data was used to broaden the experience captured in personal profiles. With or without scientific support, narrative arcs served to convey a sense of social rupture and radical change from the old China to the new.

One sees in *Minzhu qingnian* that the cult of the chairman was, in the mid-forties, still a work in progress. In the spring of 1944, Deng Tuo had

---

[6] Cheek, *Propaganda and Culture in Mao's China*, 75.
[7] Hans J. van de Ven, *From Friend to Comrade: The Founding of the Chinese Communist Party, 1920–1927* (Berkeley: University of California Press, 1991), 61, 67, 69, 85–90.

edited a compilation of Mao's *Selected Works*, which appeared just as he took up editorship of *Jin Cha Ji ribao*.[8] After running a collection of stories on Mao, the youth association members editing *Minzhu qingnian* commissioned the writer Xiao San to compose a piece on Mao's childhood in response to what Xiao called a wellspring of interest among its youngest readers. One of the first Chinese biographers of the Communist leader, Xiao had only gathered a limited amount of material on the subject, yet bowed to pressure from the editors to produce something by April 1946 in time for the magazine's fourth issue. Xiao dashed off, he explained, "The Childhood of Comrade Mao Zedong" ("Mao Zedong tongzhi de ertong shidai") without any input from Mao – who was by his own account "extremely unwilling for others to write about his personal life" – or without any permission, he stressed, from him to do so.[9] The story opens with a lengthy description of Hunan's Xiangtan county before arriving at a particular spot in the landscape:

On the river bank, hemmed by mountains, there was a simple, tile-roofed house. Consisting of a single row with two crossbeams, inside lived two families, one named Zou, and one named Mao. With the building divided down the middle, each resided in one half. In 1893, in the nineteenth year of the Qing dynasty's Guangxu reign, on November 19 of the *guiji* lunar year, inside this house Comrade Mao Zedong was born – the wise, great leader and guide of today's Chinese people, our Chairman Mao.[10]

The son of a poor peasant (*pinnong*), the story continues, Mao and four other members of his family lived off fifteen *mu* of land, purchased by his father with money painstakingly earned through small trades. In this way the figure and political status of Mao, already supreme in Yan'an since the late 1930s, was brought to the attention of young readers in other regions.

Through such stories, public interest in a rising political star was served. Stories of far humbler figures appeared in the same pages and served different purposes, such as stressing the democratic empowerment of revolutionary participation. Han Feng's "Shi Kelang's Journey from Misery to Liberation" ("Shi Kelang cong kunan zhong jiefang chulai") appeared in the magazine's second issue, a short story structured around a family's destitution and the dehumanization of its young breadwinner, a shepherd boy, followed by his political awakening. Hu Shijing's father had fled famine in their Hebei county of Raoyang to seek work, and perished on the road. Coming of age in a desperately poor family, the boy took on the name Shi ("Shit") Kelang as he struggled to support his

[8] Cheek, *Propaganda and Culture in Mao's China*, 10.
[9] Xiao San, "Mao Zedong tongzhi de ertong shidai," *Minzhu qingnian* 4 (April 1946), 40.
[10] Ibid., 41.

aging mother and young sister. Spent from overwork, threadbare, with never a full stomach, his mother is left to suffer through her tuberculosis for which she was unable to buy medicine. Struggling to maintain a family of three on only two *mu* of land, Shi carries, from the age of fourteen, a burden "like 100,000 pounds of stone on his back." For his meager income, Shi relies on Hu Zhixiu, a man who uses hired hands to work his seventy *mu* of land, while Hu indulges in other elite pursuits (his given name reads roughly "one who writes and compiles local annals.")[11]

Two episodes set in 1944 lead to Shi's transformation. While Shi subsists on scraps and is scolded as he toils, food and drink is brought expressly for his boss's cattle to enjoy in the fields. Living worse than the animals, he asks himself, "Will this always be my lot?" Then a period of dearth arrives:

Disaster struck, brought by the [Japanese] enemy and by heaven, and the masses suffered famine. Society was continually in disorder. At the time Hu Zhixiu stored grain reserves in Shi Kelang's family home (borrowing grain from the master's stock, though, was out of the question). When a spell of food shortages came and Shi Kelang's family could not cope for a few days, they ate, without making a sound, six or seven *sheng* of grain. This was surely an offense against gentlemen! A heavy rainfall followed, and Hu Zhixiu and his wife arrived at the house. Ferociously bearing sticks, they looked for their absconded grain. As his sick mother implored them from her knees again and again, they docked Shi Kelang's wages on the spot.[12]

Shi resolves to transform his life, realizing that resigning oneself to fate is the "damned lie of a fool." He takes up the call to join a rent-reduction team in his district, then returns to his village to bring all the laborers and poor together. They form a tenants' association, after which a series of struggle sessions with "landlords and bosses" secures rent returns and back pay, among other benefits; Shi's family acquires an additional five *mu* of good land, his mother and sister get new clothes, and Shi is elected head of the village workers' association. The tale ends with a beaming smile on Shi's worn face.

An Empirical Piece

Social surveys gave a broader picture in which readers could ground gritty personal narratives like Shi's. The exploitative relationship in his case is based on wage labor, one in which rich peasants were largely implicated

---

[11] Han Feng, "Shi Kelang cong kunan zhong jiefang chulai," *Minzhu qingnian* 2 (February 1946), 26.

[12] Ibid.; the parenthetical comment is in the original text.

and which defined their political status, according to Mao's 1933 social typology.[13] Shi's tormentor is referred to as "employer" (*guzhu*) or "master" (*dongjia*), leaving the larger figure of the landlord on the story's sideline. Zhao Hong's "The Miserable Life of the Jin Cha Ji Peasantry before the War of Resistance" ("Kangzhan qian Jin Cha Ji nongmin de beican shenghuo") appeared two issues later, a survey-based essay that breaks down the subject into sections on land tenure, exploitative practices and the ravages of imperialism. The marked imbalance in the economic development of the Jin Cha Ji region is put to extremely unequal property ownership and the resulting stranglehold of the "landlord-rich peasant economy" on village life. Monks and temple complexes generally comprised the region's largest landlords, the essay points out, most notably the lama monastery at Wutai shan in Shanxi. And while rich peasants contributed to the emerging, more advanced phase of capitalist development in the villages, they also joined in "feudal forms of exploitation" such as rent and high interest loans.[14]

The essay then offers a snapshot of ownership strata through a survey of eighty-eight villages in twenty-eight counties in the region undertaken before the onset of war with Japan. Before 1937, it found, nearly half of the communities surveyed consisted of worker households (2.10 percent), rental farmer households (5.82 percent) or poor farmer households (41.63 percent) owning 1.78 *mu*, 2.54 *mu* or 7.40 *mu* of land, respectively. In contrast, landlords and rich peasants comprised 1.03 percent and 7.26 percent of households with an average of 97.89 *mu* and 56.27 *mu* each. (In between sat roughly a third of households, "middle peasants," with 18.09 *mu* of farmland each.)[15]

In this context, a range of rental arrangements prevailed, often with payment made in grain although cash payment existed in more developed areas. Rent in kind regularly reached half of the year's crop, while some arrangements required a year's rent before the soil could be broken. At least seven types of loans existed, commonly charging in the area of 25 percent annual interest. A more onerous scheme – "One day one copper," attractive perhaps in its simplicity – involved an interest payment of a copper each day of the year per silver yuan borrowed when the copper-silver exchange rate was 400 to 1, an interest rate of more than 90 percent. Loans of grain, often to struggling families, could involve returns of twice, thrice, sometimes five times the original amount at a subsequent harvest.[16]

---

[13] Mao Zedong, "How to Differentiate the Classes in the Rural Areas," 137–38, in Schram, ed., *Mao's Road to Power*.
[14] Zhao Hong, "Kangzhan qian Jin Cha Ji nongmin de beican shenghuo," *Minzhu qingnian* 4 (April 1946), 24.
[15] Ibid.   [16] Ibid., 26–28.

Having summarized economic practice within rural communities, the essay brings outside imperialist forces into the picture. A combination of feudal and colonial economies led to the collapse of the peasantry, it explains, making suffering from famine an all-too-common phenomenon, with people increasingly fleeing from western Hebei into Shanxi or northward beyond the Great Wall. "Add to this the fact that politics is in the dark ages," it continues, "staring the peasantry in the face, looking on as they die in streams on the roads." With the arrival of the Eighth Route Army following Japan's surrender, the seeds of revolution nurtured by economic conditions in the villages finally grew into an "earthshaking revolutionary movement," one the reader had seen develop on an individual level in the story of Shi Kelang.[17]

A Theoretical Piece

In its magazine, the youth association of Jin Cha Ji offered a range of items for a broad readership of young adults and children, combining storytelling with the social and political exposés above. This variety extended to considerably denser essays on the theory of history. Appearing in the same issue as Mao's childhood profile, Wang Xiangsheng's essay "A Few Fundamental Issues in the Study of History" ("Xuexi lishi de jige jiben wenti") takes the reader in turn through four aspects of the historical discipline: context, materialism, agency and authorship. Yet it too begins with a story, what it calls two "very ordinary tales in fashion in the countryside":

It is said there was a peasant with a life of great hardship. One day he invited a friend over, and after they shared a bite to eat, he said with great excitement: "You know, if I ever become emperor, I'll spoon some oil onto every meal." Then there was an emperor who spent all year deep inside his palace. One day one of his ministers presented him with a memorial stating that famine had struck a part of his realm, and that the stomachs of the peasantry were starved for they had nothing to eat. Hearing this, the emperor was surprised and said, "Why don't they eat meat?"[18]

Not only do peasant and emperor live different lifestyles, the essay explains, but from this social cleavage comes different ways of thinking. Social phenomena might be complex, but they boil down to differences in outlook, which in turn stem from differences in material wealth. For this reason, even the slightest gains for the poor are invariably met with resistance. The essay continues:

Reduction in rent is an entirely just act in the eyes of the awakened peasant [*juewu de nongmin*]. Achieving incremental rent reductions is a benevolent and righteous [*da ren da yi*] concession towards landlords while doing nothing to abolish their

---

[17] Ibid., 29.
[18] Wang Xiangsheng, "Xuexi lishi de jige jiben wenti," *Minzhu qingnian* 4 (April 1946), 10.

feudal exploitation. Yet in the landlord's pigheadedness [*wangu*] that is tanta-
mount to rebellion, because their riches are built on peasant destitution.[19]

Extend this tension into questions of governance on a national scale,
the essay explains, and one quickly understands that the way political
dominance is wielded – by the Guomindang, by major landlords, bankers
and compradors – stems from the fact that people's thoughts and conduct
are merely reflections of their economic position. Or, "to put it in scientific terms, 'One's social existence determines one's social consciousness
[*shehui de yishi*].'"[20] As the essay explains:

If you are born into a feudal-landlord household, you are incapable of producing
socialist thoughts. If you are born into a capitalist household, naturally your brain
is consumed by a "self-centered and self-interested" [*zisi zili*] exploitative consciousness. If you are born in today's China, you are primed to join the tremen-
dous democratic current [*minzhu de ju liuli*], in service to Chinese democracy. In
short, whichever society you are born into shapes the kind of person you
become.[21]

Following on this, the reader could assume that relief only serves to
exalt the moneyed, degrade the penniless and reinforce the conditions
necessitating aid in the first place. Acknowledging past acts of relief is
therefore a magnanimous concession on the part of the underclass akin to
celebrating incremental rent reductions or debt amnesties: it is a sign of
revolutionary weakness.

From stressing the economic, or material, context of events, the essay
turns to historical materialism. Here it roughly follows a classical Marxist
teleology: Out of a proto-Communist society in ancient times developed
a slave society in which landlords acquired the lion's share of landed
property while "peasant-slaves" had little to none so were forced to rent
land, thereby forming feudal society. In the last stage of feudal society,
worker and capitalist classes formed, with the means of production in
capitalist hands and workers forced to sell their labor – the basis for
capitalist society. This would, in its final stage, give way to socialist
revolution and, in the end, Communist society. No nation evolves outside
of these laws, just as no person evolves outside the bounds of social law.
Students of both national and political history, then, must keep the
economic context in mind.

In its third section the essay moves onto historical agency. Here it
makes the point that recognizing the material basis for historical change
outlined above allows one to seize the moment and master history in ways
the downtrodden have done (only without knowing it) in the past. Over

[19] Ibid.   [20] Ibid., 11.   [21] Ibid., 13.

two thousand years of rule under landlords, big merchants and high interest lenders inhibited China's social progress, "putting peasants, artisans and workers in a constant state of half-starvation, not only unable to expand production, but with no choice but to leave the land and head elsewhere to beg for a living."[22] For this reason, history has been riddled with instances of peasant rebellion and the overthrow of ruling houses, each representing a small step in social development. And in this way, historical progress, slow as it might have been, has represented the exertions of "a billion people":

There exist two social camps: the exploiters and the exploited. There also exist two types of leaders: those that unite the masses and those that separate the masses. The former is a force for historical development, the latter an obstacle to it. Old style history took these types of rulers and portrayed them as "holy men" or "heroes," and depicted the people as rebels. This is erroneous. Today we study history in order to expose these deceptions for what they are, researching tirelessly towards people's true history [renmin de zhenshi lishi].[23]

The essay's final section, "true history and fake history," concerns authorship and the high stakes of historical narrative. Old-style history champions social parasites, and by its very nature disguises the true engines of change, but

if you view things from the position of the people, you'll realize the peasantry has truly been the force behind Chinese history, and that it does not need always to take this position of slavery. In order to live, in order to deliver a billion laboring people from this, they must rise up and kill these bloodsucking demons [ba naxie hexuegui dadao shasi]. This is no "rebellion". This truly is great benevolence, great justice, great kindness, and great compassion.[24]

In *Minzhu qingnian*, stories like those of Shi Kelang put faces to the injustices of society; survey essays conveyed the scale of those injustices within a wider social structure; and theoretical essays placed those injustices in a grand sweep of history, one riding on generations of social conflict that was, at last, culminating in an inexorable drive for revolution.

Maoist Morality for Urban Audiences

A range of observations might be made from these three items in the youth organ of the Jin Cha Ji Press in the years running up to Communist victory in 1949. The first concerns violence. Shi Kelang's inspirational journey from shepherd to village champion was in fact notably bloodless – at least compared to the struggle sessions playing out in land-reform

---

[22] Ibid., 15.   [23] Ibid., 16–17.   [24] Ibid., 18.

dramas at the time. Yet it is the magazine's more sober, academic essay, our third story, that ends with a call for extermination. Why Wang Xiangsheng, its author, chose to do so is unclear, but its inclusion in a periodical read by children reveals the extent to which youth had been brought to the forefront of violent revolutionary struggle.

Youth outreach strategies had been formalized as early as the first split with the Guomindang in 1927. Back then, the party had created Youth Vanguard Teams as a way of rejecting the 1920s student movement on the grounds it was allied with the urban bourgeoisie and, at the same time, as a way of co-opting its goals of social transformation. These teams, or *shaonian xianfengdui*, practiced many of the strategies used by progressive reformers in the mass literacy and rural reconstruction movement of the late 1920s and 1930s, compiling and teaching folk songs and melodies in the countryside while holding sporting events and training, and giving "basic language instruction and courses in regional history and folklore," Marcia Ristiano explains. "Music students would perform the songs at music parties sponsored by the Vanguards, and the whole village would be entertained under the auspices of the Vanguards."[25] As cultural work gave youths an instrumental role in the mediation of revolutionary goals and doctrine in the countryside over the 1930s, land reform dramas in the forties empowered youth to realize these goals in their own communities or in ones they adopted. "The really new aspect of the 'new *yangge*'" opera, explains David Holm, "was its use as a weapon in the hands of village activists, and as a vehicle through which they could produce a dramatic re-enactment of contemporary events and their own role in the revolutionary movement."[26]

Working in conjunction with these rural youth efforts, *Minzhu qingnian* was designed to mobilize youth in areas with a higher concentration of the educated urban middle class, a constituency treated with suspicion by the party in its youth strategies two decades earlier. It would make sense, then, that immediately following the essay's concluding call for blood, Wang ends the historical overview with a message to those in the political center. "The middle ground is often the standpoint of the exploiter," he explains. "Principle [*daoli*] is found here. The middle ground's signage of 'fairness' [*gongdao*] is, in truth, a way of protecting those in power."[27] In this way, the magazine tailored its calls for violence to its audience, couching it in more abstract terms than those of the stories and dramas emanating from lecterns and stages in rural Shaanbei.

[25] Ristaino, *China's Art of Revolution*, 171–72.
[26] Holm, *Art and Ideology in Revolutionary China*, 313.
[27] Wang Xiangsheng, "Xuexi lishi de jige jiben wenti," 18.

This leads us to the role of outrage in Maoist storytelling. It achieves this by adding a moral charge to materialist history, one grounded in older, more familiar and more accessible Chinese dialectics of good and evil. In each of our pieces from *Minzhu qingnian*, suffering is met with moral failure: in the case of Shi Kelang's boss, it is indifference. In the case of the political class standing aside as people fall dead in the social survey piece, it is inaction. In the case of the emperor, it is willful ignorance. In each case, what the people would expect a decent person to do – regardless of the broader socioeconomic circumstance – does not happen. The poor are effectively kicked when they are down. Crucially, these stories acquire further power through the larger history in which they are set, one that expresses a revolutionary memory that provides a reservoir of negative social precedent for activists and audience alike to tap into when validating Maoist claims, consciously or otherwise.

Moreover, Maoist stories not only pulled from conventional morality but also turned it on its head. Violence in this instance was more than a political necessity. It was a retrieval of fundamental Buddhist and Confucian concepts of benevolence (*da ren*), justice (*da yi*), kindness (*da ci*) and compassion (*da bei*), in Wang's reckoning. With his words, we see the hinges of a political discourse swing decisively toward a moral rationale for mass violence. Force had of course long been used to uphold the Confucian order. Now it would be used to engineer a new one. Revolutionary memory presented the ruins of failed communities and institutions on which it would be built.

Against whom would legitimate acts of violence be directed? With a mixture of modern scientific analysis and older dialectics, Maoist sociology distilled human personality into two essences: a rigid dichotomy of exploiter and exploited, the culpable and the innocent. Evil is personified, rendered in shorthand by class, as is goodness. ("The exploited people embody those who have moved history forward," Wang explains in his essay. "They exploit no one. They have no despicable acts to hide.")[28] Maoist *fanshen*, or transformation of the body in revolution, was accompanied by a transformation in ethical injunctions, a new morality. The result was an unleashing of interpersonal animosity, and a social setting that was at once volatile and incendiary.

Here we might revisit the words of Bishop S. G. Monseigneur Henri Lécroart, which we touched on in Chapter 3. Lécroart had written to his French readers about the moral state of those in his mission field, "above all [about] the lettered pagan who inhabits a pride from a thousand years of inertia," he explained, "[a] man degraded, congealed, mummified in

[28] Ibid., 17.

his errors; the pagan for whom justice, discretion, generosity are words meant only to hide his vices."[29]

Wang could not have made the point more clearly. The estimation of China's literati, and by implication its gentry more broadly, by the bishop of Daming in south Zhili in 1920 was as damning as those of his Communist counterpart writing a quarter century later for a publication across the province in Zhangjiakou. Equally striking are the redeeming figures shared in both Catholic and Communist texts: in Lécroart's words, the "poor, the peasant, the child."[30]

Maoist storytelling consisted of a series of innovations to the May Fourth and missionary cultural inheritances. Where student reports and missionary ethnographies had deinscribed China's lettered elite from accounts of rural life in favor of what was in the process of being conceived as the masses or the peasantry, the party did so too, only using a different regime of codes and values for the reinscription of rural accounts. Communities previously cast as morally bankrupt and socially moribund were by the 1940s repopulated with a social field viewed through dualities of good and evil; politics meanwhile was supercharged with the urgent goals of national salvation. In order to do this, Maoist narratives raised social struggle above the particularity and temporality of communal memory, placing it in an overarching firmament encoded with Marxist and moral terminology and substantiated by revolutionary memory. Abstractions could be internalized by the broader population and then acted upon in the most intimate of settings.

Two years after Wang's essay ran in *Minzhu qingnian*, its parent publication *Jin Cha Ji ribao* was transformed into *Renmin ribao*. In March of 1949, the paper moved to Beijing (then Beiping), six months before Mao announced the establishment of the People's Republic, and Deng Tuo took up the role of editor-in-chief of the national party mouthpiece.[31]

But before we consider events in the New China, it is important to get a sense of how far revolutionary perceptions of village and town life had diverged from local records since May Fourth. When *Minzhu qingnian* was launched in 1946, a quarter century had passed since *Xin Long*'s creation among Gansu student circles in the nation's capital. Back then, the journal had sought to expose the "baseness" of Gansu society to the outside world, in the words of its editor, Wang Zizhi, so that remedies for its ills might be found and its people might "awaken" to transform what he called a "filthy society."[32] A year later, urgency was added to Wang's

---

[29] Lécroart, preface to *La Légende Dorée en Chine*, by Mertens, v.   [30] Ibid.
[31] Cheek, *Propaganda and Culture in Mao's China*, 106, 124.
[32] Wang Zizhi, "Fa kan ci," 3; Chow Tse-tsung, *The May Fourth Movement*, 71.

stated mission when his home county of Jingyuan lost more than thirty thousand people, or 40 percent of its population, in the great earthquake of 1920 with which our text began. But the traumatic episode was recorded in other ways, too. We now return to Gansu in 1920 in search of these other voices.

Part IV

Politics of Oblivion in the People's Republic

10   Communal Memory

Xu Chengyao was in the final stage of a journey from Beijing to Lanzhou when he composed a series of verses on a staggering spell of destruction he witnessed along the way. A roar of the earth rattled his inn at the county seat of Dingxi, Gansu and before Xu could make it outside the outside came to him, revealing a bright moon in a clear starry sky as the "four walls fluttered and shrieked" to the ground. As he struggled for his footing, the earth gave way, rising and falling in waves "as supple as cotton cloth or leather hides, just a few inches thick, and as if creatures were howling just underneath."[1] From a jumble of ruins next door came human cries, while overhead the moon and stars turned dim behind the clouds of dust surging into the sky.

The tremors weakened as the night deepened, and local officials informed Xu of their toll: the *yamen* county offices were in ruins, a bridge had severed, parapets and battlements toppled, and cliff faces had tumbled into nearby gorges, cutting off official highways. Thousands of townsfolk, their livestock crushed in their cave pens, nursed their injuries on the streets. Then, with dawn, monumental news arrived: the collapse of mountains into valleys in the area of Haiyuan and Guyuan to the east; "whole towns" made of compacted earth "vaporized into a fine spray"; and one hundred thousand people entombed in their homes. The people of Dingxi "stared ahead in shock" as a man recited Koranic verse to the heavens and Xu hurried on to the provincial capital, "escaping the scene at double speed," with locals facing the specter of deprivation and disorder in a world disintegrating around them.[2]

A hundred miles to the east, meanwhile, Zhang Renzhi had been attending lessons – in the old style – in the village of Mafangcun near Pingliang, by an esteemed local scholar on the upper floor of a wooden house. As Guan Shiyu began to interpret the day's reading for his nineteen-year-old student, the gas lamp started swaying to a terrifying noise, and the two made for the

---

[1] Xu Chengyao, *Yi'an shi* (Hefei: Huangshan shushe, 1990), 100.   [2] Ibid., 101.

street below in a hail of flying roof tiles. People assembled on nearby fields, huddled together under tarpaulins or in cavities carved out from beds of wheat stalks. No one dared sleep, and teacher and student parted ways in search of their families.[3]

After a scramble home of five or six *li*, the student found a confusing fog of loess dust shrouding his village. A dead silence came from the crumbling cliff face out of which his family residence was hewn – its windows and door swallowed by falling soil, the courtyard spewing chunks of earth onto the path. At that point, around 11 p.m., a mild aftershock struck, and Zhang followed a burst of voices to a village square. There, at last, to his great joy, he spotted his family. Their collapsed home had begun to suffocate them all, they told him, when after a pause in the tremors, "villagers came and dug through the earth and pulled them out to safety." Following a night in the fields, people collected what food they could from the crushed gardens around the village and searched for friends and kin as a ferocious wind kicked up clouds of dust. Over two days "people presented to the earth god what sheep or chickens were left in their keep so they might escape calamity," and as the veil of dust lifted things slowly "returned to normal."[4]

Zhang, like Xu, soon learned that his location was not, in the end, the quake's focus. Ten days later a letter arrived from his teacher, who had hurried home over 100 *li* to learn the tremors had spared his sixty-year-old mother but killed his wife and seventy-year-old father. Where Guan's family home was Zhang does not say. More likely than not, it was located in the Liupanshan range to the north. There, the earth's convulsions had "brought mountains together in several locations" in Guyuan and Haiyuan, people in Pingliang learned, crushing communities in their paths.[5]

Through the twentieth century, generations of Chinese visualized disaster via a number of cultural mediums, as we have seen. These ranged from school textbooks and magazines, in the 1920s, to woodcut prints and the new "national forms" of rural *nianhua* art and opera cultivated by party cultural workers in the 1940s. Aimed at a national audience, these forms favored generalized narratives of social interaction across space and time. In the hands of party ideologues, both Guomindang and Communist, revolutionary memory would, in time, pivot on abstracted relationships and inhabit new terminological frameworks. The fact that this way of viewing the past was applicable to any context afforded it its political utility as revolutionary movements spread in the interior. It led to

---

[3] Zhang Renzhi, "Huiyi yijiuerling nian Pingliang dizhen," *Pingliang wenshi ziliao* 2 (1991), 164–65.
[4] Ibid., 165–66.   [5] Ibid., 166.

a social diagnosis of atomized communities, civic inaction and, in its Maoist form, a preponderance of evil in the running of rural life.

Over the same stretch of time, disaster experience in China – and through it, past social and cultural life and death – was commemorated through other cultural forms. Equally horrific in their capturing of disaster events, these were more particular in scope than revolutionary memory, as they were tied to localities and transmitted along community networks. The experience of the 1920 earthquake was recorded on stone monuments and markers around the affected region, carried over generations by ritual prayer and song, and inscribed into the landscape itself by toppled pagodas and scarred mountain slopes (see Figure 5).

In its textual form, communal memory appears in three main types of media: published diaries or memoirs, such as Xu Chengyao's poetic verse, composed by and for an educated elite. (A member of the Hanlin Academy – the pinnacle of erudition in the late imperial period – Xu served as the intendant [*daoyin*] of the Gansu circuit of Jingyuan, and was doubtless steeped in artistic and literary forms of cultural memory long practiced by those in literati or scholar-official circles.) As inaccessible as this form of writing may have been to the general public, elite writings maintain a presence in public spaces such as the Lanzhou Earthquake Museum, where excerpts of life amid the Haiyuan earthquake from

Figure 5 *Up from Kuyuan*, 1936. From the Rev. Claude L. Pickens Jr. Collection on Muslims in China, Harvard-Yenching Library. Used with permission.

another memoir, Zhang Shenwei's *Lanzhou chunqiu* (Lanzhou Annals), are prominently displayed.[6]

In contrast, Zhang Renzhi's three-page vernacular account appeared in a 1991 volume of *wenshi ziliao*, or Cultural and Historical Materials. An innovation of the People's Republic, *wenshi ziliao* are compendia of articles, poems, songs and testimonies on life in pre-1949 China in considerably more accessible and popular form, being readily found in bookstores and libraries – and discussed further below.

A third textual basis for communal memory is the city or district gazetteer (*difang zhi*), which served as the basis for our review of famine relief in two Zhili counties in Chapter 2. Gazetteers, in a social sense, sit somewhere in the middle between published memoirs and *wenshi ziliao* articles. A remarkably established tradition reaching as far back as the twelfth century, gazetteers under the People's Republic retain much of the organization and topical focus of their prerevolutionary counterparts – geography, official policies and institutions, popular customs and local products – only rendered in more accessible modern Mandarin. Gazetteers today also continue to offer transcriptions of local cultural miscellany, such as family gravestones or stele from temple grounds – texts sponsored, in other words, by local elites – along with biographical sketches of local notables: men and (in much more limited ways) women of various walks of life. A collective project, often by committee or a team of scholars, gazetteers vary widely in the amount of detail they might offer on any particular event; in this they share a good deal with *wenshi ziliao*, hosting a random assortment of personal recollection and literature on historical events.

One point to make clear here is that neither of these platforms presents the cultural memory of any one discrete community. By and large, gazetteers and *wenshi ziliao* are issued as town or county (*xian*, sometimes called district) publications. They are meant to encompass, in other words, political entities whose borders are drawn by the state and altered periodically. The compilers or editors of these publications bring stone stele inscriptions, village songs, epitaphs and other forms of local cultural memory into their pages for a wider public to consume. And by transcribing these forms for posterity, they also bring communal memory to light for the researcher.

Our focus here is the official historical record of the second hardest-hit district in December 1920, Guyuan (see Figures 6 and 7). The regional hub of eastern Gansu at the time, Guyuan was second only to Haiyuan in both its absolute human toll (around thirty-six thousand killed) and the

---

[6] This was the case during a personal visit to the site in Lanzhou in 2013.

Figure 6 *Kuyuan, Kansu: Entering Through the Outer South Gate*, 1936. From the Rev. Claude L. Pickens Jr. Collection on Muslims in China, Harvard-Yenching Library. Used with permission.

Figure 7 *Kuyuan, Kansu: The Open Forum*, 1936. From the Rev. Claude L. Pickens Jr. Collection on Muslims in China, Harvard-Yenching Library. Used with permission.

ratio of its earthquake dead to the total county population (45 percent).[7] Our aim is twofold: to shed light on the existence of gaps in knowledge of how communities responded to crisis in the republic – gaps that were, in many ways, cultivated by reformist, missionary, Communist and other organs of revolutionary memory examined in the last nine chapters; and to chart local cultural production up to and through the People's Republic, using Guyuan's earthquake experience as our thread. We do this for what it reveals about fundamental tensions within the historical record itself.

Two Accounts from Guyuan

Deng Tuo and Ye Chao were both native sons of coastal Fujian province, where they shared the same home county of Minhou. By the 1940s, both found themselves working in official capacities in China's deep interior: Deng along the steppes of Inner Mongolia, Ye in the southern hills of Ningxia. Both would help shape, in their respective ways, how residents there viewed society in the recent past. As Deng rotated through various posts in the administration of the Jin Cha Ji Daily Press, part of an influential career already touched on in Chapter 9, Ye presided over the production of the local history of Guyuan. Their careers allow us to chart how revolutionary and communal memory were officially practiced over the 1940s at opposite ends, in this case, of North China's loess plateau.

From 1939 to 1940, Ye headed the Guyuan county government, then in Guomindang hands. Gazetteer production was an immense task undertaken at irregular intervals over the centuries, normally by a team of local scholars and retired officials, and overseen by the magistrate. Magistrates had ready access to many of the *yamen* records used in a gazetteer's composition, and had an incentive to ensure their quality since the end product was essential to their jobs. Gazetteers were both a chance for local scholars to practice pride of place and a rich source of local information – on anything from popular customs and religion to past tax policies or households to turn to in the event of floods or banditry. Magistrates, often from provinces distant from their posts, relied on the background they offered on local practice and precedent as they rotated in and out of alien localities on assignment from the central government. In Ye's case, he was third in a line of four consecutive county heads

---

[7] Unlike the cases of some counties with fluctuating figures, Guyuan's earthquake mortality remained roughly at thirty-six thousand in numerous reports from 1921. *Zhongguo minbao*, March 1–4, 1921; *Xinlong zazhi*, April 20, 1921; Xie Jiarong, "Minguo jiu nian shi'er yue shiliu ri Gansu ji qita ge sheng zhi dizhen qingxing," 6.

overseeing the project of gazetteer production from 1937 to 1948; Ye, though, would stay on after his two-year tenure ended, joining the staff at the local middle school and teacher's college until the eve of the gazetteer's completion in 1948.

Normally, gazetteer projects were not started from scratch. Instead, they involved revisions to an existing edition from a previous reign or regime, updated with texts collected and transcribed from around the area. In 1921, a resident named Du Youren undertook to update a Guyuan gazetteer produced thirteen years earlier in the final reign of the Qing. Du went about soliciting materials from fellow residents as the quake-hit town and surrounding communities were rebuilding over the winter and spring, only to be frustrated by a weak response.[8] There is a chance that, before suspending his project, Du had obtained several items related to the calamity that had befallen the area just the year before. Or perhaps they were collected afterwards. Either way, by the late 1940s, several works by locals who lived through the cataclysm entered into the communal record by way of the county's local-history committee, which amassed 136 epitaphs, personal accounts and other miscellaneous literary items from the republican era for the literary volume of a new gazetteer.[9]

One of these is a work entitled simply "A Record of the Earthquake of 1920" ("Gengshen dizhen ji") by Shi Zuodong (aka Shi Zuoliang), a native of a rural district on Guyuan's border with Haiyuan county. Shi's narrative opens with a description of the tremor's violence to Guyuan town and the anguish of residents searching for children or parents in its immediate aftermath. He then turns to steps taken to contain the disaster:

At the time I headed the Bureau of Public Safety, which was responsible for rescue and protection services. I immediately summoned patrol officers and team leaders, and mustered the rank and file to fan out, keep order through the night, and rescue people who were still alive. Already there were those crushed to death and those who were buried but awaiting rescue, in critical condition. To make matters even worse, it was in the middle of a hard winter. The air was frigid, the winds fierce, and the ceaseless aftershocks did not stop for months.

People had put up sheds of woven grass and mats on the streets of the town to shelter themselves from the snowstorms that followed the earthquake, dispersing in daytime and coming together in them at night. Shi continues:

Men and women did not separate as they established themselves all over the streets and lanes, exchanging words with each other in a state of shock. No one dared reenter their home. I then promptly circulated an order for men and women

[8] Hu Yubing, *Ningxia jiuzhi yanjiu* (Shanghai: Shanghai guji chubanshe, 2018), 292.
[9] Ibid., 299.

to cease mixing in such disorder, and instead form their own respective groups. In light of the bitter cold, people were permitted to find ruined wood materials, regardless of who owned them, for making fires to ward off the cold until the morning light. This is the way things were on the night of the earthquake. The following day, people greeted each other with astonishment, and when hearing whether others were doing well or not, they took no time in answering. The next day it was still like this. The telegraph line was down and the postal routes blocked. Appeals for disaster relief were hard to issue as they were impossible to be heard. Suddenly, we raised our hands in alarm, unable to find peace in the face of calamity. Fortunately, Commander Lu [Hongtao] at nearby Pingliang took pity over the disaster with emergency relief, sending carts of cooking equipment and baked goods from Pingliang to the suburbs and countryside where, before they could even complete their deliveries, the disaster stricken swarmed around them, begging in columns that took up half the road. Even though there were escorts of soldiers scolding them, still they did not step back.[10]

Shi gives a figure of 934 deaths in collapsed homes in Guyuan town, and a total of 32,245 crushed to death over the whole county (somewhat lower than other reports). Authorities buried over one hundred families on an open plain outside the crumbled walls of town, and after searching for his own kin, Shi was amazed to learn they had all been spared.

Within two days, the blocked entrances to town had been dug out and traffic flowed freely again, if slowly. It would take some time for the local markets to be replenished via the region's rutted roads. Elsewhere, Shi's account continues:

Thereupon a summons was issued in the area just outside the town gates for all the grain and flour stocks that had not been crushed [by landslides] to be prepared as meals and put up for sale as a matter of great urgency, so as to support the sourcing of relief goods. [Over?] twelve days, relief affairs were arranged. Fortunately, the powerful family of Qi Ruiting in the north district [of Heichengzhen] gladly donated 20 *shi* of coarse rice, and the wealthy town-center merchant Zhang Futang answered a call for subscriptions with 10 *shi* each of wheat and beans. Then an emergency relief facility was set up at the temple to the god of war, with merchant and gentry together running its affairs. With each day rice was cooked and beans boiled in order to aid the disaster stricken. In this way truly multitudes were fed. Some did not wish to compromise the dignity of their station by coming to the facility to be served. I ordered superintendents and police to use water jugs to serve congee and beans along the lanes, sounding gongs as they dispensed it, so that people could, if at all possible, be satisfied. In this way people found much convenience.[11]

Shi's account of his performance of his public duties, which is only excerpted here, is a uniquely detailed overview of events in the quake's

[10] Shi Zuodong, "Gengshen dizhen ji," in *Guyuan xianzhi* (n.d.), vol. 10, *yiwen* [art and literature], 15a–17a, file K294, Ningxia Hui Autonomous Region Archives, Yinchuan.
[11] Shi Zuodong, "Gengshen dizhen ji," 15b–16a.

immediate wake, while also a reflection of values concerning status, sex and other things. From the glimpses it offers on efforts to mitigate the disaster, one can put names and origins to the relief actors he dealt with. We see military and official personnel like Shi working both in tandem with, and parallel to, gentry and merchant initiatives as the disaster unfolded.

The gazetteer from 1948 also included a work of rhymed prose by a native of Guyuan town, Xu Busheng. In "Guyuan's Earthquake Disaster" ("Guyuan zhenzai xing"), the Qing civil degree holder narrates the course of events over forty-two couplets in a style reflecting the highest levels of classical education – words he reportedly committed to paper before the tremors had fully calmed down.

The poem opens with a candle-lit banquet scene shattered by an enormous sound with "airborne cups and plates turning over in dance." Everything goes dark as elegant guests spill out into a broken landscape run wild with convicts freed from collapsing jails and "bent on carrying out evil designs," only to run into the magistrate and his retinue and be subdued "with the greatest of luck." "A long, slow night with no sign of morning" follows, broken only by the arrival of Lu's mounted men, "each carrying biscuit rations and grain, just as dawn rapped on the city gate," bringing calm to a town with kitchens razed, wells filled in with earth and "people lodged under blankets of morning dew."[12]

Then, halfway through, the poem turns to the destruction of the countryside where "the cracked earth shot out fiery jets of scalding water" and "in multiple spots moving mountains were set adrift," before commenting on community responses:

> Officials Lu [Hongtao] and Zhang [Gongxue, the magistrate] initiated emergency aid,
> To the pitifully thin and emaciated.
> Preserving lives, dispensing porridge and burying the dead,
> Responding speedily while striving to the utmost.
> Officials set up reed huts, the people [made] nests,
> [As they] clamored for relief, looking to their compatriots.
> With benevolence running thick [ren jiang] charity grain arrived from all over,
> Emergency aid that depended on high and low coming together [lian shang xia jiao].
> Philanthropists [da cishan jia] keeping the earthquake disaster in mind,
> Generously donating clothes and money.

---

[12] Xu Busheng, "Guyuan zhenzai xing," in *Guyuan xianzhi* (n.d.), vol. 10, *yunyue* [verse], 31b–32a; punctuation added to the translation.

> But like fur turning to shreds or rivers to drips,
> No one foresaw that this was but a cup of water tossed onto
>   a bonfire [*xinche shuijinbei*].
> For several months people cried out in distress,
> All four classes [*si min*] had no work to do but cry out in vain.
> The terrain shook without end,
> On what day would this torment be escaped?

With local responses exhausted and overwhelmed, and a mantle of earth that refused to settle, Xu goes on to lament the slow and anemic assistance from the outside world, ending on a most gruesome line:

> The people, sixty-two thousand of them,
> Living beings [turned to] dog feed [*chu gou*] in the blink of an eye.[13]

Both of these narratives, in their own way, offer eyewitness detail of horror and social responses. But their existence also says a good deal about the process behind the production of local cultural memory. In 1937, when the first of four magistrates behind the gazetteer project established a county history committee with a dedicated office for the task, both Shi and Xu were among the first ten appointees. Xu even served as head of the committee until his death later that year. Predominantly local (at least eight members were county natives) and from education circles (the same number were education officials or heads of local schools), half of the committee held civil degrees from the Qing period, and a third held positions in the county assembly. Aged fifty-one at the time of the quake, Xu, for his part, had served as an assistant head of the county assembly in the early years of the republic, and later became head of the county's agricultural association in 1923. Socially and professionally, the men were well-placed to identify and collect materials from the private collections of fellow gentry around the area.[14] The result was a ten-volume gazetteer for republican Guyuan, transcribed by hand in 1948, with the customary range and organization of subjects found in gazetteers since the late imperial era: astronomy and climate followed by geography; customs; products and manufactures; buildings; officialdom; governing bodies (parties and associations); governance (taxes, law and military matters); notable people; and, finally, art and literature.

Within a year, on August 2, 1949, the Red Army entered town; Guomindang forces retreated northward into Haiyuan two days later; and the opening of Guyuan People's Government took place the following day.[15] With this turn of events, the gazetteer went unpublished,

---

[13] Ibid., 32ab.   [14] Hu Yubing, *Ningxia jiuzhi yanjiu*, 290–93.
[15] *Guyuan xianzhi* (1993), 40, 216.

finding its way instead into state archives at the county and regional levels. A few decades later, in 1981, new life was breathed into the manuscript when the county gazetteer committee made at least one set of mimeograph copies of eighty binders worth of its contents, which made its way into the Ningxia library in Yinchuan.[16] Both Shi and Xu's writings were included in full in this new edition.[17] Five years on, the county launched a decided effort to prepare the late 1940s manuscript for publication, publishing it in 1992 with the Ningxia People's Press.[18]

In various ways, then, descriptions of life and local events in prerevolutionary society were officially conveyed to later generations in all manner of local historical publications: this includes the 1981 mimeographed version of the republican county gazetteer, its 1992 full version and the 1993 updated People's Republic gazetteer. It also includes the Guyuan city gazetteer, published in 2009. In it, Shi's description of communal responses to the 1920 tremors appears not once but twice, in both the volume's "art and literature" section and one dedicated to the 1920 earthquake.[19] Detailed accounts of republican life in past disasters are thus carried through into the post-Mao era, and on their own terms – albeit with the hard-going language and classical allusions of a bygone era (and in slightly abridged form in Shi's case).[20]

But in some ways the material *added* to Guyuan's official historical record over the course of the People's Republic is more revealing. These are stories of life in the preliberated past that were composed during (or just after) the Maoist period. Their existence reveals a fissure between different levels of party-sponsored historical production on the nature of the old society – different levels of cultural work that match the differences between revolutionary and communal memory. We view this fissure here in two ways: first, through the life sketches of two men in local histories – a member of the gentry and, more briefly, a merchant; and second, through the appearance of this new genre of historical writing on the past developed after 1959: the *wenshi ziliao*.

---

[16] *Guyuan xianzhi* (1981?). The possible date of this copy is accounted for in Niu Dasheng, "Minguo 'Guyuan xianzhi,'" 218.

[17] Shi Zuoliang, "Gengshen dizhen ji," *Guyuan xianzhi* (1981?), vol. 10, *yiwen* [art and literature], part 2, 18–21, Ningxia Library Special Collections, Yinchuan; Xu Busheng, "Guyuan zhenzai xing," *Guyuan xianzhi* (1981?), vol. 10, *yiwen*, part 1, 11–13.

[18] Hu Yubing, *Ningxia jiuzhi yanjiu*, 300.   [19] *Guyuan shizhi* (2009), 1509–11, 2663–65.

[20] *Guyuan xianzhi* (1981?), vol. 10, *yiwen*, 18–21. The author's name is rendered Shi Zuoliang in this version.

PRC Prisms onto Two Lives

One way of measuring the extent to which revolutionary memory could be at odds with communal memory is by tracing the evolution of life stories of local elites through the revolutionary period. The 1948 gazetteer bequeathed by the local-history committee under Guomindang rule to its counterpart in the People's Republic had divided 3,243 biographical entries from the late imperial and republican periods in customary fashion: into two main sections organized by virtues, or "exemplary conduct [*dexing* or *yixing*]," and occupations, or "talent [*cai*]."[21] When Ningxia People's Press produced the 1948 republican gazetteer for public distribution in 1992, a selection of these biographies was included. One of them begins like this:

Xia Jiwen was/is the second son of Ji Xuangong. A man of modest and gentle personality, with others he has/had no quarrels. In the ninth year of the republic [1920] an earthquake brought disaster. He operated soup kitchens, for which he donated 20 *shi* of autumn and summer grain, and encouraged donations for neighboring villages of 30 *shi* of autumn grain. He then donated funds to set up a market fair in [the district of] Touying, which brought abundance to the country villages of his native place, employing the people of the area both in tilling the earth and in commerce. Wealth was brought to the poor, and those who had fled returned.[22]

Xia's biography goes on to briefly summarize the ways he defended the local population from the hardships and burdens of military activity in the area later in the 1920s, and then it ends. It includes no mention of occupation, level of education, date or place of birth. Instead, by way of identification, it names his father, along with personal attributes, and does so in a way that suggests intimate knowledge of the subject's character. This was how the biographical sketch of a local figure might run during that person's lifetime, evidently serving as an example of admirable conduct in the community. Xia, it turns out, would live into the 1960s, and so it made sense that his biography remained incomplete at the time of the gazetteer's completion in 1948.

In (or around) 1981, the Guyuan local-history committee prepared a draft gazetteer updated for the People's Republic. This edition included biographies of people who had died since the 1940s, which included Xia. Only after death would subjects customarily receive more thorough biographies, serving as a form of printed epitaph or obituary. In this version we learn a good deal more about the man:

Xia Jiwen (1886–1964), who also went by the secondary name Yuqin, was from the village of Yaodonggou in the rural Guyuan district of Touying. Ethnically

---

[21] Hu Yubing, *Ningxia jiuzhi yanjiu*, 298.
[22] *Minguo Guyuan xianzhi* (1992), 692. Xia and his father appear to have different family names. It is not clear why this is the case.

Han, he was a senior licentiate [civil degree holder] in the late Qing. In the republican period he was appointed to various posts, including head of the office for the encouragement of study [*quanxuesuo*]; head of the education bureau; member of the Guyuan county standing committee under the Guomindang; head of the disaster relief society; and a member of the county council. After the establishment of the new China, he served as a representative on various county people's assemblies, and was also successively appointed to the Guyuan Hui Autonomous Area People's Committee, the People's Political Consultative Conference for Gansu Province, a representative to the Ningxia Hui Autonomous Region, and vice chair of the county's political consultative conference.[23]

After this career summary, Xia's biography turns to his character, offering a slightly different selection of acts performed for his community:

> Yuqin's attitude towards others was one of goodwill and generosity. Happy to do good, he enjoyed giving away [*leshan haoshi*]. In the winter of the ninth year of the republic, Haiyuan and Guyuan were struck by a major earthquake, a calamity such that the world has rarely seen. Residents of the towns and countryside cried out about famine and the bitter cold. He initiated and managed a soup kitchen, relieving the disaster stricken. He personally donated 20 *shi* of autumn and summer grain (roughly equal to 10,000 *jin*), and persuaded well-off families to contribute over 30 *shi* of autumn grain, saving many lives. In 1929 the area was again hit by drought and grain prices exploded. Prices for a *dou* of wheat (equal to 50 *jin*) reached 10 yuan. The famished covered the countryside; the situation was tragic to the extreme. After discussion with his older brother, Jilong, 200 *shi* of family grain stocks were both given away and loaned out, and their release helped to stabilize rising grain prices. All over the countryside, those that relied on this to survive the famine year were grateful for their kindness.[24]

From this paragraph of Xia's biography, we can glean a few things. His relief efforts extended to the countryside, presumably including his native district of Touying, halfway between Guyuan town and Haiyuan, an area especially hard hit by the tremors. His 1920 donation alone equated to a day's famine ration for twenty thousand people, or roughly half the county's entire surviving population after the initial landslides.[25] The brief also includes two episodes of relief initiative, giving a sense of how local families established a reputation for such interventions in the lives of residents, and the organizational know-how with which to do so.

But then the remaining text in his biography complicates our picture considerably. It turns out Xia, too, had been appointed to the original

---

[23] *Guyuan xianzhi* (1981?), vol. 9, *renwu zhi* [biographies], 65.
[24] Ibid. The conversion of volume to weight is in the original text.
[25] My estimate is based on the daily relief portions of half a *jin* prevailing among the international famine relief societies that year. Volumes of beans or rice could sustain more due to their higher nutritional value.

ten-man committee charged in 1937 with advancing production of the county gazetteer; he was even appointed its chair upon Xu Busheng's death, shepherding the manuscript to its longhand draft form in 1948.[26] This makes Xia the third witness to the 1920 earthquake, together with Xu and Shi Zuodong, to be memorialized, in one form or another, in the county gazetteer, while having had a major hand in its creation.

Looked at one way, this makes sense. Often sophisticated and monumental in size, gazetteers required public-spirited, well-connected personalities in their production, not to mention men with the family means to finance years of unproductive and expensive study. These were traits that also brought them into the immediate orbit of incoming magistrates, with whom they enjoyed access as social and intellectual peers. These same qualities and privileges could drive and enable major acts of relief in one's community in times of crisis.

Looked at another way, though, Xia's role in the production of his home county's gazetteer over the 1940s is a prime example of what Jin Cha Ji Press's *Minzhu qingnian*, over the same decade, dismissed as "fake history": elites using ill-gotten wealth to glorify their own kind in self-serving narratives. Xia even closely matched the class profile of the decadent boss in the magazine's story of Shi ("Shit") Kelang – the given name of the boss, Hu Zhixiu, one might recall from Chapter 9, meant "one who writes and compiles local annals." Xia also shared these elite traits with *Red Leaf River*'s landlord and rapist Lü Chengshu, whose given name translates roughly as "one who inherits and undertakes the reading and writing of books." Xia too participated in the writing of local annals, including Guyuan's earthquake literature. And in this literature, local authorities and elites come off well In his poem, Xu alludes to myriad acts of relief in a scene of extreme suffering, while by his reckoning Shi polices the crisis dutifully, and Xia is remembered for his largesse.

This makes the language used in 1981 to describe Xia's elite endeavors especially noteworthy:

In the thirtieth year of the republic [1941], he took charge of the editing and compilation of the Guyuan county gazetteer, laboriously ploughing and weeding over eight years [*xinqin gengyun ba sui*], producing in the end a draft county history of over 700,000 characters.[27]

A life sketch completed after 1964 – sometime in the mid-sixties or seventies, or at the latest by the local historical committee in 1981 – equates

[26] Hu Yubing, *Ningxia jiuzhi yanjiu*, 290, 293.
[27] *Guyuan xianzhi* (1981?), vol. 9, *renwu zhi*, 65.

the cerebral task of constructing the cultural record of prerevolutionary society to the arduous labor of the peasantry, a foundational aspect to Maoist revolution.

Xia's biography is again updated in 1993, in the new county gazetteer for the People's Republic also issued by Ningxia People's Press. This grander edition, with color maps and photographic prints, makes, for the first time, an explicit mention of his political status:

Xia Jiwen (1886–1964), who also went by the secondary name Yuqin, was from the village of Yaodonggou in the rural district of Touying. Ethnically Han, he was an enlightened member of the gentry [*kaiming shishen*]. Born into a landlord household, he graduated from the Guyuan middle school toward the end of the Qing period. For nine years starting from the seventh year of the republic (1918), he headed Guyuan's office for the encouragement of study and the education bureau, devoting himself to the reform of private home-style schooling and doing away with the study of the classics. Instead, he developed formal education, establishing thirty-two primary schools in town and countryside. He also initiated the first primary school for girls in the county (the predecessor of today's No. 6 Primary School just outside the town gate), urging girls to enroll and study. [In 1928] he was appointed to the Guomindang executive and standing committees of Guyuan county. The following year he broke away from party business [*tuoli dangwu*] to engage in local cultural and educational causes and social and public welfare [*shehui gongyi shiye*], successively heading a relief group and then an anti-footbinding society.[28]

After touching on Xia's role in compiling the gazetteer, followed by his relief acts in 1920 and 1929, the sketch ends by remarking how "after liberation, his enlightened gentry status allowed for his appointment" to a host of county and regional appointments, including as a Gansu representative to the People's Political Consultative Conference. Formed in the 1940s, when the idea of coalition government between the Guomindang and the Communists was still seen as a possibility, the PPCC continued to serve a policy-drafting function until 1954 when it was superseded by the National People's Congress and, relegated to an advisory body, formed local and regional branches around the country; Xia then served as vice chair of the PPCC for Guyuan county.[29]

Held up against Maoist storytelling on the eve of the revolution, Xia's evolving life sketches between 1948 and 1993 amounted to profoundly mixed messaging on what the fate of the prerevolutionary elite should be: a man who was at once a landlord, ex-Guomindang official and compiler of a discredited form of history could be commemorated afterwards, somehow absolved by good deeds and service to the community.

---

[28] *Guyuan xianzhi* (1993), 1067.
[29] Martin T. Fromm, *Borderland Memories: Searching for Historical Identity in Post-Mao China* (Cambridge: Cambridge University Press, 2019), 5, 31.

Xia's case reveals a harsh dissonance between different types of cultural work performed over the middle of the twentieth century, in other words between revolutionary and communal ways of perceiving local figures in the recent past. His treatment in the record, and the language used to describe him, is by no means unique. The 2011 area annals of Pingliang nearby use nearly the exact same terms – "enlightened gentry from the area [*difang kaiming shishen*]" – in its account of how local figures worked with relief societies there to fundraise for and manage relief after the 1920 earthquake.[30]

And, significantly, this dissonance between these different types of cultural memory is not limited to the treatment of those identified as gentry. It extends to accounts of Guyuan's merchant community, as well. Take, for example, the following entry from the biographical section of the 1992 (i.e., 1948) republican gazetteer, quoted here in its entirety:

Yang Xuan (aka Zhansan) is/was the boss of the Dexingming shop in the center of town. He is/was outspoken and upright in character, a man of courage and resourcefulness. He easily parts/ed with wealth and stood for justice [*shucai zhangyi*]. During the earthquake of 1920, the [Guyuan] town grain market was cut off and townspeople crying out in hunger and howling from the cold could be found everywhere. Xuan joined with the head of the merchant's association, Qiang Yongjun, and raised a sum of money to acquire several *shi* of grain and give it away as porridge at soup kitchens, saving the lives of countless of the disaster stricken.[31]

Yang's presence in the local annals evolves slightly in the People's Republic history of Guyuan published the following year. In it his relief initiative is again commemorated, only this time it is moved from the gazetteer's biographies to its "popular customs [*minqing*]" section, in the subsection entitled "good customs and moral excellence [*liangfeng meide*]." In a list of seven acts of "comfort and aid to those in peril" since the early 1800s, Yang's soup kitchen appears at the end.[32]

This merchant's inclusion in multiple local histories reveals a couple of things about the practice of communal memory. The first is that biographical sketches could revolve around a single deed, and did not require the more extensive resumés of figures such as Xia Jiwen. The continued appearance of individual relief acts in consecutive local histories (produced, no less, under different political regimes) is evidence of their worth to the community. Of course, other Guyuan actors could have made this list commemorating "comfort and aid to those in peril" for their roles in

---

[30] *Pingliang diquzhi* (2011), 1302.   [31] *Minguo Guyuan xianzhi* (1992), 689.
[32] *Guyuan xianzhi* (1993), 973.

1920. Yang's initiative was meant to be read as merely representative of communal measures taken in the past.

A second thing to note is the continued presence of certain value-laden language over the revolutionary period. The list of "good customs and moral excellence" in which this republican merchant appears is from a text compiled more than forty years into the People's Republic. What is remarkable in this is the extent to which the language and broader system of values from the republican and earlier late imperial eras persist in official local records. Xia's biographies from 1981 to 1993 use somewhat antiquated formulations to describe the personality traits driving his 1920s relief interventions: "Pleased to do good and fond of aiding those in distress [*leshan haoshi*]" and "zealous for the public interest [*jigong haoyi*]," respectively. These are variations on stock phrases, infused with Confucian and Buddhist moral terms, used in gazetteer biographies from the late imperial period of local figures across China. What was the purpose of these texts? Reflecting a tiny social circle of degree-holding scholars and literati involved in the compilation of official local histories, these sources were products of the orthodox ruling elite, men writing, if not about themselves, then about their own kind, and reflecting their values, interests and views of the world. Fundamental to this worldview was the centrality of the Confucian family unit to social order; the maintenance of stable and viable households in which Confucian values and ritual would be instilled and reproduced in the next generation was evidently a primary motivation behind elite disaster relief measures.[33]

But stories recounted in local histories also served a social, and very practical, purpose: as public standards of generosity and activism to which later generations of affluent householders might be held in crises to come. One purpose of these stories was presumably to exalt their subjects – a posthumous reward on top of those received in their lifetimes, such as official proclamations of praise regularly posted above the doors of charitable households and other awards conferred by the community or state. And poor relief undoubtedly served an array of sociopolitical objectives, among them enhancing family status, protecting private reserves from looting, and easing everyday tensions between landlords or creditors and the poor beholden to them. Cases of past largesse passed down orally or in printed annals could be used to prod, and possibly shame, later generations into action.

---

[33] William T. Rowe, "Women and the Family in Mid-Qing Social Thought: The Case of Chen Hongmou," *Late Imperial China* 13/2 (1992), 13. See also Rowe's monograph on the same subject, *Saving the World: Chen Hongmou and Elite Consciousness in Eighteenth-Century China* (Stanford, CA: Stanford University Press, 2002).

Guyuan's new gazetteer for the People's Republic, drafted in the 1980s and published the following decade, was joined by other forms of historical work revived in the reform period. The first was the initiative of provincial seismological bureaus, which in the 1980s published enormous compendia of data, gazetteer texts, newspaper reporting and archival materials concerning earthquake events over the modern period. These volumes, which included one for Ningxia in 1988 and one for Gansu in 1989, provide chronological run-throughs of regional earthquake events with extensive excerpts of primary texts over hundreds of pages, retrieving the actions, and sometimes the voices, of many of the figures from the earthquake of 1920.[34]

More significant in its reach and involvement of the public, though, was the revival of communal memory by an official body distinct from local-history committees. The *wenshi ziliao* project fully flowered over the course of the 1980s, but it had been initiated by Premier Zhou Enlai in 1959 when he served as chair of the national People's Political Consultative Conference – the body in which Xia Jiwen served for some time at both the regional and Guyuan county levels. Back then, during the throes of the Great Leap Forward, the *wenshi ziliao* involved assembling teams of interviewers to gather "firsthand testimonies covering pre-1949 events deemed historically significant" and "inviting people to tell their stories about travails they had endured in the past," Martin Fromm explains, thereby "constructing an authentic narrative based in firsthand testimonies that would remind people of the Party's liberatory role in history."[35] Incomplete, and "with limited internal circulation" in this earlier stage, the project was dropped for the duration of the Cultural Revolution but revived in 1978 when volumes were completed periodically at the county, prefectural and provincial levels of the People's Political Consultative Conference before appearing in libraries and bookstores. By the end of the eighties, Guyuan's *wenshi ziliao* committee had overseen the production of consecutive volumes on life in the pre-1949 period.

Communal Silences

In various ways described thus far, local records from the People's Republic have been built on a much older cultural inheritance. But, of course, the process we have seen behind the production of these records

---

[34] Ningxia Huizu zizhiqu dizhen ju, ed., *Ningxia Huizu zizhiqu dizhen lishi ziliao huibian* (Beijing: Dizhen chubanshe, 1988); Guojia dizhen ju Lanzhou dizhen yanjiusuo, ed., *Gansu sheng dizhen ziliao huibian* (Beijing: Dizhen chubanshe, 1989).
[35] Fromm, *Borderland Memories*, 3, 33.

raises questions about how inclusive prominent forms of communal memory, the gazetteer especially, can be of the community at large. To address this, we consider two additional figures. Their example highlights the limitations of this key window onto rural life, the gazetteer; but, at the same time, they each offer a glimpse into what might be seen as a civic sphere in this remote section of the loess plateau several decades before the 1949 revolution.

When women are named in the Guyuan gazetteer in relation to the earthquake it is in brief biographies, several sentences long, designed to highlight instances of culturally valued conduct: remaining devoted to husbands killed in the landslides, supporting infirm in-laws when their sons were killed or adopting orphaned relations.[36] Yet even these celebrated women are, out of customary female modesty, identified only by their maiden surname (which women retained after marriage) together with the full name and home village of their husband.

But even if women are nearly invisible in local histories on matters of public importance, this does not mean that women were cut off from decision-making on matters beyond the home. When women of means did involve themselves in relief interventions, they did so behind the scenes, instructing sons to take charge of aid to the community, sanctioning the use of family resources to do so and generally instilling charitable values in the men in their lives. Within a historical record dominated by male voices, it takes an incidental remark by the writer of an epitaph or biography about this maternal influence on a filial son for these household dynamics to come to light.[37]

Occasionally, though, gazetteers feature women of the republican period in lengthy biographical entries of their own. Such is the case with Li Shufang, a woman born in 1875 to a literary family in a village west of Guyuan town. Li quickly established a reputation as something of a marvel in the region for her memorable quips, having learned to read at the age of five from a father who insisted on educating his daughters. With the spread of May Fourth and New Culture ideas to the area in 1919, Li opened a primary school for girls on a lane in Guyuan town with the idea of eliminating old-fashioned private education in favor of public schooling, only to struggle to recruit students. Within a few months, through a combination of perseverance and the support of Xia Jiwen, the No. 1 Girls Primary School of Guyuan came into existence, with

---

[36] *Minguo Guyuan xianzhi* (1992), 663, 673, 674, 677.
[37] For examples of this from 1920 to the 1870s, see Fuller, *Famine Relief in Warlord China*, 147–48; Pierre Fuller, "Decentring International and Institutional Famine Relief in Late Nineteenth Century China: In Search of the Local," *European Review of History/Revue européenne d'histoire* 22/6 (2015), 879.

forty-four-year-old Li as its director. Attendance sputtered, however, until the arrival of a Sino-Muslim military officer in the Guomindang army, Su Tingrui, who enrolled his only daughter, Su Caifeng, in the school. Enrollment grew steadily afterwards to a hundred students, both Hui and Han in ethnicity, modern gazetteers explain. By 1927, much of the school's inaugural graduating class had gone on to teach at or head girl's schools in Guyuan and neighboring counties.[38]

Li's life is a window onto several things. First, it briefly but meaningfully connects a major local figure, Xia Jiwen, involved in a range of institutions and initiatives in both town and countryside in the remote Northwest to the May Fourth and New Culture movements. In doing so, it is a sign of the cross-fertilization of ideas between local actors and between the locality and national trends, while suggesting that Li was at least part of the impetus behind Xia's initiatives over his long tenure as head of education policy in the county. It also sheds light on the groundwork laid already in certain communities for the reception of ideas associated with urban, cosmopolitan change, such as female education.

Li's career story and its intersection with the Sino-Muslim community is, secondly, an incidental reminder of another markedly light presence in the Guyuan official history: those of Muslim voices. Part of the reason for the lack of a clear ethnic breakdown of earthquake death rates was the lack of ethnic census taking to begin with during the republican period. Ethnic or linguistic data collection – and classification of China's "nationalities" generally – did not start in earnest until the People's Republic, a fact that is also reflected in local histories.[39] Gazetteer biographies composed in the republican period normally begin with their subject's secondary names, native place and personality traits, while those in People's Republic gazetteers as a rule assign ethnic categories – Han or Hui, in Guyuan's case – in their opening lines. Only in the Guyuan gazetteer of 1993, then, does it become apparent that of the ten members of the original committee of Guyuan's republican gazetteer (formed in 1937), only one was identifiably Muslim – one Zhang Zuanxu.

From Zhang's appearances in local records, we can get a somewhat fuller reading of the broader community dynamic of Guyuan and the role of gazetteer committee members in that dynamic: first was a role in communal mediation. Where earthquake accounts had spoken of acts of desperation, they also gave a picture of communal solidarity in times of crisis. Yet Zhang's appearance in local records attests to the existing

---

[38] *Guyuan xianzhi* (1993), 1058–59; *Guyuan diquzhi* (1994), 674.
[39] Thomas S. Mullaney, *Coming to Terms with the Nation: Ethnic Classification in Modern China* (Berkeley and Los Angeles: University of California Press, 2011), 25–26.

tensions between communities in Guyuan, as well. In these, Zhang and his colleagues were often positioned (or, more accurately, positioned themselves) as mediators. Zhang's family were in fact newcomers to the area, having fled from an unspecified disaster in their Gansu district just south of Pingliang – most likely the drought-famine affecting the broader Wei River valley basin at the turn of the century – to settle down outside the town gates of Guyuan in 1901 when he was a child, where his father opened up a shop. As an adult, Zhang would hold various official positions in the region until his death around 1947, and was remembered in local histories for "being adept at bringing Hui and Han communities together, for which he was held in great esteem"[40] and "mourned by Hui and Han alike at his death."[41] In this, Zhang shared roles in communal mediation with other members of the gazetteer committee on which he served, such as former security official Shi Zuodong, who is recognized for initiating the renovation of rural schools later in life in order to foster local youth and remembered as one who "mediated disputes between Han and Hui," for which he was noted as "making no distinctions" between members of either community.[42]

Guyuan's gazetteer compilers also served as advocates for the community and activists in the area of education. On a petition for tax relief for the county, forwarded by the sitting magistrate to the province in the wake of the earthquake, four of the nine signees are names of those who would join the gazetteer committee sixteen years later – among them Zhang, Xia Jiwen and Xu Busheng – identified on the petition as "citizens of Guyuan."[43] At the time, Zhang served as a teacher and the head of an upper-primary school attached to a mosque in town, positions he held from 1916 to 1926.[44] And like Xia, he too is remembered for taking a lead in promoting female literacy in the region, opening a school for Sino-Muslim girls in which he enrolled his own daughters and daughters-in-law, appointing Su Caifeng (the daughter of the army officer referred to earlier and the 1927 graduate of Li Shufang's school) to run it, and attracting several dozen local Muslim girls from town to its classes.[45]

Conclusion

Communal memory is of course multifaceted, reflecting power dynamics, cultural values and influence within a community, however it might be delineated or evolve over time. Generally shaped by local elders, civic and

---

[40] *Guyuan diquzhi* (1994), 672.   [41] *Guyuan xianzhi* (1993), 1064.
[42] *Minguo Guyuan xianzhi* (1992), 692.   [43] Ibid., 821.
[44] *Guyuan xianzhi* (1993), 1064.   [45] *Guyuan diquzhi* (1994), 672.

religious leaders, and cultural and educational forums and institutions, it is a reflection of an elite with the resources to make lasting impressions through cultural production of different forms. This elite of course can have its origins in different social circles in any one locale and is by no means unitary or stable.

How can one delineate the constituency, so to speak, of communal memory? That would depend on the particular medium of communal memory, and the locality or social network constituting the community. A gazetteer, being the official history of a district, is distinct from the communicative memory of its inhabitants and instead reflects the interests and values of the district's elite projected onto a population of several tens of thousands of people. In this way, the gazetteer becomes the "shared" history of a district, one privileged by a reproducible paper form lasting generations. A stone stele in the grounds of a village temple is similarly in most cases an elite creation, one privileged by its durable nature: to what extent is its content, or that of a gazetteer for that matter, integrated into the under-standing of ordinary villagers? That is very difficult to say, and doubtless varied both between types of communities and over time. If we are to believe one biography from the 1996 gazetteer of Pingliang city, "People in the countryside [*xiangmin* ...] erected a stele to extol [*shu bei ji song*]" a departing local magistrate in 1918; another biography in the same history, that of a local man known for his famine relief and support of schools in his rural district, ends by noting how he was commemorated with a stele at his death in 1932: "the masses [*minzhong*] erected a '10,000 person tablet [*wanmin bei*]' in order to record his virtue [*zhi qi de*]," it read.[46]

However revealing such accounts may be of the culture of stele production, the actual role and nature of popular sentiment in them is of course unclear. The communal memory conveyed in these gazetteer examples, and throughout this chapter, clearly reflected a particular set of values and perspectives, both patriarchal and privileged. Stemming from a politically dominant demographic minority in the area, it was plugged into larger, national (and once imperial) networks composed of classically trained and educated men of means, many coming in and out of official service. Prominent Muslims, such as Zhang Zuanxu and the religious leader Ma Yuanzhang or army general Ma Fuxiang, partici-pated in this culture, and were often recognized for serving as a bridge between the region's politically dominant Han and the demographically larger Sino-Muslim community (the latter categorized as Hui in the People's Republic).[47]

---

[46] *Pingliang shizhi* (1996), 773, 786.
[47] See, for example, Ma Yuanzhang's biography in *Minguo Guyuan xianzhi* (1992), 688.

The new genre of *wenshi ziliao* joined the modern gazetteer in offering a window onto the tensions between communal and revolutionary memory, ones played out over the course of the People's Republic in several observable ways. In doing so, *wenshi ziliao* restored visibility to an array of social phenomena in prerevolutionary life. Characteristic of *wenshi ziliao* treatment of the past is not only dramatic detail of life experience, such as Zhang Renzhi's joy in discovering that fellow villagers had dug free his family from the rubble of their home in 1920. The genre also offered minute details often conspicuously absent from revolutionary memory, such as the origins, operations and finances of charities and civic projects. In some ways, *wenshi ziliao* also continued the use of investigative methods of both the nation-building social survey movement of the 1920s and 1930s and the Maoist concept of "seeking truth from facts" in service of revolutionary goals. But as much as they sought to advance a progressive party narrative into the reform era, Fromm explains, "*wenshi ziliao* editors in the 1980s sought political reconciliation by obscuring the moral boundary between the pre-Communist and Communist eras and emphasizing constructive continuities across the 1949 divide."[48]

In this way, compilers of the Guyuan *wenshi ziliao* included accounts that, in one example from 1988, gave a nod to the "social relief work" (*shehui jiuji gongzuo*) performed by gentry in the late Qing and early republican period – including a home for orphans and the elderly, a Muslim elementary school, and a charity society and medicine dispensary founded in 1923 to assist the local poor – while at the same time highlighting their sporadic and limited nature and critiquing the vague and formulaic way the republican gazetteer had handled the important question of financing. In this case, what the gazetteer had simply described as "financed through the interest earned on funds raised and managed by gentry from the surrounding area [*difang xiangshen*]," the *wenshi ziliao* article described as involving a murkier back story revealed later at a county meeting in 1966. Then, at the outset of the Cultural Revolution, the eighty-year-old former head of the Guyuan charity society from 1926 to 1938, Li Wenhui, explained that in fact a corrupt official (*tanguan*) – who is curiously anonymized in Li's account as "Guyuan XX county chief [*xianzhang*]" – had absconded with a fortune seized from a criminal operation. Local gentry had gone in search of the funds, and were only successful in recovering 8,000 yuan, which they then committed to the endowment of the charity.[49] What the *wenshi ziliao* account offers is a more textured picture of republican life: it exposes the

[48] Fromm, *Borderland Memories*, 113.
[49] Jing Wenyuan, "Qingmo minchu de Guyuan yangjiyuan yu cishanhui," *Guyuan wenshi ziliao* 2 (1988), 127–29.

unsavory underside of governance but, significantly, without removing the local-elite initiative behind public welfare measures, however modest they might be.

In addition to this more measured take on prerevolutionary affairs, *wenshi ziliao* can offer a crucial space for consideration of what has been lost to a community's inheritance in the political struggles of the recent past. In addition to serving as civic figure, Zhang Zuanxu stood out as a steward of the local documentary record. What clearly tied Zhang to local gazetteer writing circles was the collection of materials on Sino-Muslim communities he had amassed for more than forty years – texts from the seventeenth century on into the republic "not copied from official documents, but instead records that investigated popular, every-day concerns," in the words of a 2001 *wenshi ziliao* profile.[50] Zhang's archive of more than five hundred thousand characters of text, though, was never published. Instead, "this nearly intact set of historical materials was reduced to ashes in the 'Cultural Revolution,'" the profile explains. "Today, for any attempt to sort out the history of struggle of the Hui people of the Northwest there is no way to make up for this loss."[51]

It is unclear how much, if any, of Zhang's collection made it into Guyuan's republican gazetteer. Yet Zhang's lost trove of materials would undoubtedly have offered unique perspectives on the experience and aftermath of the earthquake of 1920, along with the bloody ethnic fighting of the nineteenth century and any number of events within and between the communities of the Northwest. Its disappearance is an example of how the tension between communal and revolutionary memory did not merely take the form of cognitive dissonance. This tension took the form of physical destruction of communal memory, as well.

---

[50] Ma Zhen, "Huizu xuezhe Zhang Zuanxu xiansheng shilüe," *Ningxia wenshi ziliao* 25 (2001), 256, quoted in Hu Yubing, *Ningxia jiuzhi yanjiu*, 291.
[51] Ibid.

The People's Republic was born in 1949 out of a quarter century of nearly continuous warfare, both with outside forces and among China's varied population. What followed over the ensuing period of Maoist rule was a bewildering complex of individual and collective mobilization that mirrored in many ways the intensity and scale of the warfare that preceded it. Only now, mobilization could be directed toward the Communist Party's vision for what was known as the New China (*xinhua*). This vision involved participation across the population in a range of new activities and forms of organization in nearly all aspects of life, from collectivization and political campaigning to intensive labor in infrastructural projects. An underlying aspect of this broad national construction effort was the elaboration and intensification, in a range of cultural forms, of a particular understanding of life in the recent past, namely revolutionary memory.

For a regime born of Sun Yat-sen's political legacy of mass mobilization, how the people perceived the world, and its past, mattered immensely.[1] On the surface, public enthusiasm for the revolution was perhaps most conspicuously reflected in aesthetic change. This was achieved through an array of representational forms over the course of the first few years of the People's Republic: from soaring monuments to new costume, badges, figurines and other items adorning bodies, workplaces and home interiors.[2] But the extent to which official symbolism and messaging mattered – the degree to which they were internalized and acted on – is a whole other question. One has to keep in mind the variability of ways in which men and women internalized official orthodoxy, in how they incorporated new or older terminology in their daily interactions, and in how they framed

---

[1] On the cultural and political precedent for "using history for mobilization" under Sun Yat-sen, see Henrietta Harrison, *The Making of the Republican Citizen: Political Ceremonies and Symbols in China, 1911–1929* (Oxford: Oxford University Press, 1999), 160–64.

[2] For a detailed overview of this world of cultural output and practice, see Chang-tai Hung, *Mao's New World: Political Culture in the Early People's Republic* (Ithaca, NY: Cornell University Press, 2011).

their own recollections of the past: these things both varied between people, regions and ethnic groups, and changed over the course of individual lives.[3]

Matthew Johnson has shown the limited capacity of what he calls the "propaganda-culture system" to dominate cultural production across the early People's Republic. In his case study of greater Shanghai, this system comprised a hierarchy of cultural and education committees and propaganda offices and ministries presiding over a range of cultural, pedagogical, recreational and religious activities. While the newly-empowered party intended on monopolizing cultural production and overseeing its consumption, Johnson demonstrates how, for a variety of reasons – including resourcing and personnel challenges – the "post-1949 local cultural landscapes remained heterogenous" in certain ways, a heterogeneity that in the 1960s would take the form of "semiprivatization" and "independent activity" at book markets, recreational halls and Hong Kong movie studios, and be expressed in the uneven uptake of propaganda films by local officials for village screenings.[4] In addition, Johnson notes how variation in state-sponsored cultural practice existed between rural and urban contexts and within official institutions themselves, "creating unresolvable internal contradictions."[5]

Of course, the experience of China's cosmopolitan metropolis of Shanghai could be seen as unique, at least in certain ways. Here we consider more rural and remote settings. In doing so, we further complicate the cultural landscape of the People's Republic by exploring tensions within officially sponsored historical production. We then consider how peak periods of Maoist revolutionary struggle were reflections of these very tensions.

The Communist Party itself was no monolith in its vision. Although naming the party as an historical actor is useful at times for us here as shorthand for the men and women deciding matters on its behalf, "the CCP" itself, David Goodman reminds us in his study of revolutionary Shanxi, "was no more a single, homogenous, political actor than the society it had emerged from and was very much part of."[6] Arunabh

---

[3] For how identity and terminology and their uses have played out in rural and urban contexts respectively, see Hershatter, *Gender of Memory*; Jishun Zhang, "Creating 'Masters of the Country' in Shanghai and Beijing: Discourse and the 1953–54 Local People's Congress Elections," *The China Quarterly* 220 (December 2014), 1071–91.

[4] Matthew D. Johnson, "Beneath the Propaganda State: Official and Unofficial Cultural Landscapes in Shanghai, 1949–1965," in Jeremy Brown and Matthew D. Johnson, eds., *Maoism at the Grassroots: Everyday Life in China's Era of High Socialism* (Cambridge, MA: Harvard University Press, 2015), 200–203; see also 220–24.

[5] Ibid., 200–201.

[6] David S. G. Goodman, *Social and Political Change in Revolutionary China: The Taihang Base Area in the War of Resistance to Japan, 1937–1945* (Lanham, MD: Rowman & Littlefield, 2000), 9.

Ghosh has shown how this lack of uniformity played out in the crucial area of statistical collection and analysis – the basis on which "social realities" were determined by state planners – in the first few decades of the People's Republic. "In the realm of statistical work [Maoist approaches] occupied at best an ancillary space during much of the 1950s," Ghosh notes. "It was only after 1958, when [the Soviet model of] socialist statistics was forsaken during the [Great Leap Forward], that the Maoist method came to occupy center stage as the principal method of social investigation."[7]

So, as we trace the reproduction of revolutionary memory of the recent past through the 1950s, our discussion should not be read as though the lens it offered was the only one available to ordinary Chinese. On the contrary, the existence of other accounts of the past should be kept in mind, communicated within families and social networks, and prepared and published by official local history committees over the course of the People's Republic. Rather than a reflection of strict ideological unity, then, revolutionary memory in its various forms was a moral *resource* for those seeking to instill ideological discipline and justify radical intervention in communities by the revolutionary state, or by activists acting on its behalf. As revolutionary memory was vested with the moral authority of the party-state apparatus taking shape over the 1950s, in other words, it became the superior prism with which to interpret and act on the past.

In this way, the appearance of cultural hegemony in the form of party orthodoxy, especially at moments of peak revolutionary praxis such as the Great Leap Forward, the Socialist Education movement and the Cultural Revolution, masked undercurrents of alternative memories and ways of perceiving the world. The clash of these currents made these episodes into hyperpolitical events, but not in the sense conventionally captured by a political spectrum of left and right. Rather, it involved conflict between frames of understanding and acting on the past: between local and national, particular and universal, abstract and concrete. At the same time, these conflicts were intensely consequential. They went far beyond intellectual sparring to involve questions of what, and who, should be targeted for reform or for immediate destruction.

This chapter, together with the two that follow, aims to complete our charting of certain threads of cultural production between the May Fourth movement of 1919 and the peak of the Cultural Revolution fifty years later. But in doing so the aim is not to invest these relationships with any sense of inevitability. Drawing connections between May Fourth and Maoist practice, to borrow the words of anthropologist Ann Anagnost, "is

---

[7] Ghosh, *Making It Count*, 49, 53.

not to suggest a linear relationship of cause and effect but to explore the contingent process of history itself, in which the origin of a thing and the ultimate uses to which it is put may indeed lie 'worlds apart.'"[8] As I argue here, revolutionary memory was instrumental in the party's seizure and establishment of symbolic power; this involved a continuation of the process of deinscription of elite symbolic structures of the May Fourth era, coupled later with the reinscription of new party-centered ones. Meanwhile, revolutionary memory would also assist the Communist program more generally in fostering acceptance of the New China's growing pains along the way, pains that in the late 1950s took, for example, the form of extreme dearth caused by state procurement policies. And it did this by offering a historical foil with which to enhance the present, however painful that might be.

Land Reform and Political Classification

The main wave of land reform campaigning occurred in the wake of Japanese surrender and the resumption of civil war in 1945, and continued as the Communist leadership swapped the cave-home communities of Shaanbei for the corridors of power in Beijing over the latter half of the forties. The aims of land reform were by no means singular, and they doubtless varied between localities and even among levels of the party hierarchy. The extent to which the process benefited particular members of society, while dispossessing or eliminating others altogether, doubtless varied too, as did the motivations behind the killing that often accompanied it. For this and other reasons, land reform and the scale of its attendant violence remain a point of interest and contention among historians, and will continue to be for some time.[9]

That said, it can be argued that peaceful land reform as a way of resolving entrenched inequalities alone was never a serious option to party decision-makers. Compensation for seized land, for example, was complicated by the rampant inflation of the late 1940s, and would have undermined the ideological purpose of land reform, which "was almost the *raison d'etre* of the early PRC state," in the words of Felix Wemheuer.[10] Land redistribution conducted in more disruptive ways

---

[8] Ann Anagnost, *National Past-Times: Narratives, Representation, and Power in Modern China* (Durham, NC: Duke University Press, 1997), 17.

[9] Recent works include Brian DeMare, *Land Wars: The Story of China's Agrarian Revolution* (Stanford, CA: Stanford University Press, 2019); Matthew Noellert, *Power over Property: The Political Economy of Communist Land Reform in China* (Ann Arbor: University of Michigan Press, 2020).

[10] Felix Wemheuer, *A Social History of Maoist China: Conflict and Change, 1949–1976* (Cambridge: Cambridge University Press, 2019), 57–58.

served additional, and arguably more pressing, goals in the context of civil war, such as seizing power militarily (by incentivizing people and mobilizing resources in the fight against the Guomindang) and politically (by restructuring and tethering communities to the party apparatus).

Our goal here is to account for the potency of discursive strategies employed in the land reform struggle meetings, namely the speak bitterness (*suku*) sessions that empowered large proportions of communities – at the price of their indebtedness to a new political order. Revolutionary memory, together with the constellation of social types suspended within it, served as the explosive ideological ether in which revolutionary practice was enacted; put another way, revolutionary memory of the recent past was methodically invoked amid the demolition of community social and economic structures by speaking bitterness, before the reconstruction of power structures under party tutelage. In short, it depicted the old society's void of beneficial communal relations in which the accused had exploited the accuser, and which party structures and forms of association would step in and fill.

One of the main purposes of struggle sessions was to stage public testimony for the naming and denunciation of individuals as part of the larger process of political classification in the early stages of Communist rule. The template for how both rural and urban populations should be differentiated along class lines had been articulated and revised by the party at least three times: once (in 1933) at the time of the Jiangsu soviet and twice (in 1948 and 1950) amid the broader land reform campaign.[11] As bewildering as this stream of party proclamations might have been for those newly initiated into local and national politics, it was only part of a larger body of legal literature that accompanied the new regime founded on the idea of mass political participation. This included a series of far-reaching laws on marriage, trade unions and policing "counter-revolutionaries," among other things, that "citizens were required to learn about and read," in the words of Jennifer Altehenger, after being rolled out with great publicity in state publishing and media in the first few years of the People's Republic. Meanwhile, trial proceedings and verdicts were made readily available in state media channels for studied consumption by the public.[12]

[11] Mark Selden, ed., *The People's Republic of China: A Documentary History of Revolutionary Change* (London: Monthly Review Press, 1979), 218–25; see also Wemheuer, *A Social History of Maoist China*, 61–65.
[12] Jennifer Altehenger, *Legal Lessons: Popularizing Laws in the People's Republic of China, 1949–1989*, Harvard East Asian Monographs (Cambridge, MA: Harvard University Asia Center, 2018), 2, 36.

Fundamental to the participatory legal system rolled out by the party was the distinction between "the People and non-People," Altehenger explains. Statutes were to be read with the assumption that transgressions naturally flowed from the ranks of the latter, to whom much of the criminal code was explicitly addressed. "Non-People needed to know the laws because, by default of their class status, they were most in danger of breaking laws," Altehenger writes.[13] Whether one fell on the side of the masses or the "landlord classes" and other questionable groups was a matter of criminality, further raising the stakes in the process of political designation.

As for class status itself, this was meant to reflect a threefold combination of one's "family origin" (i.e., pre-1949 household socioeconomic status), current occupation (on which one's "personal status" was based) and "political performance" (which included one's posture toward the revolution and with whom one socialized). But, as Wemheuer explains, "the leadership of the CCP never clearly defined how the[se] three elements [...] were weighted when evaluating individuals' class status."[14] Moreover, the malleability of class designation could be used for a reappraisal of one's class status later on, say through exhibiting greater fervor in the political campaigns ahead. This meant that even the losers of the class-naming process at land reform were motivated to buy into its logic in order to navigate or survive the performative and politically competitive nature of the Maoist world as it took shape around them.

The guidelines, while replete with caveats and supplemental explanations, broke down class status in the countryside into five basic categories: landlord, rich, middle and poor peasant, and worker (or farm laborer). Normally, attendance at land reform meetings at which these designations were assigned was by invitation; exclusion from them, except to be put on trial, suggested one was suspected of being an enemy on class (landlord or rich peasant) or political (Guomindang, cult or other affiliation) grounds. Villagers, both male and female, generally made sure to be present, especially since the criteria for enemy status was far from clear.[15] At the same time, land reform meetings were often held in the wake of visits by land reform drama troupes enacting the very dynamics of class struggle on the village stage, making them less alien to villagers than their novel, radical nature might suggest.

There are a few aspects of political classification worth drawing attention to here. First is its complexity and variability. When land reform

[13] Ibid., 33.   [14] Wemheuer, *A Social History of Maoist China*, 29.
[15] Gao Wangling and Liu Yang, "On a Slippery Roof: Chinese Farmers and the Complex Agenda of Land Reform," *Études rurales* 179 (January–June 2007), 21.

teams sought to identify whom to include under landlord status, the net they cast could be wide and deep. This was especially the case in areas of mostly poor owner-cultivators, such as China's North. (With its colder climate and generally less productive soil, the North attracted less investment in agriculture than the South; the latter, meanwhile, posed its own challenges to those charged with identifying landlords, such as the large proportions of "common" land managed by temples and lineage-hall estates.) In homogenously poor areas with low tenancy rates, the use of hired labor instead of rental income became a key criterion for landlord or rich-peasant status. So in these areas work teams might assign landlord status to members of households that had bought land with the profits from hired labor but not to those who had purchased land from money made hiring themselves (or their sons) out to neighboring farms. In places with few stand-out rich, struggle sessions cropped up what villagers later called "tattered (*polan*) landlords," people with the modest diets and patched clothes of those classified as peasants yet classed as landlords by virtue of their owning a small shop or patch of unproductive hilly land on the edge of town.[16] And then, officially, political status was meant to be based on income over the three years prior to the point of local Communist control – which did not distinguish between families whose wealth and influence were entrenched in an area or fleeting, lasting a generation or two.[17]

More fundamentally, the complicated set of evolving regulations issued from the party center was readily simplified by land reform teams in the field itself. For example, servants, concubines or anyone performing manual labor in landlord or rich-peasant homes were to be classified as laborers, according to central government directives; but in the interest of expediency or other concerns, land reform teams were free in practice to assign landlord classification to entire households rather than to individuals within them.[18] So too could artisanal workshops and other nonfarming pursuits be classed as landlord interests, depending on the discretion and calculations of local cadres.[19] Finally, class enemies were officially identified in shorthand with

---

[16] Hershatter, *Gender of Memory*, 80.

[17] Jeremy Brown, "Moving Targets: Changing Class Labels in Rural Hebei and Henan, 1960–1979," in Jeremy Brown and Matthew D. Johnson, eds., *Maoism at the Grassroots: Everyday Life in China's Era of High Socialism* (Cambridge, MA: Harvard University Press, 2015), 53.

[18] This included the "Resolution on Class Stratification in Rural Areas by the State Council of the Chinese Central Government" of August 4, 1950. For discussion of class designation studied through fieldwork conducted in 1990s rural Fujian, see Zhang Xiaojun, "Land Reform in Yang Village: Symbolic Capital and the Determination of Class Status," *Modern China* 30/1 (January 2004), 11, 15.

[19] Jacob Eyferth, *Eating Rice from Bamboo Roots: The Social History of a Community of Handicraft Papermakers in Rural Sichuan, 1920–2000*, Harvard East Asian Monographs (Cambridge, MA: Harvard University Asia Center, 2009), 124–25.

the composite classification "landlord-rich peasant [*dizhu funong*]." This "blurred the distinction between two sets of production relations – rent versus wage labor – that the Party had so carefully drawn" up until land reform, historian Philip Huang notes, by grouping landlords with those who hired laborers (mostly three to eight in number) at various points over the year.[20] In these various ways, the increasingly weaponized lexicon of land reform coincided with increased generalization in the way political labels were applied.

Of course, there could be credence to accusations of exploitative relations within communities on which political labels were based, of fortunes made on usury, of sexual predation by men of influence, or of private militia used to enforce a landowner's bidding on struggling tenants. The severe deprivation and associated injustices that land reform could address were rife in many areas of the country. But land reform teams were tasked with pinning down the source of these ills with a social schema that was somehow both remarkably rigid and, at the same time, plastic in its application. The landlord category became a catch-all term for the accused, formally applied at meetings on top of the more familiar names used by those speaking bitterness, such as "traitor" (*han*) (for having worked, say, with the Guomindang) or "bandit" (*fei*) or "local tyrant" (*tuhao*) (for exploiting or throwing one's weight around the community).[21] The result was an elasticity and arbitrariness (and in subsequent decades a surprising degree of changeability) to political classification that defied any coherent logic or standard application. Life was subjected to what Jeremy Brown has called the "class status system's dynamism, instability, extreme variation, and sheer confusion."[22]

As crucial as classification could be for the individual or family, it also had implications for the fates of entire communities. If, in order to simplify proceedings, land reform teams or local activists decided to employ a narrower set of political categories during land reform, the result could be a redrawing of the local social and economic landscape. Take, for example, villages with strong traditions of light industry, which were hardly rare in prerevolutionary China. In some cases, such as the paper-making districts of Sichuan examined by Jacob Eyferth, rural industry expanded during the 1920s and 1930s. But when local cadres chose to limit rural classification to the five-class schema promulgated before 1950, and reserve "nonagrarian, nonfeudal labels" (tied, say, to merchants or handicraft trades) only for residents of market towns, they

---

[20] Huang, "Rural Class Struggle in the Chinese Revolution," 116.
[21] Gao and Liu, "On a Slippery Roof," 22, 26.   [22] Brown, "Moving Targets," 53.

effectively reduced manufacturing communities in name, and soon in practice, to peasant economies, as Eyferth has shown.[23]

In this way, political classification and the pressures to free up resources for reallocation during land reform campaigning resulted in much wider effects, one that denied the diversity of rural commercial activities and its attendant social complexity. This reduction of civic and commercial spheres in the countryside into peasant spheres – perhaps the most significant by-product of land reform classification – completed the deinscription of rural elites as they were folded into the more limited, indeed stilted, cultural landscape of a peasantry. Through the process of classification, the old China's "feudal" nature was legislated into reality. Its simplification of the present was then extended backward through the cultivation of a suitable understanding of the past.

A Collision of Memories

The fact that revolutionary memory deinscribed rural elites from Maoist understandings of the past did not mean that all aspects of elite culture were rejected by the Maoist wing of the party. Elements of the elite literary value system were enthusiastically embraced by the revolutionary leadership, as shown by Mao's very public enthusiasm for the very pinnacle of erudition and refinement in Chinese culture to that time: calligraphy and poetry.[24] Only now, these inherited elite forms were made to cast the social context that had produced them in a different light, while making them more accessible to the general population. Ordinary people were increasingly inducted into this once-rarefied world through continued mass literacy campaigns and, in the mid-1950s, the formal adoption of simplified forms of some Chinese characters (followed by the *pinyin* system of romanization to assist students in the pronunciation of the standard Mandarin dialect, *putonghua*).[25]

But literacy and schooling take time. A further dimension was added to the deinscription of the old order – the cultural elevation of the spoken word, which lent authority to new forms of speech over older ones while equipping the masses with new subjectivities. Speaking bitterness (*suku*), a form of communicative memory transmitted through speech and personal contact, involved more democratic modes of cultural transmission:[26] speech was crucial to the subversion of existing social norms and power

---

[23] Eyferth, *Eating Rice from Bamboo Roots*, 124–25.
[24] On this, see Richard C. Kraus, *Brushes with Power: Modern Politics and the Art of Calligraphy* (Berkeley: University of California Press, 1991), 65–74.
[25] Ibid., 76–77.
[26] On this distinction, see Assmann, "Communicative and Cultural Memory," 109–118.

dynamics as speech privileged over text was arguably a radical act, both empowering the illiterate (which included most women and poor men) and subverting the long-standing veneration of the written word among upholders of the old order, namely Confucian literati and scholar-officials.

Much more, then, was at play in struggle sessions than the exercise of one party-sponsored narrative structure (revolutionary memory) at the expense of another (communal) one. A triangular set of lenses onto both past and present was being used to reconstruct the rural life experience: the communal memory of local cultural forms; the revolutionary memory of national (if locally inflected) cultural forms; and the communicative memory transmitted over interpersonal channels. Participation in bitterness speaking – by both speaker and listener – involved a personal employment of all three to varying degrees. In other words, as much as speaking bitterness was infused with official terminology and diagnostic frameworks, the practice was by no means a parroting of party doctrine by the grassroots.

One way of disentangling the hybridity of voices involved in these new forums is through the experience of new players in formal community politics at the time: poor men, and women generally. Struggle sessions were modelled on the stage dynamics of major land reform dramas like *Red Leaf River* (examined in Chapter 8), in which females, and young women in particular, often took center stage. Party stewardship of struggle sessions also echoed land reform stage dramas, which customarily presented the predation of young women in the years ahead of the intervention of the Red Army, after which female victims are emboldened to right past injustices.[27] The performative nature of bitterness speaking was facilitated by the oral, as opposed to the textual, nature of the forum. Its orality also permitted the participation of the illiterate majority of rural communities, again, predominantly women and poor men.

The latter could include struggling tenant-farmers or owner-cultivators, but in its most extreme form, it included landless laborers like Shi Kelang, whose story in *Minzhu qingnian* we followed in Chapter 9. No matter how impoverished or indebted they might be, farmers who rented or owned land or land-use rights were involved in community ritual and affairs to some degree. This was considerably less likely for landless, itinerant or seasonal laborers like Shi. Although community membership in North China was fluid relative to the South (where single-lineage villages were more common) and criteria for who "belonged" in

---

[27] Brian DeMare notes these characteristics of Communist theater in DeMare, *Mao's Cultural Army*, 125–26.

the community varied between localities and presumably changed over time, landless laborers were often too poor to find a partner and establish a family, and could well have been excluded from community member-ship and the benefits, like mutual-aid measures in times of dearth, that could come along with it.[28] Speaking bitterness, then, could have pro-vided a space for such men to decry reasons for their exclusion from communal life and, more fundamentally, for why they were denied the dignity and self-worth that certain things – paternity foremost among them – could bring them as men in their particular cultural context.

Arguably the most capable handling of the female experience of revo-lution and how it related to memory is the work of historian Gail Hershatter. Over the course of the twentieth century, what had long been understood by many women as the forces or path of "fate" governing their lives (*qishu* or *mingtu*, among many other expressions) came to be understood as feudalism (*fengjian*), a term that in its modern usage entered the language by way of Japanese. But this new way of framing social structure and organization in the old order of things came with its contradictions. "At the heart of speak bitterness stories is a paradox," Hershatter notes, based on interviews she conducted in the 1990s and 2000s with elderly rural women in Shaanxi whose lives spanned the 1949 divide. "Women often emphasize that they were confined to domestic space by feudal social norms, naming this confinement as a root cause of their suffering" before the Communist rise to power.[29] Yet any such framing of revolution as an emancipation from seclusion "entailed for-getting that girls and women were already in public space" in the old society.[30] The contradiction lay in the fact that their preexisting public exposure was a function of the breakdown of the old order as families and communities lost men to conscription, flight or death, leaving females and the young and elderly to manage what was left of household affairs, among them farm work and the marketing of family produce and handi-crafts. "In part, the speak bitterness story resolves an injury by *misrecog-nizing* it," Hershatter explains, "substituting the bitterness of feudal confinement for the bitterness of being out and about in dangerous circumstances," while asserting that the speakers "did once qualify as the sort of respectable and virtuous women who should have been shielded from harm."[31] In this way, bitterness speaking could affirm certain values of female dignity and the protection of the weak and lament

[28] Fuller, *Famine Relief in Warlord China*, 137–38.
[29] Hershatter, *Gender of Memory*, 34.   [30] Ibid., 62.
[31] Ibid., 63; emphasis added. On the ways rural women in China's reform period drew from "prerevolutionary notions of female virtue" and "culturally durable notions of 'the good woman,'" see *Gender of Memory*, 28.

the failure of one's community to uphold them while denouncing one's community as "feudal" and inherently hostile or alien to those same values.

This complicates the forsaken subjects of revolutionary memory (discussed in Chapter 7) as seen through the woodcut movement popularized through the 1940s. As these images toured in exhibitions and changed hands through the countryside, many women would have seen in them the disintegration of their own families and support networks through the war years. This led to a general conflation of social disintegration with cultural and moral ("feudal") incapacity for supportive communal relationships in times of need and the incapacity to work together toward shared goals and common interests. In this way, the total war of the 1940s not only created the political conditions favorable to Communist revolution but the ideological ones as well.

Here we turn to how the tension, conflation and interpretation of memories at a society-wide level could act on the individual level. For every number of instances of rich households shutting their granaries to bands of starving villagers or scooping up land at fire-sale prices, there were instances of others carrying their communities through years of drought or coming together to forgive debts by burning them after episodes of famine.[32] And people clearly valued such gestures: in one case, recounted by Henrietta Harrison, when a man from one of the "oldest and wealthiest families" in a Shanxi district "was arrested as a counter revolutionary by the Communists, hundreds of people in his village went to rescue him because he had distributed food to the people in his village during the Japanese occupation."[33] Intellectually, then, while relief in times of disaster could be dismissible (why care about a neighbor's largesse if it was ill-gotten to begin with, from high interest or rent charged the poor), it retained power emotionally (that a neighbor opened his granary to your family is materially significant: your family lived to a new year). In this way, the "bitterness speaking" performed on village stages during land reform, when the most marginalized people in the village spoke out against past injustices, could involve gut-wrenching emotions pulling participants in different directions at once.

In struggle sessions, the difference between life and death could just as easily be a function of perceived political necessity as it could be of the

[32] Fuller, "Decentring International and Institutional Famine Relief," 873–74; Fuller, *Famine Relief in Warlord China*, 140; see also Ralph Thaxton, *Catastrophe and Contention in Rural China: Mao's Great Leap Forward Famine and the Origins of Righteous Resistance in Da Fo Village* (Cambridge: Cambridge University Press, 2008), 35, 61.

[33] Henrietta Harrison, *The Man Awakened from Dreams: One Man's Life in a North China Village, 1857–1942* (Stanford, CA: Stanford University Press, 2005), 99.

seriousness of any personal charge. In this way, members of a community that were known to have acted in defense of communal solidarity and welfare were condemned for their influence in communal decision-making itself. This explains how, according to a study by Gao Wangling and Liu Yang, a man with landlord status named Feng Jianzi, described (much later) in interviews as "quite a nice person" who was "highly considered all over the locality," could have been executed for treachery at a land reform meeting (in this instance in the Kunyu mountains in eastern Shandong) for having joined the Guomindang during the war with Japan.[34] As one interviewee later said of Feng:

At the time, the very good guys did not survive. This man regularly helped the poor and offered money to neighbours at New Year. I even got 5 yuans [sic] from him. He had actually helped the entire neighbourhood. When he was killed, people were all grieving, who [sic] wouldn't they?[35]

Gao and Liu note that "all the despots who were executed [in land reform circa 1950] were designated as 'rich peasants' or 'landlords.' Actually, it did not matter if these people owned land or not, or how much property they had. The important thing is that they were, for various reasons, locally influential. Before land reform, people would listen to their opinions and follow them."[36]

Although their study is based on fieldwork conducted in Heilongjiang in 2003, it demonstrates that people of similar social profiles survived land reform while others did not: Xia Jiwen of Guyuan, we might recall from Chapter 10, was also of landlord status and a former Guomindang official, yet he not only survived land reform but served on local and regional committees under the new Communist regime. What lay behind his happier fate is unclear. But what is clear is the variability across localities in how the political struggles of the early People's Republic played out. Where land reform involved the weeding out of the locally influential, good or bad, the universals of revolutionary memory trumped the particulars and historical complexities of communal memory: the "good" or upstanding of the community, either in ethical terms (de or yi) of leadership or in talent (cai) of craft or trade, was contaminated by a diseased collective.

"We must read speaking bitterness narratives not as an explosive sounding of voices silenced in history," as Anagnost reminds us, "but as having emerged from a historically specific politics of representation."[37] This politics involved the interplay of memory in various forms. With the

---

[34] Gao and Liu, "On a Slippery Roof," 22. [35] Quoted in ibid., 26. [36] Ibid., 26.
[37] Anagnost, *National Past-Times*, 20.

injection of revolutionary memory into village politics, "Speaking bitterness was elevated to the status of 'history speaking itself.'" Through its performance, "local conflicts were made to stand metonymically for the historical collision of warring classes rendered in an idiom of known personalities," resulting in "a process of 'abstracting' individuals out of the complex fabric of social life and rendering them as the material embodiment of a dispersed social evil."[38] If the party went to pains at times to create caveats and a degree of nuance for class designation, the abstracted qualities of revolutionary memory were less forgiving.

Revolutionary memory thus served as the cultural conditioning for key foundational aspects of the People's Republic, starting with land reform. Through the image (woodcut prints and exhibits), voice (dramatic performances) and text (magazine articles), it served as the vehicle through which a growing share of the general population was introduced to new frameworks and terminology over the decades preceding the People's Republic. Through these new ways of seeing and speaking, revolutionary memory infused speaking bitterness with a heightened intensity and coherence in various ways: it made it easier to employ imprecise criteria or logic to the act of class labelling; this was to the advantage of both activist cadres seeking radical changes to the local power structure and novices to the revolutionary lexicon and its theoretical underpinnings. It also gave national purpose to acts of personal denunciation (tethering individuals to larger, impersonal structures of power) while enhancing a denunciation's moral authority (the old order, to which the accused belonged, was categorically devoid of communal or civic values). It performed all this before the reinscription of a new order, which, in the case of China's countryside, meant a uniquely agrarian counterpart to the nation's industrializing urban sector over the course of the 1950s.

Narratives of Construction in the 1950s

The deinscription of the old order through community struggle meetings and bitterness speaking overlapped with the proliferation of narratives of socialist construction of the New China in a range of artistic forms, accessible to both the masses and the more erudite. In the early years of the People's Republic, the mainland's mostly Shanghai-based publishing industry slowly transitioned into a field of state-run enterprises. It was not until 1954 that party cadres took formal oversight over the Commercial Press and other major private publishing houses. The 1949 revolution masked a surprisingly amount of continuity in the staffing of these

[38] Ibid., 18, 27.

formerly capitalist firms "because they advanced the PRC state's pedagogical goals," in the words of Robert Culp.[39]

Republican art forms that had suited party doctrine continued to enjoy official sponsorship and dissemination. One of the earliest moves by Mao Dun as the first culture minister of the People's Republic was to establish an official successor to the woodcut. "The very first document to be issued by the new CCP Ministry of Culture in November 1949," James Flath recounts, "was nothing other than the 'Directive Concerning the Development of New *Nianhua* work,'" which stated that new "*nianhua* should emphasize labouring people's new, happy, and hard-fought lives and their appearance of health and heroism."[40]

Woodcut perspectives on the old society would continue to serve as windows onto the preliberated past, though, providing a rear-view mirror of sorts for a nation accelerating into the myriad campaigns of the Maoist period. In some cases, this involved renaming individual pieces of art in ways to better reflect orthodox language. Five years into the revolution, the Beijing-based People's Fine Arts Publishing House reissued a collection of Yan Han's woodcuts from the civil war years. The volume included Yan's *Images of the Eighth Route Army Greeted by Villagers* from 1943, and four works from 1947: *Settling Accounts with the Landlord*, *Distributing the Grain*, *Speaking Bitterness* and *Distributing Loose Objects*. By 1954, *Distributing Loose Objects*, the depiction of villagers leisurely rifling through a wealth of fine objects forfeited by a rich family, was given the new title *This Is All the Toil* [literally blood and sweat] *of the Peasantry (Zhe dou shi nongmin de xuehan)*.[41]

Before heading the cultural organs of the People's Republic, Mao Dun was a leading figure in the literary realism movement of the May Fourth era. Writers in the movement had sought to harness popular voices to articulate their visions for the future in ways shared afterwards by the land reform and cooperative movement novels examined by the literary scholar Cai Xiang. In this way, literature in the early years of Communist rule would mirror the perspectives of bitterness speaking. But the two forms also differed fundamentally: struggle sessions were hybrid inflections of multiple forms of memory at once – communal, revolutionary and communicative. In contrast, by their very nature novels

---

[39] Robert Culp, *The Power of Print in Modern China: Intellectuals and Industrial Publishing from the Empire to Maoist State Socialism* (New York: Columbia University Press, 2019), 7; see also 185–213.
[40] Quoted in Flath, *Cult of Happiness*, 146.
[41] Yan Han, *Yan Han muke xuanji* (Beijing: Renmin meishu chubanshe, 1954), 5, 16–19, 22.

were elite projections that, in Cai's words, "transcended the experiential level to articulate intellectuals' imaginary of the nation/future."[42]

Cai's analysis sheds light on several things: the first is how the local was subsumed into national narratives over the course of the 1950s. What Cai calls a "mobilization-transformation narrative structure" originated in land reform novels of the late 1940s before becoming a standard form of composition in the "literature narrating the 1950s cooperative movement" in the run-up to collectivization.[43] The transformation, or *gaizao*, of these narratives had "the goal of reorientating the self toward the socialist project," Cai explains, which "meant that the nation started to regulate the local and to appropriate it vigorously into its own imaginary" by "interven[ing] in local social narratives."[44]

What this means in practice – both the reorientation of the "self" toward socialism and the intervention by the "nation" into the "local" – can be seen through our theme of mutual aid. "The so-called mutual support and mutual aid [of the Yan'an] period is in fact a very important narrative theme of novels that deal with the [1950s] cooperative movement," Cai writes, "and it constitutes an important ethical resource within those narratives."[45] Cai notes how character development in these stories achieves an "emptying out of the moral legitimacy of the process of becoming rich peasants" by positioning that process as "an affront to the 'cultural signifying system of rural ideals' manifested in mutual aid and assistance."[46]

At the same time, and on a more personal level, the national inflection of local politics engendered by revolutionary memory helps account for the continued potency of class labelling well into the People's Republic. With it, people were no longer condemned merely for being a bully or a predator (in other words, a community subject position); instead, their record of conduct within the community became wrapped up in a national subject position (e.g., that of a landlord). Landlords were condemned for being a hindrance to national development (in this case, out of a feudal stage) and not merely to local harmony or justice for the poor. Thus, even "good" people were caught up in the widening and deepening net of class conflict for standing in the way of revolutionary progress.

For these reasons, revolutionary memory of the recent past, which suppressed the very possibility of community mutual aid and wider civic measures within the context of the old society, was foundational to the

---

[42] Cai Xiang, *Revolution and Its Narratives: China's socialist literary and cultural imaginaries (1949–1966)*, trans. and ed. Rebecca E. Karl and Xueping Zhong (Durham, NC: Duke University Press, 2016), 48.
[43] Ibid., 49.   [44] Ibid., 34, 45.   [45] Ibid., 47.   [46] Ibid., 59.

socialist imaginary as articulated through the rural cooperative movement. The deinscription of earlier modes of mutual-aid practice from
narratives over the previous decades further enhanced the sense of youthful newness and reinvention, of self-transformation, and of revolution's
promise to community welfare more generally. The picture of rural life
engendered by decades of deinscription, in other words, sharpened the
utopic arc composed by land reform and cooperative movement nove-
lists. In this way, revolutionary memory helps account for the genuine
enthusiasm for utopia exhibited by writers over the course of the 1950s,
an enthusiasm that Cai in his study insists be taken seriously.

Conclusion

By the time of the Great Leap Forward history in its various literary and
academic forms had become a widely discussed instrument of party
politics. "Mao used the phrase 'Use the past to serve the present, the
foreign to serve China' in 1952 and 1956," Tina Mai Chen explains, "but
only at the end of the Antirightist Campaign in 1957 did it come into
widespread use in the general media."[47] It was then, on the eve of the
Great Leap, that "revolutionary romanticism" took off amid what Chen
calls "renewed attention to methodological questions and the relationship
between the past and present, particularly in the fields of philosophy and
history, as well as cultural and literary theory."[48] The retrieval of the past
by professional historians and other academics became explicitly geared
toward a succession of political campaigns and the selection of their
targets.

But scholarly discussion was only part of a much broader effort to
mobilize cultural forms and popular voices in support of national reconstruction. At its outset, the Great Leap was accompanied by "an orchestrated attempt to compose and collect 'new folk songs' (*xin minge*)
written for the campaign and celebrating a new dawn of unlimited possibility," Richard King writes. And "following the call to collect folk songs
in early 1958, 'several million pieces were collected' in Shanghai alone, of
which two thousand were published."[49] Several hundred more of these
songs appeared in an anthology entitled *Red Flag Ballads* and published in

---

[47] Tina Mai Chen, "Use the Past to Serve the Present, the Foreign to Serve China," in
Wang Ban, ed., *Words and Their Stories*, 208–9.
[48] Ibid., 210.
[49] Richard King, "Romancing the Leap: Euphoria in the Moment before Disaster," in
Kimberley Ens Manning and Felix Wemheuer, eds., *Eating Bitterness: New Perspectives
on China's Great Leap Forward and Famine* (Vancouver: University of British Columbia
Press, 2011), 52.

Beijing the following year.[50] The genre by and large sang of the country-side and the great change to life there, from the new public roles of women to the conquest of the natural world and, in King's words, "the superiority of socialist humanity to heroes of the past."[51]

The voicing of affirmative messaging through folk positions was a practice that spanned numerous art forms, the woodcut included. During the resumption of civil war in 1946, the Shanghai-based Chinese Woodcutters' Association had chosen for the title page of a major collection of prints an image of four emaciated children (as we saw in Chapter 7). Into the People's Republic, the forsaken subjects of the past, reproduced in woodcut collections, served as a visual reminder of the revolution's achievements to date. In contrast, a similar volume entitled *Amateur Woodcuts of the Masses* (*Qunzhong yeyu muke xuan*), published by the People's Fine Arts Press of Shanghai in 1959, opened with a smiling pigtailed girl balancing a pair of vegetables equal to her in size, followed by prints of a crop-dusting biplane in flight, a communal kitchen and scenes of revel in bountiful harvests. The latter included *Celebration of a Bumper Crop* by an artist identified as a miner named Cai Yi from Anhui province. In it, the artist depicts a procession of workers behind a banner adorned with flowers and streamers, all led by a man playing a traditional suona horn.[52]

Taking the tenor and vision of fifties art and literature seriously is important for anyone seeking to understand the furious energies and aspirations of the period, and their culmination in the Great Leap. By the end of the decade, nearly all of China's countryside had moved beyond cooperatives, restructuring the means of agricultural production and consumption into labor brigades and communal kitchens. The creation of the household registration (*hukou*) system in 1958 formalized the distinction between the rural-agrarian and urban-industrial sector and the duty of the former to provision the latter with essentials.[53] Narratives of construction – of what the revolution had achieved thus far – provided a romantic quality for the intensely politicized and militarized processes behind collectivization. These narratives would also serve as a way of instilling ideological discipline when challenges, large and small, set in.

---

[50] The Chinese title is *Hongqi geyao*; ibid., 68.   [51] Ibid., 54.
[52] *Qunzhong yeyu muke xuan* (Shanghai: Shanghai Renmin meishu chuban she, 1959), 3, 22, 36, 37, 39.
[53] On this relationship, see Felix Wemheuer, *Famine Politics in Maoist China and the Soviet Union* (New Haven, CT: Yale University Press, 2014), especially 121–28.

12   Culture as Historical Foil: The Great Leap Forward

One of the most jarring aspects of culture in the late fifties was the euphoric quality of artistic production just as mass starvation unfolded in communities across the People's Republic. In 1959, the same year the artist-miner Cai Yi's joyous print *Celebration of a Bumper Crop* appeared in the Shanghai publication *Amateur Woodcuts of the Masses*, his home province of Anhui had begun to experience an "unnatural death rate" of nearly 20 percent, the highest of any province over the Great Leap period.[1] Between 1958 and 1961, the population loss to starvation and other causes in one Anhui county alone, Wuwei, roughly equaled the number of residents that perished across fifty counties during the Haiyuan earthquake of 1920: 245,000 out of Wuwei's population of around 1 million.[2] This loss of life was part of a national toll that Yang Jisheng places conservatively at 36 million "unnatural deaths."[3]

But it is not only the human toll of the Great Leap that is staggering. There were also the similarities between what *seismic* activity wreaked in 1920 and what *human* activity brought on four decades later. Gansu's Tongwei county, some 180 kilometers southeast of Lanzhou, had been ravaged by the Haiyuan earthquake. By one count it had led to 20,000 human deaths, crushed 40,000 livestock in their pens and left 70 percent of homes and other structures in ruins.[4] At the time of the Great Leap – according to the 1965 report *Regarding the Historical Experience and Lessons of Tongwei* by the county party committee – from 1959 to 1960

the county suffered a population loss of 60,210; 2,168 households were completely wiped out, 1,221 children were left as orphans, 11,940 people fled the county, more than 360,000 *mu* of fields were left fallow, more than 33,000 head of livestock perished, more than 40,000 sheep were slaughtered, pigs, chickens, and

---

[1] Yang Jisheng, *Tombstone: The Great Chinese Famine, 1958–1962*, ed. Edward Friedman, Guo Jian and Stacy Mosher, trans. (from Chinese) Stacy Mosher and Guo Jian (New York: Farrar, Straus and Giroux, 2012), 3, 395.
[2] Shuji Cao, "Grain, Local Politics, and the Making of Mao's Famine in Wuwei, 1958–1961," *Modern Asian Studies* 49/6 (2015), 1676.
[3] Yang Jisheng, *Tombstone*, 430.   [4] *Zhongguo minbao*, March 1, 1921.

cats and dogs were virtually wiped out, more than 50,000 homes were demol-
ished, more than 270,000 trees were felled, agricultural production ground to
a halt, schools and factories were shut down, and society roiled with unrest.[5]

By the time of the People's Republic, Tongwei was part of Dingxi prefecture. It was in Dingxi that we started Chapter 10, following the official Xu
Chengyao's flight to Lanzhou in 1920 as his inn and the region around him
"vaporized into a fine spray" by the earth's tremors, and word spread that
100,000 people were entombed in their homes nearby. Forty years later,
human energies brought a strikingly similar litany of destruction.[6]

How this comes to be in any society and moment in history is
a mammoth question. Of course, a good deal had changed in China and
the world over the half century, including the relationship between communities and the nation (or more specifically in China's case, the national
revolution). It was this changed relationship, on both structural and ideological levels, that helps account for the fundamentally different responses
to local calls for outside assistance in the early 1920s and the late 1950s. We
see it in the expansion of the idea of self-relief (*zijiu*) for communities
during crisis. We also see it in the introduction of the household registration, or *hukou*, system in 1958. The idea of self-relief had been employed
earlier to stretch the limited resources in the Communist base areas during
the war years; during the People's Republic it was meant to free up state
resources for national construction, such as the use of grain exports to
purchase foreign industrial goods.[7] For its part, the *hukou* tied rural households to agricultural production in order to provision the industrializing
urban sector. In times of disaster, the *hukou* system also had the effect of
limiting (but by no means fully preventing) popular movement out of
stricken villages to normally better-stocked cities, leaving them with little
escape from famine or other conditions.

But none of this explains the energies behind the seismic nature of
destruction brought by the Great Leap to far-off places like Tongwei. For
this, we might return to Yang's study, which details similar events in
Zhenyuan, the county in Gansu immediately to the east of Guyuan.
Back in December 1920, Zhenyuan had suffered a reported three thousand deaths in the earthquake.[8] Authorities in the garrison city of

---

[5] Quoted in Yang Jisheng, *Tombstone*, 141; see also 535.
[6] The Tongwei county gazetteer offers a higher population loss of 78,462 from 1958 to
1961, or 28.1 percent. Yang reckons the "shortfall" in Tongwei's population due to the
famine was closer to 100,000 people, or nearly 33 percent lower than it should have been
in 1961, based on rates of population growth in the preceding years. Yang Jisheng,
Tombstone, 138.
[7] For a very capable analysis of the political causes of the Great Leap famine, see
Wemheuer, *Famine Politics*, 77–114.
[8] *Zhongguo minbao*, March 2, 1921.

Pingliang, as we have seen, dispatched a caravan of monies, tents and other relief in the direction of Guyuan and neighboring counties. It was little more than a palliative act considering the level of suffering and need there, but nonetheless it was an eagerly welcomed gesture of assistance from outside. With establishment of the People's Republic in 1949, Zhenyuan was incorporated into Pingliang prefecture. Six years later, in 1956, and again in 1958, the county reported extreme shortages of food to the prefectural seat. In response, Yang writes:

In July 1958, Pingliang Prefecture sent a work group to Zhenyuan County to launch a "political revolution" and "organizational revolution." Taking over the county leadership, the work group encouraged the masses to speak out, "pull down white flags," "oppose right deviation," counter "false reporting of output and private withholding," attack "sabotage by class enemies," and root out the source of the county's backwardness.[9]

Middle-school students were enlisted to join cadres in producing thousands of big-character placards for posting around the county while in villages farmers were "denounced" by the work group with charges of embracing capitalism, and their homes were "ransacked." "County leaders who had sought food to feed the hungry were sent to toil in the countryside," Yang writes, while many long-standing cadres and party members were unseated with charges of "right conservatism" and "localism."[10]

It was in this second charge of localism that the tension between communal and national-revolutionary interests most starkly resided. Anyone seen to be obstructing the system of state procurement and its national-revolutionary goals, either as (alleged) sabotage or lackadaisical attitudes toward collective contributions, was liable to political targeting as a rightest resisting revolutionary change. But defense of the community – by members of localities or their leaders who reported existing production shortfalls or food shortages or voiced the need for assistance – involved a different dynamic, one less clearly defined by political positioning between left and right. For localism to resonate as a criminal act associated with bygone elites, revolutionary or communal memory came into play.

How much personal or communal resistance was there? Despite the intensity and enormity of suffering across the country ten years into the 1949 revolution, it remains difficult to gauge the extent of disillusionment with the party during and after the Great Leap, either in villages or in comparatively privileged cities like Shanghai.[11] What is clear is that the

---

[9] Yang Jisheng, *Tombstone*, 116. [10] Ibid., 116–17.
[11] For social and cultural evidence of post-Leap disillusionment in rural and urban contexts, respectively, see Thaxton, *Catastrophe and Contention in Rural China*, 307; and Johnson, "Beneath the Propaganda State," 212–14.

famine was followed by intense political activity across the country, much of which took the form of drives for ideological discipline in how people perceived "how things used to be." Discipline in perceiving life and relationships in the past was especially important after the rural ideal of mutual aid and assistance, which had been celebrated during the cooperative movement as the spirit of the New China, had been thrown on its head by the Great Leap.

The reinforcement of revolutionary memory in the wake of calamity in communities across the country in the second decade of the People's Republic is the focus of this chapter. Our aim is to trace the use of cultural memory as a foil against which mass starvation under the New China, and the experience of modernization under party direction more generally, was contrasted. We begin by touching on how ideological discipline was approached in the crucial institution of the military before turning to efforts at shaping public perceptions more broadly in the early to mid-1960s, a stage in Maoist campaigning known as the Socialist Education and Four Histories movements.

The Socialist Education Movement

The People's Liberation Army (PLA) was a force that sprang in large part from rural areas, which were hit most harshly by the Great Leap famine. Its commanding officers could safely assume that the rank and file were exposed to unsettling developments in the countryside from correspondence and family visits, and from the local press over which state supervision had been relatively lax, historian Daniel Leese explains. In the middle of 1960, military authorities in affected parts of North China moved to tighten controls on personal communication with home and rein in local reportage over print and broadcasting channels. But ultimately the strategy authorities took relied less on "restrictive measures" and "confiscation of family letters or the rejection of visiting relatives" and more on discussion of "natural disasters" and "the deviations of a number of local cadres from the correct line."[12] Originating in the northwestern military command based in Gansu, the army's approach would include:

New forms of exegetical bonding at the lower ranks that emphasized the emotional aspect [Leese writes]. The Lanzhou Military Region had, after conducting a rectification of working styles among party cadres in July 1960, employed a method to strengthen the proletarian class standpoint; this method was commonly referred to as "two remembrances, three investigations" (liang yi, san cha). On [Minister of National Defense] Lin Biao's request, the report of the Lanzhou

[12] Leese, *Mao Cult*, 98–99.

Military Region was promoted throughout the army in a number of trial spots [the results of which a political department report found "highly satisfying," in Leese's words]. Within a short period of time (usually three to four weeks), the educational movement had raised the soldiers' class awareness and fuelled 'fervent love' for the socialist cause. The participants, according to the [January 1961] report, had compared their present situation with the bitterness of the past and had come to feel gratitude toward the party, despite the present hardships.[13]

Trialed in hundreds of units across the country, "the emotional bonding was implemented as the core of political work in all army units in the first months of 1961," Leese explains. Through exercises in bonding through group study, "the soldiers' passive acceptance [was] to be turned into active and self-conscious propagation of the party's interpretation of events. This type of exemplary education, according to a contemporary report [from 1961], proved to be ten times more effective than the usual frontal classroom lectures."[14]

The military's response to the ideological challenges posed by widespread calamity a decade into the People's Republic, then, included the refinement and expansion of study and socialization techniques developed at Yan'an in the formative stages of the Maoist movement. And instrumental to this endeavor was its historical aspect, which had, by 1960, reached considerably higher levels of sophistication and dissemination than the cultural production of the Yan'an period. Through such group study and bonding exercises in the "investigation" of the present through "remembrance" of the bitter past, authorities reinforced the national "intervention in local social narratives" (to return to the words of Cai Xiang) achieved by literature over the course of the 1950s. Only this time, narrative intervention had immediate and direct bearing on responses to events in localities in which millions continued to starve.

The military had tested what the Socialist Education movement would implement for the party among the general population over the following few years: ritualizing the consumption of revolutionary memory in both intimate and very public practices of recital and performance, running parallel to the way the book of *Quotations of Chairman Mao* originated in an early 1960s group study among PLA soldiers before spreading to the public at large.

This 1960s reinvigoration of revolutionary memory equipped a new generation with the resources for political combat on the basis of historical conditions many had no experience of themselves. In the countryside, work teams achieved this by sponsoring events at which older villagers spoke of the past in ways that echoed bitterness speaking. In one north

---

[13] Ibid., 99.   [14] Ibid., 99–100.

Henan community in 1964, "The village leaders cooked a big pot of wild vegetables to serve a meal for the whole village," a villager later explained, and "while we were eating, the old folks would tell us how hard life was before Liberation."[15] In cities and towns, the movement could be more elaborate, consisting of class education exhibitions (*jiezhan*) sponsored from 1963 to 1966 by party committees from the municipal on up to the provincial levels – a phenomenon studied by Denise Ho. Building on earlier practices of displaying artifacts acquired during the house raids that accompanied land reform and other campaigns of the 1950s, "the genre was intensely local," Ho writes.[16] In places, old landlord compounds were turned into walk-through dioramas depicting debt or rent collection. In a sense, woodcut images from the land reform era – such as Yan Han's *Settling Accounts with the Landlord*, reissued in the 1962 collection *Woodcuts of the Liberated Areas* by Beijing's People's Fine Art Publishing House – were brought to life for schoolchildren and the general public.[17] Via an array of cultural forms over the course of the 1960s, political messaging on what existed before the revolution was further refined and institutionalized, and through it, in Ho's words, "the ghosts of class enemies came to live in China's midst."[18]

Remaking Communal Memory on the Loess Plateau

Ideological intervention in the wake of calamity such as the Great Leap Forward would appear to be a most daunting endeavor. The Leap's consequences, especially those for rural communities, presented herculean challenges to those concerned with the cultivation of party messaging a decade into the New China. One aspect of such efforts involved cultural work on local history in ways that refashioned communal memory into the image of its revolutionary counterpart. To consider how this was done, we turn to Shanxi.

Southern Shanxi's Jin district sits within the Taihang mountain range, which forms the easternmost edge of China's loess region, whose cave home communities stretch across the mountainous landscape westward from Jin all the way to Lanzhou in central Gansu. It would make sense to

---

[15] Villager speaking in 1998, quoted in Thaxton, *Catastrophe and Contention in Rural China*, 295. For a thorough discussion of the varied ways villagers in north Henan dealt with official representations of the Great Leap years and the tortured explanations for the famine conditions it precipitated, see 292–324 of the same volume.

[16] Denise Y. Ho, *Curating Revolution: Politics on Display in Mao's China* (Cambridge: Cambridge University Press, 2018), 142; see also 150.

[17] Zou Ya and Li Pingfan, eds., *Jiefang qu muke* (Shanghai: Renmin meishu chuban she, 1962), 93.

[18] Ho, *Curating Revolution*, 137.

trace revolutionary memory's development in relation to communal memory here for several reasons. Chances are that local residents were familiar with the imagery of the woodcut movement as Jin sat in the old base area targeted by woodcut artists as early as the war of resistance against Japan, as we saw in Chapter 7. Southeastern Shanxi was also where, in the last stage of the war with Japan, the party cultural worker Ruan Zhangjing composed his play *Red Leaf River*, which became the leading land reform opera in the wider region around Jin, as we saw in Chapter 8. During the resumption of civil war that followed, the area formed the southernmost part of the Jin Cha Ji border region, whose Zhangjiakou-based newspaper and magazine unit – sketched in Chapter 9 – later evolved into the main party newspaper, *Renmin ribao*. Together, these local developments provide a sense of the types of cultural conditioning that, generally speaking, residents there were exposed to in the decades leading into the 1960s.

While the 1920 Haiyuan earthquake could be felt as far as eastern Shanxi, it did relatively little damage to communities there, if any at all; yet Shanxi, and the area around the Jin district especially, had been the center of China's most momentous famine in living memory, the Guangxu-era famine of 1876–79, which saw the death of possibly ten million people across five northern provinces over three years of drought. Fortunately, over the course of the Great Leap, Shanxi experienced possibly the lowest death rate of all provinces. But immediately to Jin's south and east was Henan, which saw nearly three million "unnatural deaths" during the Leap, according to Cao Shuji, the sixth highest toll in the country.[19] If Jin's residents were not witnessing starvation in their midst around 1960, evidence of its occurrence in such numbers nearby likely made its way over provincial borders.

To meet this concern, authorities in southern Shanxi employed the memory of disaster in several ways. The first was centered in classrooms. In 1960, two years into the Leap, officials equipped teachers with copies of stele inscriptions in which gentry had recounted horrific episodes of suicide, cannibalism and the sale of children by the starving nearly a century earlier – inscriptions the students were made to memorize. Schools in the region also "organized activity nights during which elderly villagers were invited to share stories about conditions during the Incredible Famine [of the late 1870s]," historian Kathryn Edgerton-Tarpley writes. And, in a striking parallel with the cultural practice (but of course not the context) of London Missionary Society Sunday school productions on Chinese life half a century earlier – touched on in

---

[19] Cao's estimates are cited in Yang Jisheng, *Tombstone*, 395–96.

Chapter 3 – "Students and teachers [in 1960 Shanxi] presented skits, poems, and essays that compared the dismal events" of the nineteenth century with what was unfolding in the country's reorganized countryside in a bid to make students "thankful for the government's grain rations."[20]

A second move officials in Shanxi took to head off parallels between late imperial events and the present was to dispatch staffers from "local history offices" into the countryside "to collect primary source documents about the 1876–79 famine," Edgerton-Tarpley writes. As the Great Leap famine died down in 1961 or 1962, depending on the locality, a portion of the collected materials appeared in a two-volume compendium published in the Shanxi capital.[21] "The prefaces to that compilation clearly illustrate just how desperately the famine-stricken new society needed the construct of a 'cannibalistic old China' as a dark contrast to modern troubles," Edgerton-Tarpley writes, adding how party ideologues contrasted the predatory nature of "moral famine" under the Qing with "natural disaster" in the New China.[22] "The present is totally different," the compilers assured readers. "The people are already liberated; the exploiting class has already been overthrown; we already have the leadership of the Party and Chairman Mao, a socialist system, a unified grain purchasing and marketing system."[23]

But it is a third intervention made around this time that is perhaps most revealing about the changing relationship between the national and the local, and between revolutionary and communal memory. This is the nationwide effort to produce a new generation of local history launched in the immediate wake of the Great Leap. Although the Four Histories movement took off in 1962 as part of the Socialist Education movement, like the class education exhibition, or *jiezhan*, and other cultural practices that built on earlier ones, Four Histories as a movement was amorphous in nature and difficult to date: a combination of a top-down and grassroots initiative involving both new works and ones produced over the preceding decades. Sidney Greenblatt notes that the Four Histories movement "is most accurately described as a sporadic and recurrent mobilization, over a period of nearly thirty years, of Chinese historical consciousness and historical resources in a variety of forms and for a variety of purposes."[24]

---

[20] Edgerton-Tarpley, *Tears from Iron*, 230.
[21] One of the volumes, published in Taiyuan in 1961, is *Annual Record of the Third Year of the Guangxu Reign (Guangxu sannian nianjing lu).*
[22] Edgerton-Tarpley, *Tears from Iron*, 228, 233.   [23] Quoted in ibid., 229.
[24] Sidney L. Greenblatt, introduction to *The People of Taihang: An Anthology of Family Histories,* ed. Sidney L. Greenblatt (White Plains, NY: International Arts and Sciences Press, 1976), xvii.

In the case of Jin, the movement was overseen by a Four Histories editorial committee assembled by the district, producing a "rough draft containing over seventy thousand family histories," which was winnowed down to a second draft of "ninety-six model stories" and, after a final (fourth) stage of editing, a book of seventeen stories entitled *Taihang renjia* (*The People of Taihang*), which was published by Beijing's China Youth Publishing House (Zhongguo qingnian chubanshe) in 1964.[25] Toward the end of the following year, newspapers ran articles on the movement and printed some model histories; this included a call in October by the editors of *Renmin ribao* for readers to send in additional pieces along similar lines.[26]

This aspect of the Socialist Education movement of the 1960s, then, can be seen as a continuation of cultural work of the 1940s when the party's propaganda apparatus took shape in the Jin Cha Ji border region seat of Zhangjiakou. Back then, as we saw in Chapter 9, the Jin Cha Ji Daily Press had both introduced its readership to major figures in the party, such as Mao Zedong (through a story of his childhood), and run life stories of members of the party base, such as farm hands and other workers, in its magazine *Minzhu qingnian*. *The People of Taihang* used similar narrative structures and life trajectories.

But there were important differences between Four Histories and these earlier magazine writings. Now, these histories were more explicitly the products of coproduction between local informants and outside students, activists and cultural workers. A main feature of the movement was the mobilization of "sent-down" youth and other activist-intellectuals to the countryside as cultural workers to conduct interviews with peasants, workers and cadres on which four types of histories would be based: "family, the village or street, the commune, and the factory or other institutions."[27] Authorship of the final product varied and was often layered, based on multiple stages of writing, revision and selection coordinated by local party committees and cultural officials. And now, fifteen years into the revolution that these cultural workers had helped give rise to, they met the need to shore up continued popular support in the wake of the mass calamity that followed collectivization.

For an example of what the Four Histories movement produced in the form of *The People of Taihang*, we turn to the volume's opening story. "A Home Given by Chairman Mao" ("Mao chuxi geile yi ge jia") is the account of a fifty-one-year-old woman named Ku Hua-jung from

---

[25] Greenblatt, introduction to *People of Taihang*, xx.
[26] Stephen Uhalley Jr., "The 'Four Histories' Movement: A Revolution in Writing China's Past," *Current Scene: Developments in Mainland China* 4/2 (1966), 8–9.
[27] Uhalley, "The 'Four Histories' Movement," 2.

a village in Licheng county, Shanxi, on the border of Hebei. In important ways, Ku's story reflects the memory and experience of many poor women as studied in major recent works of the social history of North China in the republic. Like those of many of the women interviewed by Gail Hershatter, Ku's story, told in the third person, is less a "family history," which requires the luxury of a degree of household stability, than one of repeated loss of home and family and exposure to hostile environments in a bid to survive. Born in a village in Wu'an county, Hebei, not far from the border with Shanxi and Henan, at times Ku lived off tree bark and other famine foods before her parents decided that selling her to a family in another village was the only way for her to survive. Here, Ku's story reflects the transactional nature of the Chinese family, which led to the exchange of young females, in particular, during periods of family distress.[28]

But then, in conveying this aspect of recent Chinese life, "A Home Given by Chairman Mao" goes considerably further. Upon her sale, Ku arrives in the home of her first tormentor, "The Living King of Hell," where she is bloodily beaten and made to kneel on broken tiles for minor carelessness; later, having grown into an attractive young woman, she refuses to become her master's concubine, for which the rejected man hangs her from a beam and flogs her. Later, after being sold to the household of another man "as diabolic as the King of Hell" she just left, Ku takes pity on a woman who begs at the door on New Year's day, only for her new master, outraged at Ku's gesture of giving some corn bread to the old woman, to take a "water-soaked rope to beat [Ku] over the head" until she bled. Finally, she makes it to Shanxi, where she settles with a kind working man, only for him to be killed later by the invading Japanese. Struggling to survive with her children, living in abandoned temples and threatened with starvation, "their lives were saved" with the arrival of the Eighth Route army "led by Chairman Mao," and the story ends. The moral of the story is captured by a line Ku says to herself: "I've met many rich people in the past. None of them treated me as a human being."[29]

The predation and hardship suffered by women like Ku were of course very real, in part a product of social practices that subordinated and commodified females and the young, especially during times of family distress when many were sold away. But then *The People of Taihang*

---

[28] On this aspect of late imperial and republican-era culture, see Johanna S. Ransmeier, *Sold People: Traffickers and Family Life in North China* (Cambridge, MA: Harvard University Press, 2017).

[29] Han Wen-Chou and Yao Lung-Ch'ang, "A Home Given by Chairman Mao," in Greenblatt, ed., *People of Taihang*, 9, 22, 25, 28, 30.

narrates this past by consistently casting only the poorest as having humanity while pointedly removing the possibility of humanity from those of higher social stations. Visceral in nature, the stories pivot on basic acts of (in)decency. Political allies and enemies in *Taihang* are identified for the reader less in terms of the technical criteria of classification, such as the exploitation of hired labor or renting out of land, although these relationships certainly have their place in the stories. Instead, identification is performed through acts of kindness or cruelty, which are in turn bound to political class. Structural positions are, in short, moral ones. For this reason, the stories hinge on acts of assistance to others, or its denial. Not only does Ku's master abuse her, a poor woman, but he denounces her instinct to assist a fellow human being. He has – by virtue of his class – no such capacity to feel.

Of course, every community had its tyrants to varying degrees. And for every act of extreme violence there were countless more of neglect and abuse permitted by power structures and social mores. For each violent act recounted in *Taihang*, a neighbor or acquaintance surely came to mind for your average reader. But, then, for every villager who had seized the (arguably increasing) opportunities to brutalize vulnerable neighbors in the changing, often chaotic circumstances of the twentieth century, there was likely his or her opposite – someone who refrained to do so and lent a hand instead (villagers in Henan affectionately referred to such figures as one's "*enren*, or benefactor, the Chinese term for a good, trustworthy patron," explains Ralph Thaxton in his oral history of this period). It goes without saying that, like anywhere, communities in China were a varying mixture of personalities and lived values.[30]

That Four Histories, in the example of *Taihang*, had no place for such nuance, and that it pivoted instead on the device of class villainy, is perhaps too obvious a point to make. More noteworthy are two characteristics of *Taihang*, ones that also have implications for the nature of political events to come later in the decade.

The first is that villainy in *Taihang* is cast in animalistic terms. "He has a jackal's heart," people say of a member of "the reactionary ruling class" in one of its stories set in the early 1920s, "although he has a man's head and is covered in human skin." Another story's villain "had the nickname of 'Black Snake,' and this venomous viper coiled around our family."[31] In

---

[30] On the array of personalities and attitudes toward the poor by "landlord" figures in a Henan village in the 1920s, '30s and '40s, recalled in interviews conducted at the end of the century, see Thaxton, *Catastrophe and Contention in Rural China*, 35; see also 33–34 and 61.

[31] Chang Ju-Yün, Kuo Shih-Kang and Li Chia-Ming, "The Tragedy of the People of 'Lucky Star Locust,'" in Greenblatt, ed., *People of Taihang*, 34; and Yüeh Feng and Wang T'ien-Ch'i, "Land," in Greenblatt, ed., *People of Taihang*, 67.

this way, the output of the Four Histories movement incorporated styles of nicknaming and other aspects of village life, giving it the granular feel of rural culture. Mao himself had popularized similar epithets a few years earlier when he spoke of "ox-monsters and snake-demons' (*niugui she-shen*)" at a propaganda conference in 1957 – a term he used at times to refer to stage characters, at others to people "out there in society," Michael Schoenhals writes.[32] And, as in land reform dramas, *Taihang* employed these names within broader Maoist narrative devices and tele-ology, pinning (in)human qualities to class positions, and rectifying things only through outside forces, namely the Red Army.

A second, arguably more significant if subtler, characteristic of *Taihang* stories is the way communities as a whole were typecast by the movement. Its collective indictment of the old society stemmed from more than the array of hedonistic characters the stories presented; the indictment was equally a function of the ugly sum of elite personalities: in other words, the communal vacuum in which the villains were allowed to operate at will.

This raises another aspect of the Maoist narrative structure: the fact that any sense of community, any organizational capacity beyond the household, does not manifest until the conclusion of the story. Only then does a semblance of community first appear with the mutual-aid teams and agricultural cooperatives formed under the protection of the Red Army. To that point, villages consist of atomized households com-peting in a field of predation. Both family- and civic-level practices are nonexistent. In these stories, there is no place, in short, for people like Guyuan's Xia Jiwen.

And yet the *Taihang* stories are often structured around major disaster events. "In her fifth year, floods struck her village and destroyed all the farmlands," Ku's story recounts, for example.[33] The reference is to the great floods that ravaged Hebei (then called Zhili) in 1917. (Any hint of civic responses to the flood along the lines of the extensive relief opera-tions orchestrated for the province by Xiong Xiling, the great philanthro-pist of the period, is absent from the narrative.) Later on, in Ku's story the 1942 drought-famine strikes the region's poor, an event that became known as the Henan famine for the great suffering it brought to that (neighboring) province during the war.[34] Another of the *Taihang* stories opens with the 1927 drought-famine that struck China's North and Northwest.[35]

---

[32] Schoenhals, "Demonising Discourse in Mao Zedong's China," 470–71.
[33] Han and Yao, "A Home Given by Chairman Mao," 9–10.   [34] Ibid., 29.
[35] Kao Feng, Chang Tso-Pin and Lang Ch'eng-Hsin, "The Story of Selling Oneself," in Greenblatt, ed., *People of Taihang*, 51.

The disasters were real in these stories, pinning the action to known events. "The *People of Taihang* is not only role-model literature," Greenblatt notes, "it is at the same time an historical document. Each phase in biographical development is linked, sometimes in the most artful ways, to environing historical conditions and events."[36] The inclusion of the historical signposts of famine and Japanese invasion without wider communal context, serves to heighten the diabolical quality of their characterization. "The greater the famine, the happier the landlords," reads one of the *Taihang* stories.[37] "The real name of 'No. 2 Magistrate' was Pao Ping-hsü," reads another, "an arch despot who could devour human flesh without spitting out the bones."[38]

In this way, through *Taihang* and similar productions, the historical foil employed by the Four Histories movement party was grafted onto the revolutionary memory of disaster responses and rural life. The use of cannibalism to understand social relations and conditions in China can be traced back to the appearance of Lu Xun's "Diary of a Madman" in the May 1918 issue of the New Culture magazine *Xin qingnian*. In the story, the protagonist comes to the realization that the entire inheritance of dynastic China – its traditions, its ethics, its social intercourse – was, in essence, a state of man eating man, and that the only people left untainted by this cannibalistic culture are the children, the youth, the generations to come.[39] The collective picture of rural life provided by May Fourth commentaries, social surveys and party literature, both Guomindang and Communist, over the ensuing decades – a rural scene devoid of indigenous civic values and effective mutual-aid practices – carried this caricature forward.

This absence of community in stories of Chinese rural life, we might recall, is something we have seen before in Pearl Buck's *The Good Earth*, only told in a much more sympathetic light. The quality of Buck's work that had alienated her from the missionary circles she had grown up in – the fact that it prescribed no Christian role in delivering Chinese communities from their current plight – was resolved in *Taihang*, only with a different source of intervention in village life: the Communist Party.

But then through *Taihang*, the Four Histories movement went even deeper in its probing of communal absence in prerevolutionary China. An underlying principle behind 1960s activism was to "Serve the People,"

---

[36] Greenblatt, introduction to *People of Taihang*, xxxviii.
[37] Yüeh and Wang, "Land," 77.
[38] Chang Feng-Ju, Li Chih-K'uan and Liu Chung, "Revolutionary Mother Pao Lien-tzu," in Greenblatt, ed., *People of Taihang*, 227.
[39] Lu Xun, "Diary of a Madman," in Lyell, trans., *Diary of a Madman and Other Stories*, 29–41.

the title of one of Mao's writings from early in the decade. "According to the particular interpretation of Marxism-Leninism that Mao and his associates were advocating in the 1960s, people were not by nature selfish," Richard Madsen explains. "Selfishness and greed came from the structure of feudal and capitalistic societies," which required the restoration of "moral thought" through reeducation and reform. "To *serve* the people was to lead them in the struggle against class enemies."[40] Revolutionary memory can be seen as the historical basis for this "fall of man" narrative, in which service to the community had ceased to exist, if it ever had at all, and class enemies were agents for the corruption of humankind.

No less important to this 1960s mission of renewal was the upending of Chinese social mores with regard to age, one suggested as far back as Lu Xun's 1918 story and the admonishment in its final line that "maybe there are some children around who still haven't eaten human flesh. Save the children."[41] The young were, ultimately, the target audience of *Taihang*'s compiler, the Four Histories' Editorial Committee of Southeast Jin District. Writing in 1964, the committee's secretary noted that among those that experienced the revolution,

some, because of the passage of time, have gradually muddled their memories of past events and have gradually forgotten class hatred. Thus, members of the older generation have to refresh their memories of the past. As for young people and adolescents, they are "doves of peace" who "have not suffered exploitation by landlords and rich peasants, witnessed the massacres by the Japanese imperialists, or experienced land reform." "Who knows what the past was like?" If they do not understand the past, then they cannot understand the present.[42]

What we see, ultimately, in the Four Histories movement is the coproduction of alternative communal memory, often written in local voices but by cultural workers from outside the community and inflected with the teleology and terminology of revolutionary memory. While they contained elements of personal testimony, the stories were team written, and compiled by committee in the way local histories were. This coproduction is shared by local informants and the outside intellectuals (students, historians and cultural workers) involved in the accumulation, selection and composition of material. Where revolutionary memory involved abstractions, the communal memory of the Four Histories movement conferred what Greenblatt calls a "concretization and personification" to

[40] Madsen, *Morality and Power in a Chinese Village*, vii, 15.
[41] Lu Xun, "Diary of a Madman," 41.
[42] Chao Chün, foreword to *People of Taihang*, ed. Greenblatt, 6–7. It is not clear whom Chao is quoting here.

the revolutionary prism onto the communal past.[43] The product of the Four Histories movement benefited, in other words, from decades' worth of deinscription of rural community and civic structures from writing on rural life, of ways of organizing constructively beyond the family or clan; most importantly, the cultural legacy of revolutionary memory made the absence of these aspects of rural life from the world of *Taihang* difficult to detect. When Buck presented a rural landscape similarly devoid of civic structures in the 1930s, she did so from the position of a long-time foreign resident; and when in the 1940s the Jin Cha Ji propaganda bureau ran profiles of the revolutionary transformation of villagers, it did so in a youth magazine published in the regional hub of Zhangjiakou; through *Taihang* and its counterparts from the Four Histories movement, by contrast, communities were made to speak for themselves.[44]

Conclusion

The reproduction and reenactment of testimonies in local-history projects in the wake of the Great Leap gave afterlives to the speaking bitterness sessions of land reform. Distributed in expensive woodcut-print volumes accessed at libraries and other institutions, hardback collections in urban bookstores or in cheap mimeograph copies circulated in workrooms and villages across the country, these stories constituted an additional layer of revolutionary memory conveyed to younger generations with no personal recollection of the revolution's early stages.

In the most fundamental terms, the historical production of the early sixties served to further subsume the local into national narratives. On this we might return to Cai Xiang, whose analysis of revolutionary narrative has shed light on the stages of the local-national relationship up to the Cultural Revolution in 1966. Cai, invoking historian Mark Selden, recognizes the "conciliation between the Chinese revolution and the local" in the revolution's early stages, such as that found in the United Front and Mao's initially moderate policy regarding richer peasants. "This conciliation preserved not only the local natural economic formation, but also the village ethical order and customary outlooks, along with their deeply embedded rural ideals," Cai observes. "What all of this generated was

---

[43] Greenblatt, introduction to *People of Taihang*, xxxvii.
[44] For an example of a Four Histories project in Hebei – a book-length story by a team of twenty Tianjin-based writers (published as *The First Flower* in 1963) of a modernizing community in Raoyang county (the neighbor of Cang county, whose relief in 1920–21 we followed in Chapter 2) – see Edward Friedman, Paul G. Pickowicz and Mark Selden, *Revolution, Resistance, and Reform in Village China* (New Haven, CT: Yale University Press, 2005), 28, 30, 37.

precisely the characteristic multiplicity of revolutionary culture of which [the literary scholar] Meng Yue writes." But then, Cai notes, this posture toward the local would change; "the conciliation originating from the flexibility and changeability of revolutionary strategy [in the 1930s and 1940s] could not completely replace the ultimate political demands of the Chinese revolution, including the demand for modernity embedded within it."[45] By the 1950s, through the bottom-up voices introduced by land reform novels and what Cai calls their mobilization-transformation narrative structure, "village politics acquired a modern expression."[46] In 1950s novels, "the local in reality ha[d] already been assimilated into the national imaginary of modernity."[47]

Within a few years of the Leap's end, the cultural assimilation examined by Cai had extended far beyond elite fiction into local history and communal memory. The "modern expression" of which Cai writes had served, in part, as a historical foil and gloss for the present. The extent to which the resulting narratives were made into a resource for a new generation of political struggle is a question we turn to next.

[45] Cai Xiang, *Revolution and Its Narratives*, 45–46.   [46] Ibid., 59.   [47] Ibid., 57.

13 Politics of Oblivion: The Cultural Revolution

On National Day in 1964, the local Shanxi party official Chao Chün explained the rationale behind his district's Four Histories movement volume *People of Taihang*, which had begun with a rough draft of seventy thousand local family histories:

Class struggle is long-term. Children grow up to be adults step by step. What is understandable to the present generation of young people may not be understood by the next generation of young people. Hence we must make long-range preparations for providing class education for succeeding generations of children and grandchildren. This is a strategic task that stands before us. According to our understanding of the socialist education movement, lecturing on village histories, family histories, communal and factory histories is a good, effective method for educating youth. In order to rescue these precious and vital materials for class education from oblivion and in order to hand them down to future generations, we have specially selected this anthology from a great volume of family histories for young people's reference.[1]

This chapter pursues several issues touched on by this local cadre in 1964. The first concerns knowledge and its survival. Chao's careful preservation of testimonies produced in the Four Histories movement had its converse in the fate of artefacts and textual accounts that offered different perspectives on the past. The late 1960s burning of Zhang Zuanxu's personal trove of half a million characters worth of Muslim records on daily life over centuries in China's Northwest – a loss touched on in Chapter 10 – represented of course only a fragment of the volume of cultural memory that would go up in smoke over the course of the Cultural Revolution. Looked at in this way, the Cultural Revolution was the manifestation of tension between different types of cultural memory, revolutionary and communal, and the unfolding of their varying fates: reproduction into the future or oblivion.

Then there is the logic to Four Histories – as expressed by Chao – of class and its instrumental role in political struggle over the long term. This

---

[1] Chao Chün, foreword to *People of Taihang*, ed. Greenblatt, 7.

point requires some additional contextualization. As we have seen, the first decade of the People's Republic sharpened the national inflection of village politics through bitterness speaking and cooperative movement narratives that framed local social dynamics in national terms. The reinvigoration of class over the sixties involved the further elevation of village politics into an articulation of geopolitics.

The literary scholar and intellectual historian Wang Hui interprets Mao's renewed emphasis on class as a way to "stimulate a renewal of the party's political culture" in the wake of the split with Moscow. The calamitous consequences of the Great Leap Forward had coincided with the Sino-Soviet split over the radical course of Maoist policies in the wake of Stalin's death in 1953 and the more conciliatory leadership of Nikita Khrushchev at the helm of the Communist Party of the Soviet Union. Party policies in China then experienced a short-lived lurch to the center in the wake of the Leap and the challenges its failure brought to Mao's supremacy. In reaction, in 1962 Mao launched a series of political campaigns that unfolded over the four years leading to the Cultural Revolution: the Socialist Education movement, its Four Histories offshoot and the Four Cleanups movement (*siqing yundong*) launched in September of the same year. Each would serve to reembolden political and cultural forces behind the Maoist vision for the country. "[Mao's] target was the Soviet notion of the 'party of the whole people,'" Wang argues, "which not only indicated confusion about the representative character of the [Communist Party of the Soviet Union], but marked the depoliticization of the party-state system."[2]

Accompanying Mao's bid to reinvigorate Communist political culture was an expansion of political targets. His denunciation of what he saw as the depoliticization of the Soviet polity was the product of a fundamentally different take on the concept of class: "In Chinese political practice," Wang writes, "class is not merely a structural category [... but] rather a political concept based on the revolutionary party's appeal for mobilization and self-renewal"; it is a concept "used to stimulate debate and struggle" that "denoted the attitudes of social or political forces toward revolutionary politics, rather than the structural situation of social class."[3]

Crucially, this expansion included those currently or formerly working the land, in other words "ordinary peasants." A series of policy documents on

[2] Wang Hui, "Depoliticised Politics, from East to West," *New Left Review* 41 (September–October 2006), 36.
[3] Ibid.

classification drafted by members of the politburo from 1963 to 1965 sent ever-evolving signals to localities, opening the door for local cadres to interpret directives in their own way; this included a policy document from 1964, which stated that "every family's status should be investigated" and "class files should be established" for all rural families for the first time. But, as Jeremy Brown explains, "because Party Center had not given a clear standard for how to reclassify people, many localities were overly punitive in assigning class labels," surpassing the vigilance taken during land reform.[4]

Added to this expansion of political targets in the sixties was the retrospective nature of class identity. The stress on personal or family *background* brought historical understanding to the fore of class struggle. By the mid-sixties the designation landlord-rich peasant had been stripped of its material meaning. A decade after the creation of communes across the vast majority of the country's agricultural land, and nearly two decades after the breakup of estates and large holdings in land reforms, what drove class politics was moral debate based on what Philip Huang calls "representational" as opposed to "subjective" realities.[5] Having outlived its material basis, class in the sixties morphed into a system of moral positioning – vis-à-vis the revolution, the masses or an accuser's standard of justice more generally, depending on the case being made. This made the moral constellation of Maoist storytelling, such as that of *Taihang*, paramount.

In his foreword Chao specifies that the intended beneficiary of his district's contribution to the Four Histories movement was the area's youth. If the Socialist Education movement and its Four Histories offshoot were vehicles for education, the Four Cleanups was a form of applied pedagogy to society at large. And Chao makes it clear that the cleansing of the country should hinge on the agency of the young.

For this, our final chapter, we explore how tensions between communal and revolutionary perceptions of the past can explain the continued potency of political labels two decades into the People's Republic. The former is limited by its particularity, weighed down by its sense of place and personality. The latter is more abstract and so freed from these constraints by its elasticity and universality. It is also empowered by its service in party-led campaigns. Revolutionary memory was given additional authority over the course of the sixties in two ways: through the supplanting of local-history production by campaigns like the Four Histories movement, as we have seen; and through the destruction of

---

[4] Brown, "Moving Targets," 59–60.
[5] Huang, "Rural Class Struggle in the Chinese Revolution," 105–43.

alternative forms of cultural memory altogether in the Cultural Revolution. We pursue this latter aspect of cultural conflict through the sixties for what it says about Maoist ideology and practice, and, more broadly, about the relationship between epistemic violence and physical violence, book burning and bloodletting.

The Cultural Revolution

The style of two deaths that occurred in the middle of the 1960s says a good deal about developments under Communist rule, including the uneven pace of change in Chinese political culture at various levels, and the limits to Maoist cultural hegemony in the years before the Cultural Revolution. The frustration that this uneven pace and these limits brought to Mao and his allies lay behind much of the political conflict that burst onto the streets of China toward the end of the decade.

In 1964, Xia Jiwen died at home of illness at the age of seventy-eight. In spite of his background as the classically educated son of a landlord family, Xia enjoyed what appears to have been a happy fate, having served in Guyuan and wider Gansu and Ningxia in various civic and official capacities for some fifty years. He was commemorated in consecutive gazetteers into the nineties as an initiator of disaster relief and employment in his rural district before the revolution, a starter of public schools around the county and as member of various advisory committees under the new Communist government. In Xia, a member of the republican-era gentry was rewarded with continued political influence in the People's Republic, despite having had a major hand in compiling Guyuan's local annals – what the Communist press dismissed in the forties as a form of "fake history," one produced by an elite that exalted its own kind in self-serving narratives.

Deng Tuo died two years after Xia, living long enough to experience the sharp side of the Cultural Revolution. A leading figure in the party's propaganda organs in their formative stages, he had presided over the Zhangjiakou-based publishing house behind *Minzhu qingnian* magazine, as we have seen, and its condemnation of the "fake history" produced by prominent local gentry like Xia, before serving as editor-in-chief at *Renmin ribao* for the first decade of the People's Republic. Deng was also a trained historian and the author, under the pen name Deng Yunte, of the pioneering book *Zhongguo jiuhuang shi* (*A History of Famine Relief in China*), published by the Commercial Press in 1937.[6]

---

[6] Deng Yunte, *Zhongguo jiuhuang shi* (Shanghai: Shangwu yinshuguan), 1937. For an English translation, see Deng Yunte, *The History of Famine Relief in China*, trans. Gao Jianwu (Cambridge: Cambridge University Press, 2020).

On one level, Deng's scholarship was compatible with Maoist doctrine. His book focused on official famine policy recommendations and practices at the highest levels of the bureaucracy. Its lack of attention to local responses to subsistence crises shed little light on communal practices, and so his work did little to offset Maoist generalizations on class conduct in rural life. For these reasons, his work, which was reissued numerous times in the People's Republic, was also used in *Renmin ribao* – for example on the eve of the Great Leap Forward in 1957 – to make favorable comparisons between socialist welfare policies and earlier periods when millions starved at times during droughts, floods, war and other disastrous events.[7]

But then, in other ways Deng's approach was fundamentally different from "later orthodox Party-approved histories," historian Timothy Cheek points out, especially in "its lack of emphasis on class struggle." Nor did Deng's materialist approach stress the "morality or venality of individual historical actors."[8] On these two crucial counts, Deng's history of disaster relief in China diverged perilously from Maoist narratives. He was removed of his leadership of *Renmin ribao* in the Hundred Flowers campaign of 1957. In May of 1966, Deng killed himself as the country's political winds picked up dramatically again.[9] That same month, the position he had held at the paper a decade earlier was taken up by Chen Boda, Mao's former aide at Yan'an, ushering in a period of extraordinary uniformity of voice in party media.[10] By one measure, references to "Mao Zedong Thought" in *Renmin ribao* went from less than a hundred in 1963 to around five thousand each year between 1967 and 1970.[11]

Despite achieving iconic stature in the world's imagination, the Cultural Revolution shared a good deal with the campaigns that had preceded it. Elements of the Socialist Education and Four Cleanups movements of the early sixties, such as investigating class background and anticorruption campaigns among cadres, had run along different time lines around the country, starting early in some places, lagging behind in others, and in some cases overlapping with the start of the Cultural Revolution in the spring of 1966. What soon distinguished what would be called the Great Proletarian Cultural Revolution was the intensity of its ritualized political struggle and cultural forms and the appearance of combat and elements of anarchy. In some ways, the forces at play behind these events make fuller sense only when we step back and look at the wider historical and global context.

---

[7] Wemheuer, *A Social History of Maoist China*, 103.
[8] Cheek, *Propaganda and Culture in Mao's China*, 50.   [9] Ibid., 236–37, 279–83.
[10] Leese, *Mao Cult*, 129.   [11] Ibid., 130; see also 18, 21.

In the two decades following the cessation of civil war in 1949, both China's fertility rate and its population grew steadily – and in rural areas especially (with the glaring exception, of course, of the Great Leap famine years of 1958–62).[12] By 1966, this first generation of revolution baby boomers was nearing adulthood. It was also the most literate in Chinese history, and the most thoroughly educated by the state. But, generally speaking, these teens also had reason for frustration with the slow pace of good jobs being created by the socialist economy, which fueled the feeling that the revolution had not fully delivered on its promises – and that something was holding it back. At the same time, the sixties generation would have been equally frustrated by a lack of purpose: while their grandparents' generation fought off Japanese invasion, and their parents' cohort created the New China by defeating the Guomindang and resisting American invasion from Korea, they had no struggle to call their own – and they had none, no less, in a Maoist society that exalted struggle above all else.

To boot, China's sixties generation was coming of age in a remarkably hostile world, surrounded by enemies just to the south in the US military, which intensified its war in Vietnam after 1964's Tonkin Bay incident, and just to the north, where increasingly fierce border clashes between Chinese and Soviet forces more than doubled in number from 1964 to 1969.[13] Moreover, for many peoples the mid-twentieth century was a moment when the growth in mass media also revealed scientific advances and the presence of microscopic germ agents never before imagined, let alone seen, along with atomic power. Both would have military applications. Strides in pathology, photographic technology and print media kept Chinese keenly aware of such threats from the US presence in Korea in the first years of the People's Republic, as Ruth Rogaski has shown.[14] The understanding of germ agents easily translated into the idea of enemy agents attacking the revolutionary body politic within. In short, the sixties in China were a moment ripe for the conflation of and interaction between modern science, global competition and age-old forces of pride and fear.

But then, amid these tensions, the huge gains in levels of classroom education for both girls and boys over the course of the fifties would come to a halt. As the Great Leap calamity eventually eased in early 1962 and

---

[12] James Z. Lee and Wang Feng, *One Quarter of Humanity: Malthusian Mythology and Chinese Realities, 1700–2000* (Cambridge, MA: Harvard University Press, 1999), 120.

[13] Roderick MacFarquhar and Michael Schoenhals, *Mao's Last Revolution* (Cambridge, MA: The Belknap Press of Harvard University Press, 2006), 309.

[14] Ruth Rogaski, "Nature, Annihilation, and Modernity: China's Korean War Germ-Warfare Experience Reconsidered," *Journal of Asian Studies* 61/2 (May 2002), 381–415.

education spending faced severe cuts, junior and senior high schools were shuttered across much of the country.[15] With the explosion of campus activism in 1966, universities across China joined in these closures – for quite different reasons – and would not reopen or take in new students until the seventies.

Stepping into this void was the Red Guard ideal, which was born partly of these massive cuts to education in the wake of the Leap and the eventual channeling of millions of teenagers into other pursuits. The generation coming of age in the mid-sixties, in other words, was largely underemployed or idle, well read and idealistic. And it was this generation whose urban members were "sent-down" to the countryside and injected into village life. This development coincided with the introduction of daily quotations of Mao in army newspapers in 1961, followed by the creation of a booklet for group study among members of the armed forces in 1964, which evolved into what has become known as the Little Red Book, published by the hundreds of millions by the end of 1966.[16] Soon, the nation's youth were encouraged to model themselves on the figure of the "selfless" soldier and martyr. With this, a generation of youth would be steeped in Mao Zedong Thought, devoting itself to self-cultivation, vigilance against perceived enemies and national sacrifice.

At first, the events of early 1966 that would develop into the Cultural Revolution would hardly have raised eyebrows, consisting mostly of denunciations of works and artists in the cultural sector by Mao and his allies. By the middle of the year, however, things would spiral into a half decade of especially complex and violent events. Andrew Walder has identified patterns to developments over this first more extreme half of the Cultural Revolution, which he breaks down into three distinct phases.

In the first phase, Red Guards materialized among students at universities and middle schools over the three months of summer 1966; Red Guards from across the country soon converged by the millions in Beijing's Tiananmen Square, where they were met by Mao and the party leadership. The frenzied rallies and struggle sessions against teachers and other forms of ritualized violence on campuses and city streets spread to communes in the capital's outskirts where militiamen and activists slaughtered hundreds by the end of summer.[17] The formation of mass organizations around the country followed over the autumn of 1966 – groups that were independent from the party but encouraged to exist at first by the center. Then, in the first three months of 1967, and

---

[15] Friedman, Pickowicz and Selden, *Revolution, Resistance, and Reform in Village China*, 21.
[16] Leese, *Mao Cult*, 108–27.
[17] MacFarquhar and Schoenhals, *Mao's Last Revolution*, 128–29. For detail on the rallies and Mao's role in them, see Leese, *Mao Cult*, 128–38.

facilitated in part by the People's Liberation Army, a form of rebellion or insurgency by mass organizations seized power at the provincial level (Guizhou, Heilongjiang, Shandong and Shanxi), municipal level (most notably Shanghai) and across "the vast majority of all local governments in China [. . .] in a remarkably concentrated period of time."[18]

Basing his findings on an exhaustive study of data from district annals across the People's Republic (minus Tibet) for 1966 to 1971, Walder finds that this first phase of Red Guard mobilization, mass insurgency and sei-zures of power saw by far the *fewest* number of deaths and victims of any period of the Cultural Revolution.[19] It should be noted that this same ten-month stretch between 1966 and 1967 was the high point of aspects of the Cultural Revolution celebrated by thinkers on the left in the decades since, perhaps most notably the philosopher Alain Badiou and sociologist Alessandro Russo as well as Wang Hui.[20] The aspects of this brief period included what Wang has called the "popular sovereignty" and "social experimentation" exercised in schools, factories and work units across the country, perhaps most notably the worker attempts to create a Shanghai Commune along the lines of what transpired a century earlier in Paris.[21] The overarching goal of these varied efforts was, in Russo's words, a "dismantling – or 'smashing' (*zerbrechen*), as Marx put it – [of] the state apparatus as an entity separated from society, and dispersing its functions among the people" after decades of party institutionalization and growing detachment from commoner concerns.[22] What had allowed for this brief explosion of heated debate was what Daniel Leese has called a "dual change" in the "highly restricted mode of political communication" at the time. This involved an unprecedented "uniformity and formalization of expression" in *Renmin ribao* and other official media that gave "little choice but to join publicly in the cult rhetoric" around Mao Zedong Thought.[23] At the same time, though, a short-lived space appeared for mass organizations

---

[18] Walder, "Rebellion and Repression in China, 1966–1971," 519; see also Wemheuer, *A Social History of Maoist China*, 205.
[19] Walder's definition of victim "includes all of those who were injured, and much larger numbers who were subjected to beatings, harsh interrogation, demotions or firings, banishment from cities, or some other form of political stigma in 'false cases.'" Walder, "Rebellion and Repression in China," 522–3, 526.
[20] Alain Badiou, "The Cultural Revolution: The Last Revolution?" *positions: east asia cultures critique* 13/3 (2005), 481–514; Alessandro Russo, "How to Translate 'Cultural Revolution,'" *Inter-Asia Cultural Studies* 7/4 (2006), 673–82; Wang Hui, "Depoliticised Politics."
[21] Wang Hui, "Depoliticised Politics," 35.
[22] Alessandro Russo, "Class Struggle," trans. David Verzoni, in Christian Sorace, Ivan Franceschini and Nicholas Loubere, eds., *Afterlives of Chinese Communism: Political Concepts from Mao to Xi* (Acton: Australian National University Press and Verso, 2019), 30.
[23] Leese, *Mao Cult*, 21.

to disseminate and debate information through nonofficial and uncensored channels, in ways that ran parallel to and often clashed with party positions.[24]

A second phase of the Cultural Revolution, overlapping with the others but with key differences, involved running battles between factions of mass organizations and defenders of local party interests, resulting in a spike in deaths. Although this phase ran for two years from April 1967 to April 1969, these battles peaked in the summer of 1967 before plummeting by mid-1968.[25] In the words of Tan Hecheng in his study of the period in one Hunan county, this spiral of conflict pitched "a hodgepodge of students and teachers, townspeople, craftsmen, lower-level intellectuals, and a few cadres" aggrieved at the "bureaucratic class and the status quo" against party "stalwarts" who came to the defense of the "entrenched political order and felt a deep antipathy toward those who boldly claimed the right to revolt."[26]

Finally, a third (again overlapping) phase involved the forced dissolution of these varied organizations that had sprouted over the previous eighteen or so months in favor of "revolutionary committees" consisting of army officers, select cadres and former insurgents, which were overseen by the military. "The sustained peak" of efforts to disband mass organizations "that begins in May 1968 and continues until early 1969 reflects direct government and army actions against insurgents and the onset of the 'Cleansing the Class Ranks,'" Walder writes. By the beginning of 1969, some 90 percent of localities had formed revolutionary committees.[27]

Crucially, this reassertion of state control brought with it the vast majority of recorded killings and general acts of victimization of the Cultural Revolution. Walder's research team culled a total of 273,934 recorded deaths from local annals and supplementary sources over the (far bloodier) first half of the Cultural Revolution. (The actual death toll over this period is doubtless much higher, perhaps as high as 1.1 million to 1.6 million.) Of these documented deaths, 176,226 "can be linked to specific events," according to Walder, and, out of these, nearly three-quarters – 130,378 – "are due to the actions of authorities in this third phase" of the Cultural Revolution.[28]

---

[24] For detail on this, see Michael Schoenhals, "China's 'Great Proletarian Information Revolution' of 1966–1967," in Brown and Johnson, eds., *Maoism at the Grassroots*, 230–58.

[25] Walder, "Rebellion and Repression in China," 518.

[26] Tan Hecheng, *The Killing Wind: A Chinese County's Descent into Madness during the Cultural Revolution*, trans. Stacy Mosher and Guo Jian (Oxford: Oxford University Press, 2017), 31.

[27] Walder, "Rebellion and Repression in China," 519.   [28] Ibid., 517, 521, 533, 536.

Significantly, the formation of army-led revolutionary committees did not merely lead to a crackdown on challenges to authority but also to a radicalization of what Yang Su calls "eliminationist killings" by the Maoist regime.[29] The official Cleansing of the Class Ranks campaign of 1968 and 1969 was by far the greatest source of official killings tallied by Walder: 96,109, or 74 percent of the 130,378 deaths presided over by the authorities, with most of these state-orchestrated killings occurring in 1968.[30]

What this makes clear is that despite the street combat and anarchic elements of the mid-to-late sixties, the decade's bloodiest episode was a result of eliminationist killings along by-gone class lines, which can be directly attributed to the hands of authorities in the form of revolutionary committees. One wonders how revolutionary memory – of evil gentry, unchecked predation and depraved communities generally – could not have played an instrumental role in these events, serving as a cultural resource informing and weaponing the pursuit of "black elements," justifying a "cleansing of the class ranks" through execution and other types of victimization by the state (on top of killings, "actions of authorities" were behind more than 90 percent of the 10,379,606 recorded acts of nonlethal victimization in the first half of the Cultural Revolution, according to Walder).[31]

What remains is the question of the rationale behind the killing of neighbors, sometimes of entire families, in this earlier stage of the Cultural Revolution when mass organizations competed with local party committees for power and factions fought in the streets. Killings within communities may have been fewer in number than those executed by the state's revolutionary committees later on, but they are in many respects more puzzling.

In the first decade and a half of the People's Republic, political killing had been largely a rural phenomenon, in the political campaigns that accompanied land reform and the Great Leap Forward. In the first few months of the Cultural Revolution, urban violence began to draw from similar forces as its rural counterpart. By 1966, the label of landlord had encompassed the urban bourgeoisie. This group had been seen as constituting "partly progressive forces" in the "new democratic alliance" of the 1950s, explains Philip Huang, and only a small minority were penalized for having owned commercial firms. Starting with the Four Cleanups movement of the early sixties, though, bourgeois elements were incorporated into the landlord class, which became a catch-all

---

[29] Yang Su, *Collective Killings in Rural China*, 29–30.
[30] Walder, "Rebellion and Repression in China," 521–22.   [31] Ibid., 521.

epithet of broad application.[32] This helps to explain the extreme *urban* violence that unfolded in the first few months of the Cultural Revolution. This form of violence, which was often very public, even performative in nature, has since become associated with the Red Guards and with the urban theater of the Cultural Revolution. This is arguably due to the more visible nature of events in major cities, like Beijing and Shanghai.

But a majority of Chinese still resided in nonurban places at the time of the Cultural Revolution. There, the nature of the violence and its reasoning during the Cultural Revolution are considerably more elusive than in the more heavily studied urban sphere. Below we continue to trace the thread of revolutionary memory and its application in rural communities for what it might reveal about the rationale for the killing of neighbors and entire families, or "collective violence" to put it in terms used by Yang Su.[33]

Rural Violence

The brief mid-1967 spike in deaths during the *first* phase of the Cultural Revolution occurred in the context of factional fighting.[34] A combat dynamic, though, does not account for the sheer range of victims caught up in the struggles of these years, especially children, the aged and villagers who appeared to have done little before their murders beyond tending to their own lives. Here we might explore the ways that revolutionary memory informed such acts within communities before the reassertion of state control at the end of the sixties. Tan Hecheng's *Killing Wind* provides possibly more quantitative and qualitative detail around one county's Cultural Revolution death toll than any other published study. He began his investigation of Hunan's Dao county in 1986, two years after the creation of a government task force in response to petitions to look into killings there two decades earlier – an effort that would come to involve contributions from 1,300 cadres by the mid-eighties.[35]

As much as Dao county's 1967 killing spree occurred amid running factional battles, such a context would not explain the range of killing methods used: many readily at hand in agricultural settings (drowning

---

[32] Huang, "Rural Class Struggle in the Chinese Revolution," 127.

[33] As Yang Su notes in his study of Guangdong and Guangxi: "Only when the Cultural Revolution overhauled local governments, however – and particularly when it created an equivalent of domestic war – did violent practices escalate to killings that included the victims' family members." Yang Su, *Collective Killings in Rural China*, 29–30.

[34] Walder, "Rebellion and Repression in China," 522.

[35] Over two years, the task force "carried out all its work behind closed doors and never made its findings public." Tan based his study on access to these records, supplemented by interviews. Tan Hecheng, *The Killing Wind*, 8, 20, 26.

victims in nearby ponds, pushing them off cliff faces or bludgeoning them with spades), nor their ingenuity and cruelty (from detonation to live burial).[36] In many of these cases, baser motivations often came into play: the reward offered by cadres for a killing (in some cases several yuan, work points and a few kilos of rice);[37] envy or lust for another's man's wife;[38] or revenge for a past grievance (sometimes in spectacularly gruesome acts).[39]

But surely these were personal motivations and impulses, and, one would assume, not the stated reason for eliminationist killing during what were ostensibly political operations. Justification is, of course, no indication of motive, but it reveals at the very least the terms in which the act was framed for public (i.e., the community's) approval (of some varying degree). And of the numerous rationales articulated in Tan's study, class labeling was paramount.

When pursuing targets in the sixties, Tan explains, perpetrators were generally free to deploy a net of twenty-one (somewhat changeable) categories inherited from and refined since previous campaigns:

There are many versions of these 21 categories, but generally speaking, they consisted of landlords, rich peasants, counterrevolutionaries, bad [or black] elements, Rightists, capitalists, and spies; people who had served in the police, military police, or Youth Corps or as military officers or functionaries under the "puppet" KMT regime; and moneylenders, concubines, peddlers, prostitutes, sorcerers, monks, Daoist priests, nuns, and vagrants.[40]

The task force found that in 1967, exactly a year after Tiananmen Square's mass parades, Dao county experienced a spree of 4,193 killings, plus 326 suicides, in a little over two months. But what is perhaps most striking is that a higher portion of Dao county's victims were classified as *offspring* of "black elements" (49.9 percent) than as "black elements" themselves (41.4 percent). In addition, the vast majority of those killed (95.2 percent) were from families that continued to work the land in the sixties as opposed to people from the ranks of educators, cadres, health workers or other more elite occupations present in rural communities at the time.[41] (As to whether Dao county was a typical Chinese county, if any is capable of being so, it was hardly centrally located, as it borders remote Guangxi; but then, as Tan notes, "scholars have established that the great modern writer Lu Xun and the PRC's first premier, Zhou Enlai, had their family roots" there.)[42]

---

[36] Ibid., 21; see also Yang Su, *Collective Killings*, 4.   [37] Ibid., 61–62.
[38] Tan finds at least forty instances of this motivation for killing in Dao county alone. Ibid., 62, 63, 68.
[39] Ibid., 105.   [40] Ibid., 475.   [41] Ibid., 20.   [42] Ibid., 24.

The targeting of offspring was in fact expressly forbidden by army circulars making the rounds in Hunan in 1967, which stressed that reeducation was the preferred official method except when "dealing with killers and the most evil, aggressive, and rebellious of the black elements."[43] But in light of slogans to "Exterminate the Seven Black Categories" that adorned school campuses around the province, such as that of Hunan University, mixed messaging was reaching activists on the street.[44]

In the words of one government task force member:

Some comrades effusively praised the random killing of innocent people as the revolutionary actions of the poor and lower-middle peasants. Some raised the killings to a theoretical level, saying they were "supplemental lessons in democratic revolution" and calling for everyone to seriously study Chairman Mao's *Investigative Report on the Hunan Peasant Movement* to enhance their ideological awareness.[45]

Mao's 1927 report – one that used the term "evil gentry" no less than sixty times – appeared in the heat of political hunts forty years later; not once, but at numerous instances of killing.[46] What is remarkable is the extent to which a moral discourse of good and evil – which flowed from Mao's own language – figured in Dao county's political hunts, as opposed to, say, the pursuit of justice for past deeds in the style of bitterness speaking.

This discourse of good and evil provided a rationale for extralegal measures. As one task force summary explained of events in 1967:

On September 14 of that same year, [a commune party secretary] Zheng Fengjiao presided over a meeting of the production brigade CCP branches, during which he said, "We need to discuss whether to kill another batch. [. . .] We have so many black elements in our production brigade, and they're so evil, we have to kill them even if it's not allowed." [. . .] That afternoon, Zheng Fengjiao organized and convened a cadre meeting to assign tasks. The next day, Zheng Fengjiao ordered the militia to take 19 landlords and rich peasants and offspring to Ningyuan's Ouchonglei Hill and kill them.[47]

Dao county killings spiked in number after mass meetings. In one district "only 40-odd people were killed before the conference," Tan writes, referring to a three-day Political and Legal Work Conference held in August 1967 to discuss calls by the army to stem the violence (instead, Mao's Hunan report was invoked at the conference and its study encouraged). "More than 400 were killed in the days immediately following," a ten-fold increase in the same district. "All in all, in the five days

[43] Quoted in ibid., 89.   [44] Quoted in ibid., 93.   [45] Quoted in ibid., 94.
[46] For another example of such use of Mao's 1927 report, see ibid., 55.
[47] Quoted in ibid., 50.

from August 26 to 30, a total of 2,454 people were killed throughout the county, comprising just over half of the killing wind's total death." In the five-day spree, "All of the county's 37 communes experienced killings, including communes that had delayed killings up until then."[48]

At times, these local operations, sometimes run by brigade operatives and at others by teams of activists, led to the elimination of entire families. In August 1967 one district saw "533 deaths, with 53 households completely extinguished," explains Tan. "Most of the people" in one "batch of victims were elderly women or minors, including a blind woman more than 60 years old and two children under 10," Tan continues. "They were buried alive in four pits on a deserted hillside, which was subsequently renamed Sigekeng, or 'Four Pits.'"[49] Remarkably, participants did not even have to harbor animosity toward their victims. In the case of one victim, a one-time primary school teacher from a middle-peasant family, participants stated that "the thing we heard most often during our inquiries was that 'Tang Yu was a good man!'" and that "one participant told us [...] 'When he was beaten, I didn't hit him hard.'"[50] Elsewhere, Tan notes that "the vast majority of the dead had been honest, law-abiding citizens who minded their own business and worked hard to maintain the most basic standard of living."[51]

So what does one make of this? In Dao county, the period saw a total of 4,519 people killed, or 1.17 percent of county residents at the time.[52] Care must be taken, of course, before generalizing about the circumstances behind the killing of possibly one million people over a period of rapid twists and turns in local political conditions. Still, it would seem that several elements were shared by the bloodletting of the Cultural Revolution in its various forms. The first is the role of rumor and fear of imminent attack. In Dao county, the threat of black elements appears to have been conjured up largely by cadres and other commune officials. But then the invitation to act evidently facilitated expression of the worst aspects of human character, providing an opportune moment for people to "settle scores" and make quick gains for themselves in communities offering limited chances to otherwise do so. In this way, political interests at the extreme top and personal interests at the bottom came together, so to speak, in the hunts of the Cultural Revolution in ways that echo previous periods: for one, how "soulstealing" accusations, score settling and imperial antisedition drives worked together in the sorcery scares of the commercializing Yangzi delta exactly two centuries earlier – an event explored masterfully by Philip Kuhn.[53] And then one wonders what

---

[48] Ibid., 96.   [49] Ibid., 50–51.   [50] Ibid., 75.   [51] Ibid., 22.   [52] Ibid., 20.
[53] Philip A. Kuhn, *Soulstealers: The Chinese Sorcery Scare of 1768* (Cambridge, MA: Harvard University Press, 1990), 228–29.

influence the proximity of a hostile American presence in Vietnam and British control of Hong Kong next door might have had in 1960s Guangxi and Guangdong (where Yang Su's study is focused), which experienced "the highest death tolls from collective killing in the country."[54]

A second element evident in 1960s political violence is the leading role of youth. In Tan's study, older killers were rare, and among them ideological reasons for their acts figured equally rarely. "In examining the data, I found that Daoxian's famous [i.e., most prolific] killers were typically around 20 years old," Tan explains, "and it was very uncommon for a killer to be over 40 years old unless revenge, material gain, or a woman was involved."[55] Here we see another coming together of interests: an appetite for acute unrest among Mao and his allies that spoke to the restlessness of a generation.

The socialist education of this new generation is not enough to explain this. Generations' worth of cultural conditioning – drawing from revolutionary memory on the ways "things used to be" – also played a vital role. Clearly, class was a license to kill, both for state organs and those acting in the name of authority, whether that was the party, Chairman Mao or the revolution cause generally. But the meaning of class, and the constellation of class labels that stemmed from it two decades after Communist victory in 1949, does not come into full relief without considering the wider cultural world these political constructions were employed in. The fact that the revolution's baby boomers – possibly China's most educated generation – appear to have enthusiastically taken to the fashion for "eliminationist killing" in both urban and rural contexts points to the significance of the inheritance of cultural memory. Revisiting the violence of the sixties with revolutionary memory as a political resource at hand for the willing, a resource not merely legitimized but exalted by authorities, allows for two seemingly contradictory explanations for the nature of Cultural Revolution violence to be reconciled: popular agency and party authority. Here we can conclude by turning to some observations about the cultural aspect of the Great Proletariat Cultural Revolution shared across China's vast social terrain.

Oblivion

The sheer uniformity of voices in official mainland Chinese media by 1968 is one of the period's most distinctive if bewildering aspects.[56] The late sixties hegemony of Maoist revolutionary praxis makes more sense when considering the decades' worth of social and cultural erasure it was

---

[54] Yang Su, *Collective Killings in Rural China*, 18, 28.
[55] Tan Hecheng, *The Killing Wind*, 64.   [56] Leese, *Mao Cult*, 21.

built on. Political actors in the sixties had ready access to a fast-growing field of revolutionary memory production – schoolbooks, village operas, woodcut volumes and other printed imagery available in Xinhua bookstores, bookstalls and libraries, and the reports and other writings of Mao himself.

Stage drama arguably epitomizes the uniformity of cultural forms and messaging that characterizes China's sixties. In it, history continued to be enacted in one of the country's most accessible mediums. Many of the land reform dramas produced earlier at Yan'an's Lu Xun Academy were converted into model operas. Such was the case with *White Haired Girl*, whose 1966 incarnation as a model work took the hybrid form of a Western-style ballet that retained many of the techniques, narrative arcs and flourishes familiar to Chinese opera theater goers. Some twenty styles of laughter were used to mark personality and moral disposition, and a spectrum of color incorporated into costume, cosmetics or lighting. White or black signified villainy, for example, and blue or green wholesomeness. The positive and energetic associations of red – devotion, daring, general happiness – carried through from older theater forms to the Communist era. More fundamentally, though, Cultural Revolution opera continued to share two fundamental traits with much older forms: role models, and a finale of "happiness and consolation, the so-called *da tuanyuan* (大团圆), the Great Reunion or Happy End in traditional Chinese theater," as Barbara Mittler explains.[57] Both traits supported age-old lessons in good and evil, but also, in the case of the finale, the teleological aspect of Maoist narrative.

But there were crucial ways in which the model opera refined the Maoist messaging of its land reform-era versions. And that was the way certain political types were eliminated altogether from village scenes, not through violence but by simply being written out of the script. "By deletion and addition, then, the model work rose above its well-known predecessors and thus fulfilled, with every revision, the political requirements made of it," Mittler notes. "Only among the villains are there landowners, literati, rich men, and 'imperialists.' [...] With further revisions, the number of appearances of negative persons is reduced. In terms of placement on the stage, they are moved farther and farther to the right" – away from center stage, hardly seen or heard, and when "they do sing, they are accompanied only by the lower, brassy sounding instruments of the orchestra" – or in some cases "only the main heroes appear; the negative characters are eliminated altogether."[58]

---

[57] Mittler, *A Continuous Revolution*, 64; see also 56–57, 59, 80.   [58] Ibid., 84.

Significantly, these class disappearances were further to *generational* disappearances that had already been built into dramas of the land reform era. Back then, "Elder peasants were portrayed as helpless in the face of feudal oppression and resigned to their fate," Brian James DeMare observes. "Even more striking is the outright absence of peasant parents in many land reform operas."[59] By the mid-sixties, opera's final scenes of reconciliation left out a large swathe of village life. Categories of people were superfluous. In the end, all that remained was the empowered youth.

This state of selective social oblivion in art was arguably the most powerful symbolic achievement of the Maoist program since Yan'an. It also constituted the moral foundation for political violence.

As Apter and Saich explain of Maoist strategies in their formative stages a quarter century earlier:

Yan'an became a unique instructional community that considered itself to be in possession of final truths ... [Mao] sought the role of Chief Agent of history in a party in which agency was the main claim to authority. From the start, *no augmentation of military force was undertaken without moral and logical infusions* [.... Mao's teaching] aimed at a form of exegetical bonding designed to convert the revolutionary simulacrum from a community of lost souls into a chosen people and, if necessary, consign the rest to the historical scrap heap.[60]

In this way, revolutionary memory can be seen as equipping generations of Chinese with the "moral and logical" bases for a variety of political acts. In the process, it nurtured both positive and negative energies simultaneously, instilling a feeling of moral exceptionalism, and the confidence and sense of mission that came with it, while at the same time positioning others as lost, even expendable. The result was a culture of political violence that did not require top-down direction, and even flourished in its absence. The collective killing experienced across rural China was, in many ways, the moral implications of revolutionary memory taken to their logical extreme.

Added to the human violence of the 1960s was an epistemic violence. Cultural vestiges of the old society were hunted down, too, emptying libraries, temple compounds and personal collections of records and artefacts from a useless and parasitic past. Of course, this phenomenon is well known, as well. But the ideological value of this erasure, the logic behind this destruction, comes into better focus when we see it as part of the struggle between revolutionary and communal memory.

---

[59] DeMare, *Mao's Cultural Army*, 129.
[60] Apter and Saich, *Revolutionary Discourse in Mao's Republic*, 34; emphasis added.

Conclusion

The twin processes of destruction and reconstruction behind China's national revolutionary project were arguably most clearly revealed during the Cultural Revolution. Here we have explored how both of these processes relied on an evolving corpus of cultural memory that reassigned values and meanings onto the recent past in ways that suited the goal of state-building. Stepping back from this aspect of Maoist China, it becomes clear that its experience was by no means unique. Parallels can be drawn, for example, between the development of the Chinese revolution and the Russian revolution earlier in the century. These parallels extend not only to cultural production and the "manufacturing of truth" in the early years of the Soviet Union but also to the incorporation of religious and messianic ideas of salvation and evil in political discourse, the nurturing of certain norms of violence, and the application of military methods to domestic politics.[61] More broadly, Mark Mazower has stressed the topic of extreme state violence over the course of the twentieth century, drawing from several scholars in the process. As Mazower explains, Nicholas Werth has pointed to "the 1919–1920 'massive extermination' of the Cossacks as a precedent for future mass killings, and argues that what the Bolsheviks did after 1920 was to extend the principle of civil war to their own society." And then Mazower continues:

As the Italian anti-fascist Carlo Rosselli first pointed out, it was a feature of mid-twentieth-century ideological states that they rather readily blurred the boundary between internal and external enemies, and thus redrew the political dividing line within their own societies between those deemed loyal and thus regarded as in practice or potentially beyond the pale. In this respect, they differed sharply from their nineteenth-century predecessors, for whom disloyalty and treachery were two separate concepts.[62]

But even more intriguing is Mazower's encouragement to "link the violence unleashed by major states in Europe itself between 1930 and 1950 with both an earlier history of imperial violence *and* a subsequent history of violent decolonization and postcolonization globally during the Cold War."[63]

Mazower speaks here of Europe (albeit in a global way). But in the case of China – and of the colonized and semicolonized parts of the world more broadly – connections might equally be drawn between the violence (both physical and epistemic) of the imperial era and civilizing missions,

---

[61] Papazian, *Manufacturing Truth*; Igal Halfin, *From Darkness to Light*.
[62] Mark Mazower, "Violence and the State in the Twentieth Century," *American Historical Review* 107/4 (2002), 1170.
[63] Ibid., 1176; emphasis in original.

the violence (again, both physical and epistemic) of the intense interstate warfare of the mid-1900s, and the violence (finally, again, both physical and epistemic) of the various types of civil, revolutionary and counterrevolutionary war fought during or after struggles for independence in the second half of the twentieth century.

That politics in newly independent states involved enormous amounts of bloodletting is well known. Accounting for its sheer scale is another matter. Walder notes similarities between China's class-based "cleansing" in 1968–69 and that of the Khmer Rouge just a few years later. In Cambodia, perhaps 1.7 million people were killed between 1975 and 1979, a death toll of around 20 percent of the population and upwards of 40 percent in some villages more closely studied by scholars.[64] Under the Cambodian Communists, political persecution and killing had achieved a marked ethnic dimension by the time they took power in 1975.[65] But they also had plenty of parallels with policies in China nearby. Although it was not until Mao's death in 1976 that Pol Pot indicated "for the first time the [Communist Party of Kampuchea]'s ideological debt to China" and Mao Zedong Thought, notes Ben Kiernan, parallels between the two sets of revolutionary ideology and practice are hard to miss: waves of eliminationist killings, the radical reorganization of communal and productive life, and round-the-clock toil to alter the environment with dams, dikes and other infrastructural projects, to name a few.[66] In these areas, the Khmer Rouge regime took on the character of an accelerated version of the Maoist one, compressed into four or so years.

But noting that millions died under the purview of "the state" or "regime" in China, Cambodia or elsewhere belies the often simple manner of their execution, with tools most readily at hand in agricultural communities: "a hoe or a large stick" and a victim "frozen and docile" with a mind grown "blurred" and hearing "gone," "easier to kill than an animal," in the words of François Bizot, the ethnologist imprisoned by the Khmer Rouge in the early seventies.[67] The method for much of the political killing in the modern period has been at anyone's disposal. As we have explored here, so has the rationale.

The Chinese revolution can in some ways be seen as a grassroots defense of the community against imperialism.[68] Imperialist interventions had distorted native social relationships and exacerbated tensions

---

[64] Ben Kiernan, *The Pol Pot Regime: Race, Power, and Genocide under the Khmer Rouge, 1975–79*, 3rd ed. (New Haven, CT: Yale University Press, 2008), 458–59.
[65] Ibid., 85–86.   [66] Ibid., 219–30.
[67] François Bizot, *Le portail* (Paris: Table Ronde, 2000), 116–17.
[68] For a compelling example of this interpretation, see for example Wang Ban, "Understanding the Chinese Revolution through Words: An Introduction," in Wang Ban, ed., *Words and Their Stories*, 8.

around the globe, and only by throwing off the coils of imperialism could communities rebuild on their own terms. But, of course, rarely were communities ever permitted to do such a thing. Reconstruction would be along the lines set by the modern party-state, a phenomenon that developed both within and in reaction to the modern colonial enterprise.

Examining the course of the Chinese revolution since the post-WWI years through the prism of revolutionary and communal memory, one sees how the *national* revolution's diagnosis and rehabilitative regimen for communities shared much with the imperialist enterprise, wreaking enormous amounts of violence in various forms while compelling communities to tie their destinies to the vision and strong hand of the party-state. In this way, revolutionary memory resembled the cultural production of colonialism from which it drew. Just as imperial authorities and writers had "discovered" native cultures around the world in periods of instability and unravelling, which the arrival of imperialist and capitalist forces had exacerbated, and then put names to the social dislocation they identified ("backward," "primitive," "savage"), in the case of China, a century of administrative and ecological crisis over the course of the nineteenth century, further intensified by a quarter century of civil war and foreign invasion, led to a conflation of social breakdown (amid imperial and military stresses) with cultural and moral ("feudal") incapacity for beneficial forms of communal organization.

In this sense, the revolutionary project was in practice less a defense of the local from imperialism than an outgrowth of colonial modernity. Viewed from this perspective, the left-right political spectrum collapses and Maoism assumes a striking proximity to rival ideologies. Only when viewed in this way could the Great Leap Forward – the culmination of Maoist economic planning – make sense as a revolutionary program, with its sacrificial demands on localities, no matter the cost, in pursuit of a larger vision of industrial progress. And only in this way could defense of the local food supply against the center make sense as an antirevolutionary act, as a form of resistance against the national revolution's absorption of the local into its designs. By the time of the Cultural Revolution, political mobilization had so detached itself from its material rationale that the national revolution came to chase phantoms and eat itself.

Conclusion

In the middle of Lucien Bianco's *Wretched Rebels: Rural Disturbances on the Eve of the Chinese Revolution* is a brief passage that brings together key themes explored here so far:

If we add natural disasters and famine [to the harshness brought by violence to rural life], we must recognize that the peasants existed in an environment where human life was cheap. It would have been surprising had this environment not influenced their behavior. Perhaps we might overlook the theories of Gustave Le Bon on the psychology of crowds (Le Bon 1895) but certainly not the modern history of China, as revisited by David Der-wei Wang: "an endless brutality," suffered and committed by a multitude of victims and executioners (Wang 2004).[1]

At first, it would seem odd that a historian – and particularly one as masterful and evidence driven as Bianco – would turn to a work of literary analysis to substantiate conditions or values in rural China. The work in question is Wang's *The Monster That Is History: History, Violence, and Fictional Writing in Twentieth-Century China*, a book that in its author's words "tackle[s] the ways Chinese writers register the manmade and natural disasters that forged a century of violence: foreign aggression, civil war, revolution, riots, clan conflict, famine, floods, and the cataclysmic collapse of time-honored establishments."[2]

But then, having *Wretched Rebels* speak in this way through *The Monster That Is History* turns out to make a good deal of sense. One cannot fully understand the course of modern China without appreciating the relationship between perception of the past and action in the present. When one inserts the urgent ideological demands put on writing over the same stretch of the twentieth century, any meaningful distinction between

---

[1] Lucien Bianco, *Wretched Rebels: Rural Disturbances on the Eve of the Chinese Revolution*, trans. Philip Liddell, Harvard East Asian Monographs (Cambridge, MA: Harvard University Asia Center, 2009), 66–67.
[2] David Der-wei Wang, *The Monster that is History: History, Violence, and Fictional Writing in Twentieth-Century China* (Berkeley: University of California Press, 2004), 3.

imaginary and evidence-based treatment of the past begins to collapse. As Wang explains:

There has always been a mutual implication of historicity and narrativity, to be sure, in Chinese historiographical and literary studies. But never have we seen such a moment as we have in modern times, when official history has been so dictated by the ideological and institutional imaginary as to verge on a discourse of make-believe, a discourse often associated with traditional fiction, and fiction so arrested by a desire to reflect the past *and* future as to appropriate the functions of traditional history with respect to completed fact. Hence the genesis of the peculiar double-bind of Chinese literary modernity.[3]

Wang begins his study with the "decapitation syndrome" that took hold of early twentieth-century Chinese writers, most famously Lu Xun but by no means limited to him. This fixation on the summary execution of Boxers, revolutionaries, "bandits" and other Chinese, often overseen by foreign powers and normalized and commodified in photographs and postcards for circulation around the world, "was to haunt Chinese literature throughout the remainder of the twentieth century."[4]

But this issue of the pervasiveness of violence in Chinese life raises the question of its converse – in the form of humaneness or mutual aid – and its disappearance from writings over the same period. As we have seen, the cultivation of perceptions of rural life within the realms of art, fiction and historical writing assisted in mobilizing political actors, exacerbating social tensions and providing the rationale for political killing and cover for systematic starvation at key moments of the People's Republic. This at root is what I have aimed to explore in this book: epistemic erasure as a catalyst for violence, and the cascading dialectic between the two. In short, I have aimed to explore how the cultural memory of revolutionary elites has been more "monstrous" – to use Wang's word – in its presentation of the past than that of communal elites, and what this difference says about China's path to modernity.

At the same time, unlike war or civil conflict, "natural" disasters like famine are often as marginal in national narratives as the communities they strike. Similar to the way refugee crises have been overlooked in histories, disasters often remain in obscurity, left out of national stories where the smallest of military engagements is not.[5] At times, famines are seen as a national shame, yet they are also deceptively complex, and the specifics of how they were responded to readily fall by the historical wayside. What often remains in mentions of famine are

---

[3] Ibid., 3; emphasis in original.   [4] Ibid., 16.
[5] On the "general absence of refugees in historical scholarship," see Peter Gatrell, *The Making of the Modern Refugee* (Oxford: Oxford University Press, 2013), 11.

social types: some combination of victims and hoarders, officials and soldiers of various stripes, and the occasional (invariably outside) relief worker. What remains of such events in revolutionary memory, in other words, are the signs and symbols of backwardness or reform that serve broader narratives of modernity or socialism or the nation, and that highlight the moral and organizational failures of the regimes and ideologies they replaced.

But, before we end on revolutionary memory's place in contemporary China, we might consider how Western writers have handled the issue of the devaluation of human life and endless brutality in China's past. As we have seen, the conversations informing revolutionary memory reached well beyond the People's Republic, beyond China's borders and to a time before the Chinese Communist Party existed. How insulated are Western grand narratives of China from revolutionary understandings of communal practice in times of crisis?

Not by much, it seems. For a good part of the twentieth century China was widely known as the "land of famine," a moniker coined by a 1926 book by the American relief worker Walter Mallory.[6] So it is especially noteworthy that famine events have a remarkably thin treatment in general histories of the country. Some Western historians limit treatment of China's disasters to a causal explanation for rebellions by the Taiping or the Boxers, or as summary context for social dislocation and class conflict between landlords and peasants.[7] In Jonathan Fenby's *Penguin History of Modern China*, flood and famine in the late Qing were events in which "special prayers in the Forbidden City failed to produce an improvement," when "moneylenders showed no pity," "bandits roamed," "parents sold their children" and people "resorted to cannibalism."[8] "At the start of the warlord era, in 1920, bad harvests and drought caused famine [and] many millions were living on sawdust, thistles" and other famine foods. "Banditry boomed" and "kidnapping became a growth industry."[9] Under the Guomindang, "famine gripped Henan, where no rain fell" in 1942, "locusts swarmed," "families sold their children" and "cannibalism spread." As phenomena, these were all too real; as signifiers of where "China was at," so to speak, they belie the element of humanity present in Chinese communities. In these approaches, famine sets the scene for

---

[6] Mallory, *China: Land of Famine.*
[7] Jack Gray, *Rebellions and Revolutions: China from the 1800s to 2000*, 2nd ed. (Oxford: Oxford University Press, 2002), 53, 135, 160; Immanuel C. Y. Hsü, *The Rise of Modern China*, 6th ed. (Oxford: Oxford University Press, 2000), 225.
[8] Jonathan Fenby, *The Penguin History of Modern China: The Fall and Rise of a Great Power, 1850 to the Present* (London: Penguin, 2013), 17.
[9] Ibid, 153–54.

broader political developments while Chinese civic or communal responses remain invisible.[10]

In other histories, Chinese disaster relief is covered in the late Qing, only to disappear thereafter. In John King Fairbank and Merle Goldman's *China: A New History*, "drought, flood, famine, and disease" figure in the nineteenth century's "long story of dynastic decline," fueling the many rebellions of the late Qing.[11] The book notes that, consequently, "welfare activities traditionally in gentry hands [...] took on a new urgency" and in the 1870s "elite activism" led to relief of the great North China famine across great distances.[12] But the authors only return to the subject of famine in 1942 Henan when the scourge "led to hoarding supplies for profit and an immense growth of corruption."[13] Similarly, Klaus Mühlhahn's *Making China Modern* details a range of state and charitable actors and institutions providing "aid for the alleviation of human misery" during famines and flooding in the late nineteenth century, only to return to the subject of famine briefly in wartime Henan and Shandong in 1942.[14] As China's national story enters its republican phase, the idea of charity or mutual aid disappears.[15] In sum, there is little chance for consumers of general histories of China to encounter the instances of relief and mutual aid the researcher finds in the documentary record.

If Western writers are not bound to the "ideological and institutional imaginary" of official People's Republic history, then why this truncated view of the past? The answer might lie in the demands of narrative itself. Capturing events in the world's largest nation over a period of rapid change is of course no easy task. Famine suffering has what one might call narrative muscle, propelling modern China toward social revolution. Famine relief, in contrast, is narrative deadweight, providing little explanation for events to come. Consequently, although the specter of famine was ever present for much of modern Chinese history, as a complex communal event it is curiously out of sight, treated more as an idea for

---

[10] The only relief initiative Fenby's history mentions is an outsider's: "Teddy White of *Time* [...] obtained an audience with Chiang [Kai-shek]. When the journalist produced photographs showing dogs eating corpses [...] grain was rushed in. The army even gave back some food." Ibid., 313–14.

[11] John King Fairbank and Merle Goldman, *China: A New History*, 2nd ed. (Cambridge, MA: The Belknap Press of Harvard University Press, 2006), 187; see also 206.

[12] Ibid., 239–40.   [13] Ibid., 314.

[14] Klaus Mühlhahn, *Making China Modern: from the Great Qing to Xi Jinping* (Cambridge, MA: The Belknap Press of Harvard University Press, 2019), 132–34; see also 317.

[15] Diana Lary's *China's Republic* does not allude to famine for the period's first thirty years. Its first mention is in the form of a box quotation from Theodore White and Annalee Jacoby's coverage of the 1940s Henan famine. Diana Lary, *China's Republic* (Cambridge: Cambridge University Press, 2007), 137.

historical subjects to behold as they come to terms with the fate of the nation.

Take the work of Jonathan Spence, one of the most capable historians the field has produced. The only mention of the great North China famine of 1920 in his *The Search for Modern China* is in the section "Marxist Stirrings," where it is relegated to the realm of impressions for May Fourth activists who "ponder such misery and its context of governmental corruption and incompetence."[16] In his earlier work on the Chinese revolution, *The Gate of Heavenly Peace*, Spence entitles a chapter "The Land of Hunger" on the period 1919 to 1923 during which the great 1920 famine occurred. In the chapter, though, no famine event is ever mentioned. The title instead comes from a poem written by the twenty-year-old *Chenbao* newspaper journalist Qu Qiubai in December 1920, seven years before he headed, briefly, the Chinese Communist Party.[17]

By and large, general histories – Western and Chinese – view disaster responses in China through some semblance of revolutionary memory. In the case of Western scholars, this is arguably for the purposes of narrative. But the effect is the same. This is by no means bad history. Revolutionary memory is historically crucial, serving as an agent of change over the past century. At the same time, however, it clouds our understanding of events at street level, of how a broad range of people related as neighbors or compatriots, and what decisions they made – in short, the interactions that are the essence of social history.

But then there is the question of more specialized histories of Chinese subjects like famine. And here the problem becomes the historical record itself. What I have in mind here is the extraordinary gulf that developed over the course of the twentieth century between the number of surviving communal records on Chinese life and the records of outsiders peering in. There are countless dimensions to this disparity, but it is perhaps best captured by events in 1968. In mid-November of that year, a staffer of the China Records Project of the National Council of the Churches of Christ addressed a letter to "former China Missionaries and Chinese Christians in the United States." "Scholars now at work on China subjects feel a great gap in resources," she explained, and so the council was aiming for a "joint effort to be made to locate, collect, and catalogue the personal reports, diaries, journals, and publications of former China missionaries," to be held under one roof and made readily "available through a central indexing system." The letter included a word of support from Fairbank,

---

[16] Jonathan D. Spence, *The Search for Modern China* (New York: Norton, 1999), 299.
[17] Jonathan D. Spence, *The Gate of Heavenly Peace: The Chinese and Their Revolution, 1895–1980* (New York: Penguin, 1981), 157–87.

at Harvard University and whose history text is quoted above, noting that "several generations of achievement [by missions] will be lost to world view," and urging contribution to the effort. The letter explained that the project's sponsors had suggested that the Missions Library of Yale University host the collection because of the legacy of Kenneth Scott Latourette – the Yale-based historian of Christian missions and of China – and the quality of its archivists. So the collection became part of Yale's Divinity Library, making a wealth of missionary documentation on China readily available to generations of scholars.[18] This consolidation of Western accounts of life in China was launched at the very moment that Red Guard raids, factional battles and the Cleansing of the Class Ranks campaign consumed an untold share of China's cultural and documentary heritage.

Of course, the bearing of this or any epistemic gulf on academic understanding is difficult to gauge. But one measure of the Yale collection's reach is its possession of the records of several key actors in the documentation of events covered in this book. This includes the papers of John D. Hayes of the Hayes-Hall Kansu Earthquake Relief Expedition of 1921 and those of Dwight W. Edwards, executive secretary of the Peking United International Famine Relief Committee from 1920 to 1922. Both men were graduates of Princeton University, an institution whose alumni had a considerable role in sociological inquiry and relief administration work in early to mid-twentieth century China. Hayes' expedition, as we have seen, resulted in two field reports for the Peking United International Famine Relief Committee and also the remarkable photographs published in the *National Geographic*'s feature story on the 1920 Haiyuan earthquake, "'Where the Mountains Walked,'" after which the seismic event largely receded into obscurity outside of geological circles. Edwards was the secretary for the same committee, and served as editor of its summary report on the famine that same year: *The North China Famine of 1920–21*. Printed by Shanghai's Commercial Press in Chinese and English editions in 1922, the book quickly made its way into library collections at universities across the United States. For nearly a century afterwards, Edwards' report served as the basis for Western scholarship on the 1920 famine, including the works of Andrew Nathan, Marie-Claire Bergère and Lillian Li.[19]

---

[18] Helen Smith, letter, November 16, 1968, box 13, folder 1, records group 8, China Records Project, Yale Divinity Library.

[19] Andrew J. Nathan, *A History of the China International Famine Relief Commission* (Cambridge, MA: East Asian Research Center, Harvard University, 1965); Marie-Claire Bergère, "Une crise de subsistence en Chine (1920–1922)," *Annales Histoire, Sciences*

But the problem with the singular position of this (and arguably any) report in historical analysis of this period is that its apparent authority – as an institutional and well-resourced summary document – disguises its limitations. Here we return to the point of departure for *Modern Erasures*. As associate general secretary of the Beijing YMCA from 1906 to 1924, Edwards' team was favorably positioned to access the accounting books of institutional relief actors in that and other major Chinese cities: among these were central government ministries, large international relief societies such as his own and the country's extensive missionary community, all of whose relief contributions receive detailed attention in his report. As for the goings-on in other circles over the famine year, however – in the capital's native charitable associations or benevolent halls, or in community networks across the North China plain – Edwards' team was in the dark.[20] It was "impossible," in their words, for them to obtain the accounts of Chinese relief groups. Consequently, *The North China Famine of 1920–21* offers "merely a guess" for what nonofficial Chinese acting independently from the foreign population generated in relief over the year – in other words, merely a guess for the communal or civic capacities considered throughout this book.[21]

As well-meaning as Edwards may have been in his endeavor, the result constitutes a social erasure that has fed into a range of understandings of this period in Chinese and international history. By way of example, the section on the 1920 drought in Li's *Fighting Famine in North China* – doubtless the most comprehensive scholarly study so far of famine over China's early modern and modern periods – relies on Edwards' report for three quarters of its forty references. The section thus frames the event in terms of "International Aid."[22] Of course, foreigners *did* do much to assist Chinese struggling to survive in the wake of drought over the winter of 1920–21, not to mention the landslides of Gansu. But such history, in this case, offers the gaze of outsiders – both urban Chinese and foreign – looking in. Stricken communities themselves remain in the shadows.

Over much of the twentieth century there was next to no Western study of indigenous human welfare or disaster-relief regimes in prerevolutionary China. Consequently, a paradoxical convergence developed between

Sociales 6 (November – December 1973), especially 1399–1402; Lillian M. Li, *Fighting Famine in North China: State, Market, and Environmental Decline, 1690s–1990s* (Stanford, CA: Stanford University Press, 2007).

[20] On this, see Fuller, *Famine Relief in Warlord China*.

[21] Dwight W. Edwards, ed., *The North China Famine of 1920–1921, with Special Reference to the West Chihli Area: Being the Report of the Peking United International Famine Relief Committee* (Beijing: Peking United International Famine Relief Committee, 1922), 24–25.

[22] Li, *Fighting Famine in North China*, 295–302, 467–68.

missionary and, later on, Cold War-era understandings of China's past and that of Maoist liberation narratives. Only in the 1990s did academic study by Chinese, Japanese and Western scholars begin in earnest to retrieve Chinese charity, disaster relief and civic legacies from historical obscurity. In the intervening years of the century, the May Fourth-New Culture take on rural communal life in China had prevailed, not only in the People's Republic but overseas as well, with a lasting grip on general understandings of Chinese life. A good deal of work on resolving this remains to be done.

Revolutionary Memory and the CCP

The Cultural Revolution, it can be said, saw the end of the peasant as a dynamic political actor. In the Maoist period, the peasant had been exalted as the propeller (conscious or otherwise) behind Chinese historical development, vacillating over time between acting toward egalitarian – or revolutionary – ends, on the one hand, and conservative goals of "class differentiation" on the other. This key "dialectical conception" fell out of favor over the course of the Cultural Revolution, Alexander Day has noted, only to be "replaced by a single-sided and static interpretation of the role of peasants in history" by "reform-period intellectuals," starting in the late 1970s, who cast them as "backward, ignorant, and the cause of China's supposed slow social and economic development."[23]

While making this key point, Day dismisses critiques made by some scholars – such as the anthropologist Myron Cohen and historian Charles Hayford – of the "invention of the peasant" by intellectuals in the early twentieth century. "Elitism cannot be transcended simply by redefining the 'peasant' as a 'farmer,' somehow evading social science categorization and reaching the real of the rural," Day writes. "Instead, we need to better account for social theorization – the continual reinvention of the peasant – within the context of the political economy of the post-socialist period, for the relationship between the peasant and history remains central to any theorization of the evolution of our global condition."[24]

In light of what I have aimed to explore with *Modern Erasures*, Day might be too quick here to dismiss the implications of the farmer-peasant distinction. The evolution of the peasant as historical subject was accompanied by the reduction of Chinese community into a social field of peasants – a "country dominated by the peasantry," in Day's words.[25]

[23] Alexander Day, "History, Capitalism, and the Making of the Postsocialist Chinese Peasant," in Arif Dirlik, Roxann Prazniak and Alexander Woodside, eds., *Global Capitalism and the Future of Agrarian Society* (London: Paradigm, 2012), 55.
[24] Ibid., 54.   [25] Ibid., 56.

Perceiving history through the prism of revolutionary memory recast communities into spheres of limited possibilities, one merely vacillating along a spectrum of reactionary and revolutionary positions.

This should have us rethink what Wang Hui has called the "theoretical disputes of the early 1930s on the social character of the Chinese revolution," what had developed by the 1960s into "a wide-ranging theoretical agenda" around Marxist-Leninist analysis of "the dynamics of history, the market economy, the means of production, class struggle, bourgeois right, the nature of Chinese society and the status of world revolution."[26] Wang has called these debates "an outstanding characteristic of 20th-century China's revolutionary transformations," namely "the continuous and intimate connection between theoretical debate and political practice." Having lost, in the era of reforms, the check these debates served on the errors of the early Chinese Communist Party, Wang suggests that retrieval of the promise of the revolution requires a reincorporation of this theory into political practice.[27]

Any revisiting of the theoretical foundation of the revolutionary project, however, must be partnered with fuller recognition of the devices used and assumptions made in its debates, which were predicated by and large on the absence of entire spheres of social activity and cultural capability in Chinese life. Only in this way can we better understand the evolution of the modern global condition – as Day rightly suggests we do. The very theorization through which revolutionary dialectics were articulated over the course of the twentieth century in this way pulled from colonial frames and discourses on the nature of native communities. The implications of this clearly reach beyond China, to a wider world experiencing various continuing forms of decolonization.

So where does this leave us, decades into a post-Mao People's Republic? To start with, local elites have regained spaces for cultural production. The ideological fervor of the sixties mellowed into the seventies, and alternative moral paradigms slowly took the place of a waning Maoism. This included a form of utilitarian individualism advanced by Mao's more centrist rivals Deng Xiaoping and Liu Shaoqi, as they reintegrated the country into the wider capitalist world.[28] In the process, social disparities resurfaced together with diasporic and religious networks and other forms of association. All of this resulted in a resurgence in local-history endeavors over the course of the eighties, reaching the point where "warlord" figures were rehabilitated in places for reasons of local pride and interest.[29]

---

[26] Wang, "Depoliticised Politics," 33–34.   [27] Ibid., 32.
[28] On this, see Madsen, *Morality and Power in a Chinese Village*, 16–17.
[29] Diana Lary, foreword to *China's Warlords*, by David Bonavia (Oxford: Oxford University Press, 199, vii–viii.

Central to these developments was the reappearance of *wenshi ziliao*, the compilations of local and regional cultural and historical materials, which had been halted in the mid-sixties. Dissolved during the Cultural Revolution, the People's Political Consultative Conference branches "were gradually reconstituted, and by the early 1980s, all provincial and most county branches had formed offices and committees specially designated for *wenshi ziliao* work," Martin Fromm writes.[30] This revival occurred in the much broader context of efforts over the eighties to rectify, or at least recognize, wrongs committed during recent periods of intense state and civil violence in Latin America, Eastern Europe and South Africa. With the Communist Party still in power in China, the country's participation in this global movement was limited. The continued focus of *wenshi ziliao* on the pre-1949 period foreclosed discussion of the Cultural Revolution and other events in the People's Republic. Nonetheless, their compilation offered a way of redressing, if not the victimization of the Maoist years, at least its epistemic violence to some degree. "As a result, while truth commissions such as South Africa's Truth and Reconciliation Commission drew a clear line between perpetrator and victim," Fromm explains, "*wenshi ziliao* editors' approach to truth and reconciliation was to blur these boundaries and to characterize people and historical events in terms of their multiple and complex dimensions."[31]

In this way, *wenshi ziliao* became a hybrid space for the practice of both revolutionary and communal memory in the post-Mao period, offering "a more complicated mapping of the past that accommodated both change and continuity across the 1949 and Communist divides," as Fromm puts it.[32] Through the project, light has been shed on the variety of social institutions and practices in the prerevolutionary past without necessarily losing the overall framework of revolutionary progress – reminding readers of "the corrupt politics and people's harsh conditions in the old society," in the words of one *wenshi ziliao* research committee vice-chair in the eighties.[33] Thus, these volumes, found readily in bookstores and libraries across the People's Republic, have joined modern district gazetteers in serving as rather unique intersections of communal and revolutionary memory, hosting elements of both types of narrative at the same time depending on the approach of any particular interviewee or writer.

This revival of local history of course builds on existing channels of communicative memory of the recent past at the family and community level. Studies of oral history based on interviews have revealed how memories contesting Maoist memory of collectivization, the Great Leap

---

[30] Fromm, *Borderland Memories*, 3.   [31] Ibid., 14.   [32] Ibid., 7.   [33] Quoted in ibid., 47.

and communal life in the deeper republican past persisted through the Maoist period.[34] In places, this revival has included the unveiling of local monuments safeguarded over the Maoist years. If we take the example of Ma Zhongtai's ritual killing in Yangjiagou, Shaanxi, with which we started our study: "After the 1980s the benevolence of the Ma landlords was once again publicly discussed," Jiangsu He writes. "In 1995 the stone tablets hidden in a wall saw daylight again," along with the "good deeds" they had recorded for posterity.[35]

Wenshi ziliao and other forms of cultural memory then have joined communicative memory in offering alternative understanding of the recent past. "Neither fabricated state propaganda nor authentic historical records," Fromm continues, "the *wenshi ziliao* constituted a highly nuanced and localized process where concepts and practices of seeking historical truths converged with post-Mao transitional political and cultural strategies and identities."[36]

So what are the party's wider political and cultural strategies in post-Mao China? It would make sense to complete our discussion with Beijing's evolving posture toward disaster, and particularly earthquake, commemoration. Through it, we see tensions between the loosening of Maoist ideology, and the tightening of political controls.

Since the Deng era, the party has staked its legitimacy in several ways. The first has been a form of performative legitimacy, basing its rule on rapid gains in economic growth, development and military strength. In 2008, after the earthquake of Wenchuan in Sichuan, a form of moral legitimacy was added to the state repertoire of legitimization strategies. For the first time under the People's Republic, the party presided over what the sociologist Bin Xu has called "mourning for the ordinary," the commemoration of "ordinary" victims of disaster, "ordinary" in the sense that they have no clear role in the national or revolutionary project – roles that were fundamental to the narrative and moral positioning of revolutionary memory.[37] This type of mourning for the ordinary had been suppressed during much of the Maoist era when disaster had been framed within the arc of revolutionary memory, in other words as a source of national humiliation and an opportunity for triumph over adversity. For example, annual collective mourning for the victims of the 1920

---

[34] Jun Jing, *The Temples of Memories: History, Power, and Morality in a Chinese Village* (Stanford, CA: Stanford University Press, 1996); Thaxton, *Catastrophe and Contention in Rural China*; Hershatter, *Gender of Memory*.
[35] Jiangsui He, "Death of a Landlord," 149.   [36] Fromm, *Borderland Memories*, 3–4.
[37] Bin Xu, "For Whom the Bell Tolls: State-Society Relations and the Sichuan Earthquake Mourning in China," *Theory and Society* 42 (2013), 509–42. I am indebted to Sarah May Comley for bringing this study to my attention along with Chen and Xu's article from 2018.

earthquake were discontinued in the fifties among Haiyuan's Muslim community, only to resume in the eighties.[38] As late as 1986, at the tenth anniversary of the Tangshan earthquake, official commemoration still took the form of a *Monument for Tangshan's Fight against Earthquake* unveiled by party general secretary Hu Yaobang. The monument to what had surpassed Haiyuan as the world's deadliest earthquake of the twentieth century extolled party responses while downplaying the "trauma of the local" experience.[39]

Late in its ritual embrace of emotional loss, the party has sought moral legitimacy through it but without compromising its bid for performative legitimacy. Perhaps the most prominent example of this was the forbidding of parents from publicly mourning the loss of their children in the rubble of Sichuan's collapsed schools in 2008.[40] In such instances, state ritual both silences and displaces communal mourning, making it clear that official "mourning for the ordinary" will only go so far.

But then semipermanent spaces do exist for the commemoration of major earthquake events, not only in Sichuan but in Gansu and Haiyuan itself. At the museums devoted to local earthquakes in both Haiyuan and Lanzhou, one finds a whole range of perspectives on events in 1920 prominently displayed: telegrams from the Gansu leadership to the central government in December of that year; memoirs from those who experienced the earthquake; photographs of people and buildings in its aftermath (including one of Zhou Tingyuan and his family that appeared in *National Geographic*) and of interviews with survivors decades afterwards; stone stele inscriptions from affected localities; copies of republican gazetteers; and poster-size reproductions of issues of *Zhongguo minbao* (the news daily that most closely followed the quake and national relief efforts from Beijing in 1921). One finds these items displayed amid material celebrating advances since made under the party to understand and relieve such cataclysmic events.[41] In this way, public museums provide hybrid spaces for the exhibiting of communal and revolutionary memory in the post-Mao period.

In the face of this and other competing narratives of the past, and the ideological incoherence it presents to the public, the party's repertoire of legitimization strategies rest on the control of mass media and communication channels. This repertoire in turn relies on a particular understanding

---

[38] *Haiyuan xianzhi* (1999), 1002.
[39] Shengrong Chen and Honggang Xu, "From Fighting against Death to Commemorating the Dead at Tangshan Earthquake Heritage Sites," *Journal of Tourism and Cultural Change* 16/5 (2018), 560–61.
[40] Bin Xu, "For Whom the Bell Tolls," 511.
[41] This was the case during personal visits to the sites in Lanzhou in 2013 and Haiyuan in 2017.

of the Maoist years, and of what existed before the party came to power. In this way, the utility of revolutionary memory lives on.

After 1989, the leadership realized it did not have sufficient "ideological education" in place to shape national identity and bolster its legitimacy in historical terms.[42] This heightened the importance of orthodox history after a period of loosened controls over intellectual activities since Mao's death. Central to this need was the cultivation of memory "about what China was like in the old days," in the words of Deng Xiaoping spoken in the week following the Tiananmen massacre of June 4, 1989.[43] Although schooling under the People's Republic to that point had stressed popular suffering under colonial and "feudal" forces, it had done so within a broader Maoist "victor narrative." In its place, the national curriculum, museums and wider cultural industry of the 1990s cultivated a "victim narrative" vis-à-vis the West and Japan. By the end of the 2000s, Chinese nationalism had developed into a rejection of the idea of universal "modern" values – embraced in the twentieth century as a way of national survival or salvation – toward a form of "Chinese exceptionalism" in the twenty-first century. The ideological basis for this exceptionalism was a particular understanding of the country's imperial past and its Confucian roots. These became inheritances the party embraced for reasons of national pride and for valorizing political authority, all while conjuring up the image of a harmonious ancient past that foreshadowed a peaceful resurgence in contrast with the West's violent rise.[44]

Looking inward, as the People's Republic evolves, revolutionary memory continues to buttress the case for the cultural necessity of strong centralized authority as an antidote to social chaos and predation in China. With the rise of Xi Jinping, challenges or "revisions" to the official line on the prerevolutionary past are dismissed as "historical nihilism." The idea of civil society or civic values are officially deemed a Western invention imposed from outside.[45] The past existence of indigenous spheres of communal or associational life before or beyond the steady hand of the party-state can be discounted.[46] In this way, the party has

---

[42] Zheng Wang, *Never Forget National Humiliation: Historical Memory in Chinese Politics and Foreign Relations* (New York: Columbia University Press, 2014), 96.

[43] Quoted in ibid., 96; see also 252.

[44] On this development, see William A. Callahan, "Sino-speak: Chinese Exceptionalism and the Politics of History," *Journal of Asian Studies* 71/1 (February 2012), 33–55.

[45] "Communiqué on the Current State of the Ideological Sphere," A Notice from the Central Committee of the Communist Party of China's General Office, April 22, 2013, Document 9: A ChinaFile Translation, ChinaFile, Center on U.S.-China Relations at Asia Society, www.chinafile.com/document-9-chinafile-translation.

[46] On the question of associational activity on the eve of Xi's rise to power, see Anthony J. Spires, "Contingent Symbiosis and Civil Society in an Authoritarian State: Understanding the

twice been served by revolutionary memory: first, by justifying the party's social hegemony and rise to power in 1949; and second, after revolutionary memory's role in fueling the bloodletting of the Cultural Revolution, by justifying continued party dominance and checks on public participation in the political realm.

To be sure, the epistemic violence of the twentieth century was not experienced equally across China. Nor was the opportunity in local-history projects to retrieve aspects of the past conferred equally. The "politics of historical memory" have played out differently in Han Chinese regions compared to the Uyghur regions of the Northwest or Tibetan regions of the Southwest, where the party's developmental narrative remains most powerfully enforced.[47]

So the tension between revolutionary and communal memory continues into the post-Mao stage of Communist rule, in uneven and ever-evolving ways: from the scar literature (*shanghen wenxue*) of the 1980s to private museums that curate alternative narratives to recent citizen investigations and documentary film on ordinary rural suffering under Mao; amid all these developments, "even critical memory narratives [can] still rely on the language of the state to criticize the state," in the words of Sebastian Veg;[48] in photographic images and other forms of visual culture online and elsewhere, the "hushing of history" persists as a "densely collective endeavor," in the words of Margaret Hillenbrand, in which the "silences of the present are conspiratorial," taking the form of state censorship and self-censorship, and only revealed in the "fleeting spaces in which public secrecy is named and outed;"[49] and finally, in textual culture the tension persists where *wenshi ziliao*, gazetteer or other accounts of life and death, of communal achievements and failures, celebration and loss come up against accounts based on party "erasing, manipulating, and rewriting" of the past into its own image.[50]

Survival of China's Grassroots NGOs," *Journal of American Sociology* 117/1 (July 2011), 1–45.

[47] Fromm, *Borderland Memories*, 77; Tom Cliff, "Refugees, Conscripts, and Constructors: Developmental Narratives and Subaltern Han in Xinjiang, China," *Modern China* (2020), 1–29.

[48] Sebastian Veg, "Introduction: Trauma, Nostalgia, Public Debate," in Sebastian Veg, ed., *Popular Memories of the Mao Era: From Critical Debate to Reassessing History* (Hong Kong: Hong Kong University Press, 2019), 9.

[49] Margaret Hillenbrand, *Negative Exposures: Knowing What Not to Know in Contemporary China* (Durham, NC: Duke University Press, 2020), 2, 7.

[50] Shan Windscript, "A Modern History of Forgetting: the Rewriting of Social and Historical Memory in Contemporary China, 1966–Present," *Quarterly Journal of Chinese Studies* (2013), 59.

The Chinese Communist Party may present its style of governance as part of a clash of civilizations, to use Samuel Huntington's phrase from some time ago.[51] But, on the contrary, the ongoing tension between revolutionary and communal memory places the heart of this clash – one between the strong hand of the party-state on the one hand and civic or communal life on the other – squarely within Chinese history itself.

[51] Samuel P. Huntington, *The Clash of Civilizations and the Remaking of World Order* (New York: Simon & Schuster, 1996).

Glossary

This list of characters for Chinese names and terms is limited to those that are sourced from Chinese-language primary sources. Also excluded here are characters found in the bibliography, provincial names and capitals, and the artist names and titles of woodcuts. The list provides traditional or simplified versions of characters depending on which appeared in the original text. The entries are alphabetized letter by letter of the romanized form, ignoring word and syllable breaks, with the exception of personal names, which are ordered first by surname and then alphabetically by given name.

aiguo 愛國

Baiyakou 白牙口
ba naxie hexuegui dadao shasi 把那些喝血鬼打倒殺死
baogao 報告
baoshou 保守
bei 碑
Beifang gongzhen xiehui 北方公振協會
bei nuyi 被奴役
bei qipian 被欺騙
beiwu 卑污
ben di tushen 本地土紳
bi gong bi yun 比公比勻
bu zhi jiuji 不知救濟

caizhu 財主
Cao Rui 曹銳
canzhuang 慘狀
Chai Yingcang 柴映仓
chaji 查記
Chen Wanli 陳萬里
chiren de yeshou 吃人的野獸
chu gou 刍狗
cishan jia 慈善家

da bei 大悲
da ci 大慈
da cishan jia 大慈善家
da de ni sui fenfen 打得你碎紛紛
Dalongwo 大龍窩
Daming 大名
daode 道德
daoli 道理
da ren 大仁
da yi 大義
Deng Chunfen 鄧春芬
Deng Chungao 鄧春膏
Deng Chunlan 鄧春蘭
Deng Chunlin 鄧春霖
Deng Tuo 鄧拓
Dexingming 德兴铭
diaocha 調查
difang kaiming shishen 地方開明士紳
difang xiangshen 地方乡绅
dizhu sijue 地主死絕
dongjia 東家
dou 斗
duangen 斷根
dui tian jietan 對天接嘆

e'ba 惡霸

fanshen 翻身
fazhan 發展
fen fuwu 分浮物
Feng Hanying 馮翰英
fengjian saowan 封建掃完
Fengtian jiuji hanzai xiehui 奉天救濟旱災協會
Fojiao chouzhen hui 佛教籌賑會
Fojiao jiaoying hui 佛教教嬰會

gailiang shehui de ji xianfeng 改良社會的急先鋒
Gan ren 甘人
gongdao 公道
gonggong daodao de fen 公公道道的分
gongmin daode 公民道德
gongshen 公審
gou caizhu 狗財主

Guangrentang 廣仁堂
Guangxu 光緒
guiji 癸己
guoren 國人
guzhu 傭主

hanhuang 旱荒
Hanzu 汉族
haoduo Xinyejiao de waiguoren 好多信耶教的外國人
Hu Zhixiu 胡志修
Hua Bancheng 花半城
Hua Hua Taisui 花花太歲
Hua Zifang 花自芳
Huang Shiren 黃世仁
Huang Xueshi 黃學史
Huayang yizhen hui *zhi waiguoren* 華洋義賑會之外國人

jiaoxun 教訓
jiazhuang 假裝
Ji Xuangong 吉轩公
jigong haoyi 急公好义
jihuang 饑荒
Jilong 际隆
jin 斤
Jingyuan 靖遠
jiushi waiguoren 就是外國人
juewu 覺悟
juewu de nongmin 覺悟的農民

kaiming shishen 开明士紳
kexiao 可笑
kong wen 空文

lao fengjian 老封建
leshan haoshi 樂善好施
Li Shufang 李淑芳
Li Wenhui 李文辉
lian shang xia jiao 联上下交
liangfeng meide 良风美德
lieshen 劣紳
Lingshan *zhenzai* 靈山賑災
Lingshou 靈壽
Longdong 隴東
Lu Hongtao 陸洪濤

Lü Chengshu 呂承書

Ma Fuxiang 馬福祥
Ma Guoming 馬國明
Ma Yuanzhang 馬元章
meide 美德
mincai 民財
minghuo 明火
minqing 民情
minzhong 民众
minzhu de ju liuli 民主的鉅流裡
mixin 迷信
mu 畝

Ning'anbao 寗安堡
nongmin 農民

pingminhua 平民化
pingtiao zhenji deng 平糶賑濟等
pinnong 貧農
putong guomin de xingzhi 普通國民的性質

Qiang Yongjun 强永浚
qingnian yundong 青年運動
qiong ren hui 窮人會
Qi Ruiting 祁瑞亭
quanxuesuo 劝学所

rendao zhuyi 人道主義
ren jiang 仁浆
renlei huzhu rensheng zhenyi ji rendao fuwu 人類互助人生真義及人
    道服務
renmin 人民
Renmin de shounan 人民的受難
renmin de zhenshi lishi 人民的真實歷史
renmin fating 人民法庭
renyi 仁義

saorao 騷擾
Shagou 沙溝
shao dongjia 少東家
sharen de mowang 殺人的魔王
shehui de yishi 社會的意識
shehui diaocha 社會調查
shehui gongyi shiye 社會公益事业

shehui jiuji gongzuo 社会救济工作
sheng 升
shenshi 紳士
shi 石
shizhou 施粥
shounan de lianyu 受難的煉獄
shu bei ji song 树碑记颂
shucai zhangyi 疏财仗義
Shunzhi hanzai jiuji hui 順直旱災救濟會
si min 四民
Su Caifeng 苏彩风
Su Tingrui 苏廷瑞
Sun 孫

tanguan 贪官
tianzai 天災
tongbao 同胞
Tongzhou 同州
Tongzijun 童子軍
Touying 头营
tufei 土匪
tuhao 土豪
tuhao lieshen chenghuayuan 土豪劣紳成化院
tuoli dangwu 脱离党务

Wang Hansan 王漢三
Wang Zizhi 王自治
wangu 頑固
wanmin bei 万民碑
weisheng 衛生
wenhua 文化
women Ouzhouren 我們歐洲人
women yao fanshen 我們要翻身
Wu Yong 仵墉
Wushanshe 悟善社
wuzhuo shehui 污濁社會
wu zuzhi 無組織

Xi Yan'er 喜燕兒
Xia Jiwen 夏际文
xiangmin 乡民
xiangren 鄉人
xianzhang 县长

Xi'er 喜兒
xinche shuijinbei 薪车水仅杯
Xingtang 行唐
xingzheng ziran fubai 行政自然腐敗
xingzhi 性質
xinqin gengyun ba sui 辛勤耕耘八歲
xin shenghuo 新生活
xuetu er ju 穴土而居

Yan Wang 閻王
Yang Xuan 杨选
Yang Zhanshan 楊占山
yaodong 窑洞
Yaodonggou 窑洞沟
yi gong dai zhen 义工代赈
yingdang de 應當的
yuan 元
Yuqin 禹勤

Zhang Futang 張福堂
Zhang Jichuan 張濟川
Zhang Zuanxu 张缵绪
Zhangjiakou 張家口
Zhansan 占三
zhe dou shi nongmin de xuehan 這都是農民的血汗
Zhengjihui 拯濟會
zhenji zhi fa 賑濟之法
zhe shi mingyun ma 這是命運嗎
Zhili yizhen hui 直隸義賑會
zhi qi de 志其德
zhiyou qiutian bai Fo 只有求天拜佛
zhong 眾
Zhongguo jisheng hui 中國急生會
Zhongguo yizhen hui 中國義賑會
zibenjia 資本家
zisi zili 自私自利
Zou 鄒
zuili 最力

Bibliography

Guyuan Gazetteers (地方志 *difang zhi*)

Guyuan diquzhi 固原地区志 (1994) Ningxia 宁夏
Guyuan shizhi 固原市志 (2009) Ningxia 宁夏
Guyuan xianzhi 固原縣誌 (n.d.) Ningxia 宁夏
Guyuan xianzhi 固原县志 (1981?) Ningxia 宁夏
Guyuan xianzhi 固原县志 (1993) Ningxia 宁夏
Minguo Guyuan xianzhi 民国固原县志 (1992) Ningxia宁夏

Other Gazetteers

Cang xianzhi 滄縣志 (1933) Hebei 河北
Haiyuan xianzhi 海原县志 (1999) Ningxia 宁夏
Jingning xianzhi 静宁县志 (1993) Gansu 甘肃
Jingxing xianzhi 井陘縣志 (1934) Hebei 河北
Lanzhou shizhi 兰州市志 (2013) Gansu 甘肃
Pingliang diquzhi 平凉地区志 (2011) Gansu 甘肃
Pingliang shizhi 平凉市志 (1996) Gansu 甘肃

Periodicals and Newspapers

Aiguo baihua bao 愛國白話報 (Beijing)
Atlantic Monthly (Boston)
Celestial Empire (Shanghai)
Chenbao 晨報, or *Morning Post* (Beijing)
Da gongbao 大公報 (Tianjin)
Dixue zazhi 地學雜誌 (Beijing)
Dongfang zazhi 東方雜誌, or *Eastern Miscellany* (Shanghai)
Fengsheng 峰聲 (Beijing)
Fengtian gongbao 奉天公報 (Shenyang)
Gansu daxue zhoukan 甘肅大學周刊 (Lanzhou)
Guobao 國報, or *Nation* (Beijing)
Guomin gonglun 國民公論 (Shanghai)
Guxin ribao 鼓昕日報 (Xi'an)
Haichao yin 海潮音 (Hangzhou)

Jiuzai zhoukan 救災周刊, or *Famine Relief Weekly* (Beijing)
Minguo ribao 民國日報, or *Republican Daily News* (Shanghai)
Minyi ribao 民意日報 (Beijing)
Minzhu qingnian 民主青年 (Zhangjiakou)
National Geographic Magazine (Washington, D.C.)
New York Times
North China Herald (Shanghai)
Qingnian liangyou 青年良友, or *Companion Pictorial* (Shanghai)
Qunbao 羣報, or *Social Reports* (Beijing)
Saturday Evening Post (Philadelphia)
Shaonian zazhi 少年雜誌 (Shanghai)
Shenghuo manhua 生活漫畫 (Shanghai)
Shengming 生命 (Beijing)
Shibao 時報, or *Eastern Times* (Shanghai)
Shihua 實話, or *Daily Truth* (Beijing)
Shuntian shibao 順天時報 (Beijing)
Times (London)
Xiangdao 向导, or *Guide Weekly* (Shanghai)
Xiao gongbao 小公報 (Beijing)
Xiao minbao 小民報 (Beijing)
Xin Long zazhi 新隴雜誌 (Beijing)
Yishibao 益世報, or *Social Welfare* (Beijing and Tianjin)
Zhengfu gongbao 政府公報 (Beijing)
Zhongguo minbao 中國民報 (Beijing)
Zhongguo nongmin 中國農民 (Guangzhou)

Primary Sources

Abegg, Lily. *The Mind of East Asia*. Translated by J. Crick and E. E. Thomas. London: Thames and Hudson, 1952. Originally published as *Ostasien Denkt Anders*, 1949.

Anonymous. Foreword to *Yan Han muke xuanji* 彦涵木刻選集. Beijing: Huabaoshe, 1949.

Anonymous. *Letters from a Chinese Magistrate*. Reprinted from the *Peking & Tientsin Times*. Tianjin: Tientsin Press, March 1920.

Anonymous. *Reminiscences of a Chinese Official: Revelations of Official Life under the Manchus*. Tianjin: Tientsin Press, 1922. Reprinted from the *Peking Gazette* and the *China Illustrated Review*.

"Beifang da hanzai 北方大旱災," *Shaonian zazhi* 少年雜誌 10/10 (1920), 4–5.

Beijing guoji tongyi jiuzai zonghui 北京國際統一救災總會. *Beijing guoji tongyi jiuzai zonghui baogao shu* 北京國際統一救災總會報告書. Beijing: Beijing guoji tongyi jiuzai zonghui, 1922.

Beijing shi difang zhi bianzuan weiyuan hui 北京市地方志編纂委员会. *Beijing zhi: baoye tongxun she zhi* 北京志 : 报业通讯社志. Beijing: Beijing chuban she, 2005.

Beijing xuesheng lianhe hui 北京學生聯合會. "Jing xuesheng diaocha zaiqing jihua 京學生調查災情計畫," *Minguo ribao* 民國日報, September 16, 1920, 3.

Beijing xuesheng lianhe hui 北京學生聯合會. "Xuesheng hui jiuzai gongqi 學生會救災公啟," *Yishibao* 益世報, September 20, 1920, 3.

"Ben she jishi 本社紀實," *Xin Long zazhi* 新隴雜誌 1/1 (May 20, 1920), 31–32.

Bizot, François. *Le portail*. Paris: Table Ronde, 2000.

Bonnard, Abel. *En Chine, 1920–1921*. Translated by Veronica Lucas. London: George Routledge & Sons, 1926.

Buck, Pearl S. Introduction to *My Country and My People*, by Lin Yutang. London: W. Heinemann, 1939.

Buck, Pearl S. *The Good Earth*. Cleveland and New York: The World Publishing Company, 1947.

Cable, A. Mildred and Francesca L. French. *Dispatches from North-West Kansu*. London: China Inland Mission, 1925.

"Cangxian jiuzai xiejinhui ganxie ge cishan jiguan shizhen beiji 滄縣救災協進會感謝個慈善機關施賑碑記," *Cang xianzhi* 滄縣志 13 (1933), 59b–60a.

Cannepin, P. M. "Les Poupées Vivantes," in Pierre Mertens, S. J., ed., *La légende de Dorée en Chine: Scènes de la vie de Missions au Tche-li Sud-est*. Lille: Societé Saint-Augustin, Desclée de Brouwer et Compagnie, 1920.

Chang Feng-Ju, Li Chih-K'uan and Liu Chung. "Revolutionary Mother Pao Lien-tzu," in Sidney L. Greenblatt, ed., *The People of Taihang: An Anthology of Family Histories*, 218–45. White Plains, NY: International Arts and Sciences Press, 1976.

Chang Ju-Yün, Kuo Shih-Kang and Li Chia-Ming. "The Tragedy of the People of 'Lucky Star Locust,'" in Sidney L. Greenblatt, ed., *The People of Taihang: An Anthology of Family Histories*, 33–50. White Plains, NY: International Arts and Sciences Press, 1976.

Chao Chün. Foreword to *The People of Taihang: An Anthology of Family Histories*, 6–7. Edited by Sidney L. Greenblatt. White Plains, NY: International Arts and Sciences Press, 1976.

Chen Bowen 陳博文. *Gansu sheng yi pie* 甘肅省一瞥. Shanghai: Shangwu yinshuguan, 1926.

Chen Gongfu 陳功甫. *Zhongguo zuijin sanshi nian shi* 中國最近三十年史. Shanghai: Shangwu yinshuguan, 1928.

Chen Zhengyu 陳崢宇. "Zhi nan Lu xibei zaiqi de qingxing he jiuji fangfa 直南魯西北災區的情形和救濟方法," *Chenbao* 晨報, October 15, 1920 2.

Close, Upton (Josef W. Hall). *In the Land of the Laughing Buddha: The Adventures of an American Barbarian in China*. New York: G. P. Putnam's Sons, 1924.

Close, Upton (Josef W. Hall) and Elsie McCormick. "'Where the Mountains Walked': An Account of the Recent Earthquake in Kansu Province, China, Which Destroyed 100,000 Lives," *National Geographic Magazine* XLI/5 (May, 1922), 445–64.

Cotton, Harold D. *Bao's Adventure: A Chinese Play in Two Acts and Six Scenes*. Westminster: London Missionary Society, [circa 1920].

Deng Chungao 鄧春膏. "Hewei daode 何謂道德?," *Gansu daxue zhoukan* 甘肅大學周刊 1/1 (1922), 23–29, and 1/2 (1922), 30–42.

Deng Yunte. *The History of Famine Relief in China*. Translated by Gao Jianwu. Cambridge: Cambridge University Press, 2020.

Deng Yunte 鄧雲特. *Zhongguo jiuhuang shi* 中國救荒史. Shanghai: Shangwu yinshuguan, 1937.

Doolittle, Justus. *Social Life of the Chinese: With Some Account of Their Religious, Governmental, Educational, and Business Customs and Opinions, with Special but Not Exclusive Reference to Fuhchau*, vol. 2. N.p.: Cheng Wen Publishing Company, 1966. First published 1865.

Du Hongguang. "Zhou Tingyuan xingshi luyao," *Jingning wenshi ziliao xuanji* 静宁文史资料选集 2 (1992),147–50.

Edwards, Dwight W., ed. *The North China Famine of 1920–1921, with Special Reference to the West Chihli Area: Being the Report of the Peking United International Famine Relief Committee*. Beijing: Peking United International Famine Relief Committee, 1922.

Egan, Eleanor Franklin. "Fighting the Chinese Famine," *Saturday Evening Post*, April 9, 1921.

Fei Xiaotong. *From the Soil: The Foundations of Chinese Society* [*Xiangtu Zhongguo*]. Translated by Gary G. Hamilton and Wang Zheng. Berkeley: University of California Press, 1992.

Fojiao chouzhen hui 佛教籌賑會, "Wei bei wu sheng zaimin gao ai 為北五省災民告哀," *Haichao yin* 海潮音 12 (December 1920).

Franck, Harry A. *Wandering in Northern China*. New York: The Century Company, 1923.

Frenz, Horst, ed. *Literature, 1901–1967: Nobel Lectures, Including Presentations, Speeches and Laureates' Biographies*. Amsterdam: Nobel Foundation/Elsevier, 1969.

Fuller, Myron and Frederick Clapp. "Loess and Rock Dwellings of Shensi, China," *Geographical Review* 14/2 (1924), 215–226.

Gamble, Sidney D. *Peking: A Social Survey*. Conducted under the auspices of the Princeton University Center in China and the Peking Young Men's Christian Association. New York: George H. Doran Co., 1921.

Gamewell, Mary Ninde. *Ming-Kwong: "City of Morning Light."* West Medford, MA: Central Committee on the United Study of Foreign Missions, 1924.

"Gansu dizhen qizai zhi diaocha 甘肅地震奇災之調查," *Xin Long zazhi* 新隴雜誌 1/4 (April 20, 1921), 28–35.

Gansu zhenzai chouzhenchu diyiqi zhengxin lü 甘肅震災籌賑處第一期徵信綠, 1–25. N.p.: 1921. Special Collections, Gansu Provincial Library.

Garland, S. J. "Earthquake in North West China: Terrible Loss of Life and Suffering," *Celestial Empire*, February 5, 1921.

Gray, John H. *China: A History of the Laws, Manners, and Customs of the People*. London: Macmillan, 1878.

Gu Jiegang 顧頡剛. *Chu ji zhong xue jiaoke shu: Guoyu bianji dayi* 初級中學教科書：國語編輯大意. Shanghai: Shangwu yinshuguan, 1929.

Gu Jiegang 顧頡剛 and Wang Zhongqi 王鐘麒. *Xiandai chuzhong jiaokeshu: benguo shi* 現代初中教科書：本國史. Shanghai: Shangwu yinshuguan, 1924–25.

Guojia dizhen ju Lanzhou dizhen yanjiusuo 国家地震局兰州地震研究所, ed. *Gansu sheng dizhen ziliao huibian* 甘肃省地震资料汇编. Beijing: Dizhen chubanshe, 1989.

Jing Wenyuan 景文源. "Qingmo minchu de Guyuan yangjiyuan yu cishanhui 清末民初的固原养济院与慈善会," *Guyuan wenshi ziliao* 固原文史资料2 (1988), 127–29.

Han Dingshan 韓定山. "Zhang Guangjian du Gan qi nian 张广建督甘七年," *Gansu wenshi ziliao xuanji* 甘肃文史资料选集 2 (1963), 17–27.

Han Feng 韓楓. "Shi Kelang cong kunan zhong jiefang chulai 屎克郎從苦難中解放出來," *Minzhu qingnian* 民主青年 2 (February 1946), 25–27.

Han Wen-Chou and Yao Lung-Ch'ang. "A Home Given by Chairman Mao," in Sidney L. Greenblatt, ed., *The People of Taihang: An Anthology of Family Histories*, 9–32. White Plains, NY: International Arts and Sciences Press, 1976.

Hayes, John D. "Report of the Shensi Investigation," Typescript. N.p.: n.d. RG127_001_005, Yale Divinity Archives.

He Jingzhi 賀敬之 and Ding Yi 丁毅. *Bai mao nü* 白毛女. Beijing: Xinhua shudian, 1951.

Hen Gong 恨工 and Zhong Jiu 仲九, eds. *Chu ji zhong xue: Guoyu wendu ben* 初級中學：國語文讀本 vol. 1. Shanghai: Minzhi shuju, 1923. Reprinted 1928.

Higgs, Phyllis M. *Blind Chang: A Missionary Drama*. Westminster: London Missionary Society, 1920.

Hinton, William. *Fanshen: A Documentary of Revolution in a Chinese Village*. New York: Monthly Review, 1966.

Hosie, Alexander. *On the Trail of the Opium Poppy: A Narrative of Travel in the Chief Opium-Producing Provinces in China*. London: G. Philip & Son, 1914.

Hovelaque, Émile. *Les Peuples d'Extrême-Orient. La Chine*. Paris: Ernest Flammarion, 1923.

Huston, J. to Secretary of State, letter, April 18, 1921. Records of the United States Department of State Relating to the Internal Affairs of China, 1910–1929, 893.48g. Microfilm.

Huston, J. to Secretary of State, letter, February 4, 1921, 2–3. Records of the United States Department of State Relating to the Internal Affairs of China, 1910–1929, 893.48g. Microfilm.

Hutchinson, Paul, ed. *A Guide to Important Mission Stations in Eastern China (Lying Along the Main Routes of Travel)*. Shanghai: The Mission Book Company, 1920.

"The Kansu Report." Typescript, unsigned. N.p.: addendum dates text to late May 1921. RG127_001_005, Yale Divinity Archives.

Kao Feng, Chang Tso-Pin and Lang Ch'eng-Hsin. "The Story of Selling Oneself," in Sidney L. Greenblatt, ed., *The People of Taihang: An Anthology of Family Histories*, 51–63. White Plains, NY: International Arts and Sciences Press, 1976.

Kemp, Emily Georgina. *Chinese Mettle*. London: Hodder and Stoughton, 1921.

Keyte, John Charles. *Andrew Young of Shensi: Adventure in Medical Missions*. London: The Carey Press, 1924.

Kipling, Rudyard. "The White Man's Burden – An Address to the United States," *Times* (London), February 4, 1899.

Lattimore, Owen. "Happiness Is among Strangers." Manuscript dated 1970. MSS80712, box 59, folder 19. Owen Lattimore Papers, 1907–1997. Library of Congress Manuscript Division.

Lécroart, Henri. Preface to *La Légende Dorée en Chine: Scènes de la vie de Mission au Tche-li Sud-est*, v. Edited by Pierre Mertens, S. J. Lille: Societé Saint-Augustin, Desclée de Brouwer et Compagnie, 1920.

Li Boyuan. *Modern Times: A Brief History of Enlightenment.* Translated by Douglas Lancashire. Hong Kong: The Chinese University of Hong Kong, 1996.

Li Hua 李樺. *Li Hua muke xuanji* 李樺木刻選集. Beijing: Xinhua shudian, 1958.

Liang Qichao 梁啟超. Preface to *Gongmin xue kecheng dawang* 公民學課程大綱, by Zhou Zhigan 周之淦, Yang Zhongming 楊中明 and Lu Duanyi 蘆段宜, 1–2. Shanghai: Shangwu yinshuguan, 1923.

Liddell, J. D. "On the Edge of the Famine: Tsangchow [Cangzhou] February 8 and 9, 1921," *The Chronicle of the London Missionary Society* 29 (June 1921), 138.

Lin Hongfei 林鴻飛. "Hanzai zhong de jidujiao fojiao he guanliao zhengke 旱災中的基督教佛教和官僚政客," *Shengming* 生命, February 15, 1921, 1–3.

Liu Xian 劉峴. *Liu Xian muke xuanji* 劉峴木刻選集. Beijing: Xinhua shudian, 1984.

Livens, Ethel S. *Women of the North China Plain.* London: London Missionary Society, 1920.

Lü Simian 呂思勉. *Baihua ben guo shi: ce 5: xiandai shi* 白話本國史: 冊5: 現代史. Shanghai: Shangwu yinshuguan, 1933.

Lü Simian 呂思勉. *Xin xuezhi gaoji zhongxue jiaokeshu: ben guo shi* 新學制高級中學教科書：本國史. Shanghai: Shangwu yinshuguan, 1927.

Lu Xun. "Ah Q – The Real Story," in *Diary of a Madman and Other Stories*, 101–72. Translated by William Lyell. Honolulu: University of Hawai'i Press, 1990.

Lu Xun. "Diary of a Madman," in *Diary of a Madman and Other Stories*, 29–41. Translated by William Lyell. Honolulu: University of Hawai'i Press, 1990.

Lu Xun. "Hometown," in *Diary of a Madman and Other Stories*, 89–100. Translated by William Lyell. Honolulu: University of Hawai'i Press, 1990.

Ma Tingxiu 馬廷秀. "Zaoqi Gansu Huizu daxue sheng fu jing jiu xue gaishu 早期甘肅回族大學生赴京就學概述," in Zhengxie Lanzhou shi weiyuan hui 政协兰州市委员会, ed., *Lanzhou Huizu yu Yisilan jiao : Lanzhou wenshi ziliao xuanji* 兰州回族与伊斯兰教:兰州文史资料选集 9 (1988), 189–93.

MacNair, Harley Farnsworth. *With the White Cross in China: The Journal of a Famine Relief Worker with a Preliminary Essay by Way of Introduction.* Beijing: Henri Vetch, 1939.

Mallory, Walter H. *China: Land of Famine.* New York: American Geographical Society, 1926.

Mallory, Walter H. *Jihuang de Zhongguo.* Shanghai: Minzhi shuju, 1929.

Mann, Ebenezer J. "The Earthquake," *Links with China and Other Lands* 31 (April 1921), 331. MS380302. Ebenezer and Mabel Mann. Papers. School of Oriental and African Studies Special Collections, London.

Mao Dun 茅盾. "Kanle Wang Renfeng de zuopin zhan 看了汪刃鋒的作品展," in Wang Renfeng 汪刃鋒. *Ren Feng muke ji* 刃鋒木刻集. Shanghai: Kaiming shudian, 1948.

Mao Qijun 毛起鵁. *Shehui xue ji shehui wenti* 社會學及社會問題. Shanghai: Minzhi shuju, 1933.

Mao Zedong. "Analysis of All the Classes in Chinese Society," December 1, 1925, in Stuart R. Schram, ed., *National Revolution and Social Revolution, December 1920–June 1927*, 249–62. Vol. 2 of *Mao's Road to Power: Revolutionary Writings 1912–1949*. Armonk, NY: M. E. Sharpe, 1992.

Mao Zedong. "An Analysis of the Various Classes among the Chinese Peasantry and Their Attitudes toward the Revolution," January 1926, in Stuart R. Schram, ed., *National Revolution and Social Revolution, December 1920–June 1927*, 303–09. Vol. 2 of *Mao's Road to Power: Revolutionary Writings 1912–1949*. Armonk, NY: M. E. Sharpe, 1992.

Mao Zedong. "The Chinese Revolution and the Chinese Communist Party," December 15, 1939, in Stuart R. Schram, ed., *New Democracy 1939–1941*, 279–308. Vol. 7 of *Mao's Road to Power: Revolutionary Writings 1912–1949*. Armonk, NY: M.E. Sharpe, 1992.

Mao Zedong. "How to Analyze Classes," October 10, 1933, in Stuart R. Schram, ed., *The Rise and Fall of the Chinese Soviet Republic 1931–1934*, 546–49. Vol. 4 of *Mao's Road to Power: Revolutionary Writings 1912–1949*. Armonk, NY: M.E. Sharpe, 1992.

Mao Zedong 毛澤東. "Hunan nongmin yundong kaocha baogao 湖南農民運動考察報告," *Xiangdao* 向导 191 (1927), 8–13.

Mao Zedong. "Letter to Yang Zhongjian," September 29, 1921, in Stuart R. Schram, ed., *National Revolution and Social Revolution, December 1920–June 1927*, 99. Vol. 2 of *Mao's Road to Power: Revolutionary Writings 1912–1949*. Armonk, NY: M. E. Sharpe, 1992.

Mao Zedong. "The National Revolution and the Peasant Movement," September 1, 1926, in Stuart R. Schram, ed., *National Revolution and Social Revolution, December 1920–June 1927*, 387–92. Vol. 2 of *Mao's Road to Power: Revolutionary Writings 1912–1949*. Armonk, NY: M. E. Sharpe, 1992.

Mao Zedong 毛澤東. "Zhongguo nongmin zhong ge jieji de fenxi ji qi duiyu geming de taidu 中國農民中各階級的分析及其對於革命的態度," *Zhongguo nongmin* 中國農民 1 (1926), 13–20.

Maugham, W. Somerset. *On a Chinese Screen*. New York: George H. Doran Co., 1922.

Mertens, Pierre. S. J., ed. *La légende de Dorée en Chine: Scènes de la vie de Missions au Tche-li sud-est*. Lille: Societé Saint-Augustin, Desclée de Brouwer et Compagnie, 1920.

Miao Jinyuan 繆金源. "Zen yang zuo hanzai diaocha de baogao 怎樣做旱災調查的報告," *Chenbao* 晨報, October 26, 1920.

"A Missionary's Wife" ("Aunt Helen"). *China and Its People: A Book for Young Readers*. London: James Nisbet and Co., 1892.

Nevius, John L. *China and the Chinese: A General Description of the Country and Its Inhabitants; Its Civilization and Form of Government; Its Religious and Social Institutions; Its Intercourse with Other Nations, and Its Present Condition and Prospects*. New York: Harper and Brothers, 1869.

Ningxia Huizu zizhiqu dizhen ju 宁夏回族自治区地震局, ed. *Ningxia Huizu zizhiqu dizhen lishi ziliao huibian* 宁夏回族自治区地震历史资料汇编. Beijing: Dizhen chubanshe, 1988.

Niu Dasheng 牛达生."Minguo 'Guyuan xianzhi' 民国 '固原县志,'" *Guyuan diqu shi zhi ziliao* 固原地区史志资料 2 (January 1987), 218–22.

"Nongmin yundong jueyi an 農民運動決議案," in Zhongyang zhixing weiyuan hui 中央執行委員會, *Zhongguo Guomindang di er ci quanguo daibiao da hui: Yiyan ji jueyi an* 中國國民黨第二次全國代表大會 : 宜言及決議案, 51–55. February 1926. Peking University Library Collections.

Pelliot, P. "Émile Hovelaque, *Les Peuples d'Extrême-Orient. La Chine*," *T'oung Pao* 20/2 (March 1920–March 1921), 157–63.

Perse, St.-John (Alexis Leger). *Anabasis*. Translated by T. S. Eliot. New York: Harcourt, Brace & Company, 1949. Translation first published 1930.

Perse, St.-John (Alexis Leger). *Letters*. Edited and translated by Arthur J. Knodel. Princeton, NJ: Princeton University Press, 1979.

Qi Tai 奇泰. "Jinzhi tuhao lieshen huodong zhi biyao 禁止土豪劣紳活動之必要," *Minguo ribao xingqi pinglun* 民國日報 星期評論, February 16, 1928, 4–5.

"Qingnian yundong jueyi an 青年運動決議案," in Zhongyang zhixing weiyuan hui 中央執行委員會, *Zhongguo Guomindang di er ci quanguo daibiao da hui: Yiyan ji jueyi an* 中國國民黨第二次全國代表大會 : 宜言及決議案, February 1926, 58–59. Peking University Library Collections.

Qunzhong yeyu muke xuan 群众业余木刻选. Shanghai: Shanghai Renmin meishu chuban she, (February) 1959.

Rodes, Jean. *Les Chinois: Essai de Psychologie ethnographique*. Paris: Librarie Felix Alcan, 1923.

Ruan Zhangjing 阮章競. *Chi ye he* 赤葉河. Shexian, Henan: Taixing qunzhong shudian, (February) 1948.

Russell, Bertrand. Preface to "The YMCA Government of China," by Rachel Brooks. 1934? Typescript 394, box 185. Manuscript Collection, New York Public Library.

Russell, Bertrand. "Some Traits in the Chinese Character," *Atlantic Monthly*, December 1921.

Russell, Bertrand (羅素). "Zhongguo minguo xing de jige tedian中國民國性的幾個特點," *Dongfang zazhi* 東方雜誌, January 10, 1922, 21–33.

Salisbury, Harrison E. "In China, 'A Little Blood,'" *New York Times*, June 13, 1989.

Salisbury, Harrison E. *The New Emperors: China in the Era of Mao and Deng*. Boston: Little Brown, 1992.

Selden, Mark, ed. *The People's Republic of China: A Documentary History of Revolutionary Change*. London: Monthly Review Press, 1979.

Shen Yanjun 申彥俊. "Tufei zhi shehui xue de kaocha 土匪之社会学的考察," *Guomin gonglun* 國民公論 1/5 (1928), 9–11.

"Shishi hua: Da dizhen 時事話 : 大地震," *Shaonian zazhi* 少年雜誌 11/2 (1921), 1–2.

"Shishi hua: Gansu Guyuan dizhen 時事話 : 甘肅固原地震," *Shaonian zazhi* 少年雜誌11/9 (1921), 1–2.

Shi Zuodong 石作棟. "Gengshen dizhen ji 庚申地震記," *Guyuan xianzhi* 固原縣誌 (handwritten; n.d.), vol. 10, *yiwen* 藝文 [art and literature], 15a–17a. File K294, Ningxia Hui Autonomous Region Archives, Yinchuan.

Shi Zuoliang 石作梁. "Gengshen dizhen ji 庚申地震记," *Guyuan xianzhi* 固原县志 (1981?), vol. 10, *yiwen* 藝文 [art and literature], part 2, 18–21. Ningxia Library Special Collections, Yinchuan.

Shi Zuoliang 石作梁. "Gengshen dizhen ji 庚申地震记," *Guyuan xianzhi* 固原县志 (1993), 891–93.

Sites, Evelyn Worthley. *Mook: True Tales About a Chinese Boy and His Friends* with an introduction by F. M. McMurry. West Medford, MA: The Central Committee on the United Study of Foreign Missions, 1918.

Smith, Arthur H. *Chinese Characteristics*. New York: F. H. Revell, 1894.

Smith, Arthur H., ed. *A Manual for Young Missionaries to China*. 2nd ed. Shanghai: The Christian Literature Society, 1924.

Smith, Helen. Letter, November 16, 1968. Box 13, folder 1, records group 8. China Records Project. Yale Divinity Library.

Snow, Edgar. *Red Star over China*. London: Victor Gollancz, 1937.

Song Zhide 宋之的, Tie Fu 鐵夫, Dong Chuan 東川 and Jin Ren 金人. *Jiu jian yi* 九件衣. Shanghai: Shanghai zazhi gongsuo, 1949.

Soothill, William Edward. *The Analects of Confucius*. Yokohama: W. E. Soothill, 1910.

Soothill, William Edward. *The Three Religions of China: Lectures Delivered at Oxford*. London: Oxford University Press, 1923.

Stauffer, Milton, ed. *The Christian Occupation of China: A General Survey of the Numerical Strength and Geographical Distribution of the Christian Forces in China*. Special Committee on Survey and Occupation, 1918–1921. Shanghai: China Continuation Committee, 1922.

"Suiru Wu xianzhang zhenzai dezheng beiji 崇如仵縣長賑災德政碑記," *Cang xianzhi* 滄縣志 13 (1933), 59ab.

Taylor, Mrs. Howard. *The Call of China's Great Northwest: Kansu and Beyond*. London, Philadelphia, Toronto, Melbourne, and Shanghai: The China Inland Mission, circa 1923.

Teichman, Eric. *Travels of a Consular Officer in North-west China*. Cambridge: Cambridge University Press, 1921.

Townsend, Ralph. *Ways that Are Dark: the Truth about China*. New York: G. P. Putnam's Sons, 1933.

Walker, Vera E. *The Way of the Merciful: A Chinese Play in Three Acts*. Westminster: London Missionary Society, circa 1920.

Wan Zhaoji 萬兆基. "Cangxian sanzhen yuan Wan Zhaoji deng baogao 滄縣散賑員萬兆基等報告," *Jiuzai zhoukan* 救災周刊, December 19, 1920, 8–9.

Wang Lie 王烈. "Diaocha Gansu dizhen zhi baogao 調查甘肅地震之報告," *Xin Long zazhi* 新隴雜誌 2/1 (July 1921), 40–42.

Wang Renfeng 汪刃鋒. *Ren Feng muke ji* 刃鋒木刻集. Shanghai: Kaiming shu-dian, 1948.

Wang Xiangsheng 王向升. "Xuexi lishi de jige jiben wenti 學習歷史的幾個基本問題," *Minzhu qingnian* 民主青年 4 (April 1946), 10–18.

Wang Zizhi 王自治. "Fa kan ci 發刊詞," *Xin Long zazhi* 新隴雜誌 1/1 (20 May 1920), 3.

Watthé, Henry. *La Belle Vie du Missionaire en Chine: Récits et croquis*. 2 vols. Vichy: Maison du Missionaire, 1930.

Wei Shaowu 魏邵武. "Lu Hongtao du Gan shimo 陆洪涛督甘始末," *Gansu wenshi ziliao xuanji* 甘肃文史资料选集 1 (1986), 58–60.

White, Theodore Harold and Annalee Jacoby. *Thunder out of China*. New York: William Sloane, 1946.

"Will of William Whiting Borden, Leaving £250,000 to China Inland Mission in North America: To Be Proved in Chicago." 1913. CIM/01/04/3/95, China Inland Mission Archives. Special Collections, School of Oriental and African Studies, University of London.

Williams, S. Wells. *The Middle Kingdom: A Survey of the Geography, Government, Literature, Social Life, Arts, and History of the Chinese Empire and Its Inhabitants*. New York: C. Scribner's sons, 1883.

Xiao San 蕭三. "Mao Zedong tongzhi de ertong shidai 毛澤東同志的兒童時代," *Minzhu qingnian* 民主青年 4 (April 1946), 40–42.

Xie Jiarong 謝家榮. "Minguo jiu nian shi'er yue shiliu ri Gansu ji qita ge sheng zhi dizhen qingxing 民國九年十二月十六日甘肅及其他個省之地震情形," *Dixue zazhi* 地學雜誌13/6–7 (1922), 1–22.

Xinren zhenzai ji 辛壬振災記, 1a–10a. N.p.: n.d. Special Collections, Gansu Provincial Library.

"*Xin Long zazhi* she tebie qishi 新隴雜誌社特別啟事," *Xin Long zazhi* 新隴雜誌 1/4 (April 20, 1921), back page.

Xin yishu she 新藝術社, ed. *Muke xuanji* 木刻選集. N.p.: Lianhe shudian, 1946.

(No name given) (Xu Busheng 徐步陞). "Guyuan zhenzai xing 固原震災行," *Guyuan xianzhi* 固原縣誌 (n.d.), vol. 10, *yunyue* 韻語 [verse], 31b–32a. File K294, Ningxia Hui Autonomous Region Archives, Yinchuan.

Xu Busheng 徐步升. "Guyuan zhenzai xing 固原震灾行," *Guyuan xianzhi* 固原县志 (1993), 886–88.

Xu Busheng 徐步陞. "Guyuan zhenzai xing 固原震災行," *Guyuan xianzhi* 固原县志 (1981?), vol. 10, *yiwen* 藝文 [art and literature], part 1, 11–13. Ningxia Library Special Collections, Yinchuan.

Xu Chengyao 許承堯. *Yi'an shi* 疑庵诗. Hefei: Huangshan shushe, 1990.

"Xuesheng hui zaiqu diaocha yuan yi chufa 學生會災區調查員已出發," *Chenbao* 晨報, September 24, 1920.

Yan Han 彥涵. *Yan Han muke xuanji* 彥涵木刻選集. Beijing: Beijing huabao she, 1949.

Yan Han 彥涵. *Yan Han muke xuanji* 彥涵木刻選集. Beijing: Renmin meishu chubanshe and Xinhua shudian, 1954.

Yang, Martin C. *A Chinese Village: Taitou, Shantung Province*. London: Kegan Paul, Trench, Trubner & Co, 1947.

Yang Zhongjian 楊鍾健. "Bei si sheng zaiqu shichaji 北四省災區實查記," *Dongfang zazhi* 東方雜誌, October 10, 1920, 24–28.

Yang Zhongjian 楊鍾健. "Bianji hanzai diaocha de suizhi 編輯旱災調查的隨志," *Chenbao* 晨報, October 14, 1920.

"Yanjing daxue xuesheng zou zhi rexin kefeng 燕京大學學生徒之熱心可風," *Qunbao* 羣報, February 24, 1921.

"Yiguo da dizhen 意國大地震," *Shaonian zazhi* 少年雜誌 10/10 (1920), 3.

Yu Bingxiang 于炳祥. "Jin nan de hanzai huangzai bingzai feizai 津南的旱災蝗災兵災匪災," *Chenbao* 晨報, September 28, 1920, 2.

Yu Guanbin 玉觀彬. "Chuangkan ci 創刊詞," *Guomin gonglun* 國民公論 1 (1928), 2–3.

Yüeh Feng and Wang T'ien-Ch'i. "Land," in Sidney L. Greenblatt, ed., *The People of Taihang: An Anthology of Family Histories*, 64–80. White Plains, NY: International Arts and Sciences Press, 1976.

"Zaiqing baogao: hanzai: Jingxing lü Jing xuesheng nianjiazhong diaocha ben xian zaimin zhuangkuang 災情報告：旱災：井陘旅京學生年假中調查本縣災民狀況," *Jiuzai zhoukan* 救災周刊, March 6, 1921, 20–21.

Zhang Renzhi 張任之. "Huiyi yijiuerling nian Pingliang dizhen 回憶一九二〇年平涼地震," *Pingliang wenshi ziliao* 平涼文史資料 2 (1991), 164–65.

Zhang Siyuan 張思源. "Shisan shiji yi lai Guyuan diqu de ba ci zhongqiang dizhen 十三世紀以來固原地區的八次中強地震," *Guyuan wenshi ziliao* 固原文史資料 1 (1987), 90–101.

Zhao Hong 趙洪. "Kangzhan qian Jin Cha Ji nongmin de beican shenghuo 抗戰前晉察冀農民的悲慘生活," *Minzhu qingnian* 民主青年 4 (April 1946), 23–29.

Zhao Jinyun 赵锦云. "Guyuan diyi suo nüzi xuexiao de chengli 固原第一所女子学校的成立," *Guyuan wenshi ziliao* 固原文史资料 3 (September 1989), 221–32.

Zhao Zongjin 趙宗晉. "Tongzijun 童子軍," *Xin Long zazhi* 新隴雜誌 1/1 (May 20, 1920), 27–31.

"Zhengjihui sanfang Dongling jizhen 拯濟會散放東陵急賑," *Qunbao* 羣報, February 21, 1921, 6.

"Zhili sheng Jingxing xian lü Jing xuesheng nianjiazhong diaocha ben xian zaimin de baogao 直隸省井陘縣旅京學生年假中調查本縣災民的報告," *Qunbao* 羣報, February 21, 1921, 6.

Zhonghua quanguo muke xiehui 中華全國木刻協會, ed. *Kangzhan ba nian muke xuanji* 抗戰八年木刻選集, or *Woodcuts of War-Time China, 1937–1945*. Shanghai: Kaiming shudian, 1946.

Zhonghua quanguo muke xiehui 中華全國木刻協會, ed. *Zhongguo banhua ji* 中國版畫集. Shanghai: Chenguang chuban gongsi, 1948.

Zhou Zhigan 周之淦, Yang Zhongming 楊中明 and Lu Duanyi 蘆段宜. *Gongmin xue kecheng dawang* 公民學課程大綱. Shanghai: Shangwu yinshu-guan, 1923.

Zou Ya 邹雅 and Li Pingfan 李平凡, eds. *Jiefang qu muke* 解放区木刻. Shanghai: Renmin meishu chuban she, 1962.

Secondary Sources

Alitto, Guy. *The Last Confucian: Liang Shuming and the Chinese Dilemma of Modernity*. Berkeley: University of California Press, 1979.

Altehenger, Jennifer. *Legal Lessons: Popularizing Laws in the People's Republic of China, 1949–1989*. Harvard East Asian Monographs. Cambridge, MA: Harvard University Asia Center, 2018.

Anagnost, Ann. *National Past-Times: Narratives, Representation, and Power in Modern China*. Durham, NC: Duke University Press, 1997.

Apter, David E. and Tony Saich. *Revolutionary Discourse in Mao's Republic.* Cambridge, MA: Harvard University Press, 1994.

Arkush, David R. *Fei Xiaotong and Sociology in Revolutionary China.* Cambridge, MA: Council on East Asian Studies, Harvard University Press, 1981.

Assmann, Jan. "Communicative and Cultural Memory," in Astrid Erll and Ansgar Nünning, eds., *Cultural Memory Studies: An International and Interdisciplinary Handbook*, 109–118. Berlin: De Gruyter, 2008.

Badiou, Alain. "The Cultural Revolution: The Last Revolution?" *positions: east asia cultures critique* 13/3 (2005), 481–514.

Bartlett, Beatrice S. "Qing Statesmen, Archivists, and Historians and the Question of Memory," in Francis X. Blouin, Jr., and William G. Rosenberg, eds., *Archives, Documentation, and Institutions of Social Memory: Essays from the Sawyer Seminar.* Ann Arbor: University of Michigan Press, 2006, 417–26.

Bellér-Hann, Ildikó. *Community Matters in Xinjiang, 1880–1949: Towards a Historical Anthropology of the Uyghur.* Leiden: Brill, 2008.

Bergère, Marie-Claire. "Une crise de subsistance en Chine (1920–1922)," *Annales. Histoire, Sciences Sociales* 6 (November–December 1973), 1361–1402.

Bianco, Lucien. "Numbers in Social History: How Credible? Counting Disturbances in Rural China (1900–1949)," in Eberhard Sandschneider, ed., *The Study of Modern China: A Volume in Honour of Jürgen Domes.* London: C. Hurst, 1999.

Bianco, Lucien. *Origins of the Chinese Revolution, 1915–1949.* Translated by Muriel Bell. Stanford, CA: Stanford University Press, 1971.

Bianco, Lucien. *Wretched Rebels: Rural Disturbances on the Eve of the Chinese Revolution.* Translated by Philip Liddell. Harvard East Asian Monographs. Cambridge, MA: Harvard University Asia Center, 2009.

Bourgon, Jérôme. "Obscene Vignettes of Truth: Constructing Photographs of Chinese Executions as Historical Documents," in Christian Henriot and Wen-hsin Yeh, eds., *Visualising China, 1845–1965: Moving and Still Images in Historical Narratives*, 39–91. Leiden: Brill, 2013.

Brokaw, Cynthia. *The Ledgers of Merit & Demerit: Social Change and Moral Order in Late Imperial China.* Princeton, NJ: Princeton University Press, 1991.

Brook, Timothy, Jérôme Bourgon and Gregory Blue. *Death by a Thousand Cuts.* Cambridge, MA: Harvard University Press, 2008.

Brown, Jeremy. "Moving Targets: Changing Class Labels in Rural Hebei and Henan, 1960–1979," in Jeremy Brown and Matthew D. Johnson, eds., *Maoism at the Grassroots: Everyday Life in China's Era of High Socialism*, 51–76. Cambridge, MA: Harvard University Press, 2015.

Brown, Jeremy. "Rebels, Rent, and Tai Xu: Local Elite Identity and Conflict during and after the Tai Ping Occupation of Jiangnan, 1860–84," *Late Imperial China* 30/2 (December 2009), 9–38.

Cai, Xiang. *Revolution and Its Narratives: China's Socialist Literary and Cultural Imaginaries (1949–1966).* Edited and translated by Rebecca E. Karl and Xueping Zhong. Durham, NC: Duke University Press, 2016.

Callahan, William A. "Sino-speak: Chinese Exceptionalism and the Politics of History," *Journal of Asian Studies* 71/1 (February 2012), 33–55.

Cao, Shuji. "Grain, Local Politics, and the Making of Mao's Famine in Wuwei, 1958–1961," *Modern Asian Studies* 49/6 (2015), 1675–1703.

Carter, James H. *Heart of Buddha, Heart of China: The Life of Tanxu, a Twentieth-Century Monk.* Oxford: Oxford University Press, 2011.

Chang, Hao. *Liang Ch'i-ch'ao and Intellectual Transition in China, 1890–1907.* Harvard East Asian Studies Series. Cambridge, MA: Harvard University Press, 1971.

Chatterjee, Partha. "Community in the East," *Economic and Political Weekly*, February 7, 1998, 277–82.

Cheek, Timothy. *Propaganda and Culture in Mao's China: Deng Tuo and the Intelligentsia.* Oxford, UK: Clarendon Press, 2011.

Chen, Shengrong and Honggang Xu. "From Fighting against Death to Commemorating the Dead at Tangshan Earthquake Heritage Sites," *Journal of Tourism and Cultural Change* 16/5 (2018), 552–573.

Chen, Tina Mai. "Use the Past to Serve the Present, the Foreign to Serve China," in Wang Ban, ed., *Words and Their Stories: Essays on the Language of the Chinese Revolution*, 206–225. Leiden: Brill, 2011.

Chen, Xiaoming. *From the May Fourth Movement to Communist Revolution: Guo Moruo and the Chinese Path to Communism.* Albany, NY: State University of New York Press, 2007.

Chow Tse-tsung. *The May Fourth Movement: Intellectual Revolution in Modern China.* Harvard East Asian Studies Series. Cambridge, MA: Harvard University Press, 1960.

Chu, Wen-Djang. *The Moslem Rebellion in Northwest China, 1862–1878: A Study of Government Minority Policy.* Paris: Mouton, 1966.

Cliff, Tom. "Refugees, Conscripts, and Constructors: Developmental Narratives and Subaltern Han in Xinjiang, China," *Modern China* (2020), 1–29.

Cochran, Sherman and Andrew C. K. Hsieh with Janis Cochran, eds. *One Day in China: May 21, 1936.* New Haven, CT: Yale University Press, 1983. Originally published as *Zhongguo de yi ri.*

Cohen, Myron. "Cultural and Political Inventions in Modern China: The Case of the Chinese "Peasant," *Daedalus* 122/2 (Spring 1993), 151–70.

Conn, Peter J. *Pearl S. Buck: A Cultural Biography.* Cambridge: Cambridge University Press, 2002.

Culp, Robert. *Articulating Citizenship: Civic Education and Student Politics in Southeastern China: 1912–1940.* Harvard East Asian Monographs. Cambridge, MA: Harvard University Asia Center, 2007.

Culp, Robert. *The Power of Print in Modern China: Intellectuals and Industrial Publishing from the Empire to Maoist State Socialism.* New York: Columbia University Press, 2019.

Culp, Robert "'Weak and Small Peoples' in a 'Europeanizing World': World History Textbooks and Chinese Intellectuals," in Robert Culp and Tze-ki Hon, eds., *The Politics of Historical Production in Late Qing and Republican China*, 211–45. Leiden: Brill, 2007.

Day, Alexander. "History, Capitalism, and the Making of the Postsocialist Chinese Peasant," in Arif Dirlik, Roxann Prazniak and Alexander Woodside, eds., *Global Capitalism and the Future of Agrarian Society*, 53–76. London: Paradigm, 2012.

de Hartog, Leo. *Genghis Khan: Conqueror of the World*. London: I. B. Tauris, 1989.

Deleuze, Gilles and Félix Guattari. *Anti-Oedipus: Capitalism and Schizophrenia*. Translated by Robert Hurley, Mark Seem and Helen R. Lane. New York: Viking Press, 1977.

DeMare, Brian. *Land Wars: The Story of China's Agrarian Revolution*. Stanford, CA: Stanford University Press, 2019.

DeMare, Brian James. *Mao's Cultural Army: Drama Troupes in China's Rural Revolution*. Cambridge: Cambridge University Press, 2017.

Duara, Prasenjit. *Culture, Power and the State: Rural North China, 1900–1942*. Stanford, CA: Stanford University Press, 1988.

Edgerton-Tarpley, Kathryn. *Tears from Iron: Cultural Responses to Famine in Nineteenth-Century China*. Berkeley: University of California Press, 2008.

Emrich, Elizabeth. "Modernity through Experimentation: Lu Xun and the Modern Chinese Woodcut Movement," in Pei-Yin Lin and Weipin Tsai, eds., *Print, Profit, and Perception: Ideas, Information and Knowledge in Chinese Societies, 1895–1949*, 64–91. Leiden: Brill, 2014.

Esherick, Joseph. "Revolution in a 'Feudal Fortress': Yangjiagou, Mizhi County, Shaanxi, 1937–1948," in Feng Chongyi and David S. G. Goodman, eds., *North China at War: The Social Ecology of Revolution, 1937–1945*. Lanham, MD: Rowman and Littlefield, 2000, 59–61.

Eyferth, Jacob. *Eating Rice from Bamboo Roots: The Social History of a Community of Handicraft Papermakers in Rural Sichuan, 1920–2000*. Harvard East Asian Monographs. Cambridge, MA: Harvard University Asia Center, 2009.

Fairbank, John King and Merle Goldman. *China: A New History*. 2nd ed. Cambridge, MA: The Belknap Press of Harvard University Press, 2006.

Fenby, Jonathan. *The Penguin History of Modern China: The Fall and Rise of a Great Power, 1850 to the Present*. London: Penguin, 2013.

Fitzgerald, John. *Awakening China: Politics, Culture, and Class in the Nationalist Revolution*. Stanford, CA: Stanford University Press, 1996.

Flath, James A. *The Cult of Happiness: Nianhua, Art and History in Rural North China*. Vancouver: University of British Columbia Press, 2014.

Friedman, Edward, Paul G. Pickowicz and Mark Selden. *Revolution, Resistance, and Reform in Village China*. New Haven, CT: Yale University Press, 2005.

Fromm, Martin T. *Borderland Memories: Searching for Historical Identity in Post-Mao China*. Cambridge: Cambridge University Press, 2019.

Fuller, Pierre. "Decentring International and Institutional Famine Relief in Late Nineteenth Century China: In Search of the Local," *European Review of History/Revue européenne d'histoire* 22/6 (2015), 873–889.

Fuller, Pierre. *Famine Relief in Warlord China*. Harvard East Asian Monographs. Cambridge, MA: Harvard University Asia Center, 2019.

Furth, Charlotte. *Ting Wen-chiang: Science and China's New Culture*. Cambridge, MA: Harvard University Press, 1970.

Gao Wangling and Liu Yang. "On a Slippery Roof: Chinese Farmers and the Complex Agenda of Land Reform," *Études rurales* 179 (January–June 2007), 19–34.

Garnaut, Anthony. "The Shaykh of the Great Northwest: The Religious and Political Life of Ma Yuanzhang (1853–1920)." PhD dissertation, Australia National University, 2010.

Garon, Sheldon. *Molding Japanese Minds: The State in Everyday Life.* Princeton, NJ: Princeton University Press, 1997.

Gatrell, Peter. *The Making of the Modern Refugee.* Oxford: Oxford University Press, 2013.

Gatu, Dagfinn. *Village China at War: The Impact of Resistance to Japan, 1937–1945.* Copenhagen: Nordic Institute for Asian Studies, 2008.

Ghosh, Arunabh. *Making It Count: Statistics and Statecraft in the Early People's Republic of China.* Princeton, NJ: Princeton University Press, 2020.

Girardot, Norman J. *The Victorian Translation of China: James Legge's Oriental Pilgrimage.* Berkeley: University of California Press, 2002.

Godement, François. "La famine de 1928 à 1930 en Chine du Nord et du Centre." Master's thesis, Université Paris VII, 1970. Microfiche.

Goodman, David S. G. *Social and Political Change in Revolutionary China: The Taihang Base Area in the War of Resistance to Japan, 1937–1945.* Lanham, MD: Rowman & Littlefield, 2000.

Gray, Jack. *Rebellions and Revolutions: China from the 1800s to 2000.* 2nd ed. Oxford: Oxford University Press, 2002.

Greenblatt, Sidney L. Introduction to *The People of Taihang: An Anthology of Family Histories.* Edited by Sidney L. Greenblatt. White Plains, NY: International Arts and Sciences Press, 1976.

Gross, Jan. *Neighbors: The Destruction of the Jewish Community in Jedwabne, Poland.* Princeton, NJ: Princeton University Press, 2001.

Halfin, Igal. *From Darkness to Light: Class, Consciousness, and Salvation in Revolutionary Russia.* Pittsburg, PA: University of Pittsburg Press, 2000.

Han, Xiaorong. *Chinese Discourses on the Peasant, 1900–1949.* Albany: State University of New York Press, 2005.

Harrison, Henrietta. *The Making of the Republican Citizen: Political Ceremonies and Symbols in China, 1911–1929.* Oxford: Oxford University Press, 1999.

Harrison, Henrietta. *The Man Awakened from Dreams: One Man's Life in a North China Village, 1857–1942.* Stanford, CA: Stanford University Press, 2005.

Harrison, Henrietta. "'A Penny for the Little Chinese': The French Holy Childhood Association in China, 1843–1951," *American Historical Review* 113/1 (2008), 72–92.

Harrison, Henrietta. "The Qianlong Emperor's Letter to George III and the Early-Twentieth Century Origins of Ideas about Traditional China's Foreign Relations," *American Historical Review* 122/3 (2017), 680–701.

Hayford, Charles W. "The Storm over the Peasant: Orientalism and Rhetoric in Construing China," in Jeffrey Cox and Shelton Stromquist, eds., *Contesting the Master Narrative: Essays in Social History*, 150–172. Iowa City: University of Iowa Press, 1998.

He, Jiangsui. "The Death of a Landlord: Moral Predicament in Rural China, 1968–1969," in Joseph W. Esherick, Paul Pickowicz and Andrew G. Walder, eds., *The Chinese Cultural Revolution as History*, 147–48. Stanford, CA: Stanford University Press, 2006.

He, Xiubin, Keli Tang and Xinbao Zhang. "Soil Erosion Dynamics on the Chinese Loess Plateau in the Last 10,000 Years," *Mountain Research and Development* 24/4 (2004), 342–47.

Heinz, Johann. *Justification and Merit: Luther vs. Catholicism*. Berrien Springs, MI: Andrews University Press, 1984.

Hershatter, Gail. *The Gender of Memory: Rural Women and China's Collective Past*. Berkeley: University of California Press, 2011.

Hevia, James. *English Lessons: The Pedagogy of Imperialism in Nineteenth-Century China*. Durham, NC: Duke University Press, 2003.

Hillenbrand, Margaret. *Negative Exposures: Knowing What Not to Know in Contemporary China*. Durham, NC: Duke University Press, 2020.

Ho, Denise Y. *Curating Revolution: Politics on Display in Mao's China*. Cambridge: Cambridge University Press, 2018.

Holm, David. *Art and Ideology in Revolutionary China*. Oxford, UK: Clarendon Press, 1991.

Hsü, Immanuel C. Y. *The Rise of Modern China*. 6th ed. Oxford: Oxford University Press, 2000.

Hu Yubing. *Ningxia jiuzhi yanjiu*. Shanghai: Shanghai guji chubanshe, 2018.

Huang, C. C. Philip. "Rural Class Struggle in the Chinese Revolution: Representational and Objective Realities from the Land Reform to the Cultural Revolution," *Modern China* 21/1 (January 1995), 105–43. Symposium: Rethinking the Chinese Revolution. Paradigmatic Issues in Chinese Studies, IV

Huang, Ko-wu. "The Origin and Evolution of the Concept of *mixin* (superstition): A Review of May Fourth Scientific Views," *Chinese Studies in History* 49/2 (2016), 54–79.

Hung, Chang-tai. *Going to the People: Chinese Intellectuals and Folk Literature, 1918–1937*. Cambridge, MA: Council on East Asian Studies, Harvard University, 1985.

Hung, Chang-tai. *Mao's New World: Political Culture in the Early People's Republic*. Ithaca, NY: Cornell University Press, 2011.

Hung, Chang-Tai. "Two Images of Socialism: Woodcuts in Chinese Communist Politics," *Comparative Studies in Society and History* 39/1 (January 1997).

Hunter, Jane. *The Gospel of Gentility: American Women Missionaries in Turn-of-the-Century China*. New Haven, CT: Yale University Press, 1984.

Huntington, Samuel P. *The Clash of Civilizations and the Remaking of World Order*. New York: Simon & Schuster, 1996.

Isaacs, Harold R. *Scratches on Our Minds: American Images of China and India*. New York: John Day, 1958.

Janku, Andrea. "From Natural to National Disaster: The Chinese Famine of 1928–1930," in Andrea Janku, Gerrit J. Schenk and Franz Mauelshagen, eds., *Historical Disasters in Context: Science, Religion and Politics*, 227–260. New York: Routledge, 2012.

Janku, Andrea. "Preparing the Ground for Revolutionary Discourse from the Statecraft Anthologies to the Periodical Press in Nineteenth-Century China," *T'oung Pao*, Second Series, 90 (2004), 65–121.

Jing, Jun. *The Temples of Memories: History, Power, and Morality in a Chinese Village*. Stanford, CA: Stanford University Press, 1996.

Johnson, Matthew D. "Beneath the Propaganda State: Official and Unofficial Cultural Landscapes in Shanghai, 1949–1965," in Jeremy Brown and Matthew D. Johnson, eds., *Maoism at the Grassroots: Everyday Life in China's Era of High Socialism*, 199–229. Cambridge, MA: Harvard University Press, 2015.

Kiernan, Ben. *The Pol Pot Regime: Race, Power, and Genocide under the Khmer Rouge, 1975–79*. 3rd ed. New Haven, CT: Yale University Press, 2008.

King, Richard. "Romancing the Leap: Euphoria in the Moment before Disaster," in Kimberley Ens Manning and Felix Wemheuer, eds., *Eating Bitterness: New Perspectives on China's Great Leap Forward and Famine*, 50–71. Vancouver: University of British Columbia Press, 2011.

Kraus, Richard C. *Brushes with Power: Modern Politics and the Art of Calligraphy*. Berkeley: University of California Press, 1991.

Kuhn, Philip A. *Soulstealers: The Chinese Sorcery Scare of 1768*. Cambridge, MA: Harvard University Press, 1990.

Lam, Tong. *A Passion for Facts: Social Surveys and the Construction of the Chinese Nation State, 1900–1949*. Berkeley: University of California Press, 2011.

Lanza, Fabio. *Behind the Gate: Inventing Students in Beijing*. New York: Columbia University Press, 2010.

Lary, Diana. *China's Republic*. Cambridge: Cambridge University Press, 2007.

Lary, Diana. Foreword to *China's Warlords*, by David Bonavia, vii–viii. Oxford: Oxford University Press, 1995.

Latour, Bruno. *Reassembling the Social: An Introduction to Actor-Network-Theory*. Oxford: Oxford University Press, 2005.

Laughlin, Charles A. *Chinese Reportage: The Aesthetics of Historical Experience*. Durham, NC: Duke University Press, 2002.

Lee, James Z. and Wang Feng. *One Quarter of Humanity: Malthusian Mythology and Chinese Realities, 1700–2000*. Cambridge, MA: Harvard University Press, 1999.

Leese, Daniel. *Mao Cult: Rhetoric and Ritual in China's Cultural Revolution*. Cambridge: Cambridge University Press, 2013.

Li, Huaiyin. *Reinventing Modern China: Imagination and Authenticity in Chinese Historical Writing*. Honolulu: University of Hawai'i Press, 2013.

Li, Huaiyin. *Village Governance in North China, 1875–1936*. Stanford, CA: Stanford University Press, 2005.

Li, Lillian M. *Fighting Famine in North China: State, Market, and Environmental Decline, 1690s–1990s*. Stanford, CA: Stanford University Press, 2007.

Li Tianchi. "Landslide Disasters and Human Responses in China," *Mountain Research and Development* 14/4, Mountain Hazard Geomorphology (1994), 341–46.

Li Xuetong. *Weng Wenhao nianpu*. Jinan: Shandong jiaoyu chubanshe, 2005.

Lin Yutang. *History of the Press and Public Opinion in China*. Shanghai: Kelly and Walsh, 1936.

Lipman, Jonathan N. *Familiar Strangers: A History of Muslims in Northwest China*. Seattle: University of Washington Press, 1997.

Lipman, Jonathan N. "Hyphenated Chinese: Sino-Muslim Identity in Modern China," in Gail Hershatter, Emily Honig, Jonathan N. Lipman and Randall Stross, eds., *Remapping China: Fissures in Historical Terrain*, 97–112. Stanford, CA: Stanford University Press, 1996.

Liu, Lydia. *Translingual Practice: Literature, National Culture and Translated Modernity*. Stanford, CA: Stanford University Press, 1995.

Liu, Tao Tao. "Perceptions of City and Country in Modern Chinese Fiction in the Early Republican Era," in David Faure and Tao Tao Liu, eds., *Town and Country in China: Identity and Perception*, 203–32. Basingstoke, UK: Palgrave, 2002.

Lü Fangshang. *Cong xuesheng yundong dao yundong xuesheng*, 1919–1929. Taipei: Zhongying yanjiuyuan jindaishi yanjiusuo, 1994.

Lu Ping. "Beyond Mr. Democracy and Mr. Science: The Introduction of Miss Moral and the Trend of Moral Revolution in the New Culture Movement," *Frontiers of History in China* 2/2 (2007), 254–86.

Lu Xun. *A Brief History of Chinese Fiction*. Beijing: Foreign Languages Press, 1959.

Karl, Rebecca. "Journalism, Social Value, and a Philosophy of the Everyday in 1920s China," *positions: east asia cultures critique* 16/3 (2008), 539–67.

Ma Yixin. "'*Xin Long zazhi* yu Gansu jindai sixiang qimeng," *Lanzhou jiaoyu xueyuan xuebao* 30/9 (September 2014), 1–10.

MacFarquhar, Roderick and Michael Schoenhals. *Mao's Last Revolution*. Cambridge, MA: The Belknap Press of Harvard University Press, 2006.

Madsen, Richard. *Morality and Power in a Chinese Village*. Berkeley and Los Angeles: University of California Press, 1984.

Man, John. *Genghis Khan: Life, Death and Resurrection*. London: Bantam Press, 2004.

Marks, Robert. *Rural Revolution in South China: Peasants and the Making of History in Haifeng County, 1570–1930*. Madison: University of Wisconsin Press, 1984.

Mazower, Mark. "Violence and the State in the Twentieth Century," *American Historical Review* 107/4 (2002), 1158–1178.

Merkel-Hess, Kate. *The Rural Modern: Reconstructing the Self and State in Republican China*. Chicago: University of Chicago Press, 2016.

Mitter, Rana. *A Bitter Revolution: China's Struggle with the Modern World*. Oxford: Oxford University Press, 2004.

Mittler, Barbara. *A Continuous Revolution: Making Sense of Cultural Revolution Culture*. Harvard East Asian Monographs. Cambridge, MA: Harvard University Asia Center, 2016.

Mullaney, Thomas S. *Coming to Terms with the Nation: Ethnic Classification in Modern China*. Berkeley and Los Angeles: University of California Press, 2011.

Mühlhahn, Klaus. *Making China Modern: From the Great Qing to Xi Jinping*. Cambridge, MA: The Belknap Press of Harvard University Press, 2019.

Nathan, Andrew J. *A History of the China International Famine Relief Commission*. Cambridge, MA: East Asian Research Center, Harvard University, 1965.

Nguyen-Marshall, Van. "The Ethics of Benevolence in French Colonial Vietnam: A Sino-Franco-Vietnamese Cultural Borderland," in Diana Lary, ed., *The*

Chinese State at the Borders, 162–180. Vancouver: University of British Columbia Press, 2007.

Noellert, Matthew. *Power over Property: The Political Economy of Communist Land Reform in China*. Ann Arbor: University of Michigan Press, 2020.

Papazian, Elizabeth Astrid. *Manufacturing Truth: The Documentary Moment in Early Soviet Culture*. Dekalb: Northern Illinois Press, 2009.

Peake, Cyrus H. *Nationalism and Education in Modern China*. New York: Columbia University Press, 1932.

Rahav, Shakhar. *The Rise of Political Intellectuals in Modern China: May Fourth Societies and the Roots of Mass Party Politics*. Oxford: Oxford University Press, 2015.

Ransmeier, Johanna S. *Sold People: Traffickers and Family Life in North China*. Cambridge, MA: Harvard University Press, 2017.

Reinders, Eric. *Borrowed Gods and Foreign Bodies: Christian Missionaries Imagine Chinese Religion*. Berkeley: University of California Press, 2004.

Ristaino, Marcia R. *China's Art of Revolution: The Art of Mobilization of Discontent, 1927 and 1928*. Durham, NC: Duke University Press, 1987.

Rogaski, Ruth. *Hygienic Modernity: Meanings of Health and Disease in Treaty-Port China*. Berkeley: University of California Press, 2004.

Rogaski, Ruth. "Nature, Annihilation, and Modernity: China's Korean War Germ-Warfare Experience Reconsidered," *Journal of Asian Studies* 61/2 (May 2002), 381–415.

Russo, Alessandro. "Class Struggle." Translated by David Verzoni, in Christian Sorace, Ivan Franceschini and Nicholas Loubere, eds., *Afterlives of Chinese Communism: Political Concepts from Mao to Xi*, 29–35. Acton: Australian National University Press and Verso, 2019.

Russo, Alessandro. "How to Translate 'Cultural Revolution,'" *Inter-Asia Cultural Studies* 7/4 (2006), 673–82.

Rowe, William T. *Saving the World: Chen Hongmou and Elite Consciousness in Eighteenth-Century China*. Stanford, CA: Stanford University Press, 2002.

Rowe, William T. "Women and the Family in Mid-Qing Social Thought: The Case of Chen Hongmou," *Late Imperial China* 13/2 (1992), 1–41.

Schoenhals, Michael. "China's 'Great Proletarian Information Revolution' of 1966–1967," in Jeremy Brown and Matthew D. Johnson, eds., *Maoism at the Grassroots: Everyday Life in China's Era of High Socialism*, 230–58. Cambridge, MA: Harvard University Press, 2015.

Schoenhals, Michael. "Demonising Discourse in Mao Zedong's China: People vs Non-People," *Totalitarian Movements and Political Religions* 8/3–4 (September – December 2007), 465–82.

Schwarcz, Vera. *The Chinese Enlightenment, Intellectuals and the Legacy of the May Fourth Movement*. Berkeley: University of California Press, 1986.

Schwarcz, Vera. *Time for Telling Truth is Running Out: Conversations with Zhang Shenfu*. New Haven, CT: Yale University Press, 1992.

Schwartz, Benjamin I. *In Search of Wealth and Power: Yen Fu and the West*. Harvard East Asian Series. Cambridge, MA: The Belknap Press of Harvard University Press, 1969.

Scott, James C. *Seeing Like a State: How Certain Schemes to Improve the Human Condition Have Failed*. New Haven, CT: Yale University Press, 1998.

Selden, Mark. *The Yenan Way in Revolutionary China.* Cambridge, MA: Harvard University Press, 1974.

Shaw, Caroline. *Britannia's Embrace: Modern Humanitarianism and the Imperial Origins of Refugee Relief.* Oxford: Oxford University Press, 2015.

Shen, Grace Yen. *Unearthing the Nation: Modern Geology and Nationalism in Republican China.* Chicago: The University of Chicago Press, 2014.

Shi, Xia. *At Home in the World: Women and Charity in Late Qing and Early Republican China.* New York: Columbia University Press, 2018.

Skinner, G. William. "Marketing and Social Structure in Rural China: Part I," *Journal of Asian Studies* 24/1 (November 1964), 3–42.

Smith, Joanna Handlin. *The Art of Doing Good: Charity in Late Ming China.* Berkeley: University of California Press, 2009.

Spence, Jonathan D. *The Gate of Heavenly Peace: The Chinese and Their Revolution, 1895–1980.* New York: Penguin, 1981.

Spence, Jonathan D. *The Search for Modern China.* New York: Norton, 1999.

Spires, Anthony J. "Contingent Symbiosis and Civil Society in an Authoritarian State: Understanding the Survival of China's Grassroots NGOs," *Journal of American Sociology* 117/1 (July 2011), 1–45.

Strand, David. "Community, Society, and History in Sun Yat-sen's *Sanmin zhuyi,*" in Theodore Huters, R. Bin Wong and Pauline Yu, eds., *Culture and State in Chinese History: Conventions, Accommodations, and Critiques,* 326–45. Irvine Studies in the Humanities. Stanford, CA: Stanford University Press 1997.

Straus, Scott. *The Order of Genocide: Race, Power and War in Rwanda.* Ithaca, NY: Cornell University Press, 2006.

Su, Yang. *Collective Killings in Rural China during the Cultural Revolution.* Cambridge: Cambridge University Press, 2011.

Tan Hecheng. *The Killing Wind: A Chinese County's Descent into Madness during the Cultural Revolution.* Translated by Stacy Mosher and Guo Jian. Oxford: Oxford University Press, 2017.

Tang, Xiaobing. *Origins of the Chinese Avant-Garde: The Modern Woodcut Movement.* Berkeley and Los Angeles: University of California Press, 2008.

Thaxton, Ralph. *Catastrophe and Contention in Rural China: Mao's Great Leap Forward Famine and the Origins of Righteous Resistance in Da Fo Village.* Cambridge: Cambridge University Press, 2008.

Thornton, Patricia M. *Disciplining the State: Virtue, Violence, and State-Making in Modern China.* Harvard East Asian Monographs. Cambridge, MA: Harvard University Asia Center, 2007.

Thum, Rian. *The Sacred Routes of Uyghur History.* Cambridge, MA: Harvard University Press, 2014.

Tuchman, Barbara W. *Sand Against the Wind: Stilwel and the American experience in China: 1911–45.* London: Macmillan, 1971.

Tyrell, Ian. *Reforming the World: The Creation of American's Moral Empire.* Princeton, NJ: Princeton University Press, 2010.

Uhalley Jr., Stephen. "The 'Four Histories' Movement: A Revolution in Writing China's Past," *Current Scene: Developments in Mainland China* 4/2 (1966), 1–10.

van de Ven, Hans J. *From Friend to Comrade: The Founding of the Chinese Communist Party, 1920–1927.* Berkeley: University of California Press, 1991.

Veg, Sebastian. "Introduction: Trauma, Nostalgia, Public Debate," in Sebastian Veg, ed., *Popular Memories of the Mao Era: From Critical Debate to Reassessing History*, 1–18. Hong Kong: Hong Kong University Press, 2019.

Vernon, James. *Hunger: A Modern History*. Cambridge, MA: The Belknap Press of Harvard University Press, 2007.

Walder, Andrew G. "Rebellion and Repression in China, 1966–1971," *Social Science History* 38 (Winter 2014), 513–39.

Wang Ban. "Socialist Realism," in Wang Ban, ed., *Words and Their Stories: Essays on the Language of the Chinese Revolution*, 101–118. Leiden: Brill, 2011.

Wang Ban. "Understanding the Chinese Revolution through Words: An Introduction," in Wang Ban, ed., *Words and Their Stories: Essays on the Language of the Chinese Revolution*, 1–13. Leiden: Brill, 2011.

Wang Ban, ed. *Words and Their Stories: Essays on the Language of the Chinese Revolution*. Leiden: Brill, 2011.

Wang, David Der-wei. *The Monster That Is History: History, Violence, and Fictional Writing in Twentieth-Century China*. Berkeley: University of California Press, 2004.

Wang Hui. "Depoliticised Politics, from East to West," *New Left Review* 41 (September–October 2006), 29–45.

Wang Hui. "The Fate of 'Mr. Science' in China: The Concept of Science and Its Application in Modern China Thought," *positions: east asia cultures critique* 3/1 (1995), 1–68.

Wang Jin and Yang Hongwei. *Gan Ning Qing minguo renwu*. Beijing: Zhongguo shehui kexue chubanshe, 2013.

Wang Runze. *Zhang Liluan yu Da gongbao*. Beijing: Zhonghua shiju, 2008.

Wang, Zheng. *Never Forget National Humiliation: Historical Memory in Chinese Politics and Foreign Relations*. New York: Columbia University Press, 2014.

Wang, Zuoyue. "Saving China Through Science: The Science Society in China, Scientific Nationalism, and Civil Society in Republican China," *Osiris* 17 (2002), 291–322.

Wemheuer, Felix. *Famine Politics in Maoist China and the Soviet Union*. New Haven, CT: Yale University Press, 2015.

Wemheuer, Felix. *A Social History of Maoist China: Conflict and Change, 1949–1976*. Cambridge: Cambridge University Press, 2019.

Weston, Timothy B. *The Power of Position: Beijing University, Intellectuals, and Chinese Political Culture, 1898–1929*. Berkeley: University of California Press, 2004.

Will, Pierre-Étienne. *Handbooks and Anthologies for Officials in Imperial China: A Descriptive and Critical Bibliography*. 2 vols. Handbook of Oriental Studies, Section Four China, vol. 36. Leiden: Brill, 2020.

Windscript, Shan. "A Modern History of Forgetting: The Rewriting of Social and Historical Memory in Contemporary China, 1966–Present," *Quarterly Journal of Chinese Studies* (2013), 59–68.

Wong, Lawrence Wang-chi. "A Literary Organization with a Clear Political Agenda: The Chinese League of Left-Wing Writers, 1930–1936," in Kirk A. Denton and Michel Hockx, eds., *Literary Societies of Republican China*. Lanham, MD: Lexington Books, 2008.

Wood, Michael. Introduction to *On a Chinese Screen*, by W. Somerset Maugham. New York: Arno Press, 1977.

Woodside, Alexander. *Lost Modernities: China, Vietnam, Korea, and the Hazards of World History*. Cambridge, MA: Harvard University Press, 2006.

Wu, Shellen Xiao. *Empires of Coal: Fueling China's Entry into the Modern World Order, 1860–1920*. Stanford, CA: Stanford University Press, 2015.

Xu, Bin. "For Whom the Bell Tolls: State-Society Relations and the Sichuan Earthquake Mourning in China," *Theory and Society* 42 (2013), 509–42.

Xu Guoqi. *Strangers on the Western Front: Chinese Workers in the Great War*. Cambridge, MA: Harvard University Press, 2011.

Xu, Xiaoqun. "The Rule of Law without Due Process: Punishing Robbers and Bandits in Early-Twentieth Century China," *Modern China* 33/2 (2007), 230–57.

Xu Youchun, ed. *Minguo renwu da cidian*. Shijiazhuang: Hebei renmin chuban she, 2007.

Yan Geng. *Mao's Images: Artists and China's 1949 Transition*. Wiesbaden: J. B. Metzler, 2018.

Yang Jisheng. *Tombstone: The Great Chinese Famine, 1958–1962*. Edited by Edward Friedman, Guo Jian and Stacy Mosher. Translated by Stacy Mosher and Guo Jian. New York: Farrar, Straus and Giroux, 2012.

Yeh, Wen-hsin. *Provincial Passages: Culture, Space and the Origins of Chinese Communism*. Berkeley: University of California Press, 1996.

Yu, Lingbo, ed. *Xiandai Fojiao renwu cidian*. Sanzhong, Taibei: Foguang chuban she, 2004.

Yue, Gang. *The Mouth That Begs: Hunger, Cannibalism, and the Politics of Eating in Modern China*. Durham, NC: Duke University Press, 1999.

Zarrow, Peter. *Educating China: Knowledge, Society and Textbooks in a Modernizing World, 1902–1937*. Cambridge: Cambridge University Press, 2017.

Zhang, Jishun. "Creating 'Masters of the Country' in Shanghai and Beijing: Discourse and the 1953–54 Local People's Congress Elections," *The China Quarterly* 220 (December 2014), 1071–91.

Zhang Jianqiu. *Zhongguo hongshizi hui chuqi fazhan zhi yanjiu*. Beijing: Zhonghua shuju, 2007.

Zhang, Jing. "Regulating Popular Political Knowledge: The Presence of a Central Government in the Late 1910s," *Twentieth Century China* 47/1 (January 2022), 30–39.

Zhang Juling. "Qingmo minchu qiren de jinghua xiaoshuo," *Zhongguo wenhua yanjiu* 23 (Spring 1999), 104–10.

Zhang Xiaojun. "Land Reform in Yang Village: Symbolic Capital and the Determination of Class Status," *Modern China* 30/1 (2004), 3–45.

Zhang, Zhenzong and Lanmin Wang. "Geological Disasters in Loess Areas during the 1920 Haiyuan Earthquake, China," *GeoJournal* 36.2/3 (1995), 269–72.

Zhao, Lidong. "Feudal and Feudalism in Modern China," *Journal of Modern Chinese History* 6/2 (2012), 198–216.

Zhou Aimin. "Matisse and the modernity of Yan'an woodcuts." Translated by Matt A. Hale. *Inter-Asia Cultural Studies* 7/3 (2006), 513–18.

Index

Saint Vincent de Paul, 95
Salisbury, Harrison E., 6
Sand Against the Wind: Stilwell and the American Experience in China, 102
Saturday Evening Post, 87
scar literature (*shanghen wenxue*), 306
School of Oriental and African Studies, London, 45
Search for Modern China, 297
Second Vatican Council, 95
Selection of Dingxian Yangge Plays, 189
self-relief (*zijiu*), 258
Sha Qingquan, 167
Shaan Gan Ning border region
development of Maoism in, 181–87
Shaanxi province, 4, 54, 57
development of *yangge* drama, 190
foreign tour of 1921 famine conditions, 190
Qing removal of Muslims from, 42
See also Yan'an
Shagou, 65
Shandong province, 2, 3
Shanghai Merchant Association, 80, 82
Shanxi Imperial University, 93
Shanxi province, 172, 262–71
development of *yangge* drama, 193–95
Shaonian zazhi
disaster coverage in, 120–22
Shen Yanjun, 145
Shenbao, 165
Shenghuo manhua, 167
Shengming, 109, 118–19
Shi Zuodong
1920 earthquake account by, 221–23
mediation of ethnic relations and, 235
Shi Zuoliang. *See* Shi Zuodong
Shihua, 32
Shirokogoroff, Sergei Mikhailovich, 158
Shoumaying, 31
Shunzhi Disaster Relief Society, 77
Shunzhi Drought Relief Society, 82
Sichuan province, 14, 246
silk road, 42
Sino-Muslims. *See* Gansu: Sino-Muslims
Sino-Soviet split, 274
Smith, Adam, 274
Smith, Arthur H., 2
Snow, Edgar, 182
Social Darwinism, 61
Social Life of the Chinese, 92
social sciences, 61–62
colonialism and, 22

development of statistics in China, 140, 241
limited influence of, 159
social surveys
movement of, 8, 61, 70, 73, 103–06, 157
use in Communist youth magazines, 203–5
Socialist Education movement, 260–71
Four Histories movement, 264–71
socialist realism, 9
origins of, 165
society (*shehui*)
appearance of concept, 57
Society for Awakening Goodness, 77
sociology, 8
Chinese textbooks on, 149–51
rise of, 61–62
Sidney Gamble and study of Beijing, 103–4
See also Fei Xiaotong
Soothill, William Edward, 93
soup kitchens (*zhouchang*), 5, 11, 16, 152, 222–23, 226–27, 230. *See also* relief
Soviet Writers' Congress,
and origins of socialist realism, 165
speak bitterness sessions. *See* bitterness speaking (*suku*)
Spencer, Herbert, 61
Standard Oil, 57
Stanford University, 56
statistics. *See* social sciences
stele. *See* media: stone stele
Stilwell, Joseph W.
involvement in relief work, 102
Strand bookstore, Manhattan, 45
struggle sessions. *See* bitterness speaking (*suku*)
students
creation of geological society and, 58
famine relief contributions by Japanese students, 76, 82
famine relief mobilization and, 36–37
Guomindang policy toward, 135
journalistic initiatives of, 12, 55, 62–70, 71–73
Su Caifeng, 234–35
Su Tingrui, 234
Sun Yat-sen, 19, 61, 63, 165, 239
superstition (*mixin*), 55, 58, 97, 127, 150

Taiyuan, 33
Tang Yingwei, 165
Taylor, Mrs. Howard, 45
Three Character Classic, 188
Thunder out of China, 2

Milton Keynes UK
Ingram Content Group UK Ltd.
UKHW020721280124
436796UK00022B/110